Weaving *Te Whāriki*

Aotearoa New Zealand's Early Childhood Curriculum
Framework in Theory and Practice (2nd edition)

Edited by Joce Nuttall

NZCER PRESS

NZCER PRESS

New Zealand Council for Educational Research
PO Box 3237
Wellington

National Library of New Zealand Cataloguing-in-Publication Data

Weaving Te whāriki : Aotearoa New Zealand's early childhood
curriculum framework in theory and practice / edited by Joce Nuttall.
2nd ed.
Previous ed.: 2003.
Includes index.
ISBN 978-1-927151-81-5
1. New Zealand. Ministry of Education. Whāriki. 2. Early childhood
Education—New Zealand—Curricula. 3. Early childhood education
—New Zealand. I. Nuttall, J. G. (Jocelyn Grace)
II. New Zealand Council for Educational Research. III. Title.
372.190993—dc 23

Designed by Cluster Creative

Printed by Lithoprint, Wellington

Distributed by NZCER
PO Box 3237
Wellington
New Zealand
www.nzcer.org.nz

Contents

About the authors

Stig Broström is Professor of Early Childhood Education and Care and Head of the Research Unit in Childhood, Learning and Didaktik in the Department of Education at Aarhus University, Copenhagen. His background is as a preschool teacher and his current work is in the areas of preschool teacher education and the supervision of masters and doctoral degrees in Education.

Margaret Carr is Professor of Education in the Faculty of Education and Director of the Early Years Research Centre at the University of Waikato. Since the development of *Te Whāriki* she has worked with Wendy Lee on a number of action research projects with early childhood teachers, including a Centre of Innovation research project with Karen Ramsey and the teachers at Roskill South Kindergarten.

Marilyn Fleer holds the Foundation Chair of Early Childhood Education at Monash University, Australia, and is the President of the International Society for Cultural Activity Research (ISCAR). Her research interests focus on early years learning and development, with special attention to pedagogy, culture, science and technology.

Helen Hedges is Deputy Head of School (Research) for the School of Curriculum and Pedagogy in the Faculty of Education at the University of Auckland. Helen's research programme explores children's and teachers' interests, knowledge and learning in the contexts of early childhood education and teacher education.

Wendy Lee is the Director of the Educational Leadership Project (Ltd), a professional learning provider for the early childhood sector in New Zealand. For the past 40 years, she has been involved in early childhood education as a teacher, tutor, lecturer, manager, professional development facilitator and researcher. Wendy recently co-authored a book on Learning Stories with Professor Margaret Carr.

Jude MacArthur is a Senior Lecturer in the School of Education, Massey University (Albany Campus). She is part of the joint Massey University and University of Canterbury team delivering the Postgraduate Diploma in Specialist Teaching, and coordinates the endorsement in Complex Educational Needs. Jude's research interests are in inclusive education and the perspectives of disabled children and young people on their school experiences.

Bernadette Macartney's doctoral research explored the effects of normalising discourses in education and society on young disabled children and their families. She is an early childhood teacher, mother of a disabled child, and an advocate for critical and sociocultural pedagogies as an alternative to limiting and deficit views and explanations of difference.

Diane Mara is Associate Dean (Pasifika) in the Faculty of Education at the University of Auckland. Diane has over 30 years' experience as a teacher, lecturer, policy analyst and researcher. Her published work in Pasifika early childhood education and in Pasifika research methodologies is well-known and used in many undergraduate teacher education courses.

Carl Mika (Tūhourangi, Ngāti Whanaunga) is a Lecturer in the Department of Policy, Culture and Social Studies in Education at the University of Waikato. Carl's research interests are in German Romanticism, phenomenology, and Māori metaphysics.

Carol Mutch is an Associate Professor in the School of Critical Studies in Education in the Faculty of Education at the University of Auckland. Her research and teaching interests are in educational policy, curriculum development, research and evaluation methodology, and social education.

Joce Nuttall is Associate Professor and Principal Research Fellow in the Faculty of Education at Australian Catholic University, where she leads the Faculty's Senior Proven Researcher Team. Joce's research interests are in the initial education and continuing professional development of early childhood teachers.

Vanessa Paki is of Tainui (Ngāti Mahuta) and Taranaki (Te Ātiawa) descent. Vanessa is a Lecturer in the Department of Human Development and Counselling at the University of Waikato. Her research interests are Matauranga Māori, transition from early childhood into school, assessment and curriculum.

Sally Peters is an Associate Professor at the University of Waikato. She is the Associate Director of the Faculty of Education's Early Years Research Centre and the co-director of a 3-year research project exploring children's learning journeys from early childhood education to school. Her research interests focus on transitions, children's development, and teaching and learning.

Kerry Purdue is a Lecturer in early childhood education at the University of Canterbury College of Education and a former teacher. She is interested in a wide range of issues related to policy and practice in early childhood education including inclusive education and social justice. Kerry is currently researching and writing in the area of disability and children and families' rights.

Karen Ramsey was the Lead Researcher of the 3-year action research project undertaken as a Centre of Innovation (COI) at Roskill South Kindergarten, where she has been Head Teacher since 1997. She has presented at several national and international conferences and authored and co-authored a number of early childhood papers and articles. Karen's pedagogical practice deeply embeds the principles of *Te Whāriki*.

Lady Tilly Reedy (Ngāti Porou), with her husband Sir Tamati, spearheaded the development of *Te Whāriki* in its Māori form. Together they were instrumental in the development of early childhood Māori-language immersion education in Aotearoa New Zealand through the Te Kōhanga Reo National Trust.

Jenny Ritchie has a background as a child-care educator and kindergarten teacher, followed by 23 years' experience in early childhood teacher education. She is currently Associate Professor in Early Childhood Teacher Education at Te Whare Wānanga o Wairaka—Unitec Institute of Technology, Auckland. Her teaching, research, and writing has focused on supporting early childhood educators and teacher educators to enhance their praxis in terms of enacting an awareness of cultural, environmental and social justice issues.

Sarah Te One has over 25 years' experience in early education as a teacher, researcher, lecturer, unionist and parent. Sarah was Principal Advisor, Education, in the Office of the Children's Commissioner. She is currently a Senior Lecturer in the Faculty of Education at Victoria University of Wellington. Her research interests focus on children's perspectives and influence on social and education policy, and parent and community partnerships in education.

Bev Trim is a Professional Teaching Fellow in the School of Critical Studies in Education in the Faculty of Education at the University of Auckland. She brings a wide experience of early childhood teaching to her work with pre-service teacher education students in early childhood studies, and educational history and policy.

Jayne White is a Senior Lecturer in the Faculty of Education at the University of Waikato. Jayne has a long-standing interest in education, with a particular emphasis on early years pedagogy and dialogism. Her interests span infant and toddler education, play, democracy, environmental education, classroom education, assessment and evaluation.

Elizabeth Wood is Professor of Education and Director of Research in the School of Education at the University of Sheffield. Her research and teaching focuses on learning, pedagogy and curriculum; play and learning; policy analysis and critique; equity and diversity; teachers' beliefs and practices; and professionalism and critical perspectives in education

Weaving *Te Whāriki:* Ten years on

Joce Nuttall

In preparing an introduction for the second edition of a book, it is customary to revisit the introduction to the first edition and reflect on changes in the intervening period. In the case of *Weaving Te Whāriki* this has been a fascinating exercise. It is almost 20 years since the *Draft Guidelines for Developmentally Appropriate Programmes in Early Childhood Services* (Ministry of Education, 1993) were released as the precursor to *Te Whāriki: He Whāriki Mātauranga mō ngā Mokopuna o Aotearoa: Early Childhood Curriculum* (Ministry of Education, 1996). What has changed in early childhood education during this time? What has stayed the same? And what are the issues to which we must remain alert in 2013 and beyond?

In the introduction to the first edition I identified three main themes across the book's chapters: the centrality of culture in the authors' analyses of the impact of *Te Whāriki*, the increasing influence of socio-constructivist theories of learning on early childhood curriculum since the 1980s, and ongoing issues in the implementation of *Te Whāriki*, largely due to its non-prescriptive nature. As I write in 2012 the first two of these issues now seem taken for granted in the work of teachers and academics in early childhood education (ECE) in Aotearoa New Zealand, and there is now a large international literature on the relationship between culture and early learning, informed by sociocultural, cultural-historical and constructivist perspectives. The issue of the implementation of *Te Whāriki*, however, is less resolved. In their final report to the Ministry of Education in 2012, *An Agenda for Amazing Children*, the ECE Task Force dedicated one of their essays on policy design to 'Enhancing ECE through *Te Whāriki*' (pp. 106–113). In this they stated, "*Te Whāriki* is considered a model of best practice, nationally and internationally, but could benefit from a comprehensive review of its implementation" (p. 106). This reads as somewhat contradictory: if *Te Whāriki* is a model of best practice, why are there persistent issues with its implementation?

In the report's recommendations the rationale behind this claim becomes clear. The Task Force remains concerned about the place of *Te Whāriki* in supporting teachers to foster

> success for Māori and Pasifika children, children who have English as an additional language, and children with special education needs; and … the level and quality of the early childhood education sector's assessment practices. (Recommendation 26, p. 106)

They go on to recommend reviews of how the schooling sector builds on children's achievements prior to school (Recommendation 27), preparation and support for teachers in implementing *Te Whāriki* (Recommendation 28), and the "development of a framework … that measures the extent to which the outcomes of *Te Whāriki* are being achieved. This framework should be linked to sector performance monitoring" (Recommendation 29, p. 106). In this final recommendation, and in the commentary that follows in the report, there is an intensification of the language of risk, performance, measurement and accountability, which the early childhood field in Aotearoa New Zealand first encountered head-on in the late 1980s. The policy reforms that preceded the development of *Te Whāriki* have been well documented elsewhere, but it is worth remembering that, amidst positive moves towards enhanced qualifications, increased professional development opportunities and increased sector funding, the price of these initiatives also had to be paid, chiefly through a reduction in professional trust, and an increase in accountability and bureaucratic intervention that now seems commonplace.

This hardening of the neo-liberal discourse of mistrust of the teaching profession is underscored not only by what is said in the report of the Task Force, but by what is not said. Despite support for the centrality of *Te Whāriki*, the report is silent about the issue of children's universal human rights, including their right to an optimal education. The language of rights is sidelined by the language of vulnerability and risk, underpinned by the influence of theories of human capital. Early childhood education is no longer seen as a public good but as a vehicle for risk minimisation for government, now and in the future. This is not a new or original analysis. Such analyses can be traced in response to changes in educational provision in Australia, New Zealand and the United Kingdom that reflect the shifting role of governments away from their post-war role of attempting to provide a 'level playing field' of access and opportunity across class and other divides toward more targeted forms of provision (Tingle, 2012).

What is relevant in the context of this book is the place of *Te Whāriki* as a key cultural artefact in this shifting sociopolitical landscape, and what it means for educators who remain committed to ideals of equity and access to early childhood services. The language of *Te Whāriki* is not one of risk, vulnerability and competition.

It speaks, instead, of opportunity, respect and relationships. In 2003 I wrote that early childhood education was experiencing a "relatively benign period" (Nuttall, 2003, p. 9). In hindsight, the word 'relatively' stands out, as early childhood educators in New Zealand in 2012 campaign against attempts to roll back standards of qualifications and other hard-won gains across the sector that are known to have an effect on the experiences of children and families in early childhood services.

Amidst these changes *Te Whāriki* remains a highly valued feature of the early childhood landscape in Aotearoa New Zealand. Its capacity to support teachers to respond to the changing life-worlds of today's young children, who will face challenges such as globalisation, climate change and fast technologies in ways we are only just beginning to recognise, will be tested in years to come. Although the relevance and status of *Te Whāriki* itself seem assured for the time being, the field remains alert to the potential for further change, and one of the functions of *Te Whāriki* has been to provide one of the rallying points for the profession in the face of change.

Not only has early childhood education developed and changed nationally and internationally in the past 20 years; so has the study of early childhood education as an academic field. Many of the authors contributing to this second edition of *Weaving Te Whāriki* were intimately involved in the development and early implementation of *Te Whāriki*; others have come to understand the document more recently in their work as teachers, researchers and academics. The ongoing development of research and curriculum scholarship in early childhood education is represented not only in the updating of previous chapters, but also by the inclusion of new chapters on topics absent from the first edition. These include Diane Mara's description (Chapter 3) of emerging Pasifika perspectives on early childhood education research. Mara identifies the challenges that have historically faced Pasifika early childhood education services and, more recently, the complexity of building and sustaining the teacher education, professional development and research expertise within Pasifika communities. Mara reminds us that these efforts always have a spiritual dimension, and challenges the field to pay attention to the spiritual nature of our relationships.

Sally Peters and Vanessa Paki also contribute a new chapter to this edition (Chapter 10). They describe their research on the transition to school and how this can be informed by the principles found in *Te Whāriki*. Transition to school from an early childhood perspective is a growing area of research interest—there is now a Special Interest Group within the European Early Childhood Education Research Association dedicated to transitions—and Peters and Paki's work is important because it makes explicit links between teachers' practices in relation to transition and curriculum frameworks. Elizabeth Wood (Chapter 13) also draws on formal curriculum frameworks, but from a critical stance. Her analysis of how play is positioned variously within the United Kingdom's *Early Years Foundation Stage* and *Te Whāriki* is not only important retrospectively but sounds a warning to policy makers and practitioners in New Zealand to be clear about what we think play can (and cannot) do for young children. The fourth new chapter in this volume is by Jayne White and Carl Mika (Chapter 5) and focuses on infants and toddlers in child care. As philosophers, White and Mika bring powerful conceptual tools to their analysis of the mysterious nature of very young children and how *Te Whāriki* can inform this specialised area of early childhood education work.

Although the remaining chapters (except one) are revisions of those in the first edition, they also reflect important developments in the field. In the intervening period Australia has also developed its own early childhood curriculum framework. The writers of Australia's *Early Years Learning Framework* (*EYLF*) explicitly acknowledge their debt to *Te Whāriki* and, in Chapter 11, Marilyn Fleer extends her analysis of the theoretical bases of *Te Whāriki* in the first edition to reflect on those of the *EYLF*. Sarah Te One (Chapter 1), Carol Mutch and Bev Trim (Chapter 4) and Stig Bröstrom (Chapter 12) all contribute significant updates of their chapters in the first edition, and Karen Ramsay, Wendy Lee and Margaret Carr (Chapter 8) update their account of Karen's assessment practice. This chapter, in particular, reflects the exciting teacher development opportunities that were available to many teachers during the 2000s. Helen Hedges, in Chapter 14, traces the decline of these programmes and the implications of this decline, at the same time as the Early Childhood Taskforce is calling for more effective implementation of *Te Whāriki* and the possibility of national standards waits in the wings.

My own work, like that of Hedges, focuses on the thinking and development of teachers. In Chapter 9 I re-cast my chapter from the first edition in a more strongly sociocultural vein by thinking about curriculum concepts as cultural tools available to teachers. This shift to socioculturalism, detectable in the 2003 edition, is even stronger in this volume. One other family of theoretical perspectives—post-structuralism—is also strongly represented in this volume, chiefly in Jenny Ritchie's discussion of implementing a bicultural curriculum (Chapter 7) and in the chapter on disability by Bernadette Macartney, Kerry Purdue and Jude MacArthur (Chapter 6). These chapters complete a rich picture of the kinds of theoretical perspectives informing early childhood education in 2013 and beyond. The one chapter that remains unchanged, that by Lady Tilly Reedy (Chapter 2), is reprinted here with thanks to Lady Reedy and to the Te Kōhanga Reo National Trust. Some aspects of the chapter, such as the statistics quoted by Lady Reedy, are no longer current, but this is a strength of this chapter: it provides an important contemporary account of the development of *Te Whāriki* and a historical marker against which to track the achievement of Māori aspirations in early childhood education.

Some topics still await future editions, particularly the perspectives of parents, the experiences of educators in parent-led services, and the voices of students in teacher education programmes as they encounter *Te Whāriki* for the first time. Many of the readers of this volume, as with the first edition, will be students in early childhood teacher education programmes. Your engagement with the chapters in this edition is warmly welcomed. Like the first edition, this volume is an artefact of its place and time, and one aspect of your teacher education will inevitably be to prepare you for change during your career. It may seem baffling to you that there was a time when the early childhood sector in Aotearoa New Zealand did not have a curriculum framework, and that the principles and strands of *Te Whāriki* became mandatory as late as 2008. I hope the chapters in this volume will help you gain a sense of the significance and relevance of *Te Whāriki*, both nationally and internationally, but also help you make your own professional judgements about its place within your practice.

Since 2003, *Weaving Te Whāriki* has become a key resource in early childhood education in New Zealand and elsewhere, particularly in the preparation of early childhood educators, and it sits alongside the original drafts and working papers developed by the writers of *Te Whāriki* as a resource for scholars interested in the history, interpretation and implementation of *Te Whāriki*. I thank the contributing authors, the reviewers of the draft chapters and the publication team at the NZCER for their willingness to continue the conversation.

References

Early Childhood Education Taskforce. (2011). *An agenda for amazing children: Final report of the early childhood education taskforce*. Wellington: Early Childhood Education Taskforce.

Ministry of Education. (1993). *Te whāriki: Draft guidelines for developmentally appropriate programmes in early childhood services*. Wellington: Learning Media.

Ministry of Education. (1996). *Te whāriki: He whāriki mātauranga mō ngā mokopuna o Aotearoa: Early childhood curriculum*. Wellington: Learning Media.

Nuttall, J. (2003). Introduction. In J. Nuttall (Ed.) *Weaving Te whāriki: Aotearoa New Zealand's early childhood curriculum document in theory and practice* (pp. 7–15). Wellington: New Zealand Council for Educational Research.

Tingle, L. (2012). Great expectations: Government, entitlement and an angry nation. *Quarterly Essay, 46*, 1–65.

CHAPTER 1

Te Whāriki:
Historical accounts and contemporary influences 1990–2012

Sarah Te One

ABSTRACT

This chapter describes the historical context for the development of *Te Whāriki* and gives an account of how the document was written. Links are made between the initial design and development of the document and some of the ideological, educational and cultural issues of the time. The chapter concludes with a description of the 2012 context and draws some parallels with influences present at the time *Te Whāriki* was written.

Introduction

On 15 September 1990 the *New Zealand Education Gazette* advertised for proposals for a contract to "develop curriculum guidelines for early childhood education" (Ministry of Education, 1990, p. 4) and invited interested persons or organisations to apply. Part One of this chapter describes the contexts in which *Te Whāriki*, the early childhood curriculum document for Aotearoa New Zealand (Ministry of Education, 1993a, 1996), was developed in the early 1990s. The ideological, educational and cultural agendas of that time led to the emergence of an idea that was, prior to the late 1980s, almost anathema to early childhood education: national curriculum guidelines.

Part Two describes how the draft version of *Te Whāriki* was developed (Ministry of Education, 1993a) and its impact on early childhood education in Aotearoa New Zealand during that era. It includes responses to questionnaires and interviews with some of the people who, from 1990 to 1993, were involved in the working groups that drafted *Te Whāriki*, and with people in the Ministry of Education. Part Three then discusses the impact and influence of *Te Whāriki* in its third decade and looks at why this document has had such longevity, the challenges to *Te Whāriki*, and what the future of this internationally ground-breaking curriculum might be.

PART ONE
Contexts for the development of Te Whāriki
The ideological context

The education reforms of the late 1980s—variously described as "technicist", "ideologically new right" and "monetarist" (Willis, 1994)—focused initially on administration and secondly on curriculum and assessment. During the 1980s there had been growing criticism of the administrative framework of the Department of Education from both the political left and right (Boston, 1990; Grace, 1990). The education system was considered to be over-centralised and unresponsive to community needs, and to have failed to deliver social and educational equity. Indeed, the educational failure of Māori had become a "statistical artefact" (Benton, 1990). Change was inevitable given the agenda of the fourth Labour Government. Almost every aspect of the public sector underwent some form of restructuring, driven by an economic ideology that devolved responsibility for service delivery yet retained fiscal control. Advisers to the government suggested that New Zealand's long-standing 'cradle to the grave' approach did not work; instead, a bold social experiment was necessary, based on a philosophy of individualism and the supremacy of the free market (Kelsey, 1995).

The 1987 briefing papers to the incoming government (New Zealand Treasury, 1987) advocated the market-driven provision of government services, including education. The role of the state was to provide minimal backstop services for people who were unable to exercise 'choice'. Liberal ideals of social equity and equality of opportunity were replaced by a consumerist approach that presented education as discrete packages of services available to anyone to buy. It was argued that, since the choice to have children was a personal one, educating them was a private responsibility; it followed that the provision of education was also in the private domain. This argument created tension between two conflicting assumptions: first, that families were ready, willing and able to exercise choice; and, secondly, that communities were in a position to provide them with choice. Little was done to address vocal concerns from educational organisations, other than a clear message from within government to hasten the process of reform. The views of teachers, union representatives, academics, researchers and parents were considered to be biased because they clearly had a vested interest in the outcome: children's education (Douglas, 1993).

In 1988 the Labour Government established a working group to "provide a short restatement of the purpose, place, form and function of early childhood education" (Department of Education, 1988a, p. iv). The resulting document, *Education to be More: Report of the Early Childhood Care and Education Working Group* (Department of Education, 1988b), was based on the five themes identified in the 1987 Royal Commission on Social Policy as underpinning all areas of social policy reform in New Zealand:
- implementing the Treaty of Waitangi
- improving the social and economic status of women
- providing a legislative environment which safeguards basic human rights and freedoms, and works towards the removal of discrimination
- recognising the needs, contributions and traditions of Pacific Island peoples and other minority cultures residing in New Zealand
- enhancing the family unit in New Zealand society
  (Department of Education, 1988a, p. v).

The release of *Education to be More* (known as 'the Meade Report') was followed by the Government's response, *Before Five: Early Childhood Care and Education in New Zealand* (Lange, 1988), written concurrently with other policy reforms in the state education sector. *Before Five* gave early childhood education the same status as primary and secondary education, and was sanctioned by David Lange, who was both Prime Minister and Minister of Education at that time. Although its policy blueprint was not universally welcomed (Mitchell, 1996), its longer-term vision had been supported by early childhood educators in both community-based and privately owned services during wide consultation with the sector.

When the National Party won the 1990 election, Labour's policy initiatives to improve the quality of early childhood education were quickly rescinded. The influential private sector lobby challenged well-established indicators of quality, such as qualified staff and reasonable pay and conditions. The lobbyists argued that the increased costs of qualified staff would be passed on to families, thereby undermining another plank of the reforms: equitable access to early childhood services. This pressure led to changes to the licensing regulations governing centres and polarised the ensuing debates between state-funded and privately owned services as to what quality early childhood education was and how it might be achieved. Ironically, at a time when many aspects of service quality were under threat, the professional status of early childhood education was to be enhanced by the development of a national early childhood curriculum.

The educational context

Alongside the administrative reforms there began a process of curriculum reform. Although the development of *Te Whāriki* was not the beginning of the debate on early childhood curriculum in Aotearoa New Zealand, there had been no national agreement on the issue. Child-care centres, the kindergarten movement and Playcentre associations had developed distinct approaches to curriculum, but these were generally not formalised.

During the late 1980s the Department of Education ran a series of week-long residential courses at Lopdell House in Auckland to help develop its policy initiatives in early childhood education. Those invited to participate were broadly representative of the sector, and reports based on their discussions and recommendations from the courses were cited in the *Te Whāriki* proposal document as significant initial influences (particularly on the issues of infants and toddlers, a Pacific Island curriculum and home-based care). One such report contained a statement on early childhood curriculum, which included a list of principles to underpin any future development of a curriculum document (Department of Education, 1988b).

These reports reflected a concern that "downward pressure" from the school curriculum was a threat to the early childhood sector's concepts of what made a "good child" (Department of Education, 1988a). May and Carr (1996) argue that *Te Whāriki* was developed as much to protect the interests of children before school as it was to promote and define a curriculum for early childhood, especially since the proposed *New Zealand Curriculum Framework* (Ministry of Education, 1993b), by prompting more systematic assessment in early childhood education, was potentially dangerous (Carr & May, 1993). They acknowledged, however, that the sector could gain additional strength and status by having clear links with the schools' curriculum framework:

> The issue here is that such dovetailing or interconnecting will now need to be a two way street ... initiatives in curriculum and assessment for the early school years, for example recommendations on the collection of information at school entry, will from now on need to take into account the curriculum for the first five years. (Carr & May, 1993, pp. 43, 49)

Cultural contexts

The cultural make-up of Aotearoa New Zealand added further complexity to the educational and economic reforms. The country's colonial past and its traditional ties to the United Kingdom were no longer the only influences on the population in the early 1990s. Successive waves of immigration, particularly from Pacific nations, had created an increasingly pluralist nation that was demanding recognition. This trend was coupled with a Māori renaissance epitomised by the kōhanga reo movement, which aimed to create "language nests" for mokopuna/tamariki Māori.

For decades Māori had been arguing against the assimilationist policies that had fuelled growing discontent among their people. During the 1980s Māori throughout Aotearoa New Zealand supported the development of kōhanga reo in a serious attempt to save te reo Māori (the Māori language). Hailed as a grass-roots revolutionary movement (Irwin, 1990), kōhanga reo focused on mokopuna/tamariki as the future speakers of te reo Māori. Immersion in te reo and tikanga Māori (Māori customary conduct) would empower these children, along with their whānau, hapū and iwi, to maintain the language and thus ensure its survival. Although the concept concerned young children, it did not identify itself as an early childhood education movement. Māori leaders argued that it was a social justice movement, a manifestation of tino rangatiratanga (self-determination) under the Treaty of Waitangi.[1] Māori activists and academics alike were clear that the existing system of education disadvantaged Māori and that the kōhanga reo movement was an example of a solution to this situation: by Māori, for Māori.

In response to concerns from Māori, the Minister of Education appointed an advisory body, known as the Rūnanga Matua, to the Ministry of Education.[2] Its role was to oversee the reform implementation process from a Māori perspective. Among its members was Tilly Reedy, who was to be one of the two Māori lead writers of *Te Whāriki*, and who was appointed to the early childhood curriculum development project by Te Kōhanga Reo National Trust (along with her husband, Dr Tamati Reedy). Even before work on *Te Whāriki* began, the Rūnanga Matua had identified concepts central to the promotion of mana Māori in education. Seeing *Te Whāriki* as a guide to "fulfilling the intent of the Treaty of Waitangi", the Rūnanga proposed "an infusion approach ... whereby mana tangata, mana atua, mana whenua and mana o te reo are considered as key factors".[3] Thus the final form of *Te Whāriki* had its beginnings in Māori pedagogical and philosophical beliefs.

---

1 The Treaty of Waitangi is Aotearoa New Zealand's founding document. Based on the principle of equal partnership, it is a contract between some Māori tribes and the Crown, signed on 6 February 1840.
2 Correspondence from Rūnanga Matua to Ministry of Education, c. 1989. New Zealand Childcare Association/Te Tari Puna Ora Archive, Alexander Turnbull Library.
3 Ibid.

From the outset, the writers of *Te Whāriki* were committed to producing a document that honoured the Treaty of Waitangi. Compared to other early childhood services, kōhanga reo had a well-defined curriculum based on the survival of te reo Māori and ngā tikanga Māori. Helen May and Margaret Carr, as the two Pākehā (non-Māori) lead writers of *Te Whāriki*, challenged the way in which previous government funding had "not so far addressed the need for a Māori curriculum, although it has looked at Taha Māori in the mainstream curriculum" (Carr & May, 1990, p. 19). This shortcoming was something they intended to redress.

Te Whāriki went on to represent and reflect Māori politics and pedagogy. "I have a dream," said Tilly Reedy (1993) at the launch of the draft version of *Te Whāriki* (see Chapter 2, this volume). This dream, articulated in the document's framework for a curriculum, drew all early childhood services in Aotearoa New Zealand into the wider world of social and political contribution and participation. Traditional approaches to planning and programming for play, which focused on activities such as collage and play-dough, were challenged by broad educational ideals about democracy and social justice.

PART TWO:
Writing *Te Whāriki*
The contract

The request for proposal (Ministry of Education, 1990) called for tenders from potential contractors "to develop curriculum guidelines for developmentally appropriate programmes for early childhood education" (p. 4). Under "Responsibilities: Contractor" were requirements to:

- direct the development, review and evaluation of curriculum guidelines for early childhood education to produce a final draft. This process of development and evaluation should involve meetings with a consultative group of approximately 10–12 early childhood practitioners and persons with special expertise;
- select the reference group to achieve appropriate geographical, gender and cultural balance, including representatives of experienced primary, intermediate and secondary teachers. The names shall be approved by the Ministry;
- consult with … organisations[4] during the development of the final draft. (Ministry of Education, 1990, pp. 6 & 7)

The proposal

Helen May, a senior lecturer and chair of the Department of Early Childhood at the University of Waikato, had signalled to the early childhood field her intention to

---

4 The organisations listed here represented national early childhood organisations, unions and training providers.

spearhead a proposal from the Waikato region and received support from the sector to do so (Wells, 1990). When May and Margaret Carr drew up the proposed process within their contract proposal, it represented a re-conceptualisation of the curriculum development process, which had previously been dominated by Western models (May, 2002). This new model treated content, process, context and evaluation as interdependent features, an idea that could be traced back to the *Basic Principles for an Early Childhood Curriculum* developed at Lopdell House (Department of Education, 1988a).

The task was now to present this ambitious and complex vision in a format that would be acceptable to the Ministry of Education. The proposal used the metaphor of a native forest to illustrate both the model's strengths and the potential barriers to curriculum development. Key theorists—Piaget, Erikson, Vygotsky and Bruner—were likened to kauri trees, famous for their great height, but "because of the immaturity of very young children, and the non-compulsory nature of the services, the forest is also strewn with ideological disputes and conflicting beliefs" (Carr & May, 1990, p. 10). The kauri were signposts for a pathway through these "dangers", but they were also representative: "[We] were concerned with the whole child and a developmental framework (Piaget and Erikson), and with learning in a social and cultural context (Bruner and Vygotsky)" (Carr & May, 1990, p. 10).

The writers claimed it was "concern for high quality early childhood care and education that prompts us to put forward this proposal" (Carr & May, 1990, p. 11). Two arguments were especially significant. One was a challenge to the dominant view that child care was a "second best" option:

> We do not subscribe to that theory, and would like to set another in its place …
> the child who has good quality care at centre and at home has a richer 'tool-kit' of
> learning strategies, friends and interests for making sense of the world than a child
> who is mostly cared for in one environment. (p. 11)

The second argument was that cultural sensitivity and equity were factors in the quality debate. Citing research that demonstrated that "the child who is bilingual has a cognitive advantage, in comparison with a mono-lingual child" (p. 11), the proposal indicated that the bicultural context was separate from the European curriculum, and distinct from the Māori curriculum. The Pacific Island context was a further consideration:

> We wanted to present an inclusive framework in which Pacific Island language
> nests were able to negotiate statements about curriculum. At that time they were the
> only cohesive immigrant group. Our contact, Iole Tagoilelagi, was able to negotiate
> with PIECA (Pacific Island Early Childhood Association) on behalf of Pacific Island
> centres. It was a strategic endeavour to recognise a different type of context. (H. May,
> personal communication, August 2002)

The issue was indeed strategic. By highlighting these discrete philosophical positions, the proposal enabled the sector to "negotiate from a position of power. We wanted to reveal issues, not silence them" (H. May, personal communication, August 2002). Previous debates about early childhood curriculum at a national level had established a positive dynamic, and broad philosophical agreement was possible. "It was really important to have a vision for children—what made a 'good' child" (ibid.). This vision became part of *Te Whāriki's* aspirations for children:

> To grow up as competent and confident learners and communicators, healthy in mind, body and spirit, secure in their sense of belonging and in the knowledge that they make a valued contribution to society. (Ministry of Education, 1996, p. 9)

The proposal also covered the development of specialist curricula for home-based care and special education. The final proposal offered inclusive guidelines designed to enable a diversity of services to strategically position their own beliefs about "what made a good child in the warp and weft of the framework" (H. May, personal communication, August 2002).

The relationship with ngā kōhanga reo

The proposal indicated a clear commitment to the Treaty of Waitangi and to a separate Māori curriculum. The principle of equal partnership embodied in the Treaty of Waitangi required that "any proposal for early childhood curriculum must include a specialist and separate Māori curriculum, developed by and for ngā Kōhanga Reo" (Carr & May, 1990, p. 12). It was proposed that the development of the curriculum guidelines be a "joint endeavour between ourselves and Te Kōhanga Reo Trust" (p. 12). As Carr and May explained:

> Ngā Kōhanga Reo has consolidated a lot of previous work towards the establishment of a Māori curriculum and it is intended that there be an identifiable Māori curriculum as well as a curriculum which reflects our growth towards a bicultural society ... our proposed contracting of Te Kōhanga Reo and our budget considerations reflect this viewpoint. (Carr & May, 1990, p. 19)

The implications of this were profound. The Māori curriculum was not to be an 'add-on', nor was it to be 'integrated': it was to be separate. This fundamental shift gave new status to Māori pedagogy within early childhood education. A decade later May (2002) wrote:

> This was a challenge. There were no New Zealand or international models for guidance. This became possible due to collaboration with Te Kōhanga National Trust and the foresight of Dr Tamati Reedy and Tilly Reedy who developed the curriculum for Māori immersion centres. (p. 31)

In an interview for this chapter, May added:

We had discussions with Te Kōhanga Reo Trust and we were clear that the Māori context was separate. We worked with Maureen Locke and Rita Walker on the bicultural curriculum, not on the Māori immersion curriculum for kōhanga. Tamati and Tilly Reedy worked on that with Rose Pere. Margaret and I often met with Tamati and Tilly to discuss how to weave the Māori and Pākehā concepts together. (H. May, personal communication, August 2002)

In addition, the writers established a set of reciprocal arrangements between the writers, researchers, working groups and the sector, and suggested there were longer-term implications for research and the production of resources. These implications included recommendations for professional development to support the implementation of the curriculum guidelines and proposals for research on assessment guidelines as part of the future development phase.

The contract: A Ministry perspective

The contract for developing the curriculum was the first early childhood contract managed by the Curriculum Division in the newly formed Ministry of Education. Caryl Hamer, previously employed in the Early Childhood Division of the Department of Education, was one of seven curriculum facilitators within the Ministry of Education who were responsible for developing curriculum documents across the education sector. A background in early childhood education gave Hamer extensive networks, including in Playcentre and child care. She described the curriculum development process as:

culture shock for us in early childhood. We were suddenly in the big wide world and that made it impossible not to have a curriculum or a framework. Right from the start *Te Whāriki* was a political document. (C. Hamer, personal communication, September 2002)

After consultation between the Ministry and the sector, a contract selection panel was set up to consider the proposals. Hamer recalled the panel's reaction to the Waikato proposal:

We were just blown away … We had never seen anything like it in early childhood. It was very detailed and clear. I remember our main concern was the working groups—the Ministry was concerned that the contractors would end up with several curriculum documents. (C. Hamer, personal communication, September 2002).

The status conferred by her position within Waikato University was well understood by May. Moreover, the tertiary sector was used to preparing tenders for research, and this experience was helpful in writing the early childhood proposal. University funding was also available:

There was a budget for travel for the working groups and, while not enough, paid release days were allocated for meetings to discuss initiatives and directions, and we budgeted for meetings with the Ministry in Wellington. (H. May, personal communication, August 2002)

Within the Ministry of Education, however, there were problems. Curriculum facilitators were not contract managers. According to Hamer, "the universities taught us about contract negotiations":

> We had no idea about costs. But it was an excellent proposal and we felt it would work because it was unaligned to any early childhood group, being based in a university, but also Helen May had childcare experience and Margaret Carr was from kindergarten. So we felt they would be acceptable to the sector. (C. Hamer, personal communication, September 2002)

May agreed that being non-aligned strengthened their proposal: "We didn't choose organisations. We deliberately chose people we knew we could work with" (H. May, personal communication, August 2002). The contract was signed in December 1990 and the process of developing *Te Whāriki* started in earnest.

Background discussion papers, working documents and working groups

Once the contract was signed, the writers embarked on an ambitious 14-month consultative exercise that aimed to identify existing discourses on early childhood in all their diversity. The curriculum development process outlined in the contract was organised around specialist working groups in the areas of infants and toddlers, preschoolers, special education, home-based care, Pacific Island people, and Māori. These working groups were to develop guidelines that could be trialled, moderated and re-worked for the Ministry of Education's advisory group.[5] They would also consult with their networks for selective feedback on the early drafts of the guidelines.

A critical component was a set of background discussion papers prepared by the co-ordinators of the working groups. While these have not been published in their original form, most of the ideas they contain have appeared in subsequent writing about *Te Whāriki*. During 1991 and 1992 May wrote several papers (May, 1991b; 1991c; Early Childhood Curriculum Project, 1992h, 1992i) that outlined the considerations of a curriculum for infants and toddlers. These papers "acknowledge the international heritage of the early childhood curriculum as well as noting the distinctive features of early childhood education in Aotearoa–New Zealand" (May, 1991b, p. 2). In the conclusion to the same paper she wrote:

> One of the tasks of the curriculum project will be to demonstrate a continuity of learning, caring, and development, (i.e. curriculum) from infancy to school age, but

---

5 The Ministry of Education selected its own advisory group, to some extent representative of the sector. This was originally chaired by Caryl Hamer and met regularly over 2 years to discuss the draft versions submitted by the Early Childhood Curriculum Project as part of milestone reports to the Ministry. Several of these meetings involved Helen May and Margaret Carr presenting material for consideration.

it will be important to ensure that within the common goals, the arrangement of the curriculum guidelines can articulate the distinctiveness of different developmental stages as well as different philosophical approaches to meeting these needs. (p. 7)

Carr (1991) identified several sources for the curriculum concepts:
- the United Nations Convention on the Rights of the Child
- our knowledge of child development
- the role of the environment
- historical and cultural contexts. (p. 2)

She also identified three broad issues for consideration in the curriculum project. The first was the range of influences that had changed societal perspectives on the roles of families and of early childhood centres (or home-based care services) "that can provide a rich and responsive learning environment" (p. 3). The second issue was the complexity of an urbanised democracy:

We may still see ourselves as a democracy with unlimited social mobility and equality of opportunity, but the reality in the 1990s is one of increasing polarisation, unemployment and competition for jobs. (p. 4)

The third issue was the pluralist nature of multicultural society, "with a diversity of belief systems" (p. 5). These issues did not create "technical questions (how to do it), they create[d] philosophical questions (what are the goals)" (p. 2). Consequently, *Te Whāriki* would not be about content but would provide a framework for action, guided by philosophical principles. Underpinning these principles were universal goals and beliefs about the wellbeing of children and the culture of Aotearoa New Zealand as it affected early childhood care and education.

By the end of 1991 there was a set of draft principles and aims. May recalled an early meeting at which the Māori working group and the Māori members of other groups joined as one:

Tamati and Tilly Reedy presented the Project with a Māori curriculum framework based on the principle of empowerment. I can remember Tamati Reedy spent a day explaining ... the concepts and their origins in Te Ao Māori. It was a complete framework and included the five 'wero'—aims for children. Margaret and I then worked with this framework to position the parallel domains for Pākehā, which later became the goals. These were not translations. (H. May, personal communication, August 2002)

May (2002) has also explained the origins of the document's final name:

The title, Te Whāriki, suggested by Tamati Reedy, was a central metaphor. The early childhood curriculum was envisaged as a whāriki [which] translated as a woven mat for all to stand on. The Principles, Strands and Goals provided the framework which allowed for different programme perspectives to be woven into the fabric. (p. 32)

Subsequent discussions among the four lead writers focused on pedagogical assumptions, coupled with cultural and political aspirations. The curriculum for kōhanga reo focused on empowerment, contribution, and participation in society, and encompassed tino rangatiratanga (self-determination). It also went beyond a focus on the child to include whānau, hapū and iwi. The final version of *Te Whāriki* (Ministry of Education, 1996) reflects these discussions. As Carr and May (1999) explained:

> The principles and aims of the curriculum are expressed in both Māori and English languages, but neither is an exact translation of the other: an acceptable cross-cultural structure ... was discussed, debated and transacted early in the curriculum development process. (pp. 57–58)

Working Document One: The Framework (Early Childhood Curriculum Project, 1992c) set out the guiding principles, aims and goals for the curriculum document, with a rider that:

> further elaborations will be added to show what this means in the following contexts or settings: Māori Immersion; Tagata Pasifika; Infant Programmes; Home-Based; Toddler Programmes; Special Needs; Preschool Programmes; Bicultural [Programmes]. (p.1)

During 1992 the working groups developed these 'elaborations' in their own specialist areas and trialled them within their networks.

Jill Mitchell (1991), co-ordinator of the Special Needs Working Group, wrote that the project appeared to recognise "the right of all children to participate in a national curriculum irrespective of the extent or degree of their special needs" (p. 1). The group's role was to elaborate on "what the curriculum statements and aims might mean in relation to children with special needs" (Early Childhood Curriculum Project, 1992g, p. 1). Each of the working groups was doing this work "firstly to test out the appropriateness of the framework and secondly, to provide a resource for the final document which will have a section on children with special needs" (p. 1). The section on special needs made it to the draft curriculum document (Ministry of Education, 1993a) but was removed in the final rewrite (Ministry of Education, 1996). Statements in the revised aims and goals about inclusion were seen by the Ministry as compensation for this omission. Not everyone saw this as adequate, though, arguing that the effect was to conceal (as opposed to revealing) the status of children with special needs.

The theme of a curriculum that merged developmental theory and sociocultural theory continued in Carr's *Working Document Six* and *Working Document Seven* (Early Childhood Curriculum Project, 1992e, 1992f, 1992d). These examine the learning issues affecting preschoolers, as identified in the contemporary literature and by the team's Preschool Programmes Working Group. These learning issues were categorised as: knowledge about people, places and things, and 'know-how' (skills and strategies); and attitudes towards learning:

The idea that children are developing more elaborated and useful 'mini-theories' or 'working models' about people, places and things in their lives is a useful one: such working theories contain a combination of knowledge-about, know-how, strategies, attitudes and expectations. (Early Childhood Curriculum Project, 1992e, p. 2)

This concept was expanded in *Working Document Seven*. Working theories were regarded as

increasingly empowering: useful for making sense of the world, having some control over what happens, problem-solving and further learning. Many of them will retain a magical and creative quality, and for many communities, such working theories about the world will be infused with a spiritual dimension. (p. 1)

The draft guidelines

Te Whāriki: Draft Guidelines for Developmentally Appropriate Programmes in Early Childhood Services (Ministry of Education, 1993a) was finally released in November 1993 and sent to all early childhood training providers, organisations and centres for a trial. May and Carr (1996) recalled that the Minister would not allow it to be called a draft curriculum "because it looked so different to the national school curriculum documents" (p. 63). The Ministry was also making a significant political statement in presenting two parallel curriculum documents that were "married" but retained a distinctive identity as Pākehā and Māori. Hamer recalled that it wasn't a problem at the draft stage:

But when [the Māori document] went to the Minister before its final re-write, he refused to sign it off and demanded a translation. Well, it was sent to [the publishers] Learning Media who reported back that it was neither easy, nor appropriate to translate because the concepts were deeply Māori. (C. Hamer, personal communication, September 2002)

Eventually the Māori version was accepted and *Te Whāriki* became the first Ministry of Education document published in both Māori and English. It also broke new ground internationally: here was a national curriculum whose conceptual framework was based on the cultural and political beliefs of the minority indigenous people.

What happened between the draft and the final version?

Questions remain about what happened to the text of *Te Whāriki* once it had been trialled and evaluated by the sector. One can only speculate about the direction the Ministry of Education received from the then Minister, Lockwood Smith, during the final rewriting process. Examination of the text suggests that the political and economic agenda of the day was accommodated by including the language of accountability (Grace, 1990). The inclusion of learning outcomes had implications for assessment, a highly contested area that pits accountability and achievement measures against beliefs about reflective teaching and qualitative understanding of children's learning. Hamer described the final part of the process:

> Once the Ministry had collated the submissions on the draft, *Te Whāriki* then went to the Minister who set up his own advisory group. We didn't know who was on this group. After that, the Ministry contracted a writer who worked on the final draft. (C. Hamer, personal communication, September 2002)

There are marked differences between the draft and the final version, the major ones being the deletion of curricula developed by specialist working groups, the developmental continuum, the references, and the addition of "learning outcomes". These changes were regarded as a loss and were opposed by the writers (Carr and May, 1999, p. 63). However,

> the early childhood community was relieved and somewhat surprised that the integral philosophy and framework of *Te Whāriki* survived the long complex political process from draft to final document. (p. 62)

A national curriculum for early childhood education was a cause for celebration in the sector. Aotearoa New Zealand's early childhood sector led the way internationally with a curriculum founded on an indigenous conceptual framework, which somehow managed to incorporate Māori and Western principles of learning and teaching alongside views of children as rights holders and citizens in a democratic society, and very 'kiwi' values about childhood in a country with a great backyard.

Embedding *Te Whāriki*

Despite the losses between the draft and final versions, there were some gains. Part of the negotiations for the development of *Te Whāriki* (Ministry of Education, 1996) included an undertaking by government to support the development of an assessment framework. Through research undertaken in the late 1990s, a formative assessment tool was developed, Learning Stories, based on a process of identifying children's learning dispositions and writing narratives about them (Carr, 2001). This resulted in a new set of resources, *Kei Tua o te Pae Assessment for Learning: Early Childhood Assessment Exemplars* (Ministry of Education, 2005). Both *Te Whāriki* and *Kei Tua o te Pae* have received international recognition as innovative examples of curriculum and assessment.

However, a quick overview of recent history illustrates that early childhood education policies, even when esteemed internationally, are vulnerable to political changes. The 1990s were dominated by neo-liberal economic theories, driving policies designed to enhance choice in a (supposedly) free market environment. The early childhood education (ECE) sector was adversely affected by a raft of policies dominated by a hands-off regulatory framework. Significant gains made to enhance the quality of provision during the 1980s were lost during the National Government's administration from 1990 to 1993, which returned to the argument that the choice to have a child was private, and therefore education for that child was a private interest.

Under a Labour-led coalition government (1999–2008), spending in the New Zealand early childhood sector increased from NZ$4 billion to more than NZ$7 billion between 2002 and 2008, representing a shift both in fiscal priorities and in philosophical principles. A main driver underpinning the increased spending emerged from within the sector through the development of *Ngā Huarahi Arataki: Pathways to the Future* (Ministry of Education, 2002), a long-term strategic plan for early childhood. Consistent with government aims to increase participation in the workforce, and therefore access to early childhood services for working families, the strategic plan was founded on three key platforms: to promote children's participation in ECE services; to improve the quality of ECE services; and to increase collaboration between agencies with an interest in ECE. *Te Whāriki* was firmly embedded within the discourse of quality, participation and collaboration, and research initiatives such as the Centres of Innovation (Ministry of Education, 2002) reflected this.

PART THREE:
Te Whāriki in 2012

At the time of preparing this chapter the current National-led led coalition government has also earmarked the ECE sector for investment and notes that, since the 2006/07 financial year, government subsidies have doubled from NZ$617 million to $1.3 billion in 2012 (Trevett, 2012). Minister of Education Hekia Parata has announced a budget freeze for most centres, but an injection of NZ$110.9 million over the next 4 years for high-priority communities, with a particular focus on increasing participation rates from 94.7 percent to 98 percent by 2016 (Trevett, 2012).

So where does this leave *Te Whāriki*? Part Three (see also Chapter 14 of this volume) analyses the current economic, social and political landscape and its impact on policy in the early childhood sector to note similarities and differences between the early 1990s and 2012.

Current contexts

In 2009 Anne Smith claimed *Te Whāriki* as a taonga (treasure) encapsulating aspirations for children based on children's rights. On a more sobering note, she observed that 2009 Budget cuts had effectively stalled the momentum towards improving quality services for children and for communities that had built up over recent years. The world-wide recession provided the Government with a rationale to alter and cut existing early childhood education policies (Te One & Dalli, 2010).

In 2012 there appears to be an unprecedented interest in the critical importance of the early years of a child's life and the value of high-quality ECE. Substantial research recognises that ECE of good quality has long-term beneficial educational, social, cultural and economic outcomes (see Mitchell, Wylie, & Carr, 2008). More recent research notes the high social and economic cost of a poor start in life (Commission on the Social Determinants of Health, 2008; Grimmond, 2011; New Zealand Government, 2011; Office of the Prime Minister's Science Advisory Committee, 2011; Poulton, 2012) and identifies research gaps and issues within policy development and evaluation in the current climate. Overall, childhood is now considered a key period for investing in human capital development and reducing social inequities (Economist Intelligence Unit, 2012).

In response to this finding, Gluckman (Office of the Prime Minister's Science Advisory Committee, 2011) recommended targeted investment for "increased access to and increased quality of, early childhood education for Māori and Pasifika whānau/families and for low decile communities" (p. 16). A targeted approach is supported in the Treasury's 2012 Briefing to the Incoming Ministers (BIM), which argues for a smaller, more effective and efficient state services sector, with better expenditure prioritisation. Treasury recommends "further targeting of existing ECE funding to children from lower socioeconomic backgrounds" (New Zealand Treasury, 2012, p. 12). The Ministry of Education's BIM states the need to strengthen links between the education system and the Government's social and economic objectives through "carefully managed trade-offs" (Ministry of Education, 2012). The BIM promotes a vision of New Zealanders with the skills, knowledge and values to contribute to economic growth and prosperity.

At the heart of these briefings is an economic argument for targeted services. Arguments against this stance adopt a universal approach, based on all children's right to services, and suggest that social equality is achieved through equitable funding arrangements (Herczog, 2012; May & Mitchell, 2009; Mitchell, 2012; Smith, 2012). In other words, ECE services for some children will cost more, but these costs should be as well as, not instead of, costs for ECE services for all children.

The current National-led coalition government has a goal of 98 percent of children participating in ECE by the time they start school and has recently announced substantial funding to support services in low socioeconomic areas to particularly encourage Māori and Pasifika children and families to engage in ECE (Te One, 2012). The relatively low participation rate in ECE for these target groups has been well documented by the Early Childhood Taskforce for Amazing Children (2011a). Not surprisingly, whānau/fanau want services that are culturally responsive and that respect reciprocal relationships inclusive of jointly negotiated goals for learning; in other words, where the principles of *Te Whāriki* are evident and clearly still relevant.

However, over the past 3 years policy changes in ECE have: reduced funding based on incentives for hiring qualified staff; cut requirements for qualified staff from

100 percent to 80 percent for over-2-year-olds, and to 50 percent for under-2-year-olds; ended the Centres of Innovation research programme; and reduced centrally funded professional development. Long-held aspirations for improved staff:child ratios for under-2s were quickly shattered in 2009 by announcements by the then Minister of Education, Anne Tolley. While some hope was restored that the level of trained staff would be raised over time, there have been no new announcements to indicate progress here. Many of these changes took effect immediately. Carmen Dalli reflected:

> The regulatory environment in New Zealand does not help; in other words, centres are not compelled by regulations to staff their under-twos areas with qualified teachers and thus the age-old practice of putting your least-experienced staff in the under-twos area persists in many centres. In this way, *Te Whāriki* has not resulted in improving the quality of under-two year olds' experiences in group-based ECE as it has for older children. (C. Dalli, personal communication, July 2012)

Current practices

After almost 20 years as a national curriculum, *Te Whāriki* is now embedded in the early childhood sector. Its durability perhaps lies in an underlying philosophy based on principles of equity, empowerment, community engagement and holistic development. Dalli notes:

> These are all still relevant and will continue to be so. Its status as an 'open curriculum' to me is a key strength; that it is a bicultural curriculum is another; that it reflects key values of this country; that it treats learning holistically rather than as discrete domains of knowledge. (C. Dalli, personal communication, July 2012)

Maureen Woodhams, National President of the New Zealand Playcentre Federation, suggests that *Te Whāriki* has not only created a coherent, agreed-upon focus for ECE; it has protected the sector from

> increased 'technicalisation' of ECE practice. Te Whāriki has forced us as ECE educators (both of young students and of adults teaching students) to remain holistic, open-ended, and construct our own whāriki. (M. Woodhams, personal communication, July 2012)

Woodhams believes that *Te Whāriki* has been relatively unchallenged in New Zealand because:

> Its development was not dominated by one part of the sector, such as a theoretical perspective, but actively included tangata whenua, parent-led, teacher-led perspectives although some of the inclusiveness was lost in the transition from draft to final. *Te Whāriki* foregrounds the right and opportunity for communities of families (I include their professional support in this) to define and work out the aspirations they have for their children. (M. Woodhams, personal communication, July 2012)

Norma Roberts and Helen Keats, both kindergarten senior teachers with more than 20 years' experience, comment:

Te Whāriki has had a really strong influence. We've now got a generation of teachers who only know Te Whāriki. Before we tried to adjust to the new curriculum by saying it was what we had always done and we used Piaget's theories which seemed to focus on individuals making their own choices about what to do and how to do it. Now we have moved to using sociocultural theories and teachers are only trained using Te Whāriki (H. Keats & N. Roberts, personal communication, July 2012).

When Te Whāriki was first released, the main focus of professional development was familiarisation with the framework. In 2003 Maggie Haggerty, a senior lecturer at Victoria University, described the response to the 1993 Te Whāriki trial as "overwhelmingly positive" (M. Haggerty, personal communication, September 2002). Dalli acknowledges that professional development to support Te Whāriki since its introduction has helped teachers to interpret it within their practice in a more sophisticated way than in the 1990s:

Resources based on the framework of Te Whāriki—like Kei Tua o te Pae, the Quality Journey, the Learning Stories approach to assessment and evaluation—have contributed to broadening teachers' talk and practice beyond the terminology of traditional areas of play and table top activities to include a wider understanding of the holistic nature of early childhood learning. (C. Dalli, personal communication, July 2012)

In 2007 Peter Moss observed that New Zealand was "leading a wave of early childhood innovation" (p. 27). More particularly, he argued that New Zealand's integrated system of ECE services brought some coherence to delivery as well as addressing issues of equity and access. His analysis clearly links the principles of Te Whāriki to early education as

a broad and holistic concept that covers children, families and communities, a concept of 'education-in-its-broadest-sense' in which learning and care really are inseparable and connected to many other purposes besides. (Moss, 2008, pp. 7–8)

Dalli noted this wider impact alongside her other concerns:

I think this broader understanding is evident in the reports from the Centre of Innovation projects which illustrate how some teaching teams have run with the ideas in Te Whāriki—the principles and strands—to create very exciting ECE programmes. (C. Dalli, personal communication, July 2012)

The fact that the national curriculum was based on principles and had no prescriptive content (e.g., disciplinary domains such as mathematics or science) was, and to some extent remains, challenging for the sector, particularly when asked to articulate what children are learning:

Initially we worked only with the goals and strands but now we focus much more on the principles. Now we see more and more evidence of the principles of Te Whāriki in the statements about philosophy. Teachers are always discussing the principles and referring to them, sometimes at the expense of content knowledge. (A. Collings, H. Keats, & N. Robertson, personal communication, July 2012)

This is reinforced by Dalli's observations:

Teacher education programmes have changed dramatically too because of *Te Whāriki* and these have had flow-on effects—such as creating a more articulate workforce. On the downside, the danger has been that the skills associated with using 'table top' activities to their full potential may not be getting the full attention they traditionally had in teacher education programmes—with the risk that they become time-fillers rather that activities/experiences that are understood for their full learning potential. (C. Dalli, personal communication, July 2012)

Challenges: From concept to reality

Dalli (2011) is one of many to observe that, despite widespread acceptance at the time, possibly tinged with relief, the curriculum did not explicate aims, objectives and measureable outcomes for learning. *Te Whāriki's* child-centred pedagogy, with its rights-based framework (Te One, 2009), is "neither a guaranteed outcome in day-to-day practice, nor necessarily an unproblematic one" (Dalli, 2011, p. 3). As early as 1996 Joy Cullen identified tensions between theoretical understanding and practice arising from *Te Whāriki*. While this has been ameliorated to some extent, new critiques of *Te Whāriki* have emerged (see, for example, Alvestad, Duncan, & Berge, 2009; Dalli, 2011). Challenges for the past decade have been *how* to recognise learning, *what* to record, and *how* to document. In terms of current thinking, Natalie Cook, an experienced professional development facilitator with a background in education and care services, comments:

Te Whāriki is the lens through which teachers recognise learning. Sometimes it is the only lens by which learning is recognised. Content knowledge and additional theories and frameworks can be overlooked as valuable tools for understanding how children learn. (N. Cook, personal communication, July 2012)

Woodhams adds a different perspective:

Being non-prescriptive has been identified as a weakness by some, but I disagree—it is only a weakness if one approaches education from a managerial perspective of expecting the exact implementation of practices in every case. This is anti the empowerment of parents/children/whānau which is the foundation of Playcentre (and anti-professionalism in the teacher-led part of the sector). Being non-prescriptive does mean that it is harder to 'teach'. In my experience this is equally true for qualified/trained teachers as for trained Playcentre educators, and depends on applying theory to practice and experience/confidence. (M. Woodhams, personal communication, July 2012)

Assessment in the early years was revolutionised by Margaret Carr's dispositional, transactional framework for Learning Stories, which arguably bridged the gap between curriculum and practice because Carr positioned assessment as *embedded* in curriculum rather than as a separate process. Considerable resources have been invested in developing Learning Stories (Carr, Lee, & Jones, 2004, 2007, 2009; Carr & Lee, 2012). Smith (2011) notes *Te Whāriki's* focus on motivational aspects of learning rather than on fragmented skills and knowledge, and argues that:

> It encourages teachers to support children's ongoing learning dispositions—for example, to persevere with difficulties rather than giving up and avoiding failure, difficulty or negative judgements from others. Dispositions to learn are 'habits of mind that dispose the learner to interpret, edit, and respond to experiences in characteristic ways'. (Carr, 1997, p.2) (cited in Smith, 2011, p. 153)

This is not always straightforward for teachers, and has proved challenging:

> The curriculum provides us with little support to effectively recognise and document progression in children's learning. For example, how learning becomes increasingly complex with higher order thinking resulting in transformation, creativity and innovation are difficult constructs to identify within *Te Whāriki*. Teachers need to understand the theories. (N. Cook, personal communication, July 2012)

The change to assessment practices as a result of Learning Stories has been profound, and, notwithstanding ongoing critique (see Blaiklock, 2008; Hedges, 2007), Learning Stories and the exemplars provided in *Kei Tua o te Pae*

> help turn *Te Whāriki* into a reality … they preserve the holistic nature of children's learning, are sensitive to context and acknowledge the complexity of children's learning. (Smith, 2011, p. 156)

Challenges have also emerged from recent OECD reporting on early childhood education in Aotearoa New Zealand (Taguma, Litjens, & Makowiecki, 2012). The OECD regularly appraises, among other measures, the quality of early childhood education provision across its member states. According to the OECD (Taguma et al., 2012),

> a common curriculum framework helps ensure an even level of quality across different providers, supports staff to provide stimulating environments for children and supports parents to better engage. (p. 7)

They describe *Te Whāriki* as "a progressive and cogent document regarding the orientation and aims of ECE" and one which "emphasises the importance of and respect for cultural values and diversity" (Taguma et al., 2012, p. 25). Overall, New Zealand ranks highly on international measures (Economist Intelligence Unit, 2012). Dalli suggests that a key reason for its continued good press is that it is based on principles that are universally valued within the sector as well as more generally in New Zealand society. (C. Dalli, personal communication, July 2012)

That said, the OECD report suggested that implementation of *Te Whāriki* could be strengthened by learning from other countries' approaches to:

- strengthening parental involvement in curriculum design or implementation;
- reflecting on children's agency (rights) and child-initiated play; and
- further improving the communication and leadership skills of staff for effective implementation. (p. 25)

The Early Childhood Taskforce, while acknowledging the ongoing relevance of *Te Whāriki's* content, recommends a comprehensive review of its implementation (New Zealand Government, 2011, p. 106). Drawing on national Education Review Office (ERO) reports, the Taskforce notes that reports "while valuable, are insufficient for an informed assessment [of the implementation of *Te Whāriki* in practice] to be made" (p. 111). For example, the ERO report *Implementing Self Review in Early Childhood Services* (2009) noted ERO's own limitations, arguing that the wide variation between services indicated that more work to support effective implementation of self-review was needed to realise the full potential of *Te Whāriki*.[6] For example, in attending to children's social and emotional competence, 45 percent of services were highly effective and the remaining 55 percent ranged from mostly effective (38 percent), through somewhat effective (14 percent) to ineffective (3 percent) (Education Review Office, 2011).

One further challenge remains. The ERO review of partnership with Māori whānau in 2012 noted that, while 78 percent of services had built positive relationships with whānau, only 10 percent had built the "effective and culturally responsive partnerships" required for meaningful dialogue and exchange (Education Review Office, 2012, n.p.). *Te Whāriki's* status as an international 'first' that gave primacy to the image of an empowered Māori child with a rich, meaningful and relevant cultural repertoire is contradicted by current discourses that class Māori tamariki as "at risk and under privileged" (May, 2009, p. 300). Dalli (personal communication, July 2012) notes that the aim of a truly bicultural curriculum remains "a distant lodestar".

Emerging critique: A sign of good health

Many have noted the recent accumulation of critical evaluations of *Te Whāriki*. These range from pedagogical, pragmatic concerns about a disconnect between aims and content, where teachers use *Te Whāriki* to justify existing practices, to concerns that the transformational potential of *Te Whāriki's* aspirations towards a socially just society remain unrealised. Duhn (2006) reminds us also of the function of a curriculum as

---

6 The Education Review Office is trialling a new self-review process in 2012/13.

a potentially technicist instrument. In the same vein, Gibbons notes that, on the one hand, by drawing on the sociology of childhood the intent of *Te Whāriki's* principles can be seen as empowering the child to learn and grow; while, on the other hand, there is an image of an endangered child, subject to increased surveillance authorised by government policies and practices (Gibbons, 2005, cited in May, 2009). Sandy Farquhar (2010) extends the debate with her critical interpretation of *Te Whāriki's* aspirations, seen in current terms:

> The competent capable learner is now a child suited to the needs of capitalism; a flexible worker adapted to the ever-changing requirements of the market … Each child must become a private citizen, self-responsible, self-governing, multicultural and cosmopolitan. This child is managed by centralised mechanisms, such as standards and testing. (Farquhar, 2010, p. 192)

The new imperative for education to be focused on skills and knowledge for the economy is clear in the Ministry of Education's BIM (2012). Carmen Dalli (personal communication, July 2012) noted that

> the current educational discourse of 'measuring outcomes' within a context of economic austerity and fiscal constraint is putting increased pressure on educational agencies to produce evidence of the difference that the educational 'spend' makes on outcomes.

This could be a challenge for an open-ended curriculum that resists predetermined outcomes. When set alongside Farquhar's analysis, this possibility signals a distinct change in educational priorities. Concerns about this sea change were expressed by a group of kindergarten senior teachers:

> The current government focus seems to be on quantifying outcomes rather than qualifying learning. We need to make sure *Te Whāriki* sits in context with other early childhood lenses. Teachers fear National Standards may replace *Te Whāriki*—that the government wants us to prove educational outcomes rather than improve them. Introducing National Standards into primary school is really concerning. How will that affect the early childhood curriculum framework? What pressure will [the] National [Government] place on ECE? How will *Te Whāriki* be placed in response to these? Will training providers gear teachers up to talk about this? (A. Collings, H. Keats, & N. Roberts, personal communication, July 2012)

Equally concerning is the lack of progress towards developing distinctive practices for under-2-year-olds, the biggest growth area in the sector and one in need of urgent attention if the present government's priorities are to be taken seriously:

> One disappointment I have about ECE in 2012 is that despite *Te Whāriki* highlighting that the curriculum for under-2 is a specialised one, and not a scaled-down version of the 3- or 4-year-old programme, the transformations that have occurred in programmes

for 3- to 4-year-olds are not visible to the same extent for younger children. For example, there is not enough study focused on the under-2s in teacher education programmes across the country. (C. Dalli, personal communication, July 2012)

Conclusion

Te Whāriki has been analysed, admired, praised, criticized, deconstructed and debunked, but it has not been a dead document lying on a shelf. (Smith, 2011, p. 157)

This chapter in the previous edition ended with a warning:

the early childhood sector in Aotearoa New Zealand would do well to remember that previous governments have overturned widely agreed longer-term policy directions in the past, as the experiences of the education sector in the late 1980s and early 1990s show. (Te One, 2003, p. 42)

When first released in 1996 as the official curriculum for early childhood education in Aotearoa New Zealand, *Te Whāriki* gained widespread acceptance throughout the early childhood sector. At that time both sides of the political spectrum used the economic crisis of the late 1980s as a rationale for retrenchment, restructuring and reform of the state education sector. Similar reforms are expected in the political and economic environment of 2012. Gains made in the early childhood sector under the previous Labour-led coalition government are under threat as the vision espoused by *Pathways to the Future* (Ministry of Education, 2002), the long-term early childhood education strategic plan, are superseded by the findings of the Early Childhood Taskforce (New Zealand Government, 2011). Debates about targeted (as opposed to universal) services, the need for trained teachers and learning outcomes—similar issues to those debated during the times in which *Te Whāriki* emerged—are on the education agenda once more. The school sector has had National Standards imposed and charter schools are mooted.

These policies bring new challenges to the education service, its teaching force and its national curriculum documents. The ECE sector is not immune to the trickle-down effects of school sector impacts but, unlike during the activism of the 1980s and 1990s, when key influencers in the sector strategically and deliberately united to cement the status of *Te Whāriki* and to influence *Pathways to the Future*, the question now is: Can the ECE sector push back as the hard-won status of the profession is threatened?

This chapter presents an overview of the socio-political environment at the time *Te Whāriki* was developed and first released, as well as an account of perspectives on *Te Whāriki* today. The draft version of *Te Whāriki* reflected the idea that curricula need to be culturally and nationally appropriate. Internationally this notion has been widely recognised and supported, and *Te Whāriki* remains a model curriculum (OECD,

2012). In the 1990s *Te Whāriki* created a point of solidarity in an unsympathetic and at times adverse political climate (Dalli, 2002). In 2002 the release of *Ngā Huarahi Arataki: Pathways to the Future* (Ministry of Education, 2002), the long-term strategic plan, influenced the regulatory environment so that the principles of *Te Whāriki* were included as measures assessed for compliance within the regulations governing licensed early childhood services. Now the sector faces an uncertain future as it awaits policy announcements following the Early Childhood Taskforce's recommendations to the Government. The question of the full realisation of *Te Whāriki* requires multiple-level actions through integrated policy (regulations and funding), research, and ongoing training and qualifications.

With or without administrative sanctions, *Te Whāriki* is on the educational map. Its durability lies in a conceptual framework that interweaves educational theory, political standpoints and a profound acknowledgement of the importance of culture. That remains unchallenged. The last words of this chapter are left to one of its original authors:

> Broadly, I would say *Te Whāriki*'s strengths are that it continues to fascinate and interest and challenge—both internationally and amongst teachers in New Zealand. (H. May, personal communication, June 2012)

References

Alvestad, M., Duncan, J., & Berge, A. (2009). New Zealand ECE teachers talk about *Te whāriki*. *New Zealand Journal of Teachers' Work, 6*(1) 3–19.

Benton, R. (1990). Biculturalism in education: Policy and practice under the fourth Labour government. In M. Holland & J. Boston (Eds.), *The fourth Labour government*. Auckland: Oxford University Press.

Blaiklock, K. (2008). The invisible alphabet: *Te whāriki*, letter knowledge, and the development of reading skills. *Early Education, 43*, 5–12.

Boston, J. (1990). The theoretical underpinnings of public sector restructuring in New Zealand. In J. Boston, J. Martin, J. Pallot & P. J. Walsh. (Eds.), *Reshaping the state: New Zealand's bureaucratic revolution*. Auckland: Oxford University Press.

Carr, M. (1991, November). *Developing a curriculum for early childhood: Establishing a framework*. Paper presented at the NZARE Conference, Dunedin.

Carr, M. (1992, March). *Preschool background paper*. Department of Early Childhood Studies, University of Waikato.

Carr, M. (2001). *Assessment in Early Childhood Settings: Learning Stories*. London: Sage

Carr, M., & Lee, W. (2012). *Learning Stories: Constructing learner identities in early education*. London: Sage.

Carr, M., Lee, W., & Jones, C. (2004, 2007, & 2009). *Kei tua o te pae: Assessment for learning: Early childhood exemplars: (Books 1–20): A resource prepared for the Ministry of Education*. Wellington: Learning Media.

Carr, M., & May, H. (1990). *Curriculum development contract: Curriculum guidelines for early childhood education.* Hamilton: Te Kohungahungatanga—Te Atawhai me Te Akoranga, Centre for Early Childhood, Hamilton Teachers College.

Carr, M., & May. H. (1993). Choosing a model: Reflecting on the development process of *Te whaariki,* national early childhood curriculum guidelines in Aotearoa-New Zealand. *International Journal of Early Years Education, 1*(3), 7–22.

Carr, M., & May, H. (1999). Te whāriki: Curriculum voices. In H. Penn (Ed.), *Early childhood services: Theory, policy and practice* (pp. 54–73). Buckingham, UK; Philadelphia, PA: Oxford University Press.

Commission on the Social Determinants of Health. (2008). *Closing the gap in a generation: Final Report of the Commission on Social Determinants of Health.* Geneva: World Health Organization.

Cullen, J. (1996). The challenge of *Te whāriki* for future developments in early childhood education. *delta, 48*(1), 113–125.

Dalli, C. (2002, October). *Early childhood policy: Stories of collaborative action in the 1990s.* Paper presented at OECD Country Seminar on Education and Trade Union policy in Aotearoa New Zealand, Wellington.

Dalli, C. (2011). A curriculum of open possibilities: A New Zealand kindergarten teacher's view of professional practice. *Early Years.* doi: 10.1080/09575146.2011.604841

Department of Education. (1988a). *The curriculum: An early childhood statement.* Wellington: Author.

Department of Education. (1988b). *Education to be more: Report of the early childhood care and education working group* [the Meade Report]. Wellington: Government Print.

Douglas, R. (1993). *Unfinished business.* Auckland: Random House.

Duhn, I. (2006). The making of global citizens: Traces of cosmopolitanism in the New Zealand early childhood curriculum. *Te Whāriki: Contemporary Issues in Early Childhood, 7*(3), 191–201.

Early Childhood Curriculum Project. (1992a). *Working document five: Pacific Island curriculum [draft].* Department of Early Childhood Studies, University of Waikato.

Early Childhood Curriculum Project. (1992b). *Working document four: Home based care and education [draft].* Department of Early Childhood Studies, University of Waikato.

Early Childhood Curriculum Project. (1992c). *Working document one: The framework:* Department of Early Childhood Studies, University of Waikato.

Early Childhood Curriculum Project. (1992d). *Working document seven: Knowledge, skills and attitudes: Infants, toddlers and preschoolers [draft].* Department of Early Childhood Studies, University of Waikato.

Early Childhood Curriculum Project. (1992e). *Working document six: Part one: Preschoolers special characteristics [draft].* Department of Early Childhood Studies, University of Waikato.

Early Childhood Curriculum Project. (1992f). *Working document six: Part two: Preschoolers elaboration of goals [draft].* Department of Early Childhood Studies, University of Waikato.

Early Childhood Curriculum Project. (1992g). *Working document three: Children with special needs [draft].* Department of Early Childhood Studies, University of Waikato.

Early Childhood Curriculum Project. (1992h). *Working document two: Part one: Infants and toddlers [draft].* Department of Early Childhood Studies, University of Waikato.

Early Childhood Curriculum Project. (1992i). *Working document two: Part two: Infants and toddlers [draft]*. Department of Early Childhood Studies, University of Waikato.

Economist Intelligence Unit. (2012). Starting well: Benchmarking early education across the world: A report from the Economist Intelligence Unit commissioned by the Lien Foundation. *The Economist*. Retrieved from http://www.lienfoundation.org/pdf/publications/sw_report.pdf

Education Review Office. (2011). *Positive foundations for learning: Confident and competent children in early childhood services*. Retrieved from http://www.ero.govt.nz/National-Reports/Positive-Foundations-for-Learning-Confident-and-Competent-Children-in-Early-Childhood-Services-October-2011

Education Review Office. (2009). *Implementing self review in early childhood services*. Retrieved from http://www.ero.govt.nz/National-Reports/Implementing-Self-Review-in-Early-Childhood-Services-January-2009

Farquhar, S. (2010). *Ricoeur, identity and early childhood*. MD: Rowman & Littlefield Publishers.

Grace, G. (1990). Labour and education: The crisis and settlements of education policy. In M. Holland & J. Boston (Eds.), *The fourth Labour government*. Auckland: Oxford University Press.

Grimmond, D. (2011). *1000 days to get it right for every child: The effectiveness of public investment in New Zealand children*. Every Child Counts Discussion Paper No. 2. Wellington: Every Child Counts.

Hedges, H. (2007). *Funds of knowledge in early childhood communities of inquiry*. Unpublished doctoral thesis, Massey University, Palmerston North. Retrieved from http://hdl.handle.net/10179/580

Herczog, M. (2012). Rights of children to quality care. In S. Te One (Ed.), *Who gets to play?: Promoting participation in ECE for all children: Children, 81, 17–21*. Wellington: Office of the Commissioner for Children.

Irwin, K. (1990). The politics of kohanga reo. In S. Middleton, J. Codd, & A. Jones (Eds.), *New Zealand educational policy today: Critical perspectives*. Auckland: Allen & Unwin.

Kelsey, J. (1995). *The New Zealand experiment: A world model for structural adjustment?* Auckland: Auckland University Press/Bridget Williams.

Lange, D. (1988). *Before Five: Early childhood care and education* in New Zealand Wellington: Department of Education.

May, H. (1991b). *Developing a curriculum for infants and toddlers in early childhood centres in Aotearoa/New Zealand*. Paper presented at the New Zealand Association for Research in Education, Dunedin.

May, H. (1991c). *Preliminary thoughts towards developing a curriculum for infants and toddlers in early childhood centres in Aotearoa/New Zealand*. Unpublished paper. Department of Early Childhood Studies, University of Waikato.

May, H. (2002). Aotearoa-New Zealand: An overview of history, policy and curriculum. *Magill Journal of Education, 37*(1), 19–36.

May, H. (2009). *Politics in the playground: The world of early childhood in New Zealand*. Dunedin: Otago University Press.

May, H., & Carr, M. (Eds.). (1996). *Implementing* Te whāriki: *Te Whāriki papers: Two*. Institute for Early Childhood Studies, Victoria University of Wellington/Department of Early Childhood Studies, University of Waikato.

May, H., & Mitchell, L. (2009). *Strengthening community-based early childhood education in Aotearoa New Zealand: Report of the Quality Public Early Childhood Education Project*. Wellington: Te Riu Roa/New Zealand Educational Institute.

Ministry of Education. (1990). *Curriculum development contract: Curriculum guidelines for early childhood education: Request for proposal*. Wellington: Author.

Ministry of Education. (1993a). *Te whāriki: Draft guidelines for developmentally appropriate programmes in early childhood services*. Wellington: Learning Media.

Ministry of Education. (1993b). *The New Zealand curriculum framework*. Wellington: Learning Media.

Ministry of Education. (1996). *Te whāriki: He whāriki mātauranga mō ngā mokopuna o Aotearoa: Early childhood curriculum*. Wellington: Learning Media.

Ministry of Education. (2002). *Nga huarahi arataki: Pathways to the future*. Wellington: Learning Media.

Ministry of Education. (2005). *Kei tua o te pae assessment for learning: Early childhood exemplars*. Wellington: Learning Media.

Ministry of Education. (2012). *Briefing to the incoming Minister*. Retrieved from http://www.beehive.govt.nz/sites/all/files/MinEdu_BIM.pdf

Mitchell, J. (1991, December). *Issues concerning the development of a curriculum for children with special needs in ECCE*. Paper presented to the New Zealand Association for Research in Education Conference, Dunedin.

Mitchell, L. (1996). Early childhood education at the crossroads. *New Zealand Annual Review of Education, 5*, 75–91

Mitchell, L. (2012). Participation in early childhood education. In S. Te One (Ed.), *Who gets to play?: Promoting participation in ECE for all children: Children 81* (pp. 27–29). Wellington: Office of the Commissioner for Children.

Mitchell, L., Wylie, C., & Carr, M. (2008). *Outcomes of early childhood education: Literature review*. Wellington: Ministry of Education.

Moss, P. (2007, May). Leading the wave: New Zealand in an international context. In *Travelling pathways to the future—Ngā huarahi arataki: Early childhood education symposium proceedings 2–3 May* (pp. 27–36). Wellington: Ministry of Education.

Moss, P. (2008). Beyond childcare, markets and technical practice: Re-politicising early childhood. In *Early childhood education and care in Ireland: Getting it right for children* (pp. 5–14). Early Childhood Care and Education Seminar Series 2. Dublin: Centre for Social and Educational Research.

New Zealand Government. (2011). *An agenda for amazing children: Final report of the ECE taskforce*. Retrieved from http://www.taskforce.ece.govt.nz/wp-content/uploads/2011/06/Final_Report_ECE_Taskforce.pdf

New Zealand Treasury. (1987). *Government management: Brief to the incoming government 1987: Volume II: Education issues*. Wellington: Author.

New Zealand Treasury. (2012). *Briefing to the incoming Minister*. Retrieved from http://www.beehive.govt.nz/sites/all/files/MinEdu_BIM.pdf

OECD. (2012). *Starting strong 111: A quality toolbox for early childhood education and care*. Paris, France: OECD. Retrieved from http://www.oecd.org/edu/preschoolandschool/startingstrongiii-aqualitytoolboxforearlychildhoodeducationandcare.htm

Office of the Prime Minister's Science Advisory Committee. (2011). *Improving the transition: Reducing social and psychological morbidity during adolescence: A report from the Prime Minister's Chief Science Advisor* [the Gluckman report]. Auckland: Author.

Poulton, R. (2012). The early childhood education (ECE) sector in New Zealand: Opportunities galore? In S. Te One (Ed.). *Who gets to play?: Promoting participation in ECE for all children: Children 81* (pp. 37–39). Wellington: Office of the Children's Commissioner.

Reedy, T. (1993). I have a dream. In *Proceedings of the Combined Early Childhood Union of Aotearoa Early Childhood Conference* (pp. 1–7). Christchurch: CECUA.

Smith, A. B. (2009, November). *Implementing the UNCRC in New Zealand: How are we doing in early childhood?* Keynote address to the Early Childhood Special Interest Group, New Zealand Association for Research in Education, Hamilton. Retrieved from http://www.nzare.org.nz/pdfs/ece/Anne-Smith-keynote.pdf

Smith, A. B. (2011). 'Relationships with people, places and things'—*Te whāriki*. In L. Millar & L. Pound (Eds.), *Theories and approaches to learning in the early years* (pp. 149–162). London, UK: Sage.

Smith, A. B. (2012). A good start for all children: The case for universal, accessible, high quality early childhood education. In S. Te One (Ed.), *Who gets to play?: Promoting participation in ECE for all children: Children 81* (pp. 22–24). Wellington: Office of the Commissioner for Children.

Taguma, M., Litjens, I., & Makowiecki, K. (2012). *Quality matters in early childhood education and care: New Zealand.* Paris, France: OECD. Retrieved from http://www.oecd.org/edu/preschoolandschool/NEW%20ZEALAND%20policy%20profile%20-%20published%20 3-8-2012.pdf

Te One, S. (2003). Te Whāriki: Contemporary issues of influence. In J. Nuttall (Ed.). *Weaving Te Whāriki: Aoteoroa New Zealand's early childhood curriculum document in theory and in practice* (pp. 17 – 49). Wellington: New Zealand Council for Educational Research.

Te One, S. (2009). *Perceptions of children's rights in early childhood.* Unpublished doctoral thesis, Victoria University of Wellington.

Te One, S. (2012). Who gets to play? [editorial]. *Children 81* (pp. 3–5). Wellington: Office of the Commissioner for Children.

Te One, S., & Dalli, C. (2010). The status of children's rights in early childhood education policy 2009. *New Zealand Annual Review of Education, 20,* 1–35.

Trevett, C. (2012, 24 May). Budget 2012: Funds frozen on early childhood subsidies. *New Zealand Herald.* Retrieved from http://www.nzherald.co.nz/politics/news/article.cfm?c_id=280&objetid=10808184

Wells, C. (1990). *Memorandum to early childhood organisations and training providers. Re: curriculum guideline in early childhood education.* New Zealand Childcare Association/Te Tari Puna Ora Archive, Alexander Turnbull Library.

Wells C. (1991, September). *The impact of change: Against the odds.* Keynote address to the Fifth Early Childhood Convention, Dunedin.

Willis, D. (1994). School based assessment: Underlying ideologies and their implications for teachers and learners. *New Zealand Journal of Educational Studies, 29*(2), 161–174.

CHAPTER 2

Tōku Rangatiratanga nā te Mana Mātauranga: "Knowledge and Power Set Me Free ..."

Tilly Reedy

ABSTRACT

This chapter, originally delivered as a keynote presentation to the 1995 Early Childhood Convention in Auckland, reflects on the sources of the Māori concepts that underpin *Te Whāriki*, both from the perspective of the author's own life and from her deep understanding of the Māori world view. The author expands on the meanings of these key concepts, sharing them with non-Māori readers whilst emphasising that they remain deeply and uniquely Māori. The chapter concludes with a reminder of the challenges that face Aotearoa New Zealand to develop and implement curricula that enhance the lives of all children.

Tilly Reedy's chapter is based on her keynote presentation to the 1995 Early Childhood Convention. We are grateful to Mrs Reedy and to the Te Kōhanga Reo National Trust for permission to reprint this material.

Tēnā rā koutou ngā kanohi ora ō ngā mātua-tīpuna kua ngaro atu ki te pō e …

Tēnā koutou, tēnā ra koutou katoa …

I believe in a freedom of the mind and spirit that is fearless yet controlled:

… a freedom that dreams dreams and seeks answers on distant horizons;

… a freedom that takes responsibility for the footprints left behind;

… a freedom that recognises the beauty of individuality;

… a freedom that weaves nations together for tomorrow's unity.

I believe in a freedom of the mind and of the spirit. That is my horizon—the heritage left to me by my ancestors who walked the ancient paths. Their horizon is my heritage.

They left me many treasures. They left me a heritage to set me free.

Ko Hikurangi te maunga	Hikurangi is my mountain
Ko Waiapu te awa	Waiapu is my river
Ko Ngāti Porou te iwi	Ngāti Porou is my people
Ko au e tū atu nei—	And I stand here before you—
He uri nā Porourangi …	A descendant of Porourangi …

They left me my whakapapa, my genealogical links: to Māui, the demigod of Māori mythology; to Paikea, the god who arrived in New Zealand on the back of a whale about 750 years ago; to our waka, *Horouta, Takitimu, Nukutere, Nukutaimemeha, Tereanini*, their leaders and their crews; to our larger-than-life ancestors, Toi, Rauru, Irakaiputahi, Kupe; to our eponymous ancestor Porourangi and his vibrant descendants, Materoa, Hinekehu, Te Rangitawaea, Pakanui, Te Aowera, Kapohanga …

I can trace my ancestry back to Māui, who "fished" this land up out of the sea. His canoe rests in petrified form on top of our famous mountain Hikurangi, the first place in the world to see the sun; Hikurangi, of special spiritual significance to us of Ngāti Porou. The magnificent birds of Ruakapanga, Tiungarangi, and Horongarangi rest there also. My 5-year-old granddaughter knows them well, and meets them often in creative, imaginative stories. She is also conversant with our famous ancestor Paikea and his whale. The whale is now an island at Whangara on the East Coast. They also left me their traditions and histories—about our waka *Horouta*, with its precious cargo of women and kūmara, and the very tapu *Takitimu*. They identified Porourangi as our eponymous ancestor, the culmination of our traditions, and the beginning of our "modern" histories.

Their horizon, my heritage

I grew up in a Māori-speaking community and Māori is my first language. It was the language of our home, the songs that were sung, the stories that were told. It was (and still is) the language of our marae, Hiruharama, and our meeting house, Kapohanga, the spiritual and emotional sanctuary of many. Kapohanga and the memories … of a young girl surrounded by powerful women who managed the marae and the community while their men were at war in Europe. I thought "women-in-charge" was the norm! My daughters think so too. I wonder where they got that crazy idea from.

Last year, my daughter Riripeti wrote this poem for my birthday:

Poem To My Mother
He wahine toa!

Ngāti Porou woman
that sees to the future
with children,
mokopuna,
and mokopuna more

Shaped from behind
Jagged hills that drop to sea
Roll on inwards
to a "promised land"

Where embers glow
and a fire is poked
For warmth
welcome,
food,
and stories

to fill the imagined
the fantasy
the free
MINDS

of children,
mokopuna,
and mokopuna more

It was here also that I learnt about the power of place, tūrangawaewae, and of knowing I belonged. To know is to be empowered. To be empowered is to be free. It all seemed so simple then. Nothing was impossible. I think it was the sharing, the caring, the collective living and learning. But as with all things, there was a flip-side—and for me, learning to accommodate the idiosyncrasies of aunts, elders and those "big kids" was tough! I resented being "seen and not heard", and developed this belief that people least able to help themselves needed me to fly their flags. The arrogance of it! I was forever challenging my elders, my aunts and my uncles, and questioning decisions they made that smacked of injustice and unfairness. I was a constant embarrassment to my family, especially my mother. Today I still carry that legacy of non-acceptance of injustice, as I see it. I hope that age has mellowed the tone and the arrogance, but not the commitment to a fair and just society that recognises the beauty in differences as much as the comfort in similarities.

A tangata whenua perspective of early learning
The Māori child

E tipu e rea mo nga ra o tou ao …
Grow up oh tender shoot and fulfil the needs of your generation …
  (Sir Apirana Ngata, 1949)[1]

Māori tradition identified the Māori child as a valued member of the Māori world—before conception, before birth, before time. The child was the personification of the worlds of yesterday:

He purapura i ruia mai i Rangiātea
E kore e ngaro.

Precious seeds dispersed from Rangiātea [the famed homeland of the Māori gods]
Will never be lost.

As with all precious seeds, the child was nurtured for survival and inculcated with an understanding of their own importance, through the reciting of genealogies and stories of folk heroes. The indoctrination of their undisputed rights to their place in their time and age was also part of their teaching. They were left in no doubt that someone cared for them physically, mentally, spiritually.

Much of this indoctrination—of mana and pride, of knowledge of their aristocratic lineage, of histories, of descriptions of chiefly ornaments and cloaks—took place through the many lullabies that were composed on the birth of the child and sung to the child constantly. The following is the first verse of a very long, very well-known oriori which I learnt as a child. It is our tribal version of how the kūmara was brought to New Zealand, and makes many references to our Pacific ancestors and their stories. It identifies our genealogical ties to ancient times, and our historical knowledge base.

Po! Po!

E tangi ana Tama ki te kai mana
Waiho me tiki atu ki te Pou-a-hao-kai
Hei a mai te pakake ki uta ra
He waiu mo Tama
Kia homai e to tipuna e Uenuku
Whakarongo. Ko te kumara ko Parinui-te-Ra
Ka hikimata te tapuae o Tangaroa
Ka whaimata te tapuae o Tangaroa
Tangaroa! Ka haruru!
    (Ngata & Jones (eds), 1974, pp. 152–161)

My son, Tama, is crying for food!
Wait until it is fetched from the Pillars-of-netted food.
And the whale is driven ashore,
To give milk for you, my son.
Verily, your ancestor Uenuku will give freely.
Now listen! The kumara is from the Beetling-Cliff-of-the-Sun
Beyond the eager bounding strides of Tangaroa, God of the Sea;
Lo, striding to and fro is Tangaroa,
Tangaroa! Listen to his resounding roar!
    (Translation by P. Te Hurunui)

For some, indoctrination took place before they were born …

"E takatakahi koe i roto ia a au he tāne, māu e ngaki te mate ō tō tipuna o Poroumata."
Thus spoke Te Atakura to the unborn Tuwhakairiora as she set the path for his
leadership role in a world of honour and revenge. He eventually avenged her father's
death, and his prowess as a warrior and as a man is recited and recalled in Ngāti Porou
today. A very powerful subtribe bears his name, and one of our most beautiful carved
meeting houses is named for him as well.

The child was, and still is, "te uri a Papatūānuku", the child of Papatūānuku, the
Earth Mother. When a child is born the placenta, whenua, is returned to the earth,
also whenua. The umbilical cord is put in the special place selected long before by the
child's ancestors, marking that child irrevocably for that tribe. The child is claimed. The
child claims! Their tūrangawaewae, their right to a "standing place", is undisputed.
They belong. But there are obligations also.

Take the word "aroha", for example. As I wrote in *He Matapuna*:

Aroha is an overworked and misunderstood concept … Misuse of this word is a
result of our lack of responsibility to teach the rule of reciprocity on which aroha

flourishes. Aroha is not something anyone can command from others because they imagine it's their right. To accept and enjoy the loving, the sharing, the caring of aroha means you give back a little more than you received. This keeps the networks alive and functioning. The acceptance of aroha in any shape or form places one unequivocally under obligation to that person, that family, that group. Perhaps it is not too late for us to spell out the meaning of aroha, more especially the obligation and responsibility that go with it. (Reedy, 1979, p. 42)

The child was, and still is, the incarnation of the ancestors: te kanohi ora, "the living face". The child was, and still is, the living link with yesterday and the bridge to tomorrow: te taura here tangata, "the binding rope that ties people together over time". The child is the kāwai tangata, the "genealogical link" that strengthens whanaungatanga, "family relationships", of that time and place. The child is also te ūkaipō, "the favoured, the special". The child is also the repository of the teachings of yesterday, the enhancement of the dreams of today, and the embodiment of the aspirations for tomorrow—the hope for the survival of the family.

The following translation of a song by a modern songwriter encapsulates these ideas:[2]

Whiringa Wairua

Many Te Kōhanga Reo whānau have flourished
Enabling this sacred vine
To weave us to those departed
This woven fibre is the spirituality of man
Since time began
The fibre comes in many colours
Red, brown, purple, ochre
Weaving the spiritual link
To our ancestors departed
This woven fibre is the spirituality of man
Since time began
The path is crystal clear
For all Te Kōhanga Reo whānau
It is our genealogical links with our gods
Our relationships with each other
And to those departed
This woven fibre is the spirituality of man
Since time began
This is the call of Te Kōhanga Reo
This is the call of Aotearoa
Let us all weave together into the spiritual realm.
  (M. Reedy, 1990)

A further waiata expresses the aspirations for the high-born child Tutere Moana, and the absolute belief of his people that all things are achieved by the power of the mind. The disciplined power of the mind was a highly accomplished skill practised by the Māori for both good and not-so-good reasons. The translation of three lines of this very long lullaby is as follows:

Listen O son; there was only one determination

That transported Tāne to the uppermost heavens

And that was the determination of the mind …

In the same song, Tutere is encouraged to take hold of the three baskets of knowledge—te kete tūāuri, te kete tūātea, te kete aronui—procured by Tāne from the twelfth heaven.

The training that was promised was rigorous and precise. Mistakes meant death, so only the best survived. The training extended to all facets of life, with specialist teachers working with selected youth. It covered both the esoteric and the exoteric: from black magic to memorising traditions and genealogies; from carving, weaving and food-gathering to warfare. Every child was a valued member of the community. Every community was valued by the child.

The following is another well-known poem which explains the importance of the child in the Māori world. It likens the child to the central shoots of the flax plant, which are protected by the outer leaves to ensure its survival. If the shoots are removed, the plant will die. The Māori drew fibre from the flax plant to weave their mats, their clothing and their baskets, and from its roots they made medicine. The flax plant was vital to the survival of the Māori, as was the child—as is the child. As the leaves protected the central shoots, so did the family protect the child. This protection, along with the nurturing, the teaching and the training, was the responsibility of the whole family, not just the parents.

Unuhia te rito ō te harakeke
Kei hea te kōmako e kō?
Kī mai ki a au
He aha te mea nui ō te ao nei?
Māku e kī atu
He tangata, he tangata, he tangata.

Strip away the central shoots from the flax plant
Where will the bellbird sing?
Tell me
What is the most valued thing in this world?
I will say
Man, man, man.

For our ancestors, one could replace the last line with the words "He tamaiti, he tamaiti, he tamaiti"—"A child, a child, a child". The child was indeed a valued member of the Māori world of yesterday.

But what about today?

Today we witness the parlous state of the Māori child in a world without the "outer leaves" of the family. No protection. No sustenance. No nurturing. What has brought them to this state?

Dr Tamati Reedy, a former Secretary for Māori Affairs, in his submission to the Royal Commission on Social Policy in 1987, identified "the historical experience of the Māori people since the signing of the Treaty of Waitangi" as one possible reason. He saw the period 1840–90 as "the era of demoralisation", in which the aim of the colonial government was to amalgamate Māori and settlers as quickly as possible. Despite the skills of the Māori and their adaptation to the agricultural, animal husbandry, trading, and marketing worlds opened up by the Pākehā, the Māori by the 1890s were overwhelmed by the process of colonisation. The sheer extent and intensity of demographic and economic change hit them hard. The Māori ceased to command the process of change.

The period 1890–1940 was viewed by Reedy as "the era of social reconstruction", in which British-educated Māori began to appear, and to present and defend Māori interests in Pākehā institutions. Land development schemes, health and house-building programmes were implemented; tribal trust boards, the Māori Arts and Crafts Board, and the Māori Purposes Fund Board were set up to help the Māori economically, socially, and culturally.

Reedy identified the period from the 1940s to the 1980s as "the era of dislocation". As he saw it, the big problem for the Māori people was the loss of their lands by confiscation or sale. With the rising Māori population, there were not the opportunities for employment in the shrinking rural economy, so Māori moved into the cities. By the late 1950s, it was a government policy to encourage this trend. Māori institutions, including the transmission of language and cultural skills, were disrupted.

It is acknowledged that the government took responsibility for developing Māori land assets in the late 1920s, but no real effort has gone into developing the human resource of the Māori people. Educational under-achievement, coupled with a lack of resources, means that Māori are largely confined to unskilled and semi-skilled wage work. Access to professional careers and participation in new commercial opportunities are strictly limited. The Māori people bear a disproportionate share of the consequences of the depressed labour market of the 1980s, and face the grim prospect of permanent unemployment. They are severely disadvantaged.

This disadvantage is shown in research carried out by the New Zealand Planning Council (1989, 1990a, 1990b), and the effect on our target group. Census figures (1986) show that Māori children still live in extended family households, but that 43 percent of those aged 1–4 years and 50 percent of those aged 5–9 years live in families with two parents. Nearly 30 percent of all Māori children live with single adults. Māori families have shown the greatest increase in one-parent families, from 19 percent in 1976 to nearly 30 percent in 1986. In 1986 women made up 84 percent of all sole parents. So women are taking on the full responsibility for rearing the children in their early years. No extended family. No male role models.

This social disadvantage is exacerbated by economic disadvantage, with 70–80 percent of Māori children aged 1–9 years coming from families in the two lowest income quintiles. One-parent families are significantly worse off than their two-parent counterparts; in 1986 they had average incomes of less than $15,000 before tax. The relationship between social and economic disadvantage and family stress and instability is well researched. A poor start in life does not augur well for any child.

The economic disadvantage experienced by Māori children extends to the type of housing available to them. Māori children are more likely to be living in flats, units, and rental accommodation. Their health is adversely affected, and Māori infants are more likely to die in their first year of life. Those who survive are likely to require more hospital treatment for illnesses associated with poverty.

Economically, socially, and culturally, Māori children and their Māori world are disadvantaged. In the following poem, Rawiri Paratene captures the Māori situation graphically:

A Tribute to the Living Māori Race

The Pākehā
with his "steal" blades
has tried to gut us.
He almost succeeded.
A lot of blood has been lost
and our dangling hearts
are tied with flax
to our knees.
We are busy now
gathering severed limbs
transplanting vital organs
regenerating rich brown skin
re-embowelling disembowelled
bowels

And soon we'll be together
and we will stand as one
No longer hollow-stomached
For we are not extinct
Nor are we endangered!

The Pākehā
with his "beehive" matches
has tried to burn
our parents' tongues
He wants to slice ours out
with his brand new
rust resistant, ever efficient
disposable, bic-thinking
all new, all purpose, all empowering
all-uminium blades.

We are busy now
gathering scattered pieces
of the riddle of our language
Yes
all those pidgin-remnants
of an acrobatic tongue
that once was fluent as a river
And soon we'll be together
and we will speak as one
No longer tongue-tied
For we are not mutes
Nor are we illiterate!

The Pākehā
with his barter (and his bullets)
has tried to banish us.
And not content with that
he came armed with Holy Bible
to take possession of our souls.
We are busy now
gathering our people
reviving and recruiting
reclaiming what is ours

And soon we'll be together
and we will RISE as one
No longer razzle-dazzled
For we are not homeless
Nor are we lacking spirit!
Nor are we lacking spirit …

The Māori people have, in the last decade, decided to take hold of their own destiny, despite the almost insurmountable hurdles placed before them. They have decided to return to their cultural roots for solutions to the issues they face. To return to their language, their culture, their values, and their practices for their identity—to return to their tribal roots to strengthen their minds and spirits. This return is the only hope for the survival of our young, the Māori child.

We have almost come full circle, and it has taken some of us 150 years to wake up to the fact that "the answer lies within us" (the catch-phrase of the World Indigenous Peoples Conference in 1990).

This challenge for the survival of the young Māori child, with an assured place in the twenty-first century, created the most vigorous and innovative educational movement in this country (dare one suggest, in the world): Te Kōhanga Reo, the Māori language nests. The movement is unique, imaginative. It has succeeded where nothing else has succeeded to unite us as a Māori people, working towards a common goal, and to motivate us to do something for ourselves. The language is us and it is ours. We are in control. Yet the language nests have done more than arrest the demise of a language— they have focused attention on the need to revitalise a generally dissipating culture and the marae, the last bastion of that culture. The marae is the cultural setting for the growing child.

Te Kōhanga Reo has brought together the child and a wide range of caregivers and teachers, and provided management and administration skills which have opened up exciting possibilities for the child's family.

The challenge has been carried into the primary schools of New Zealand—in immersion classes and Kura Kaupapa Māori. The latter continue the philosophy of Te Kōhanga Reo, with teachings only in Māori, and in an entirely Māori-speaking environment. Māori universities are being discussed, and one is operating with Ngāti Raukawa ki te Tonga. We have come full circle.

Yet all these achievements have had their difficulties. Hostility to the revival of Māori language and culture remains. Obstacles to the rebuilding and reinforcement of the Māori child's identity continue. Overt and covert racism persists.

Our Māori ancestors, in one of their many proverbs, provide an answer:

Whaia te iti kahurangi
Ki te tuohu koe, me he maunga teitei.

Seek ye the treasures of your heart
If you bow your head, let it be to a lofty mountain.

In other words, nothing worthwhile ever comes easy. The survival of the Māori in New Zealand is imperative for the survival of the Māori child. We must fight for that right as tangata whenua of New Zealand, as the first peoples of Aotearoa.

Nor are we lacking spirit . . .

Dimensions of the learner

Te Whāriki projects four dimensions for the holistic development of the child at all times—the physical (tinana), the mental (hinengaro), the spiritual (wairua), and the emotional (whatumanawa) (see Table 2.1).

Tinana

This dimension deals with the physical power and health of the body. The child learns that play, sport, and enjoyment are fundamental to good health; that knowledge of the biological functions and processes of the body is necessary; that the daily maintenance of the body, using old and new learnings, is important.

Hinengaro

This dimension deals with the power of the mind. The child learns about thoughts; about controlling their inner and external worlds, which builds this power of the mind; about "belief systems" that empower the mind; about explanations of the universe, from ancient Māori philosophies of te pō and te kore, to modern explanations of black holes and future/past time zones; about understanding themselves and their purpose in life.

To meet these needs, the Māori developed the very useful tool of karakia/incantation and affirmation. The karakia imprints within the mind the ability to focus on the purpose at hand, which may be to seek help for oneself or for someone else; to find a job; or to achieve some goal. This imprinting is similar to the rituals performed in the cultivation of the kūmara. It is no different from prayers calling on some divine agent, such as Jesus Christ, God or Allah, for guidance.

Wairua

This dimension deals with spiritual power and the sense of oneness with the universe. The child learns that all things are part of the universe; that all matter is made up of the same energy forces. They learn that past, present, and future are sources of trust, confidence, and self-esteem; that eternal questions about atua/gods and their place in the universe are challenges for the mind to explore; that tradition, religious beliefs, philosophy and modern science are not necessarily incompatible.

Whatumanawa

This dimension deals with the power of the emotions. The child, through knowledge and experience, builds an understanding of the range of human emotions—from love and happiness to hate and sorrow. These emotions manifest our inner world. If the child's experiences are positive and happy, the emotional responses will produce a child who is positive and happy, who is confident and has a positive self-image.

Ngā Taumata Whakahirahira

The following achievement aims will ensure that the learner is empowered in every possible way. The main achievement occurs in the development of the child's mana. The child is nurtured in the knowledge that they are loved and respected; that their physical, mental, spiritual, and emotional strength will build mana, influence, and control; that having mana is the enabling and empowering tool to controlling their own destiny.

Mana Atua

This is the development of personal wellbeing in the child, through an understanding of their own uniqueness and divine "specialness".

According to Māori there is a divine spirit, a spark of godliness, in each child born into this world. This belief is rooted in the teachings of old. When Tāne fashioned the human form from Papatūānuku, he breathed godliness into mankind. From that time to this, the teachings and understanding are that the essence of God is transmitted to each child born into this world. The Māori mind also determined that all things, both animate and inanimate, have their own mauri, their own spark of godliness. John Kehoe, in his book *Mind Power* (1991), reflects that "even a rock is a dance of energy".

It is therefore imperative that the teacher constantly celebrates and praises the learner. Whenever the child feels respected and accepted, their mauri thrives. When anything is correct, no matter how small, we must applaud and praise it! Only the child knows and feels the intensity and importance of this celebration.

We must also instil within the child the belief that they too can celebrate themselves. They need to be encouraged, each day and at all times, to use their own space to contemplate and ponder their own needs and successes.

Mana Tangata

This is the development of self-esteem through the individual's confidence to contribute to life. It encompasses the spirit of generosity and reciprocity; of caring for others and creating enduring personal relationships; of developing beliefs about prosperity that bring about the learning of skills for success and achievement; of developing physical powers through a strong and healthy body; of developing emotional maturity and awareness; of learning to deal with fears and inhibitions, which leads to joy and happiness. Children must learn early that life is a once-only experience. It is not a practice run.

Mana Reo

This is the development of communication, which enhances personal mana and wellbeing. The aim here is to empower the child in their ability to speak and to elucidate their learnings, knowledge, and abstract thoughts in te reo Māori. It is in the fluency of their delivery that their mana is enhanced.

Language is the window to a culture, and transmits the values and beliefs of its people. The many languages in this world have their own sounds and their own structures, yet they have but one purpose—to convey messages between the speaker and the listener.

Mana Whenua

This is the development of a sense of sovereignty, of identity, and of belonging. According to Māori, when a child is born their umbilical cord is cut and buried along with the placenta in their own land. In te reo Māori, the land and the placenta are both "whenua". Because of these traditions, the child has a spiritual unity with the land, with its people, and with the universe at large. A sense of identity with the land of their birth is inculcated in the child; love and respect for the land and its environment, and the geographic features of home, are learnt and imprinted in the child's mind. The spirit of the land lives in the child; their physical and emotional identification with the land is strengthened through myths, song, dance, and karakia. Confidence and self-esteem are the outcomes.

Mana Aotūroa

This is the development of a desire to explore and understand all aspects of this world and the universe; the development of curiosity, and of seeking answers.

The child learns and understands their uniqueness and their similarity with the rest of the universe. They learn that conquering the unknown through the power of the mind is possible; that understanding the physical world is exciting and challenging; that developing and practising the universal ideals of peace, compassion and harmony are a responsibility for us all.

Conclusion

Te Whāriki, the curriculum for early childhood education, is such a challenge for all of us. Our rights are recognised, and so are the rights of everyone else. For me, *Te Whāriki* encapsulates my horizon and the dreams I have for my mokopuna's heritage. It can be your horizon as well, and the heritage you leave behind, because *Te Whāriki* recognises my right to choose, and your right to choose. It encourages the transmission of my cultural values, my language and tikanga, and your cultural values, your language and customs. It validates my belief systems and your belief systems. It is also "home-grown".

Te Whāriki has a theoretical framework that is appropriate for all; common yet individual; for everyone, yet only for one; a whāriki woven by loving hands that can cross cultures with respect, that can weave people and nations together. *Te Whāriki* teaches us to respect ourselves and ultimately to respect others. It aims to ensure that children are empowered in every way possible, particularly in the development of their mana. They are nurtured in the knowledge that they are loved and respected; that their physical, mental, spiritual, and emotional strength will build mana, influence, and control; that having mana is the enabling and empowering tool to controlling their own destiny.

Te Whāriki encompasses the child in their uniqueness, as well as their being part of a whole. It reflects the child's holistic development, and the effect of the total environment on that development. In all of this, *Te Whāriki* also recognises the child as the living link to the past, the embodiment of the present, and the hope for the future. *Te Whāriki* perpetuates the cultural belief held by many Māori that the mokopuna is special.

Table 2.1

Te Whāriki: The Explanations

NGĀ TAUMATA WHAKAHIRAHIRA

Mana Atua
- The spiritual and sacred
- The unique and divine sense
- Developing a sense of wellbeing

Mana Tangata
- One's contribution to people, places, and things
- Developing self-esteem
- Developing ability to control

Mana Reo
- Speaking the language
- Communication
- Knowing the sacredness of the language

Mana Whenua
- Identity and belonging
- Rootedness
- Developing a sense of sovereignty with land

Mana Aotūroa
- Exploration
- Curiosity and adventure
- Developing understandings of self and the universe

TINANA

Power of the Body
- The body manifests its own atua/god
- The body projects its own powers

Physical Powers
Exercise and good nutrition build:
- A healthy body
- A strong body
- A fit body.

Body of Communication
- Language and its many forms—voice, sign, mind (telepathy)
- Language and its physical structures
- Expresses culture and people's mana

Physical Identity
- Cultural symbolism—houses, food, music
- Researching health of land and people
- Identifying with land of one's birth/ancestry

The Physical Universe
- Exploration of self, mankind, earth, and the universe
- Knowledge of the old and new
- Exploration of "large" and "small"

HINENGARO

Power of the Mind
- Training the mind to inquire, understand, and progress one's destiny through life
- Belief in "self"

Intellectual Powers
- Imprint belief systems
- Develop skills and knowledge for success
- Belief that opportunities abound in life
- No trials—this is life!

Power of Language
- Medium organised by the mind for communication
- Use of language skills enhances mana of the medium and person

Intellectual Identity
- Recognition and imprinting of home and place—land, rivers, mountains, people
- Self-esteem and love of "home"

Time and Space Orientation
- Conquering the unknown—internal or external
- Exploring and understanding one's uniqueness and similarity with the rest of the universe

WAIRUA

Power of the Spirit
- The spark of godliness in each human being
- Each is unique
- Mauri is in all things—animate and inanimate

Spiritual Powers
- Spirit of giving
- Caring for others
- Creating firm relationships

Spiritual Communications
- Every language carries its own spirit
- Every language is precious
- Language must be spoken to survive

Spiritual Identity
- Land, people, and universe are one
- Spirit of the land is in the person

Spiritual Universe
- The source of all energy in the universe is one
- Exploring and discovering is a spiritual experience

WHATUMANAWA

Power of Emotions
- Emotions express our inner and outer worlds
- Positive thoughts fuel happiness, success
- Negative thoughts fuel negative outcomes

Emotional Powers
- Encouraging joy and happiness
- Removing fears and inhibitions
- Supporting fairness and justice

Emotional Communication
- Conveying emotions powerfully—love, happiness, sorrow, fear, hate
- Language and a strong identity develop a healthy, confident person

Emotional Identity
- Identity with the land is developed through art, music, language, poetry, drama, and history
- Understanding wars over land

Exploring the Emotional Universe
- Recognising universal "laws" of the emotions – love, greed …
- Developing those that bring peace, harmony, balance

References

Government Review Team (1988). *Government review of Te Kohanga Reo. Ripoata o te whakamatau o nga mahi a Te Kohanga Reo.* Wellington: Author.

Kehoe, J. (1991). *Mind power.* Toronto: Zoetic.

New Zealand Planning Council (1989). *From birth to death II.* Wellington: Author.

New Zealand Planning Council (1990a). *Māori information booklets 1, 2, 3, 4.* Wellington: Author.

New Zealand Planning Council (1990b). *Who gets what?* Wellington: Author.

New Zealand Planning Council (1990c). *Puna wairere.* Wellington: Author.

Ngata, A. T., & Jones, P. T. H. (Eds.). (1974). *Ngā mō teatea: He maramara rere nō ngā waka maha.* Part II. Auckland: Polynesian Society.

Reedy, M. (1990). 'Whiringa Wairua'. In Te Kohanga Reo booklet for World Indigenous Peoples Conference. Hamilton, New Zealand: The Conference.

Reedy, T. (1979). *He matapuna.* Wellington: New Zealand Planning Council.

Endnotes

1 The full text of Sir Apirana Ngata's poroporoaki is as follows:

> E tipu e rea mo nga ra o tou ao
> Ko to ringa ki nga rakau a te Pākehā
> Hei ara mo to tinana
> Ko to ngakau ki nga taonga
> A o tipuna Māori
> Hei tikitiki mo to mahuna
> A ko to wairua ki te Atua
> Nana nei nga mea katoa.

> Grow up oh tender shoot and fulfil the needs of your generation
> Your hand mastering the skills of the Pākehā
> For your material well-being
> Your affections centred on the treasures
> Of your Māori ancestors
> As a plume upon your head
> Your soul given to God
> Creator of all things.

2 The original text of *Whiringa Wairua*, by Moehau Reedy, is as follows:

> Kua pua nga tini mano kawai
> O nga Kohanga Reo
> He whiriwhiri ano ki te putahi-tanga
> O rehua

> Whiringa wairua
> He muka tangata
> Whiria mai tawhiti nui i pamaomao
> He muka whero he parauri
> He muka papura kokowai
> Hei whiriwhiri ano ki te putahi-tanga
> O rehua

> Marakerake te huarahi
> Mo nga Kohanga Reo
> Ko te wairua ki te atua
> Ki te putahi-tanga
> O rehua

> Whiringa wairua, he muka tangata
> Whiria mai tawhiti nui i pamaomao
> Whiringa wairua he muka tangata
> Kohanga Reo karanga ra whiria mai
> Hei whakahoki ano ki te whiria mai
> Hei whakahoki ano ki te putahi-tanga
> O rehua

> Ki te putahi-tanga o rehua
> O rehua.

CHAPTER 3

Teu Le Va: A cultural knowledge paradigm for Pasifika early childhood education in Aotearoa New Zealand

Diane Mara

ABSTRACT

The involvement of Pacific women in the consultation process and publication of *Te Whāriki* provided 'a place to stand' for the diverse Pacific communities described in policy discourse as 'Pasifika'. The pan Pacific concept of *Teu Le Va* situates dialogue about theory and practice, community cultural knowledge and values, the place of Pacific languages, culturally responsive pedagogy, and the authentic implementation of *Te Whāriki*. Pasifika early childhood scholarship is emerging that focuses on the role of spirituality within the holistic bicultural curriculum and a critique of the notions of 'play' as understood and practised within a Pacific paradigm of teaching and learning.

Introduction

Pasifika early childhood provision has had a unique place in New Zealand's early childhood education sector since 1972, when the first Cook Islands punanga reo play group was set up in Tokoroa (May, 2003). However, over the following four decades the sector has struggled to maintain community-based services through which Pacific languages and cultural values can be fostered and maintained. As minority immigrant groups with high aspirations for their children and their future lives in New Zealand, Pacific families have long wanted their children to be supported in their own ethnic identity/identities and languages while being prepared for educational success within the New Zealand education system. The diversity of ethnic and community languages within the umbrella of 'Pacific' is also a distinctive feature of Pasifika early childhood education (ECE).

The challenges facing Pasifika services since the release of *Te Whāriki* in 1996 (Ministry of Education, 1996) have been the same as for other ECE providers:

- advocacy for quality early childhood education for children and their families in Aotearoa New Zealand
- the viability and sustainability of services
- building a pool of qualified Pasifika teachers, teacher-educators and researchers
- accessing funding for the establishment of buildings and venues within which quality early childhood education can take place.

However, the challenges have been qualitatively different for Pasifika groups given the particular ethnic identity agendas that continue to be shaped by socioeconomic factors, higher levels of unemployment, poorer-quality housing, and other social indicators that have contributed to the positioning of Pasifika learners within the underachieving tail of educational success. Most importantly, if high-quality early childhood education can mitigate aspects of early social disadvantage, then striving for and attaining excellence in ECE is all the more essential for Pasifika children, parents and communities in Aotearoa New Zealand. The high stakes and societal outcomes affect all groups within our society.

As more of our Pasifika ECE founding mothers pass on, there are fewer left to recall the aspirations that were present during the 1970s and 1980s, and fewer still who are able to recall the contributions of Pasifika women who have gone before. I would like to dedicate this chapter to pioneers such as Teupoko Morgan, Eti Laufiso and Materena George, as well as those in 'retirement', including Fereni Ete, Tuiataga Faafua Tautolo, Feaua'i Burgess, Telesia McDonald, Tepaeru Tereora, Taonefou Falesima and Iole Tagileloilagi. Many of these women were an integral part of the *Before Five* (Lange,

1988) policy developments in the 1980s, and were involved in certificate and diploma training of Pasifika ECE teachers, as well as the development of the draft (Ministry of Education, 1993) and final versions (Ministry of Education, 1996) of *Te Whāriki*.

It is important to record that the 1993 draft contained specific reference to Tagata Pasifika, special educational needs and home-based services, which helped teachers to interpret *Te Whāriki* and to respond to the particular priorities and interests of those groups. The reasons for the omission of these sections in the final document has never been fully clarified (see Chapter One, this volume). However, this decision meant that the possibilities for accessing and implementing appropriate professional practice among all teachers working with Pasifika children and their families received a setback. It could be argued that the articulation of valid Pasifika pedagogical links to the ECE curriculum was also held back. However, as this chapter later argues, contemporary Pasifika ECE researchers, teachers and teacher-educators are increasingly beginning to create a uniquely Pasifika 'space' within *Te Whāriki*.

This chapter begins by considering how themes from research in the 1990s are still relevant to current curriculum developments in Pasifika ECE. One of the major shifts in Pasifika educational research has been the use of metaphors and paradigms to advocate for Pasifika knowledges, beliefs and values as credible frameworks for pedagogy and practice. In particular, the metaphor of *Te Whāriki* as a woven mat and the embodiment of knowledge in the act of weaving (or raranga) has always been a relevant and appropriate symbol for Pacific ethnic groups in the social construction of knowledge.

In 2010 a group of Pasifika researchers (Airini, Anae, & Mila-Schaaf, 2010) published *Teu Le Va* as a call for the creation of spaces for all those engaged with Pasifika learners to work together for educational achievement and success. The resonances of this work within *Te Whāriki* as a holistic curriculum are elaborated on a conceptual level, and also with specific reference to contemporary Pasifika ECE curriculum and pedagogy. It is within the dimension of spirituality that a growth in Pasifika ECE pedagogy has recently emerged, and this chapter highlights that work. One of the remaining challenges, however, is the need for more comprehensive Pasifika centre-based research. This and other issues are discussed in the concluding sections of the chapter as part of speculation on the future of Pasifika ECE in Aotearoa New Zealand.

Research from the 1990s

Interest in the implementation of *Te Whāriki* within Pasifika ECE centres and services dates back to the 1990s, when the author of this chapter was commissioned by the New Zealand Council for Educational Research (NZCER) to carry out a small-scale study on this topic (Mara, 1999). This work arose from a previous examination of progress towards the licensing and chartering of Pasifika ECE centres and services (Mara, 1998). The findings are still relevant to present debates and the re-consideration of *Te Whāriki* as the curriculum framework for all ECE services in Aotearoa New Zealand.

Focus groups were convened in Auckland, Wellington and Christchurch, representing 20 Pasifika early childhood centres. Participants commented on the need for professional development for the implementation of *Te Whāriki* to be more specific to Pasifika ECE centre needs, and to be responsive and appropriate to each centre (Mara, 1999, p. 36). At that time professional development was provided through the Early Childhood Development Unit (ECDU) and, although the ECE centres appreciated the provisions being made, they also wanted recognition of the need to translate the curriculum and to make explicit the aims, philosophies and values held by each of the main Pasifika ethnic groups. The response by the ECDU was to provide professional development by Pasifika ECE practitioners. This was recognised by the sector as being a positive development, although providing coverage for all six Pacific cultures and languages has been, and continues to be, a challenge for educational agencies and professional development providers.

The priorities of the Pasifika ECE sector at the end of the 1990s included the translation of *Te Whāriki* into Pacific languages, which was achieved through the concerted efforts of the Samoan and Tongan Early Childhood Associations. Other needs related to the level and quality of professional development and the approaches used to assist teachers in ECE centres, and the need for action research approaches to enhance Pasifika pedagogy, including that in Pacific language immersion provision. Obstacles to full implementation included improving the qualifications of Pasifika teachers (from certificate to diploma), and the licensing and chartering of Pasifika early childhood play groups so that they could become fully funded services (Mara, 1998). This often included planning and building (or renovating) premises.

Pasifika parents and communities also faced the complexity of policies and compliance expectations being placed on ECE centres, including becoming employers. Without the benefits of national umbrella organisations, such as those for kindergartens and child care under the various Kindergarten Associations and the New Zealand Childcare Association Te Tari Puna Ora, each Pasifika centre had to act autonomously and draw heavily on church, community and volunteer contributions to establish and maintain its services. Not surprisingly, two decades later many of these challenges remain in terms of maintaining fully sustainable Pasifika services (Mitchell & Mara, 2010).

Equally importantly, the challenge remains to explicitly articulate the definitions and meanings of quality Pasifika ECE in its own collective and ethnic-specific terms, particularly in terms of culturally inclusive curriculum and pedagogy. Research is one of the ways in which this challenge can be addressed. However, until relatively recently the volume of research within Pasifika ECE centres that follows the Pasifika

Research Guidelines (Anae, Coxon, Mara, Wendt Samu, & Finau et al, 2001), and which
articulates distinctive Pasifika pedagogies and the implementation of curriculum, has
been low. This situation is changing as more Pasifika early childhood teachers move
into research and teacher education or engage in postgraduate study, and as greater
provision of professional development in centres becomes available. Before turning
to a discussion of Pasifika ECE curriculum and pedagogy, it is necessary to consider
the nature of Pasifika knowledge and how it is socially constructed and articulated.

Metaphors and paradigms: The situating of knowledge in Pasifika research

Increasingly, Pasifika research in education, including early childhood education,
has featured the use of Pasifika knowledge, metaphors and methodologies as ways
of making more explicit Pasifika values, beliefs and traditional knowledge bases. As
suggested by Amituanai-Toloa (2009):

> The existing literature on indigenous methodologies, ways of doing things and ways
> of acting are majorly premised on the underlying beliefs and assumptions of Western
> research paradigms which do not reflect the values and beliefs of research participants
> such as Pasifika people. (2009, p. 46)

Furthermore, in order for Pasifika researchers to promote Pasifika indigenous beliefs
and assumptions, they have increasingly relied on the articulation and use of cultural
metaphors in order to take ownership of, and retain control over, their traditional
cultural knowledge base within a more academic and scholarly context. Amituanai-
Toloa (2009) provides a summary of such metaphors, including *talanoa* (Vaioleti, 2006),
the *kakala* (Thaman, 1995) and the *tivaevae* model (Maua Hodges, 2000). Metaphors can
be useful in helping to explain concepts or areas of unfamiliar knowledge, to increase
the understanding of a different frame of reference, or to increase access to new sets
of ideas, perspectives or paradigms.

Such directly visual or commonly understood representations of knowledge as
well as ethnic group priorities are highly relevant in establishing and maintaining
collaborative relationships between all ECE teachers and professionals, and with
Pasifika families and communities in Aotearoa New Zealand. Many Samoan, Tongan,
Cook Islands, Niuean, Tokelauan, Fijian and other Pasifika children and their families
are well acquainted with living across at least two paradigms or ways of knowing and
being while maintaining lives that have some internal integrity, expressed as ethnic
identity. As members of cultural and ethnic minorities, Pacific people in Aotearoa
live much of their lives within a second paradigm, and move across and between
paradigms all the time with relative success, although examples of social and cultural
disconnection and disengagement still occur for some young urban Pasifika.

Such cultural and political experiences by members of Pacific ethnic group
members—some now third- and fourth-generation New Zealanders—become

opportunities for pan-Pacific and ethnic-specific consciousness to be articulated and communicated. Expressing that consciousness through Pasifika metaphors such as the Cook Islands *tivaevae* model (hand-sewn quilting) and the Tongan *kakala* model (the construction of flower adornment) has made more visible knowledge systems and ways of learning and teaching that were previously invisible. Accordingly, Pasifika teachers, teacher-educators and researchers have claimed a unique set of Pasifika knowledge frameworks and Pasifika research methodology as domains and mechanisms of control over their cultural indigeneity, and as a source of self-definition that potentially (in academic terms) can become a distinct disciplinary domain or body of knowledge.

Within the context of Pasifika ECE the national early childhood curriculum *Te Whāriki* provides an inclusive and ecological framework of principles and strands, within which Pacific knowledge and pedagogy are able to grow and develop. This is because the metaphor of a woven mat is a significant and appropriate one to Pasifika knowledge paradigms, since it represents an authentic creative and artistic artefact embodying many social and cultural meanings related to social relationships and the sharing of knowledge. The metaphor allows for the inclusion of the selection and preparation of weaving materials, and the design and techniques of the weaving itself, through to the purpose and utility of the finished product, as well as cultural practices of gift giving or ceremonial presentation that complete the process. The appropriateness of the woven mat metaphor is consistent and meaningful across all Pacific ethnic groups. The whāriki metaphor and all its levels of meaning were well received and understood by the Pasifika ECE sector, dating back to the initial development of *Te Whāriki* and during associated consultation across the sector in the 1990s.

Barriers to articulation of Pasifika knowledge in the ECE sector

It is important to ask, then, why Pasifika knowledge and pedagogy in ECE are still not well known or understood. There are many reasons for a historical paucity of Pasifika ECE research, knowledge, evidence-based practice and articulated pedagogy, despite synergies with *Te Whāriki* as a curriculum document. However, a primary reason is that it takes time, opportunity and resources to build an academic and research evidence base, resources that have largely been unavailable to Pasifika ECE teachers.

There is also the reality of ethnic and cultural diversity across at least six main Pacific groups and the high proportion of Samoan people, followed by Tongan people, in Pasifika communities in Aotearoa New Zealand. It is not surprising, therefore, that Samoan and Tongan ECE services are the most numerous. A closely related point is that the relatively small size and the diversity of the Pasifika ECE sector has meant that the growth and development of services has largely taken place around individual ethnic groups, employing a range of forms of community leadership, or as isolated initiatives that have not been widely shared across the Pasifika ECE sector. Nor has the

sector had the benefit of overarching co-ordination through national networks, except
that incidentally provided by the Ministry of Education and government agencies in
relation to policy, the setting of regulations, funding requirements and professional
development—when available.

The historical patterns of teacher training and qualifications for the Pasifika sector
have also been characterised by the sector playing catch-up throughout the preceding
decades with the continually evolving certificate, diploma and degree qualifications
required of ECE teachers. This has affected the Pasifika ECE workforce to the extent
that Pasifika ECE teachers as a group are still the least qualified sector of the profession
and the most vulnerable in terms of achieving any parity with other ECE sector
professional standards (Mitchell & Mara, 2010).

In addition, the professional expertise that can only be built up through tertiary
education and academic research to inform evidence-based practice for Pasifika ECE
has been scattered across institutions and providers of teacher education. Only national
organisations, in particular Te Tari Puna Ora New Zealand Childcare Association,
have been able to consistently recognise and contribute to raising the quality of teacher
education programmes and qualifications for Pasifika ECE across the last three decades,
closely followed by the Pacific Islands Early Childhood Council Aotearoa (PIECCA),
Auckland College of Education, Wellington College of Education, several polytechnics,
private providers and today's universities. Only recently has it been possible to gather
together a critical mass of Pasifika ECE teachers and researchers in one institution,
where the time and resources have been available to create the conditions for writing
and research and for growing Pasifika ECE evidence-based professional practice.

Teu Le Va and Te Whāriki

The increase in the use of metaphors in Pasifika ECE research has been a response by
Pasifika researchers to a need to give Pasifika values and practices a central position
while validating and legitimising cultural and social knowledge in ways that allow
other researchers, teachers, parents and families to be involved and feel a measure of
connection. The development of *Teu Le Va* (Airini et al., 2010) spanned several years
of discussion, reflection and consultation by a task group of Pasifika educators and
researchers, sponsored by the Ministry of Education, Research Division.

The pan-Pacific concept or notion of *va, va'a* or *vaha* can be translated as a space
that transcends a physical dimension or construct. This culturally defined space is
characterised as a place or space or site of action in which productive social relationships
are enacted. Social interactions can be accomplished in a win-win situation that benefits
all stakeholders that enter into the *va*, and in situations that uphold the moral, ethical,
cultural and spiritual dimensions of social relationships. *Teu Le Va* also describes the
valuing, nurturing and guardianship of any space in which the relationships of all

stakeholders play out. The word *teu* in Samoan literally means 'to keep the space': to place something in a safe place, to carefully look after the space, to tidy up the place, and place everything in harmonious order.

The Samoan self, for example, is reliant on the state of the relationships within the *va* and on the sacredness of the *va* in human relationships. In the Tongan meaning of *va*, the spaces between any two individuals or groups are defined by and within the context in which they are taking place. Hence the metaphor or image of a flower, which is used to represent the concept of *va* as being surrounded by time, environment and contexts that set the boundaries of the *va* and of the relationships within it (Airini et al., 2010, p. 19). The context in the 2010 document is an educational one, in which the Pasifika child and his/her family are at the centre. It is considered important that sufficient time be set aside to nurture the relationships between all of the stakeholders, which in educational contexts are between and among Pasifika families and the community, teachers/educators, researchers and policy makers. It is also important that these relationships occur within a space or *va* that remains strong and robust, yet flexible.

In Pasifika cultural knowledge paradigms, connection and collaboration for shared visions of educational success are always geared towards attaining and maintaining harmony and balance in all human interconnections, in the expectations held of each other, in our behaviours, and in the ways in which we communicate verbally and non-verbally. The *va* itself can be described as being the place where aesthetic balance exists, as it does in an artistic or architectural sense. All who enter the *va* make a commitment to cherish, nurture and take care of all aspects of human relationships: spiritual, social, cultural, emotional, psychological and what can only be referred to as the tapu or sacred spaces of human relationship formation. Therefore, the expression of personal and professional ethics and behaviour required of teachers becomes an important aspect of taking care of all stakeholders within the *va*.

Knowledge and understanding of the concept of *Teu Le Va*, the ways in which most Pacific community members prefer to behave and the contexts that are congruent with their values, place certain requirements on all teachers, researchers, and policy makers committed to educational success. It requires nothing less than examining our professional and personal ethical conduct in any joint endeavours. Although *Teu Le Va* was not specifically developed for Pasifika ECE, the principles and strands of *Te Whāriki*—including collaboration, co-construction of knowledge, and respectful and responsive relationships—are equally appropriate and are upheld.

Creating spaces within the *va* for Pasifika early childhood curriculum and pedagogies

In 2000 Mara and Burgess argued that the development of Pasifika ECE would only be successful with ECE cross-sector support and collaboration. This theme was

continued when the present author argued for collaboration with Pacific and other
ethnic communities as part of implementation of the ECE Strategic Plan *Pathways to the
Future Ngā Huarahi Arataki* (Ministry of Education, 2002) and its crucial importance in
improving quality provision (Mara, 2006). This theme of collaboration and community
is central to understanding the *va*.

Two further articles by Samoan teachers and researchers have described the nature
of the *va* in Pasifika ECE from a Pasifika knowledge perspective. McDonald's (2004)
paper articulates aspects of cultural values and beliefs, including spirituality, which
many Pasifika teacher-educators have used in the course of their work. McDonald
provides an accessible working definition of what Pasifika pedagogy entails and the
ways in which these beliefs and values are transmitted pedagogically through the
Samoan language in all its various nuances and meanings. That is why immersion in
Samoan or in any other Pacific language in early childhood education is eminently
preferable in Aotearoa New Zealand, not only in terms of laying down the fundamental
mechanics and skills of early literacy, but also in laying the foundations of ethnic
identity, collective wisdom, and those values and beliefs that are essential in the
diaspora Samoan aiga or family. As McDonald asserts, it is through engagement in
the important rituals, ceremonies and knowledge of genealogy that the Samoan child
comes to an understanding of his/her relational self.

McDonald and other Pasifika ECE educators and researchers observe that in Pasifika
families children are never alone physically, emotionally, culturally or spiritually.
Children are always involved within a range of groupings and affiliations, where the
purpose of life is to be of service to others and to think of others before themselves at
all times and in all circumstances. Unfortunately, there are times when such goodwill
can be exploited or taken for granted within and outside of Pasifika networks, or when
it prevents the assertion of needs by individuals who may wish to raise questions or
who have ideas that challenge the status quo.

In Pacific communities, spirituality existed before the arrival of Christian missionaries
in the form of reverence for the sea, the land, the stars, the fish, and man's relationship
with natural forces. Since the 18th century, however, and introduction to the European
Christian God by missionaries, Pasifika understandings of spirituality have remained
very important, although their expression and literacies may have changed in line with
Western beliefs. In whatever way Pasifika spirituality is expressed, there are many
layers to a person's being and, as McDonald suggests, Samoan and other Pasifika are
always able to return to a spiritual core that provides a measure of solace, peace and
protection—a space or *va* that restores and affirms.

Tuafuti (2010) has described the nature of silences within the *va* in relation to the
relationships between teachers and parents. Samoan children are expected to learn
when it is appropriate to speak and when it is appropriate not to speak (by implication,

listening and observing are equally, if not more, important within the *va*). In many instances silence is based on respect for the other party in the interaction rather than an assumed withdrawal from the matter being discussed within the *va*. Some aspects of silence are culturally affirming and have powerful spiritual and sacred meanings. Further, Tuafuti argues, silence cannot always be interpreted as agreement, since the Samoan parents in her study felt they were *being* silenced. This did not occur consciously or deliberately, but often the parents felt too shy to speak because of their lack of fluency in English, lack of understanding of what the teacher was communicating, or respect for the palagi teacher in case the parents' own questions were interpreted as critical of the teacher's status. Conversely, Samoan parents, through their keen perceptions of body language and sensitivity to a subtext of feelings, reported an impression of not always being told the truth about their child or, from their perspective, detecting an underestimation by the teacher of what their child could do or achieve.

Insights from studies such as those by McDonald and Tuafuti help all stakeholders to understand that when some of the partners enter into the *va* with rigid preconceptions or assumptions so that the *va* is no longer a safe, equitable space, then relationships aimed at facilitating growth, development and learning of the child become less possible.

Spirituality in the early childhood holistic curriculum

As previously mentioned, during the development of *Te Whāriki* in the 1990s Pasifika ECE educators such as Fereni Ete began to translate the document into the Samoan language, and there were similar moves within the Tongan community. In both communities there was also a call to add a further strand: "Our children are gifts from God". On reflection, this assertion was, at its base, a claim for spirituality and uniquely Pasifika views of the child to be considered as important as all the other strands in *Te Whāriki*. In fact the bicultural curriculum, based on Māori dimensions of spirituality and the weaving metaphor, does permit space for a spiritual dimension in child development, but this has only recently been explored more fully by non-Pasifika teachers and researchers.

Bone, Cullen and Loveridge (2007) considered dimensions of spirituality within one Montessori, one Steiner and one privately owned preschool by observing the behaviours, practices and pedagogy around expressions of hospitality. Bone et al. cite Maria Montessori's belief that the child absorbs his/her environment and that experiences and things witnessed are not just remembered but become part of the soul. Montessori's view of learning and interacting with the environment was a spiritual one. The researchers found the centre staff created a sense of order, and the maintenance of a calm environment was considered very important. Unlike many

ECE centres, collective silence was encouraged and deemed to provide a powerful experience of 'one-ness'. Courtesy and the care of others helped children and adults to forget themselves when welcoming new children and adults.

The aim was to provide opportunities to connect with aspects of relationships beyond the material and the surface, such that the centre was a space where everyone had the chance to replenish and re-energise their spirit. In other words, the spiritual dimension involved a connection with feelings and concepts that have no material manifestation, except we know that when these connections are absent, life can be a struggle for both children and adults. Most importantly, if, within the early childhood learning context, we live as if there is enough regard, respect and integrity, then newness and difference are welcomed and not rejected. Bone et al. (2007) suggest that the spirituality they were able to observe through noting hospitality rituals provides some "in between space" that "constitutes a place of transition and opportunity for transformation" (p. 350). When wholeness is affirmed, professional practice that alienates and fragments becomes inappropriate and unacceptable. Not only is the space or centre a place of safety, restoration and replenishment, but it permits collective and transformative practice. The conclusions of the study by Bone et al. closely align and resonate with the Pasifika concept of *teu le va.*

Spirituality and implications for pedagogy

All reflective practitioners interrogate their daily practice. When spirituality and holistic development in every aspect are incorporated in that act of reflection, teaching can be considered to be a sacred and timeless vocation. As a result, teachers retain a measure of consistency and integrity whatever the latest policy or strategic directions set for the early childhood sector. Bone et al. rightly remind us of Dahlberg and Moss's call for a pedagogy "where we examine the question of being together" (Bone, et al, 2007, p. 351) and where teachers provide spaces where there is no room for exclusion of any kind. Do our present ECE centres and services prescribe curriculum parameters so tightly that what we offer leaves no room for the next child or family who arrive to add anything? What do new and successive children add to the spaces in terms of energy, their background, their hopes for the future—in other words, the non-material contributions to the learning and knowledge building of the centre?

Pedagogy that is inclusive of spirituality has some distinctive features: there is freedom to change, question and examine what it means for teachers, children and families to be together within the learning space or *va*. There is also a respect for difference that affirms social justice principles because of the calmness and wholeness that is present. In so doing, tension and hesitancy to engage and learn—by children and adults alike—are marginalised.

Implications for Pasifika ECE

Interest in spirituality and its implications for pedagogy permits Pasifika ECE to engage in an articulation and celebration of the spiritual dimension of the holistic curriculum. In Pasifika ECE, caring for and nurturing the spiritual wellbeing and growth of children and their families resonates with the cultural, social and community knowledge building that is facilitated by teachers within ECE centres and services. Not only is there a respect for silences and for the appropriateness of cessation of silencing, but also an active creating, maintaining and guarding of the spaces or *va* in which we all work together for children.

Pasifika ECE services have experience and skill in catering for cultural diversity across at least six main ethnic groups, including their languages and cultural beliefs and practices. The context of ECE in Aotearoa New Zealand has provided those opportunities because of the relative size of Pasifika minority groups, their geographic location, and the lack of supply of suitably qualified Pasifika teachers to implement quality curriculum. Pasifika ECE centres have worked tirelessly within relentless waves of policy, regulatory and funding changes to continue to be guardians of shared values, beliefs, cultural identities and Pacific languages.

Just as tangata whenua place centrality on wairua (spirit) and on spiritual growth and development, so do Pacific communities in Aotearoa New Zealand. It is a positive development that there is a growing corpus of knowledge now emerging from the Pasifika ECE sector that affirms such philosophical paradigms. Unfortunately, there is only anecdotal evidence of how spirituality is expressed in Pasifika pedagogies and ECE centres, beyond the daily practice of rituals such as lotu (prayer) in Samoan aoga amata (early childhood centres). There is an assumption made about how the significant adults in a child's life, including Pasifika ECE teachers, model and express spirituality through their own conduct so that these values and beliefs are transmitted to children. Elements of power and empowerment through such relationships need to be further researched.

Conclusion: Looking towards the future of Pasifika knowledge and pedagogy

Tuafuti (2011) describes a personal journey of challenge and possibility as she adopted a set of *fa'asamoa* protocols in her study of the establishment of bilingual and immersion centres in Auckland Pasifika communities. She reinforces the need for the time and patience required to search for multiple culturally appropriate research protocols while ensuring the specific methodologies and methods of research are commensurate with Pasifika cultural and historical traditions. Such research becomes transformative for stakeholders even though it requires much collaboration, conversation, reflection and ethical respect among all participants.

Leaupepe (2011) challenges Cook Islands and other Pasifika ECE teachers to reconsider the traditional and widely accepted definitions and understandings of play in the light of their own professional practice. It is argued that where teachers have not made conscious some of their own values and beliefs about play and its place in the growth and development of the child, then implementing pedagogy within a culturally inclusive curriculum may be adversely affected. Although play has been one aspect of a binary of work/play in traditional communal settings, there is no place for play within the Cook Islands cultural and community contexts and there remains a suspicion that play is down time that allows opportunity for off-task, even anti-social, behaviours. The processes suggested and modelled by Leaupepe are creating new and innovative approaches to Pasifika ECE pedagogies and the implementation of *Te Whāriki*, whereby children are encouraged to question and to follow their own interests through play and exploration.

The most comprehensive work that places Samoan spirituality within the implementation of *Te Whāriki* has been published by Toso (2011). Toso reconceptualises spirituality as a philosophy of practice, arguing from traditional Samoan values and beliefs about the child and developmental growth, and the relationship of those beliefs and values to professional practice in 21st century Pasifika ECE. Toso has developed some practical approaches and ideas for pedagogical innovation that can be used as indicators for culturally inclusive pedagogy and practice, primarily in early childhood but with relevance for primary and secondary classroom pedagogies (Toso, 2011, p. 135). She suggests that there is a well-argued basis for incorporating spirituality within the early childhood curriculum and Pasifika ECE, and that this articulation must be done by and with Pasifika teachers, researchers and communities. This articulation must also take into account the diverse cultural knowledge from Samoan and other Pasifika traditions, languages and values.

Although we are witnessing some innovation and progress in the sector, many challenges remain for Pasifika ECE. This chapter has described some of the recent work being produced by Pasifika ECE teachers, researchers and practitioners in which the *va* concept is reinforced as an authentic notion that can act as a rallying point to engage in questioning and interrogating prevailing pedagogies and areas of educational knowledge. There is no doubt that realising a holistic curriculum such as *Te Whāriki* can include enhancing and facilitating the spiritual wellbeing of children as an important learning outcome, and that it is a dimension to which Pasifika ECE can continue to make significant contributions.

This historical and pedagogical review of contemporary Pasifika early childhood education in Aotearoa provides a mosaic of areas of progress in some quarters—as well as areas of relative frustration—in the seemingly endless pursuit of high-quality educational provision for Pasifika children and their families. This situation remains despite the best (but isolated) efforts of some key (but limited) Pasifika ECE services. Despite the increase in funding provided by government to the development of play groups in areas with a high concentration of Pasifika families, and despite assurances that the play groups are 'following *Te Whariki*' despite the lack of professional, qualified leadership (which in Pasifika terms means fluent speakers and those who are respected cultural leaders), the sustainability as well as the quality of such well-meaning, staged development remains in question.

Questions of the sustainability of present Pasifika ECE provision must be addressed in the light of centres being forced to close down, centres with ongoing supplementary reviews by the Education Review Office, governance and management issues, lower levels of qualified Pasifika staff in Pasifika centres, and centres that have high levels of Pasifika participation. Meanwhile, the current government policy goal is for 98 percent participation in ECE for Pasifika children, but it is unclear, given the aforementioned factors, how rates of participation will be in quality Pasifika ECE. An analysis of Pasifika data from across a number of research findings by Mitchell and colleagues (Mitchell, Tangaere Royal, et al., 2006a, 2006b, 2008; Mitchell, Meagher-Lindberg, et al., 2011) provides compelling evidence that this is an unrealistic expectation.

The need for overarching policy and implementation in the sector remains, but this has to move beyond the national level of policy making or target setting. It is not only the Ministry of Education or the Ministry of Pacific Island Affairs that should set the agendas in Pasifika ECE. Pasifika communities and education stakeholders themselves (as demonstrated in recent petitions to government by Pasifika community networks to officially recognise Pasifika languages) must work in collaboration with the agencies responsible for providing resources and cross-agency co-operation. Only such co-ordination will result in substantial and sustainable progress and change.

The development of educational policy, research, practice and curriculum implementation infrastructure, and the production of qualified professionals to provide a critical mass of expert leadership, is still some time away. Pasifika ECE researchers, academics and educators in the tertiary sector are scattered and yet informally provide networking for change. Cross-institutional supervision of student teachers, and those Pasifika teachers wanting to pursue postgraduate qualifications, will need to continue for some time, as will collaborative Pasifika centre-based research, if further benchmarks for quality are to be established and achieved in Pasifika ECE in Aotearoa New Zealand. *Te Whāriki* remains the ECE curriculum within which Pasifika ECE can continue to make significant progress in the education and wellbeing of Pasifika children and their families in Aotearoa New Zealand.

References

Airini, Anae, M., Mila-Schaaf, K., with Coxon, E., Mara, D., & Sanga, K. (2010). *Teu le va: Relationships across research and policy in Pasifika education: Report to the Ministry of Education.* Wellington: Ministry of Education.

Amituanai-Toloa, M. (2009). What is a Pasifika research methodology?: The tupua in the winds of change. *Journal of the Pacific Circle Consortium for Education, 21*(2), 45–53.

Anae, M., Coxon, E., Mara, D., Wendt Samu, T., & Finau, C. (2001). *Pasifika education research guidelines: Report to the Ministry of Education.* Auckland: Auckland Uniservices.

Bone, J., Cullen, J., & Loveridge, J. (2007). Everyday spirituality: An aspect of the holistic curriculum in action. *Contemporary Issues in Early Childhood, 8*(4), 344–354.

Lange, D. (1988). *Before five.* Wellington: Government Printer.

Leaupepe, M. (2011). Professional development in the Cook Islands: Confronting and challenging Cook Islands early childhood teachers' understandings of play. *Pacific-Asian Education, 23*(2), 23–32.

Mara, D. (1998). *Progress towards licensing and chartering Pacific Islands early childhood centres in New Zealand: Final report to Ministry of Education.* Wellington: New Zealand Council for Educational Research.

Mara, D. (1999). *Implementation of* Te whāriki *in Pacific Islands early childhood centres: Final report to the Ministry of Education.* Wellington: New Zealand Council for Educational Research.

Mara, D. (2006). Relationships with Pacific and other ethnic communities. *Childrenz Issues, 10*(2), 32–34, 42.

Maua Hodges, T. (2000). *Ako pai ki aitutaki: Transporting or weaving cultures.* Unpublished research report of field experiences to the Cook Islands. Wellington: Wellington College of Education.

May, H. (2003). *Concerning women; considering children: Battles of the Childcare Association 1963–2003.* Wellington: Te Tari Puna Ora Aotearoa/New Zealand Childcare Association.

McDonald, A. T. (2004). *Spirituality an important quality in Pasifika early childhood education: A Samoan perspective.* Paper presented to the Pasifika International Conference, Samoa.

Ministry of Education. (1993). *Te whāriki: Developmentally appropriate programmes in early childhood education services.* Wellington: Learning Media.

Ministry of Education. (1996). *Te whāriki: He whāriki mātauranga mō ngā mokopuna o Aotearoa: Early childhood curriculum.* Wellington: Learning Media.

Ministry of Education. (2002). *Pathways to the future: Ngā huarahi arataki.* Wellington, New Zealand: Learning Media.

Mitchell, L., & Mara, D. (2010, September). *Pacific children and families in early childhood education in New Zealand.* Paper presented to the European Early Childhood Education Research Association, Birmingham University.

Mitchell, L., Meagher-Lindberg, P., Mara, D., Cubey, P., & Whitford, M. (2011). *Locality-based evaluation of Pathways to the Future: Ngā Huarahi Arataki: Integrated report 2004, 2006 and 2009.* Wellington: Ministry of Education. Retrieved from http://www.educationcounts.govt.nz/publications/ece/locality

Mitchell, L., Tangaere Royal, A., Mara, D., & Wylie, C. (2006a). *An evaluation of initial uses and impact of equity funding: Report to the Ministry of Education.* Wellington: New Zealand Council for Educational Research & Ministry of Education.

Mitchell, L., Tangaere Royal, A., Mara, D., & Wylie, C. (2006b). *Quality in parent/whānau-led services: Summary research report.* Wellington: New Zealand Council for Educational Research & Ministry of Education.

Mitchell, L., Tangaere Royal, A., Mara, D., & Wylie, C. (2008). *Locality-based evaluation of Pathways to the Future: Ngā Huarahi Arataki: Stage 1 baseline report.* Wellington: Ministry of Education.

Thaman, K. (1995). Concepts of learning, knowledge and wisdom in Tonga and their relevance to modern education. *Prospects: A Quarterly Review of Comparative Education, 15*(4), 723–733.

Toso, V. T. (2011). Reconceptualising spirituality as a philosophy of practice for Pasifika early childhood education in New Zealand: A Samoan perspective. *Pacific-Asian Education, 23*(2), 129–138.

Tuafuti, P. (2010). Additive bilingual education: Unlocking the culture of silence. *MAI Review, 1*. Retrieved from http://review.mai.ac.nz

Tuafuti, P. (2011). Multiple challenges in research within the *fa'asamoa* context. *Pacific-Asian Education, 23*(2), 33–42.

Vaioleti, T. (2006). Talanoa, a research methodology: A developing position on Pasifika research. *Waikato Journal of Education, 12*, 21–34.

CHAPTER 4

Improvement, accountability and sustainability: A comparison of developments in the early childhood and schooling sectors

Carol Mutch and Bev Trim

ABSTRACT

In this chapter, the authors argue that the contemporary political setting for both early childhood education and schooling in New Zealand has made the sectors more similar than different. They have both been subject to increased policy surveillance, accountability dictates and market forces. This, in turn, affects curriculum and pedagogy. The chapter takes an historical approach to discuss how this situation came to be but ends by reminding readers that models of collaborative endeavour such as the development of *Te Whāriki* or the *New Zealand Curriculum* offer beacons of hope for the future.

Introduction

The first edition of *Weaving Te Whāriki* included a chapter titled 'One context, two outcomes: A comparison of *Te Whāriki* and the *New Zealand Curriculum Framework*'. In that chapter Carol Mutch argued that, despite the two curriculum documents being prepared in a similar political context, there were significant differences in terms of how the concept of curriculum was defined, what the purpose of the curriculum was, what principles underpinned its development and what content was included. A decade on from writing that chapter there is a new curriculum for the schooling sector and renewed discussion about the early childhood curriculum in Aotearoa New Zealand's changing society.

This chapter puts recent changes into a longer-term perspective by examining developments in both sectors over the past three decades or so. This will be done through the lenses of improvement, accountability and sustainability (Cheng & Mok, 2008). We argue that the political and economic context in which both sectors now operate has meant that, while there are still interesting differences, in many respects the two sectors, their policies and the contexts for their respective curricula have come to have more in common. We begin by outlining the theoretical and conceptual framework which we have brought to the preparation of this chapter.

The theoretical framework underpinning this chapter

Much has been written about the impact of market-led forces on education, and on New Zealand education in particular (see, for example, Butterworth & Butterworth, 1998; Fiske & Ladd, 2000; Langley, 2009; Mutch, 2003; Thrupp, 1999b). New Right ideologies that have come to dominate educational decision making, through neo-liberal and neo-conservative discourses, have threatened to overtake New Zealand's social egalitarian ethos and liberal progressive educational tradition in both the schooling and early childhood education sectors. These discourses have been challenged at each turn—sometimes successfully, sometimes not. This chapter retraces some of the earlier developments outlined in the Mutch (2003) chapter but brings the discussion up to date before considering courses of action for the future. We use a framework from the schooling effectiveness movement literature to unpack the neo-liberal and neo-conservative forces at work since the 1970s and the socially critical responses to these.

In their paper on schooling effectiveness, Cheng and Mok (2008) posit a theory that education systems have faced three consecutive waves over the past 30 years: (1) *effective* school movements, (2) *quality* school movements, and (3) *world-class* school movements. The effective school movements, arising from the protest movements of the 1970s and gaining hold in the 1980s, had a strong focus on the *improvement* of school processes, because they appeared not to be providing equitable outcomes for all students. This first wave was characterised by approaches aimed at improving individual schools' performance through initiatives such as the "self-managing school" (Caldwell & Spinks, 1988). The emphasis was on autonomous, school-based decision making, but it was very much left to individual schools or school districts to implement, with little support from education ministries or departments. Success was therefore sporadic.

Because autonomous school decision-making on its own did not appear to be providing the answer, the second wave focused on ensuring that schools were more accountable. The *quality* (or competitive) school movements, beginning in the late 1980s and reaching a peak in the early 2000s, focused on the "quality and accountability of educational services provided by the schools meeting the multiple stakeholders' expectations and needs" (Cheng & Mok, 2008, p. 366). Improvement was still a key outcome, but the *accountability* wave brought with it the need for external validation and judgement of both individual school and system-wide decision making. This saw the proliferation of external evaluation agencies and the rise of performance benchmarks and standards.

Cheng and Mok argue that now, in the 2000s and beyond, *world-class* school movements need to ensure that schooling leads to *sustainability* of good practice in a context of globalisation and change. (In more recent writing in this area this is often referred to "21st century schooling".) The importance placed on school system rankings in international comparative studies has led to education systems scrutinising their own internal systems and looking at other external systems they deem to be successful: since we have gathered plenty of evidence about 'what works' over the last three decades, how do we now embed these principles into systems that can build on this knowledge, yet be flexible enough for whatever the future may hold? The third wave focuses on producing a research-informed, practice-driven, sustainable educational system to meet multiple and flexible local and global needs.

Our interpretation of Cheng and Mok's model, drawn from our research and experience within the New Zealand education system, does not view the aim of sustainable world-class schools as a finite phase but one of several overlapping aims in current education policy making. One of the interesting features of Cheng and Mok's wave model is that they suggest that the notion of 'effectiveness' has changed with each wave. In the improvement wave, success was measured by 'internal effectiveness': how well did the school perceive that systems functioned within their school and what could they do to improve them? In the accountability wave, success was measured by 'interface effectiveness': how involved in, and how well informed were all the stakeholders of, the success (or otherwise) of the school's systems? In the sustainability wave, 'future effectiveness' takes on a more global outlook.

The concepts in this chapter appear as overlapping waves (see Figure 4.1) that rise and fall and carry forward in time the assumptions underpinning each interpretation of effectiveness, creating a more complex and contested educational environment.

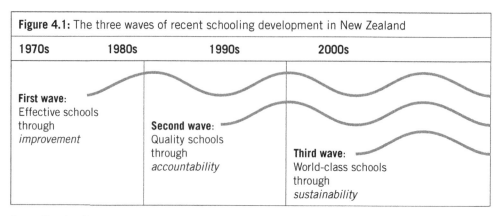

Figure 4.1: The three waves of recent schooling development in New Zealand

| 1970s | 1980s | 1990s | 2000s |

First wave:
Effective schools through *improvement*

Second wave:
Quality schools through *accountability*

Third wave:
World-class schools through *sustainability*

Source: Based on Cheng & Mok, 2008

The 'three waves' metaphor will be used to frame the discussion in the rest of this chapter. For clarity, we will outline the effects of each wave on the schooling sector first, followed by the early childhood education sector, and draw the discussion together at the end before considering possibilities for the future.

Wave 1: The improvement wave

Schools

After a period of economic growth and social stability in the 1960s, the 1970s heralded the stirrings of social, cultural and economic dissatisfaction. "The welfare state bred new problems, inflation, and with it new inequalities and new anxieties" (Dunstall, 1981, p. 398). Māori cultural resurgence, opposition to the Vietnam War and a rising feminist movement created "a new wave of protest that brought a new hue to the social fabric" (p. 428). Schools were not immune to calls for a shake-up of the status quo. This was reflected in the curriculum through the promotion of new conceptual approaches, such as 'new maths' and the 1974 social studies curriculum. As prosperity declined, education was seen as a convenient scapegoat, and the business sector was quick to propose solutions to the economic crisis. Snook (1995) gives examples of the talk of discontent at this time, including talk of "declining standards", "basics and frills" and "social engineering". Snook notes that the National Government's Minister of Education at the time was conducting a strong personal campaign to improve standards and reinstitute traditional values.

The downturn in the world economy was also calling into question the Keynesian economic policies of previous governments. In 1984 the Labour Government came to power with a mandate to undertake major social and economic change, but they were to do so in a way that would dismantle the foundations of the Welfare State set in place by the first Labour Government in 1936. Before both the 1984 and 1987 elections, the New Zealand Treasury issued briefing papers to the incoming government advising them of how this expenditure could be decreased and the economy strengthened (see Chapter One, this volume). Treasury advice was accepted and the ideological approach known as 'New Right' began to pervade government policy. The New Right was not alone in calling for reform, however. Research showed the education system was disadvantaging Māori, Pacific Island students and girls (see, for example, Alton-Lee, Nuthall & Patrick, 1987; Benton, 1986).

While improvement was called for from many quarters, there were differing perspectives on the nature of the problem and the best solutions. Throughout the 1980s there was a range of initiatives designed to address inequality in education—including the 'Girls can do anything' campaign and taha Māori in schools—and, the most radical, the notion of 'self-managing schools'. Self-managing schools (Caldwell & Spinks, 1988) were seen as a way of lessening educational bureaucracy and putting decision making into the hands of those who knew the context best and could implement new policies and programmes unimpeded by the slow machinery of government. While some individual schools embraced this approach, it was not, in its early incarnations, supported by giving schools the necessary autonomy.

New Right ideology, however, was to provide a place for the self-managing school concept to flourish. Two of the tenets of New Right thinking were that there should be minimal state support and that competition would lead to more efficient production (Lauder, 1987). In New Zealand, health, education and welfare services were seen as a major drain on government funds and therefore reform would make them more cost effective. The Prime Minister, David Lange, considered the need for reform so important that he took over the Education portfolio and set up a taskforce to review educational administration. Led by a prominent businessman, *Administering for Excellence* (Taskforce to Review Education Administration, 1988, "the Picot Report") would provide a justification for the reforms. Lange followed this with his policy document, *Tomorrow's Schools* (Lange, 1988), which set the reforms in motion.

Despite the rhetoric of minimal state intervention, the Government would retain control of much of what happened in schools because it still controlled education policy, curriculum content, student assessment and senior qualifications. This is explained by Dale (1989) and Trowler (1998), who claim that the New Right contained two forces: the neo-liberals and the neo-conservatives. The neo-liberals wanted freedom for the market to dictate direction and had no particular views on moral issues, as they believed market forces would lead the way. The neo-conservatives, by contrast, wanted to prescribe and regulate, preferring carefully monitored accountability and 'old-fashioned' values. The tensions between the two views and the way they both attempted to shape education policy, yet give concessions to each other in order to keep a strong alliance, led to some of the contradictory directions education policy was to take.

Early childhood education

The history of early childhood education in New Zealand followed a separate course to that of education for children in compulsory schooling until it became caught up in the reforms of the 1980s (May, 1991) because it was tied to society's views about the role of women in the home and workforce. Two main strands appear in the development of early childhood services. One focused on the care of young children; the other focused on education and was influenced by the philosophies of Rousseau, Pestalozzi, Froebel and, later, Montessori (May, 1997). The first kindergarten in New Zealand was established in 1889, to be followed by other services such as crèches (1903), playcentres (1941) and kōhanga reo (1982), so that by the time of the consultation period which laid the groundwork for *Te Whāriki* there were 20 different forms of early childhood services (Carr & May, 1993).

This diversity of services—and accompanying diversity of standards of provision of services—led to a rethink of the place of early childhood education within the wider system. Moving oversight of early childhood education from the Department of Social Welfare to the Department of Education in 1986 was a major and significant decision at that time. It meant that the measurement of the effectiveness of early childhood education shifted from a common micro-management style in many early childhood centres, to system-wide decision making. The rationale for this included a clear focus on improvement of provision, increased consistency across services, and an ability to monitor these improvements through a more concerted approach.

As the Labour Government (1984–1990) began its reform of social and educational services, the time was ripe for early childhood educators and supporters to lay the groundwork for a coherent and distinctive statement of the aims and practices of the early childhood community. "The bonus for early childhood was, however, to be swept on board a new upheaval of restructuring that it did not have to drive, just steer in the right direction" (May, 1991, p. 7). From 1982 a series of national in-service courses took place, an outcome of which was an affirmation of 15 basic principles for an early childhood curriculum. Carr and May (1994, p. 26) state, "it was perhaps the first time that the word 'curriculum' was applied nationally to all early childhood, to all services and to all ages from birth to school age".

This was followed by the Meade Report, *Education to be More* (Early Childhood Care and Education Working Group, 1988), in which the writers were committed to preserving equity across the variety of early childhood education services in

New Zealand (Meade, 1997). In 1989 *Education to Be More*, with some amendments, became the policy document *Before Five* (Lange, 1989). Government policies focused on giving early childhood education the same recognition as primary and secondary education. For example, bulk funding would be available for chartered early childhood services, conditional upon them meeting their negotiated charters with the Ministry of Education. The Meade working group recommended that these charters reflect curriculum objectives and aims. May was to comment that

> despite the dictates of wider political and administrative agendas, the early childhood concepts of diversity and the integration of care and education are not only intact but have been incorporated into a system which is more equitable to all. (1991, p. 10)

Although early childhood centres were able to retain their individual philosophies, in the next wave there were measures put in place to provide a greater degree of consistency of care and quality of education. These included a set of national operational regulations, a national curriculum, and the requirement that monitoring be undertaken by the Education Review Office (the same agency that conducts reviews of the compulsory schooling sector).

Wave 2: The accountability wave

Schools

The wave metaphor is appropriate for talking about educational policy in schools because it is difficult to state exactly when one phase began and another ended; rather, they merged and overlapped. Although 1989 is often cited as the date when the reforms began, the 1989 Education Act was, in fact, merely turning the earlier policy recommendations in the Picot Report and *Tomorrow's Schools* into legislation. The Act replaced the Department of Education and its regional offices with the Ministry of Education, formed self-managing schools by giving governance to boards of trustees, established the Education Review Office (ERO) to evaluate and report on the quality of educational provision within state-funded pre-tertiary education institutions and services, and created the New Zealand Qualifications Authority (NZQA) to oversee the development and monitoring of a secondary assessment and qualifications system for secondary and vocational education. The Act also made provision for school governance bodies, known as boards of trustees, to become Crown entities ultimately responsible to the government of the day.

The tensions becoming apparent in the 1980s, between neo-liberals wanting more freedom and neo-conservatives wanting more control, were not resolved with the establishment of self-managing schools. The low-trust environment that emerged meant that although schools were given more autonomy on the one hand, they were constricted by greater accountability measures on the other. The regulatory framework for schools' accountabilities was (and still is) provided by the National Education Guidelines (NEGs) and National Administration Guidelines (NAGs). Schools were required to gather information on student progress and achievement and to report to students, parents, the board of trustees, the school community and the Ministry of Education.

However, New Zealand's egalitarian ethos was not completely over-ridden. The opposing ideology, dubbed by Barr (1997) the "liberal left", was "a fusion of earlier liberal progressive and more recent socially critical perspectives" (Mutch, 2004, p. 194). Government policies attempted to overpower the voices of the liberal left; for example, by diminishing the strength of the teacher unions and discouraging collective bargaining through the Employment Contracts Act 1991. However, this was not completely successful, and at various times over the next two decades the voices of teacher unions, principals associations, academics and parents were to ameliorate or even counter proposed government policy directions.

These ideological tensions were very apparent in the school curriculum developments of the 1980s and 1990s. In 1985 a curriculum review had been conducted with wide educational, academic and community consultation. It led to a proposed curriculum that departed, in the main, from traditional subject divisions. The essence of the proposed curriculum sat more within the liberal left ideology. Instead of mathematics, science, English and so on, it suggested culture and heritage; language; creative and aesthetic development; mathematics; practical abilities; living in society; science, technology and the environment; and health and wellbeing (Department of Education, 1987). It was never implemented, and by 1991, as New Right ideologies became more entrenched with the change to a National Party-led government, the Minister of Education was talking instead of a "core curriculum" of English, mathematics, science and technology. Curriculum had gone from an integrated and progressive concept to one based in the neo-conservative (back to basics) and neo-liberal (importance of science and innovation) rhetoric of the time. The final version, the *New Zealand Curriculum Framework* (Ministry of Education, 1993b), was to appeal to a wider range of interests by returning to a broader subject base, which included essential skills and underpinning principles and values.

The *New Zealand Curriculum Framework* was only an overarching policy document, so more detailed guidance was needed, and over the next decade each curriculum learning area would receive its own curriculum statement. Again, this was a contested process. The writing of these curriculum statements was put out to competitive tender. In the case of social studies, for example, the statement went through three full revisions before all parties could agree on the final version. The polarisation of ideological views was to dominate the 1990s, but if anything the results of the New Right policies showed deepening social divisions and little improvement in student achievement by marginalised groups (Thrupp, 1999a).

Alongside the trend for more curriculum control was the call for more accountability. In the *New Zealand Curriculum Framework* (Ministry of Education, 1993b, p. 3) the Government set out its intentions:

> to ensure that the quality of teaching and learning in New Zealand schools is of the highest international standard. It [the curriculum] identifies for boards of trustees, teachers, students, parents and the wider community a progression of desirable standards of learning throughout the years of schooling, against which students' progress can be measured.

While the United States was implementing curriculum standards and the United Kingdom was instituting national testing, New Zealand managed to avoid going down the path of 'high stakes' testing by, instead, developing a local solution. To address the question of how well students were achieving throughout the country, the document *Assessment: Policy to Practice* (Ministry of Education, 1994) signalled the introduction of a national sampling assessment programme. This became the National Educational Monitoring Project (NEMP), which subjects a randomly chosen but representative sample of school students at Years 4 and 8 to a series of assessments. Each curriculum area is assessed on a 4-yearly cycle. As well as providing a snapshot of achievement and understanding, it highlights curriculum areas where improvement is needed. NEMP reports provide a national picture of student achievement and progress, but the identity of students, classes and schools remains confidential. The focus is not on how well particular students or schools achieve, but on what a representative sample of students are able to do; how this compares across gender, ethnicity, geographic location or other variables; and what trends are apparent over time. As an accountability tool this gives a general picture of what is happening in New Zealand schools, but it does not go far enough for those who wish to identify underperforming individual students, teachers or schools.

As the accountability wave moved into the 2000s, the overwhelming pace of change slowed a little. The Ministry undertook a 'stocktake' of the curriculum, which included wide consultation and various iterations of a new, streamlined curriculum. Again, tensions between the various ideological factions can be seen. While a broad curriculum based on conceptual understanding was being promoted on the one hand, an increased emphasis on numeracy and literacy was being implemented on the other. Part of the reason for this can be found in the increasing impact of international comparative assessments, which highlighted New Zealand's 'long tail of underachievement'.

Early childhood education

Since the 1990s two sets of policy direction have influenced early childhood education at a global level. The first was the *Education for All* (UNESCO, 1990) policies endorsed by most governments. These aimed to "ensure access to basic education for all, reduce gender disparities at all levels of education, and eliminate illiteracy" (Stromquist, 2005, p. 105). The second was the *Millennium Development Goals*, unanimously agreed by members of the United Nations in 2000, which reinforced the earlier goals and set 2015 as the date to aim for their full implementation. While the focus of these goals has been on basic public education, they have had a marked influence on what countries do in the early childhood education realm.

The Organisation for Economic Co-operation and Development (OECD) report, *Starting Strong* (2001), highlighted the "surge of policy attention over the past decade" (p. 7) to early childhood education. The report continued: "There is a need to strengthen the knowledge of the range of approaches adopted by different countries, along with successes and challenges encountered" (2001, p. 7). By now it was universally agreed that early childhood education was a significant feature of children's development and wellbeing (Koralek, 2007; Meade, 2001; OECD, 2001, 2006). Studies also showed that access to early childhood education substantially increased a child's likelihood of success at school and in later life (Wylie & Hodgen, 2006; Wylie & Thompson, 2003). This was supported by the OECD, which stated:

> Policy makers have recognized that equitable access to quality early childhood education and care can strengthen the foundations of lifelong learning for all children and support broad educational and social needs of families. (2001, p. 7)

In New Zealand over the 1990s more children began attending early childhood services, and by the year 2000 over 153,000 children were enrolled in a wide range of services (Ministry of Education, 2012). There was also increasing recognition of the impact of early childhood education on schools and children's learning, especially in relation to the transition to school. When oversight of early childhood education was moved to the Ministry of Education, it instantly 'lifted the bar' in terms of recognition that early-years education was about education *and* care. With that, however, came increased accountability for the sector. In 1990 regulations were mandated (Ministry of Education, 1990) and indicators for quality programmes (*Statement of Desirable Objectives and Practices for Chartered Early Childhood Services in New Zealand*, Ministry of Education, 1991), known as the DOPs, were established. ERO was given responsibility for monitoring the quality of delivery. This increased accountability was consistent with neo-conservative thinking, which supports government intervention and close scrutiny, but a challenge was to come from the other arm of New Right thinking—the neo-liberals. When a National government was returned to power in 1991, the growing privately owned early childhood sector began to question the policy directives of qualified teachers and increased pay and conditions. Neo-liberal ideology required the market to expand and profits to increase in a competitive environment, and with this came the freedom to manage centres as businesses.

At this time, as is now well documented (see, for example, Carr & May, 1993, 1994; Nuttall, 2003), the development of an innovative, holistic and inclusive national curriculum for children in early childhood education and care from birth to age 5 was able to proceed. Mutch (2003) argued that the National Government of the time was not as interested in early childhood as the previous government, as it was seen to be the domain of women and children, and so *Te Whāriki* was able to be developed without government interference. A draft was released in 1993 (Ministry of Education, 1993a), followed by professional development, research trials and further consultation. The final version, *Te Whāriki: He Whāriki Mātauranga mō ngā Mokopuna o Aotearoa: Early childhood curriculum*, was released in 1996 (Ministry of Education, 1996b) and the DOPs, the administrative guidelines for early childhood centres (Ministry of Education, 1996a), were amended to take account of this new curriculum.

The title *Te Whāriki* was chosen with care—literally translated it means a woven flax mat. This metaphor works at several levels. At a national level it represents the diversity of early childhood services as a coherent whole, and, in particular, acknowledges the place of Māori culture and language in New Zealand society. In relation to the curriculum itself it is an interlocking of the four underpinning principles and five strands and goals. Finally, it represents the curriculum (or course of learning) that each child will undertake—not as a linear and structured progression, but as a complex interweaving of experiences and developments.

Te Whāriki received international acclaim. Germany, Norway and Denmark (Fleer, 2003) and the United Kingdom (Siraj-Blatchford & Clarke, 2000) are countries that have examined *Te Whāriki* in depth when considering the development of their own early childhood curricula. But what impact will 21st century expectations have on *Te Whāriki*?

Wave 3: The sustainability wave

Schools

The sustainability wave introduced the language of 'evidence-based' practice and 'what works' to educational policy making. Early in the 2000s the Ministry of Education set out on an ambitious search for the evidence that would support development in key educational areas. The Iterative Best Evidence Synthesis (BES) programme was born. To date it has synthesised relevant national and international research to produce key findings on many different topics, such as teaching and learning (Alton-Lee, 2003), teacher professional learning (Timperley, Wilson, Barrar, & Fung, 2007), and school leadership (Robinson, Hohepa, & Lloyd, 2009).

The first of these, *Quality Teaching for Diverse Students in Schooling: Best Evidence Synthesis* (Alton-Lee, 2003), was to have a profound impact on pedagogy and curriculum. The outcome of curriculum development undertaken throughout the 2000s, the *New Zealand Curriculum* (Ministry of Education, 2007) was not only a set of learning areas underpinned by a vision and guiding principles, but also included guidance on effective pedagogy by reframing teaching as an ongoing inquiry. This inquiry process has three stages. *Focusing inquiry* establishes the baseline and direction. Teachers ask the question: What is important (and therefore worth spending more time on) given where my students are? *Teaching inquiry* uses evidence from research and practice to design teaching and learning opportunities and asks the question: What evidence-based strategies are most likely to help my students learn this? *Learning inquiry* investigates the success of the teaching in terms of the prioritised direction by asking the question: What happened as a result of the teaching, and what are the implications for further teaching?

Another aspect of the sustainability wave related to the way countries seek to achieve the status of world-class education systems, as judged by their performance in comparative international studies such as Trends in International Mathematics and Science Study (TIMSS), the Progress in International Reading Literacy Study (PIRLS) and the Programme for International Student Assessment (PISA). Such international comparisons have had a major impact on government policies and Ministry strategies in New Zealand. The Minister of Education stated in the foreword to the *2010–2015 Statement of Intent* (Ministry of Education, 2010, p. 2):

> New Zealanders are rightly proud of our education system. We are home to some of the best schools, the best teachers and the best students in the world. But the gap between our high performing and our low performing students is one of the widest in the Organisation for Economic Co-operation and Development (OECD), and this government is determined to address underachievement in our schools, and to drive improved educational performance right across the system to improve education outcomes for all New Zealanders.

The call for evidence-based practices that would prepare students for the 21st century and lift the achievement of 'underperforming' groups had both improvement and accountability aims, and these would soon clash head-on. After three terms in office, in 2008 the Labour Government was replaced by a National-led coalition. Having a single government in power for most of the 2000s (Labour) had given some stability to education. The implementation of the 2007 curriculum as the outcome of long, ongoing consultation with the education sector had met with little resistance. This stream-lined curriculum, which focused more on important principles and conceptual development, left schools with a high degree of autonomy in terms of how they would use the guidelines to devise and implement a school-based curriculum to meet the varying needs of their student populations. As soon as National came to power in 2008, a new (neo-conservative) policy to introduce National Standards was announced.

National Standards were seen as a way of providing parents of primary students with benchmarks against which the progress and achievement of their children could be judged, and teachers and schools could be made more accountable for their students' results. National Standards in reading, writing and mathematics for English-medium schools, and similar standards in Māori-medium settings, set out the expectations for student achievement and progress for Years 1–8.

Lack of consultation and the rapid implementation of National Standards meant they were met with fierce resistance from schools. Although the Ministry was able to soften the original expectations by allowing teachers to make 'overall teacher judgements' using a range of assessment tools to determine whether a student had met the standards, this compromise was not enough for some schools, who simply refused to comply. This standoff between the Government and the education sector was to grow even fiercer as National was returned 3 years later with talk of charter schools (neo-liberal), league tables (neo-conservative) and teacher performance pay (neo-conservative/neo-liberal). In 2012, as part of a coalition promise, charter schools are going ahead. They will receive government funding but will not be bound by regulations about class size, teacher pay, curriculum or assessment. One bright spot in 2012, however, was the resistance to the government announcement about increasing class sizes. As would be expected, teacher unions, principals' associations, students and academics vociferously opposed the policy, supported by unexpected allies—parents. From fear of losing electoral support, the government quickly dropped the class sizes policy and instead floated a policy that would be more divisive: league tables to rank school 'performance'.

From a promising start in the early 2000s, when New Zealand was performing well by international standards and finding innovative ways to address the underachievement of marginalised groups, the sustainability wave has become very rocky as it hits up against the neo-liberal and neo-conservative forces that threaten to overturn the progress made. Will the re-emphasis on New Right ideology underpinning education policy making enhance or diminish New Zealand's ability to build a sustainable education system that prepares young people for a complex and fast-changing future? Only time will tell.

Early childhood education

As the early childhood sector entered the sustainability phase, many would claim it was already riding the crest of the world-class wave. While the rest of the world looked on in admiration at "our integrated approach to early childhood qualifications, funding, regulation and curriculum" (Duhn, 2010, p. 49), at home we were more aware of the work still to be done.

In 2002 *Pathways to the Future: Ngā Huarahi Arataki* (Ministry of Education, 2002) set out a 10-year strategic plan for improving the quality of early childhood education and care. Plans for improvement were intended to increase participation, improve the quality of early childhood education services and promote collaborative relationships. Accountability measures were to include new regulatory and funding systems. Action-based strategies were set in place and progress against the plan was to be assessed in 10 years. The strategies promoted at the time included increasing the number of registered teachers, supporting services and families, improving ratio and group sizes, establishing and reflecting on quality practices, and integrating other services. Also identified in detail was the need to promote coherence in education provision from birth to 8 years with a better understanding between primary and early childhood in relation to curricula, pedagogical approaches and transition from early childhood to school. The expectation was that all early childhood teachers would be fully qualified by 2012. The plan was followed several years later by a process that set in place the chance for qualified early childhood teachers to gain pay relativity with their school counterparts (May, 2007).

May (2007) claims that the policy context for early childhood education in New Zealand has changed considerably over the years. Since the days of the development of *Te Whāriki*, and the accumulation of research findings that highlighted the benefits of early childhood education (see, for example, Wylie & Thompson, 2003; Wylie & Hodgen, 2006), early childhood education had come under more scrutiny. As the more recent OECD report, *Starting Strong II* (2006), stated:

> The provision of quality early childhood education and care (ECEC) has remained firmly on government agendas in recent years. Public awareness of gaps in provision and of insufficient quality in services has moved the issue of childcare and after-school care onto electoral agendas in many countries. (p. 12)

Concern over variation in quality led to a strengthening of teachers' knowledge and understanding of assessment, enhanced centre self-review and increasing teacher professional learning. ERO was also to play a role in increased scrutiny by focusing both on improvement (through centre self-review) and accountability (through ERO's external reviews). One of the issues that remains contested within these processes is that of the private for-profit provision of early childhood services.

The public/private divide in early childhood education provision has had a long history. Public provision, represented by kindergartens, makes up just 5 percent of the early childhood sector (Duhn, 2010). The remainder is split between community-based, not-for-profit and private services, mainly providing long-day child care. Private and corporate centres make up 60 percent of service provision. With the policy of providing funding for 20 hours of free ECE for all children, introduced by Labour in 2008 and continued (with adaptation) by National, and a range of subsidies available to families, "early childhood education is potentially a sound business investment" (Duhn, 2010, p. 51). Because private and corporate centres are free to respond to the market, there is potential for some private centres, especially if fewer- or lower-qualified teachers are employed, to forget the spirit of *Te Whāriki*. While many private centres understand the importance of implementing an age-appropriate curriculum, there are reports of others focusing on worksheets and preparation for school to the detriment of creative child-initiated play and exploration. A concern is that there could also be a trickle-down effect from National Standards that could narrow the curriculum further. In this way, New Right ideology drives not just the management of centres but pedagogy and curriculum. Duhn (2010, p. 51) explains the way neo-liberal ideology can influence early childhood provision:

> The underlying rationale is quite clear: private providers will respond to the market and consumer demand will dictate what kind of early childhood education services are required.

The increased corporatisation of early childhood education has meant there is growing competition in the sector, and, as a result, the policies proposed early in the decade have not all come to fruition. With the change of government, the current requirement is that only 50 per cent of all teachers employed in early childhood education will need to hold a recognised qualification (Parliamentary Counsel Office, 2008). The current government has also set a target that by 2015, 98 percent of new entrants in school will have participated in early childhood education (National Party, 2011), but this may be at the expense of quality within centres by, for example, increasing group sizes. Part of the National Party manifesto is to promote diversity and choice, control spiralling costs by reducing the expectations for teacher qualifications, introduce a funding model that is flexible, and reduce bureaucracy (National Party, 2011). The discourse is very neo-liberal. Although the word 'sustainable' is used, it is in the context of financial sustainability— quality is not mentioned.

Not all changes are politically driven. Some kindergartens, for example, have changed to a 6-hour session per day model to better meet the needs of working families, and the response has been positive. Mitchell (2010) is still optimistic about the changes in early childhood education over the decade and feels that the various initiatives, such as the 10-year strategic plan, were "a step towards the government viewing ECE as a child's right, a public good and a governmental responsibility" (p. 329). However, she acknowledges that reviews of early childhood services, budget cuts and the language of 'efficiency', 'cost-effectiveness' and 'evidence-based' are coming to dominate the policy landscape.

Where to from here?

Where do we find ourselves in the year 2012? We, the authors, would argue that after a long history of separate development, the schooling and early childhood sectors have been drawn closer together as they confront the New Right forces of neo-liberalism and neo-conservatism. While advances in embedding good practice were made in the early to mid-2000s through consultative curriculum development in the schooling sector and considered long-term planning in early childhood, these advances slowed as the decade came to a close. In the schooling sector, schools were barely able to implement and consolidate school-based curriculum design before the ground shifted and National Standards heralded a narrowing of the curriculum. In early childhood education the proliferation of new centres has left the capacity of the sector to offer consistent quality severely compromised.

How does the Cheng and Mok (2008) framework help us make sense of where we are now? Achieving *effective* schools and early childhood centres through a focus on *improvement* is still a key aim of the system. Teachers across the sectors are committed to enhancing the life chances of all children and young people through equitable and effective education provision. To be fair, the Government is too. Our concern is not with their lack of commitment to education, but rather the lack of understanding of what the evidence tells us and their seemingly random selection of policies which they consider will bring about the best results. National Standards and charter schools have not lived up to expectations overseas and it makes little sense that they will be any more successful in New Zealand. While 20 free hours and 98 percent participation seem like laudable aims for early childhood, if they lead to higher child:teacher ratios, fewer qualified staff and decreased quality of provision then it is hard to see how improvement will follow.

Achieving *quality* schools and centres through *accountability* is also still a key aim of the system. The problem is not with accountability *per se* but rather with the top-down imposition of multiple accountabilities. Taxpayers and parents have a right to expect their money will be spent wisely—and what could be more important than sound investment in the next generation? Schools and early childhood services take accountability seriously through assessment of learning, self-review, professional development, and planning and reporting requirements. Introducing policies such as league tables will only move accountability from something that is intrinsically motivating, for the good of teaching and learning, to something that is externally driven and extrinsically motivating—or demotivating. And can lowering the qualifications expectations of early childhood teachers really maintain or increase quality outcomes for children?

Ensuring a *world class* system through *sustainability* of good practice is also a key aim. We have a world-class system, we use evidence to guide our practice, and we have skilled and committed teachers. While neo-conservative ideology promotes a back-to-basics curriculum with one-size-fits-all standards, and neo-liberal ideology espouses freedom, choice and market forces, the sustainability of good practice is under threat. But not all is lost. The voices of the liberal left continue to critique policies that attempt to narrow the curriculum, de-professionalise teachers or lower quality provision. But the policy situation in 2012 can best be likened to a child's computer game: no sooner do you zap one alien than another pops up to take its place. Constant vigilance and a steady hand are required.

Long term, where is the answer to be found? Can a balance between improvement, accountability and sustainability lead to a system that is effective, delivers quality and maintains our place as world leaders in preparing children and young people for the 21st century? We believe it can, but it cannot be achieved while New Right policies dominate, demonise and demoralise. How do we bring all parties together to build on the strengths in the system and use the available evidence to promote policies that will bring about the necessary improvements?

We already have two sound models of how this can be achieved. One is *The New Zealand Curriculum*; the other is *Te Whāriki*. Each of these documents was the result of ongoing, wide-ranging consultation and iterative refinement. They provide an insight into the vision that teachers and wider society have for the education of our children and young people, along with the principles and values that we wish to underpin curriculum and pedagogy. Although they are the products of their time, they have captured many concepts that are timeless and, in the case of *Te Whāriki*, have stood the test of time. Table 4.1 outlines some of these important concepts.

Table 4.1: Important concepts in *The New Zealand Curriculum* and *Te Whāriki*	
New Zealand Curriculum (Ministry of Education, 2007)	**Te Whāriki (Ministry of Education, 1996b)**
"Our vision is for young people: • who will be creative, energetic, and enterprising; • who will seize the opportunities offered by new knowledge and technologies to secure a sustainable social, cultural, economic, and environmental future for our country; • who will work to create an Aotearoa New Zealand in which Māori and Pākehā recognise each other as full Treaty partners, and in which all cultures are valued for the contributions they bring; • who, in their school years, will continue to develop the values, knowledge and skills that will enable them to live satisfying lives; • who will be confident, connected, actively involved, and lifelong learners." (p. 8)	"This curriculum is founded on the following aspirations for our children: *to grow up as competent and confident learners and communicators, healthy in mind, body, and spirit, secure in their sense of belonging and in the knowledge that they make a valued contribution to society."* (p. 9)

"The principles set out below embody beliefs about what is important and desirable in school curriculum—...
    High expectations
    Treaty of Waitangi
    Cultural diversity
    Inclusion
    Learning to learn
    Community engagement
    Coherence
    Future focus." (p. 9)
	"The term 'curriculum' is used in this document to describe the sum total of experiences, activities, and events, whether direct or indirect, which occur within an environment designed to foster children's learning and development." (p. 10)
	
	"There are four broad principles at the centre of the early childhood curriculum.
	    Empowerment
	    Holistic Development
	    Family and Community
	    Relationships." (p. 14)

There it is, in a nutshell: what New Zealanders want for their children. We know what works, we have evidence from research and good practice about how best to achieve this. We now want a mandate to get on with meeting these visions, goals and aspirations in an environment of trust, respect and professionalism without being at the mercy of the buffeting winds of ideologically driven change.

Conclusion

This chapter comes full circle: through decades of educational policy making when schooling and early childhood education curricula have reflected particular historical, social, political and economic contexts; to the present, when the forces of New Right ideology meet the voices of the liberal left as we strive to forge an educational future for our children and young people. Although teachers feel under threat, we can be optimistic. What this overview of the last three decades has shown is that our vision and commitment has not wavered. *Te Whāriki*, not just as a curriculum but as a philosophy, has left an enduring legacy which has reminded the schooling sector that education should be child-centred, culturally sensitive and holistic. *The New Zealand Curriculum* has shown that we can bring curriculum design into the 21st century and encapsulate diverse perspectives into a statement of what we value as New Zealanders. The two curriculum documents outline the basis on which to make wise educational policy decisions. Let us use them. Our children and young people deserve no less.

References

Alton-Lee, A. (2003). *Quality teaching for diverse learners in schooling: Best evidence synthesis.* Wellington: Ministry of Education.

Alton-Lee, A., Nuthall, G., & Patrick, J. (1987). Take your brown hand off my book: Racism in the classroom. *set: Research Information for Teachers, 1*, item 8.

Barr, H. (1997). From the editor. *New Zealand Journal of Social Studies, 6*(2), 2.

Benton, R. (1986). Now fades the glimmering: Research in classrooms in New Zealand. *set: Research Information for Teachers, 2*, item 12.

Butterworth, G., & Butterworth, S. (1998). *Reforming education: The New Zealand experience 1984–1996*. Palmerston North: Dunmore Press.

Carr, M., & May, H. (1993). Choosing a model: Reflecting on the development process of *Te whāriki:* National early childhood guidelines in New Zealand. *International Journal of Early Years, 1*(3) 7–21.

Carr, M., & May, H. (1994). Weaving patterns: Developing national early childhood curriculum guidelines in Aotearoa-New Zealand. *Australian Journal of Early Childhood, 19*(1), 25–39.

Caldwell, B., & Spinks, J. (1988). *The self-managing school*. London, UK: Falmer Press.

Cheng, Y., & Mok, M. (2008). What effective classroom?: Towards a paradigm shift. *School Effectiveness and School Improvement, 19*(4), 365–385.

Dale, R. (1989). *The state and educational policy*. Buckingham, UK: Open University Press.

Department of Education. (1987). *The curriculum review*. Wellington: Government Printer.

Duhn, I. (2010). 'The centre is my business': Neo-liberal politics, privatisation and discourses of professionalism in New Zealand. *Contemporary Issues in Early Childhood, 11*(1), 49–59.

Dunstall, G. (1981). The social pattern. In W. Oliver (Ed.), *The Oxford history of New Zealand* (pp. 396–429). Wellington: Oxford University Press.

Early Childhood Care and Education Working Group. (1988). *Education to be more* [the Meade Report]. Wellington: Learning Media.

Fiske, E., & Ladd, H. (2000). *When schools compete: A cautionary tale*. Washington, DC: Brookings.

Fleer, M. (2003). The many voices of *Te whāriki*: Kaupapa Māori, socio-cultural, developmental, constructivist, and...?: Australians listen carefully. In J. Nuttall (Ed.), *Weaving* Te whāriki: *Aotearoa New Zealand's early childhood curriculum document in theory and practice* (pp. 243–268). Wellington: New Zealand Council for Educational Research.

Koralek, D. (2007). Early childhood development: A global movement. *Young Children, 62*(6), 10–11.

Lange, D. (1988). *Tomorrow's schools*. Wellington: Department of Education.

Lange, D. (1988). *Before five: Early childhood care and education in New Zealand*. Wellington: Department of Education.

Langley, J. (Ed.). (2009). *Tomorrow's schools: 20 years on*. Auckland: Cognition Institute.

Lauder, H. (1987). The new right and educational policy in New Zealand. *New Zealand Journal of Educational Studies, 22*, 3–23.

May, H. (1991). "From a floor to a drawer"—a story of administrative upheaval: A post-Meade reflection on early childhood policy. *Te Timitanga, 9*(2).

May, H. (1997). *The discovery of early childhood*. Wellington: New Zealand Council for Educational Research.

May, H. (2007). 'Minding', 'working', 'teaching': Childcare in Aotearoa New Zealand, 1940s–2000s. *Contemporary Issues in Early Childhood, 8*(2), 133–143.

Meade, A. (1997). Good practice to best practice: Extending policies and children's minds. *Early Childhood Folio, 3*, 33.

Meade, A. (2001). One hundred billion neurons: How do they become organised? In T. David (Ed.), *Promoting evidence-based practice in early childhood education: Research and its implications*. Kilvington, UK: Elsevier Science Ltd.

Ministry of Education. (1990). *Education (early childhood centres) regulations.* Wellington: Author.

Ministry of Education. (1991). *Statement of desirable objectives and practices for chartered early childhood services in New Zealand.* Wellington: Learning Media.

Ministry of Education. (1993a). *Te whāriki: Draft guidelines for developmentally appropriate programmes in early childhood services.* Wellington: Author.

Ministry of Education. (1993b). *The New Zealand curriculum framework.* Wellington: Author.

Ministry of Education. (1994). *Assessment policy to practice.* Wellington: Learning Media.

Ministry of Education. (1996a). *Revised statement of desirable objectives and practices for chartered early childhood services in New Zealand* [supplement to the *Education Gazette*]. Wellington: Learning Media.

Ministry of Education. (1996b). *Te whāriki: He whāriki mātauranga mo ngā mokopuna o Aotearoa: Early childhood curriculum.* Wellington: Learning Media.

Ministry of Education. (2002). *Pathways to the future: Ngā huarahi arataki.* Wellington: Author.

Ministry of Education. (2007). *The New Zealand curriculum.* Wellington: Author.

Ministry of Education. (2010). *Statement of intent 2010–2015.* Wellington: Author.

Ministry of Education. (2012). *ECE participation.* Retrieved from http://www.educationcounts.govt.nz/statistics/ece2/participation

Mitchell, L. (2010). Constructions of childhood in early childhood education policy debate in New Zealand. *Contemporary Issues in Early Childhood, 11*(4), 328–341.

Mutch, C. (2003). One context, two outcomes: A comparison of *Te whāriki* and the *New Zealand Curriculum Framework*. In J. Nuttall (Ed.), *Weaving* Te whāriki: *Aotearoa New Zealand's early childhood curriculum document in theory and practice.* Wellington: New Zealand Council for Educational Research.

Mutch, C. (2004). The rise and rise of early childhood education in New Zealand. *Citizenship, Social and Economics Education: An International Journal, 6*(1), 1–11.

National Party. (2011). *Education in schools policy.* Retrieved from http://www.national.org.nz/policy.aspx

Nuttall, J. (Ed.). (2003). *Weaving* Te whāriki: *Aotearoa New Zealand's early childhood curriculum document in theory and practice.* Wellington: New Zealand Council for Educational Research.

OECD. (2001). *Starting strong: Early childhood education and care.* Paris, France: Author.

OECD. (2006). *Starting strong II: Early childhood education and care.* Paris, France: Author.

Parliamentary Counsel Office. (2008). Retrieved from http://www.legislation.govt.nz/regulation/public/2008/0204/latest/DLM1412635.html

Robinson, V., Hohepa, N., & Lloyd, C. (2009). *School leadership and student outcomes: Identifying what works and why: Best evidence synthesis iteration.* Wellington: Ministry of Education.

Siraj-Blatchford, I., & Clarke, P. (2000). *Supporting identity, diversity and language in the early years.* Buckingham, UK: Open University Press.

Snook, I. (1995). Re-forming the curriculum in New Zealand. In D. Carter & M.O'Neill (Eds.), *International perspectives on education reform and policy implementation* (pp. 158–168). London: Falmer Press.

Stromquist, N. (2005). Comparative and international education: A journey toward equality and equity. *Harvard Educational Review, 75*(1), 89–111.

Taskforce to Review Education Administration. (1988*). Administering for excellence: Effective administration and education* [the Picot Report]. Wellington: Government Printer. Thrupp, M. (Ed.). (1999a). *A decade of reform in New Zealand education: Where to now?* Hamilton: University of Waikato.

Thrupp, M. (1999b). *Schools making a difference: Let's be realistic!: School mix, school effectiveness and the social limits of reform.* Buckingham, UK; Philadelphia, PA: Open University Press.

Timperley, H., Wilson, A., Barrar, H., & Fung, I. (2007). *Teacher professional learning and development: Best evidence synthesis iteration.* Wellington: Ministry of Education.

Trowler, P. (1998). *Education policy: A policy sociology approach.* London, UK: Routledge.

UNESCO. (1990). *World declaration on education for all and framework for action to meet basic earning needs.* New York, NY: Author.

Wylie, C., & Hodgen, E. (2006). *The continuing contribution of early childhood education to young people's competency levels.* Wellington: New Zealand Council for Educational Research.

Wylie, C., & Thompson, J. (2003). *The long-term contribution of early childhood education for children's performance: Evidence from New Zealand.* Wellington: New Zealand Council for Educational Research.

CHAPTER 5

Coming of age?: Infants and toddlers in curriculum

Jayne White and Carl Mika

ABSTRACT

Te Whāriki was the first early childhood framework to give infants and toddlers an inclusive position within a curriculum for teaching and learning. Since it was introduced, several other countries have adopted a similar stance, either by following suit or by developing separate curricula for under-2-year-olds. This chapter explores the implications of this positioning, and the associated role that *Te Whāriki* has played in shifting the status of infants and toddlers in New Zealand early childhood education, and beyond. Future directions for the curriculum based on research and theory that were not readily available in 1996 are discussed for both Māori and tauiwi (non-Māori) learners. The simultaneous interplay of living texts—both te reo Māori and English—and the agency of very young child are seen as a source of clarification in this regard. These insights call for a conceptualisation of infants and toddlers as more complex and mysterious than has previously been envisaged. The chapter concludes by considering the implications for the educational experience of infants and toddlers in early childhood education settings and the associated role of the teacher. These, if taken seriously, herald a 'coming of age' for under-3-year olds within a curriculum that *is* infant and toddler pedagogy.

Introduction

> It's obvious—you're not only giving a baby a bottle, you're interacting with another child, you're scanning the environment, you're thinking about who is going to need what in the near future and it all looks like you are just feeding the baby. Yeah, so … it's very involved what's going on. (Rachel, Infant Teacher, in White, 2012, p.14)

Rachel's articulation of her own practice sets the scene for an examination of *Te Whāriki* (Ministry of Education, 1996) and its aftermath for infant and toddler teaching and learning in the 21st century. From its inception *Te Whāriki* signalled a radical turning point in the way teachers of infants and toddlers conceptualised their pedagogy. With the advent of this document, infants and toddlers were granted a position as competent and capable learners alongside their 3- and 4-year-old peers, and infant teachers were afforded a special status. Pushing beyond Cartesian principles of the separation of mind and body that had dominated the study of infants and excluded them from curriculum altogether, *Te Whāriki* took the bold position that learning and development are inseparable. The document reconciled these principles in the education of infants and toddlers by foregrounding the artistry of care-giving and the 'unknowability' of the infant in contexts beyond the home. The curriculum thus validated aspects of learning that went beyond an exclusive focus on cognition and gave teachers of infants permission to consider the significance of their work as "inter-subjective" and "emotional", as well as "intellectual", in a new era of "professionalism" (Dalli, 2006).

Since *Te Whāriki*, unprecedented national and international attention has been paid to understanding how infants and toddlers learn. Drawing on the rich multi-disciplinary, theoretical and philosophical 'post-*Whāriki*' literature base, there is now overwhelming support for an emphasis on *relationships* as central to learning, thus expanding on the ideas established by *Te Whāriki*. There is also a growing body of philosophical and socio-cultural research that suggests infants and toddlers are agentic subjects (rather than just objects for adult intervention) in their own right. New ways of studying infants and toddlers reveal their significance as subjective participants who draw on systems of meaning-making that often exceed the grasp of adults (Johansson & White, 2011).

Such a view is implicit in both the draft and final versions of *Te Whāriki*. A Māori notion of care is expressed through the representation of the child's mysterious presence in language. The transformation of key terms in the document and its practical application are therefore crucial for both the wielders of that language and those who must act on its interpretation. An appreciation of the tensions that exist within the text represents a further opportunity for adults—especially those who work with infants and toddlers in educational services[1]—to prioritise their work as deeply aligned to emotional attunement and care, mystery and wonder, uncertainty, and, above all, hope.

In the chapter that follows, an examination of *Te Whāriki's* treatment of infants and toddlers—in text and in practice—illuminates critical shifts the document continues to herald for infant and toddler pedagogy. These shifts are not merely concerned with flexible programmes or routines that respond to cultural, developmental and individual differences, but also relate to responsive pedagogies that give primacy to the voices of infants and toddlers. The strength of such pedagogies can be at least partially attributed to Māori theorisation of learning as a holistic concept enshrining principles that form the basis of knowledge, such as security, respect and a sense of belonging, within fundamental notions of mystery and wonder.

This claim is not made lightly when text is brought into practice. From a Māori viewpoint the infant or toddler may be cast as vulnerable when the wording of the text is misappropriated or misunderstood. As a result, the 'mystery' of the Māori child is seldom reflected in mainstream educational practice (Thrupp & Mika, 2011). Just as the young child is misinterpreted in and through unmysterious text, so, too, is the language of the text and the pedagogy it encapsulates undermined. In the regimes of accountability that permeate the educational landscape, the wisdom of the teacher can become harnessed to learning outcomes that are devoid of emotive or 'unscientific' interpretations (White, 2011). On this basis, we argue that *Te Whāriki*, as a living document and as a source of identity, must be continually theorised so that the child retains a sense of autonomous, yet interdependent, development, fluidity and mystery. We begin by examining the location of infants and toddlers within the educational tenets of *Te Whāriki.*

Te Whāriki's positioning of infants and toddlers

Until *Te Whāriki* was introduced, the concept of pedagogy for infant care was ignored due to the emphasis on the task of keeping infants safe and cared for, focusing on development rather than understanding the diverse ways in which infants eagerly engage with their world. (Rockel, 2010, p. 99)

From the outset, *Te Whāriki's* construction of infancy offered a serious challenge to the education sector in two fundamental ways. First, by acknowledging care as a central element of learning through curriculum, *Te Whāriki* challenged traditional curriculum models that had previously dismissed infants and toddlers altogether

---

1 Since *Te Whāriki's* inception, infants and toddlers feature much more strongly in the early childhood education landscape and, as such, represent a policy and research priority in New Zealand (Dalli, White, Rockel, & Duhn, 2011) and elsewhere (see, for example, Elfer, 2006; Greve & Solheim, 2010; Hannikainen, 2010; Musatti & Picchio, 2010).

from education. Secondly, *Te Whāriki* employed a koru (an unfolding fern) metaphor of development and learning that made a fundamental shift from ages and stages to "a spiral which takes into account developmental delays and spurts, diversity as well as universal stages" (Victorian Curriculum and Assessment Authority, 2008, p. 16). By placing infants and toddlers alongside their older peers, *Te Whāriki* made a strong statement about the inclusion of 'babies' in the education system, and about the nature of teaching and learning.

Dispensing with what were seen as limiting developmental constraints, *Te Whāriki* invited teachers to consider infants and toddlers as inquisitive learners first and foremost, each with individual preferences, needs and desires. Also, teaching was expanded well beyond subject domains that had historically dominated curricula. Both of these ideas were radical at a time when infants and toddlers were beginning to make a marked entrance into formal education and care services in New Zealand, and when notions of care as private 'women's work' prevailed. In the section that follows we explore these various positionings of infants and toddlers within *Te Whāriki* and the implications they pose for practice. We start with the premise of the infant and/or toddler as a developmental subject: a child in the making.

A child in the making

The notion of infancy and toddlerhood as discrete and distinctive developmental periods in the human lifespan is present in the text of *Te Whāriki*. While the curriculum framework—aspirations, principles, strands and goals—is shared across all age groups, *Te Whāriki* provides specific guidance, in the form of examples for teachers working with each age category, to meet curriculum outcomes. The inevitable tension between not wanting to limit the individual and specific potential of very young children while simultaneously acknowledging critical developmental differences is reconciled in the development of three distinct, yet overlapping, age categories:

- infant/ngā pēpi: birth to 18 months
- toddler/ngā mokopuna kei te hāereere: one year to 3 years
- young child/ngā mokopuna i mua o te haerenga ki te kura: 2½ years to school entry age. (Ministry of Education, 1996, p. 20)

An analysis of the "examples of experiences which help to meet these outcomes" (ibid, p. 45) for each age category in *Te Whāriki* reveals a view of infants as having a greater need for adult intervention, while toddlers are described as fluctuating between needy and independent. The terms 'infant' and 'toddler' themselves are not unproblematic. Morss (2003) suggests that such terms represent a form of reductive labelling, while others (see, for example, Lokken, 1999) argue in favour of such language as a form of identification and therefore a means of celebration. This distinction is reconciled in the text of *Te Whāriki*, which states that

[t]he goals should be interpreted according to the individual needs of each child, but it is implicit that many of the examples which apply to younger children continue to apply to children of an older age group. (Ministry of Education, 1996, p. 45)

Yet the suggestion that the reverse may be true—that examples that apply to children in the older age group might apply to younger children—is not found in the text. Taken literally, this view of the infant as more vulnerable and less independent appears at first glance to be inconsistent with a view of the reciprocal learner that *Te Whāriki* promotes elsewhere in the text. Similarly, the toddler is located somewhere in between infancy and childhood, a position that disregards the unique characteristics of the toddler beyond their "fluctuating needs" and "desires" (Ministry of Education, 1996, pp. 23–24).

In this sense, infants and toddlers feature as *known* objects, "something 'over and done with' that has nothing more to teach us" (Deleuze, 1995, p. 106). Such a position is reflected in practices that assign untrained adults to the younger child, based on a view of infant care as something 'natural', where little or no staff education is required, or in practices where toddlers are placed in programmes that are more suited to older children. That the New Zealand Government recently chose to reduce the number of untrained staff working with infants and toddlers to 50 percent (from a previous goal of 100 percent) suggests that this view is still prevalent (Ministry of Education, 2010; see also Carroll-Lind & Angus, 2011; Johnston, 2011).

A view of the infant and toddler as 'not quite there' or 'in progress' is arguably reinforced by *Te Whāriki*'s employment of the koru (Ministry of Education, 1996, p. 21), a metaphor that portrays the developing child as the unfolding frond of the fern. One interpretation of the koru metaphor positions learning as progressive development, and implies that the infant and, to a lesser extent, the toddler are at the lower (i.e. deficit) end of a developmental continuum. Yet from a Māori perspective this metaphor suggests that the infant and toddler are already innately and fully developed: they simply need time and the right conditions to flourish.

Marsden's (2003) analysis of the metaphysical terms 'kore' and 'korekore' reconcile this notion. Both terms refer to identifiable phases of the process of creation. They are metaphors for the child in the making, such that the infant and toddler are seen as reflections of the continuous active process of renewal. They also signal the simultaneous presence of being and not being, with oppositional characteristics, since 'kore' signals nothingness, and 'korekore', with the doubling, signifies the positive attributes of this position. Although 'korekore' seems to follow 'kore', in fact 'kore' already contains elements of its predecessor.

This is further explicated through an examination of the term 'whakapapa', which suggests that time is far from linear, since what is anticipated—the forthcoming generation—is already contained in the essence of the present. This presence is more than just the ability to create one thing from another in a scientific or linear sense (Mika, 2011b): it encompasses the existence of the unborn child in all aspects for those who are present in both word and deed. Seen in this light, *Te Whāriki*'s term for toddler, "kei te hāereere", could equally be applied to all age groups, since all are in a similar process of becoming and the distinction between age groups becomes redundant.

A Māori view of language incorporates this notion of the already present with the belief that the words a person directs at another have a real effect. Instead of being arbitrarily named through human intervention, the object of the words has agency in bringing about the words to begin with. Royal (2011, n.p.) notes the tendency of the object to induce words in the utterer with his assertion that whenua (land), viewed not just as a noun but as an active participant, "sparked the Māori imagination", and that

> [m]ā te ao te tangata e tohu e oho ai tōna ngākau, tōna wairua e mārama ai ia ki ētahi mea [it is the world that provides signs to humanity and that awakens humanity's heart and spirit, such that understanding occurs]. (Royal, 2008, p. 37)

In both cases, words used about or towards the world are already provided by the world or elements of the world. More specific to the learning situation, the Māori child is viewed as a creator *with*, not *of*, language. This is an effect of wairua (spirit), in which the child is moved to think and become involved in the world through the prompts provided by that world, seen and unseen, in the first instance. As such, early learning is an embodied experience as much as transmitted and received knowledge.

The pōkeka metaphor invoked in New Zealand's recent kaupapa Māori early childhood assessment guidelines (Ministry of Education, 2009) supports this principle. Pōkeka is a traditional baby wrap that "takes the shape of the child as he or she learns and grows" (Walker, 2008, p. 5). Here, the paradox of Māori metaphysics offers the possibility that the fully formed person is already here, even though he or she may reveal him- or herself more fully at a later point. Seen in this light, the role of the teacher is one of dialogic partner in an unpredictable encounter rather than a transmitter of knowledge in known territory.

Approaches to teaching and learning that seek to shift the learner towards a shared way of thinking give way to those that celebrate the infant or toddler as a source of wonderment and awe. Emphasis is given to interactions within naturally occurring events, such as routines, movement and play. Where a group of well-meaning adults take a more limiting developmental view of the infant or toddler as a 'child in the making', however, the co-creative nature of dialogue within these interactions is potentially blocked. As a result, the teacher persists with an 'outcomes' agenda that drives learners towards certain educational endpoints (White, 2009). If, on the other hand, all things flow from that primordial moment, as Marsden suggests, then even apparently banal entities such as curriculum documents are open to the voice of the smallest infant. It is here the true intent of *Te Whāriki's* koru may be realised, and the tenets of education and care liberated through practice.

The child as a treasure to be cared for

The relationship between the mystery of the child and the text of *Te Whāriki* may be further theorised in relation to the notion and practice of care. *Te Whāriki's* treatment of care as the primary educational act for teachers of infants and toddlers was a contentious position in an era when a professional and highly political agenda was being pursued in the early childhood sector. In order for *Te Whāriki* to build a convincing case for the relationship between care as educative and education as caring, "a theoretical position had to be promoted that would integrate care and education in *praxis* [our emphasis] as a professional skill" (OECD, 2006, p. 30).

Cullen (2003) notes that there were few theoretical clues in *Te Whāriki* to support this position, but the positive philosophical influence of American infant programmes on the development of *Te Whāriki* cannot be understated. One of the key writers of *Te Whāriki*, Helen May, had studied with Magda Gerber, Ron Lally and Alice Honig in the United States, and had attended the Infancy Centre at Bank Street College. May wrote at the time of *Te Whāriki's* development:

> It is important that the Curriculum Guidelines reflect the values and style of programmes in Aotearoa/New Zealand as well as incorporate some excellent research and writing from overseas on curriculum and programmes for infants and toddlers. (May, n.d. p. 2)

In an address to the 1991 early childhood convention, May suggested that Gerber's Resources for Infant Educarers (RIE) philosophy, in particular, could offer much to an infant curriculum that went beyond a focus on activities or programmes. May explained that "Although never one to buy a philosophy in its entirety I was much impressed by some of the philosophical principles" (H. May, personal communication, 21 May 2012). Combined with the local models of Playcentre and Plunket that were influencing mainstream infant and toddler practice in New Zealand at that time, *Te Whāriki's* attention to relationships, routines and individualised care activities, and a resistance to 'teaching' beyond traditional forms of education, can be more than partially attributed to these sources as a means of developing a "deeper and deeper relationship" (Tardos, 2012, p. 4).

The work of feminist writers, drawn on by New Zealand researchers (see, for example, Dalli, 2006; Rockel, 2009, 2010), has also contributed to the theorisation of care in curricula for under-3-year-olds. Noddings (1998, 2011), a primary source of inspiration for these discussions at the national level, interprets relationships as the primary focus for pedagogy, describing care as an act of "motivational displacement" whereby the educator is drawn to pedagogical concern for the learner based on the learner's priorities rather than their own. Nodding emphasises modelling and dialogue rather than instruction and monologue, characterised by a move towards "values as living, learning and loving" (Semetsky, 2012, p. 48), highlighting an *attitude* towards care alongside *acts* of care.

Yet in this understanding little attention is given to the distinctive nature of each person's subjectivity, the construction of care as a value, and the associated and highly complex demands on teachers. As Brownlee (2012) states:

> We have all done/still do things to babies and young children, instead of *with* babies and young children … [we are] perplexed as to why we would do to babies and young children that which we would not like done to us. (p. 27)

Her perplexity supports Johnston's (2011) proposition that infant teachers require significant support to "unravel the complicated and emotional nature of infant pedagogy" (p. 98).

Inevitably, the issue of pedagogy is brought into question when curriculum is discussed, as Rockel (2009) explains when she notes that "when curriculum is in place it follows that pedagogy is essential for its interpretation and implementation" (p. 3). Yet the conscious reflection on pedagogy that Rockel proposes may not occur automatically in debates about curriculum. For instance, a critical aspect of pedagogy is not evident in the Education Review Office's (2009) articulation of 'quality' infant and toddler practice: their suggestion that 'quality' infant and toddler practice exists in centres where there is "a focus on relationships between children, teachers and families" provides few clues about what this might mean in reality. Instead, emphasis is given to "a safe and nurturing environment; programmes that focused on the individual needs of children; and an attractive well-resourced learning environment" (p. 14).

However, to teach in a caring manner is not simply a case of responding to a set of indicators: it is a complex practice which summons the tenets of *Te Whāriki* through empowerment (Johnston, 2011), and mutual dialogue and respect (Akast, 2012). Dalli, Rockel, Duhn and Craw (2011) suggest a further lack of clarity about the teacher's pedagogy based on their investigations of infant teachers who, they argue, tend to oscillate between intuitive and intentional practice when describing their work. The difficulty that reflection on pedagogy poses due to its frequent location within discourses of accountability can only to some extent be mitigated by broad principles of engagement, such as "watching over time" (Dalli & Doyle, 2011, p. 18) or "being in the moment" (Duhn, 2011, p. 26). However the concept does not sit with ease in a pedagogical location. It is here, especially, that the active presence of the infant/toddler and the teacher becomes vital, as the Māori view of the holistic development of the child as taonga shows, and as a much more mysterious and spiritual view of the relationship between the 'object' (child) and the 'describer' or interpreter (language and text—*Te Whāriki*), hints at. By adopting a view of praxis as both wisdom and knowledge within the metaphysical approach to learning signalled in *Te Whāriki*, there is the potential to view teaching and learning as *both* intuition and intention. In a recent study by one of the authors (White, 2012) involving two infant 'key teachers'[2] working with a 4-month-old and an 8-month-old infant in a New Zealand education and care service, this view of praxis was clearly evident. Teachers described their pedagogy as a series of inter-subjective acts comprising mutual gazes, shared rituals, physical and emotional presence, and the constant seeking of cues through physical and verbal language. In these dialogues no sense of pedagogical certainty regarding outcomes or criteria for engagement was articulated. Instead teachers celebrated their relational presence—a concept also proposed by Brownless, & Berthelson, (2007); see also Biesta (2010). Taken together, these practices articulate a pedagogy that is unapologetically presented as an inter-subjective process of intuition and intentionality, with the teachers invoking terms such as 'love' in describing the process:

> Lynnette: You give them your heart and soul. It is, honestly, it's like that and I don't think people get that really. And it comes back to that notion of love, of the child.
>
> Jayne: So what is this love? Can you name it? Frame it?
>
> Rachel: It's a different love. It's a different love than from your own children. Completely, cos I've worked with my own children as well. It's a different love, but it's still a, like a nurturing love. The thing is that, you know, they're in care. Like [L] and [H] they are there like five days a week. Nine-hour days, or something, and so you think "if you were at home what would you be getting? Well you'd be getting love from your mum, your dad, your grandparents" and so why not make our environment a loving place to be where there is physical touch, kisses.
>
> Lynnette: Blowing raspberries on their tummy. Like I would do with any child I had a close relationship with.
>
> Jayne: Yes you seem to be the one who does raspberry blowing and Rachel does kisses so I guess the children know what they will get when they are with each of you?
>
> Rachel: Yeah, I kiss a lot [laughs]. Once upon a time, maybe even now in some centres, would that be OK? But that's part of me as a teacher and everyone knows that about me and so that is OK.
>
> (Lynnette, Rachel and Jayne, in White, 2012, p. 12)

---

2 At the time of writing, a key teacher system was not legislated practice in New Zealand but many ECE services were convinced of its relevance to infant and toddler education and had put systems in place. A key teacher system is one where each infant has a designated adult who takes overall responsibility for their education and care as a means of promoting secure attachments in ECE (Elfer, 2006; Rockel, 2003). The role of a key teacher was significant in this ECE centre context because it represented an organisational and philosophical commitment to primary attachments as the "keystone in a block wall or arch" (Hose, in Ormond, 2010, p. 3). A commitment to the key teacher system was evident throughout all practices in the centre, from initial settling-in arrangements and liaison with families, to important decisions regarding the infant's daily care during the day—all of which were undertaken by the key teacher.

Despite the ease with which these teachers discuss love as a central element of their pedagogy, the language of love is absent in the text of *Te Whāriki*. This may be due to an understanding of love as an abstract concept in educational discourse rather than an appreciation of its treatment in the lived world of teaching and learning (White, 2012). In the language of *Te Whāriki*, a return to the koru image offers a means of examining the latter. Here, the role of the adult is to protect and sustain growth through loving acts that respond to the infant as a subjective partner in ways that are likely to have benefits for all society.

Yet if this concept is taken out of context, there is a risk that the infant and toddler are seen as objects for adult intervention, with pedagogy playing a transmissive, manipulative or surveillance role. In curricula of this nature, infants and toddlers are not granted the authority to *participate* in the curriculum, but instead are seen as the *recipients* of it—coerced through the promise, or threat, of love. As taonga (treasured things), however, infants and toddlers are deeply treasured within *Te Whāriki* due to their capacity and potential to forge links between the past and the future (Reedy, 2003), and the teacher thus acts as a guardian in the absence of a loving parent; pedagogy is re-envisaged as "a deed of care" (Bakhtin, 1990, p. 89).

When seen as loving partners in a dialogical process, as the teachers in White's study explain, the notion of taonga is realised in this fuller sense. *Te Whāriki's* treatment of the term 'aroha' (love or compassion) lends support to this claim, since it derives from the insight that is gained in deep relationships where one looks or 'breathes' into another (Brownlee, 2012). Jenkins, Harte and Ririki (2011) suggest that love is the essence of "the ihi, the wehi and the wana" (p. 29) of Māori child-rearing practices, and represents "a total commitment to the child" (p. 30). Such expression was conveyed by one of the teachers in White's study, who, when asked to describe her pedagogy, chose to articulate a lingering gaze exchanged between herself and a 4-month-old infant before sleep as a significant pedagogical act

> that signified the trust that he has in me, the trust to know him, to respond to him and to care for him. That's how I wrote it, and that's how I feel, is that you know, that one last look, 'You're ok, I'm ok', and off he goes to sleep. (Lynnette, in White, 2012, p. 11)

Kidwell's (2005) analysis of infant–caregiver interactions reinforces the significance of 'the look' as a sustained inter-subjective act of intentionality. As such, emphasis is placed on infants' use of mutual gaze to regulate the nature of their response (Beier & Spelke, 2012) towards joint attention (Gaffan, Martins, Healy & Murray, 2009). From this standpoint the gaze is no accidental meeting but an orienting experience for the infant and adult alike. While conveyed in different terms (for a fuller discussion, see Page, 2011), this view is consistent with contemporary cross-disciplinary research that highlights the long- and short-term impact of positive early experience on mental, physical and intellectual health (Dalli, White, Rockel, & Duhn, 2011). As Manning-Morton (2006) explains, "These synchronized interactions both deepen bonds and expand the baby's curiosity and interest in the world" (p. 47). According to neurological research such interactions play a significant role in learning by sparking synaptic processes in the brain (see, for example, Fox, Leavitt, & Nelson, 2010).

Through such an orientation to pedagogy, it is possible to argue that the nature of care as a reciprocal relationship in *Te Whāriki's* education model is upheld and the fullest expression of aroha is legitimised in practice. Yet, as with all aspects of *Te Whāriki*, approaches to such expressions are not prescribed. New Zealand teachers adopt a number of different practices to achieve this goal, ranging from whānau models, where all adults share responsibility for infants and toddlers (White, 2009), to primary care-giving systems that promote key teacher relationships (see, for example, Rockel, 2003; Christie, 2011). The Māori concept of ūkaipō (mother, source of sustenance) is helpful in this regard (Reedy, 2003), because it signifies the importance of reliable, intimate and embodied relationships that support the infant or toddler as they interact with the wider world. Seen in this way, care is neither exclusive nor dismissive, neither intuitive nor intentional, but resides within *Te Whāriki's* educational landscape of "people, places and things"; in other words, it is first and foremost relational. In the section that follows we suggest that this aspect is downplayed in *Te Whariki's* treatment of infants and toddlers as social agents in their own right.

The social infant and toddler

Despite what was already known and promoted about peer-to-peer and adult–child relationships for older children during the development of *Te Whāriki*, the social world of the infant and toddler was not explored in the text beyond a brief mention of infants' inclusion in "social happenings", or toddlers' "*attempts* to initiate social interactions with other children and adults" (Ministry of Education, 1996, p. 71, our emphasis). Movement beyond an emphasis on learning theories focusing on the individual or on infant–mother dyads in the post-*Te Whāriki* era has been promoted by re-conceptualising perspectives on curriculum that "look beyond theories of learning for their explanation of what goes on in early childhood education" (Nuttall, 2003, p. 12). Paying attention to the significance of infant and toddler relationships with peers and adults in group settings is a recent example of this phenomenon in educational research.

There are now a small number of studies that illuminate the complex nature of these relationships from a diverse range of philosophical standpoints (see, for example, Johansson & White, 2011). These studies argue that mutual non-verbal and verbal communication regularly takes place between infants and toddlers in early childhood education settings, and that this communication successfully facilitates meaningful friendships between peers and inter-subjective relationships with adults.

These relationships support the infant and toddler within dialogic communities that exceed traditional boundaries of self/other. In a recent study, White (in press, b) concludes that very young children are not merely mimicking the behaviour of others as a mean of emotional regulation, but are drawing on the acts of others as a kind of compass or map for their own actions (see also Stephenson, 2011). White's (2009, 2011) video portrayals of the social acts of toddlers in New Zealand early childhood settings highlight the complex and agentic nature of social engagements that often exceed adult comprehension.

These findings go well beyond *Te Whāriki's* attention to infants' need for "physical and emotional security with at least one other person within each setting" (Ministry of Education, 1996, p. 22). Based on the idea that, like anyone else, infants are strategically orienting themselves within social situations, this more complex view expands on *Te Whāriki's* notion that infants and toddlers are capable and confident, to encompass a view of under-3-year-olds as *dialogic agents* in social settings. This view reinforces the socio-cultural concept that, like Vygotsky's (1976) young child, an infant or toddler may be "a head taller than themselves" (p. 102) in social engagement with others. It also goes further to suggest that infancy is "a complex, ungraspable period of deep wonderment that resides in axiologic relationships rather than finalized regimes of truth" (White, 2011, p. 383).

Seen in this light, infant and toddler curriculum involves a more sophisticated exchange with the social world than was previously conceptualised, and reinforces Marsden's thesis that the young child *creates* language rather than merely receives it. The delicate problem of retaining the integrity of Māori concepts to ensure that the wellbeing of the child is undisturbed is beyond mere theory in a Māori world view (although it must indeed be theorised). Browne (2005) notes that the wairua of language is uppermost in the learning process for Māori. The application of this is twofold: language is to be respected as a phenomenon in its own right, but, equally, language has an impact on the object of its intentions, regardless of how indirectly this may occur. Even the language of curriculum documents has implications for human beings in practice. These implications are not just realised through the execution of what the language calls for—although this factor is important—but the language itself has a residual, metaphysical effect on the distant subject.

In an examination of *Te Whāriki*, this point is particularly relevant for the infant or toddler. Although the writers produce text *about* and *towards* the infant or toddler, it is teachers (or untrained adults) who must carry out the intentions of the text for the wellbeing of the young child. The English-speaking teacher is told that this is to be applied in a way that "recognises the distinct role of an identifiable Māori curriculum" (Ministry of Education, 1996, p. 12). Yet, in this reading, it appears that the infant or toddler is voiceless, because the curriculum is devoid of the embodied wairua of the young child it purports to represent: the dialogue moves in only one direction. Taken from a Māori metaphysical standpoint, the voice of the child, although quiet (or perhaps even as yet un-uttered), should be free to respond to those words in the document that are proclaimed as being imbued with something special.

Te Whāriki invokes multiple dialogues: between text and infant, between text and teacher, between text and theories, and between text and cultures. These dialogues collectively call for a lived response to curriculum that exceeds the text, or practice, alone. In this sense, curriculum is represented through the young child in dialogue with others. In an infant and toddler curriculum that foregrounds relationships, it is a pedagogy that relies heavily on contextualised knowledge, language and practice in *this* moment, in dialogue with *this* infant or toddler. It is not a curriculum that pays lip service to Māori world views, but one that is imbued with an essence that lives and breathes the languages of kei te hāereere as citizens with voice(s) in a bicultural society.

The challenge facing those who work with *Te Whāriki* has always been how to hold off consuming (perhaps even colonising) Māori content and then regurgitating it as universally relevant or applicable. As the words of the Māori content maintain their integrity in the document, so too the infant or toddler retains his/her own sense of mystery, wonder and awe. This is especially true for those who retain a special place in a Māori world view—our very youngest—in dialogue with adults, peers and the wider world.

Challenges and opportunities for infant and toddler pedagogy

The curious mix of *Te Whāriki* as a mat for all to stand on and a call for an acknowledgement of the presence of mystery presents a unique challenge for infant and toddler pedagogy. As soon as the infant or toddler of *Te Whāriki* is literally and unproblematically theorised as a 'child in the making', a 'treasure', an 'isolated subject' or any other construct summoned with little regard for the Māori text, a set of characteristics are instantly attributed to teaching practice.

One consequence of this literal interpretation for the young child is that they may become illuminated for the purpose of discussion *about* him or her, with the language used to discuss the child aimed at the needs of this suddenly highly visible, knowable entity that the child has become. The words that make up this language are contained in a document that is 'dead on arrival', and adults are brought into the text with an intention to discuss the infant and toddler in certain, and as a result limiting, ways. In these colonised spaces, the aim is to make the infant or toddler known and utterly knowable through adult scrutiny. Pedagogy becomes a form of accountability rather than a relationship, and the teacher's practice is made a public source of evidence.

Perhaps, however, the prescriptive approach of the Māori component of *Te Whāriki* is beneficial because it provides a space for the infant or toddler to be 'present'. Here we see that the Māori component of *Te Whāriki* tries to cater for the unseen world as well as the perceptible world by introducing terms such as mātauranga huna (mysteries) and pūngao (energy), no sense of which is present in the English text. Nearly all of these sorts of terms, which have the greatest ability to preserve an openness towards the child, are moved into a right-hand column of the glossary at the end of the document. Here, the more outcomes-focused terms are to the left, possibly indicating a desire on the part of the authors to draw attention to them and to demarcate them from those in the other column. Their separation does not necessarily mean that the terms enjoy their own domain; another possibility is that they inform each other. To that extent, mātauranga huna could influence whakaputanga (outcomes), and the openness of the document towards the child could be even more emphasised if whakaputanga, for example, were considered to mean 'revelation' rather than the calculative translation given in the glossary.

The issue then becomes what effect the (admittedly colonising) translation of traditional Māori terms will have on the freer character of other terms. Does the 'whakangaromanga Ao'—described in *Te Whariki*'s glossary as Black Holes (Universe) (Ministry of Education, 1996, p. 38)—and the substantive text indeed have a gravitational tug on whakamātau (assess) and pull its meaning away from an outcomes focus towards the mysterious? Or does the overall philosophical configuration of the document support 'assessment', so that any sense of mystery and unknowability is resistible and, ultimately, able to be ignored? In the first scenario, 'assessment' is affected by its involvement with the mysterious realm of the universe and becomes less about setting out to measure the child and much more about an intuitive response to the child and to things around the child. In this conceputalisation, the objective is to work alongside the child so that they engage with things around them in an open and exciting way—one that delights in the awe of the infant as an expression of life (Jenkins et al., 2011). In the second conceptualisation, however, there is little room for the mystery and awe that epitomise a metaphysical relationship between adults and very young children.

The extent to which these terms are treated as 'Māori sounds' for a basically un-mysterious message, or act as thresholds for transformation (White, in press, a), will shape the pedagogy for infants and toddlers that *Te Whāriki* heralds. The Māori version of *Te Whāriki* aims to deal with the mystery of the child through the use of terms that understand teaching and learning as a reciprocal engagement that seeks to preserve that mystery. Yet in mentioning the prized terms that are associated with Māori existence—whānau, mana, kotahitanga, hononga, and so on—the absence of the political reality of the child, and hence their voice, still occurs. It is as if those rather optimistic Māori terms stand in for the less pleasant colonised experiences and inheritance of the seemingly untouched infant or toddler.

Schleiermacher (1969) noted, with his preference for a view of the self as a bearer of one's own history, that "you should not only consider humanity in its static appearance but also in its state of becoming" (p. 67). All that has gone before the child—and, indeed, all that occurs simultaneously, as Marsden reminds us—is part of that child's existence. This accords with the socio-cultural tenets that underpin *Te Whāriki* and are closely aligned with the term 'arorangi' (unrestricted) in the document, to the extent that the child that is imagined in the document is always in a state of change. This state of change should be supported by the *full extent* of the Māori terms. As a colonised being, and as an inheritor of that colonised history (Reedy, 2003), the child needs to be reflected in and through the document as an unfamiliar, yet powerful, presence. This is especially true for the infant and toddler, who bring their unique forms to the text.

The potential for the kind of openness to the child's mysterious voice evident in the Māori text relies on making certain terms deliberately opaque so that the apparently "non-prescriptive" (Ritchie, 2003, p. 91) character of the document is emphasised. Rockel (2010) suggests that an appropriate response to *Te Whāriki* is more a case of the teacher "'being with' rather than 'doing to'" (p. 105). If this were true, a metaphysical approach could be summoned and teaching would be a deeply appreciative encounter and a "meeting of two consciousnesses which are in principle distinct from one another" (Bakhtin, 1990, p. 89). For example, kaupapa whakahaere (the agenda for moving forward) would be less about principles and more about the disclosure "for the first time" (Marsden, 2003, p. 66) of a metaphysical ground of becoming.

Rather than emphasising infant and toddler learning outcomes or desperately trying to identify 'interests' (a problematic concept for many infant and toddler teachers; see White, 2009), whāinga (goals) would be to do with *movement* towards a desirable endpoint rather than the endpoint itself; and 'whakamana' could take on aspects of engagement with the hidden autonomy of things around the child, thereby replacing (but also encapsulating) the usual 'empowerment' translation that it is usually given. Although the assessment document *Te Whatu Pōkeka* (Ministry of Education, 2009) goes some way towards bringing these ideas to life, even this provides little room for the tentative *becoming* voice of infants and toddlers (as opposed to the being, knowing and doing framework that is currently promoted).

Te Whāriki's expanded views of learning and teaching are consistent with contemporary studies that understand infants and toddlers as inter-subjective players in an educational dance (Dalli et al., 2011). Where the relationship between care and education is recognised as both implicit within the text and explicit in practice, a view of infant and toddler pedagogy as a specialised domain emerges strongly. The voice of the infant or toddler is celebrated *because* it is elusive, based on the premise that babies are persons of culture in their own right. Such a stance calls for more than an attention to routines and rosters, and programmes and practices inherited from elsewhere.

With this view come significant challenges for the *Te Whāriki* teacher of infants and toddlers. For her or him, education is less about endpoints than about engagement with multiple voices, including living text and the autonomous infant, and therefore relies on a revised conceptualisation of inter-subjectivity as a moral imperative (White & Nuttall, 2007). Seen in this light, *Te Whāriki* represents an opportunity to bring together diverse principles, issues and dilemmas that characterise a curriculum that responds to the aspirations of society (as Yates, 2009, notes). In a curriculum of this nature, the teacher of infants and toddlers needs to be

a critically reflexive, theoretical boundary crosser: a boundary crosser who can see young children as powerfully active learners (with autonomy and agency) and yet still hold their independent and vulnerable selves in mind. (Morton-Manning, 2006, p. 50)

In the case of teachers like Rachel, whose words began this chapter, there are considerable cultural, philosophical and intangible boundaries to cross in seeing (and celebrating) the mysterious unknowability, vulnerability and wonder of *Te Whāriki* infants and toddlers. Such a pedagogical stance legitimates the role of teachers in appreciating the infant or toddler through a curious mix of care and education that at first glance seems conflicted, but in *Te Whāriki's* fullest sense reconciles itself as "obvious". For Rachel, as for her colleagues, there is an ongoing and urgent need for those who work with infants and toddlers to continually theorise their position and the conditions that give it (and infants or toddlers) their status.

Though difficult to articulate in a literal sense, the metaphysical nature of the language of *Te Whāriki* suggests that, like the infant and the unfurling fern, an infant and toddler pedagogy is 'already there' for those who are willing to engage with these messages in the spirit with which they were given. The teacher holds on to the principle that infants and toddlers are elusive and mysterious, even when they reside within regimes of certainty that threaten the integrity of the text and its lived reality. With the very young child at the heart of *Te Whāriki*, curriculum and pedagogy align as a relationship, a practice, a future and a hope. For infants and toddlers, who are seldom given voice in their own lives, this is a document that, in spirit and practice, takes them very seriously indeed.

This chapter concludes with the proposition that a literal interpretation of *Te Whāriki* as a set of guidelines for practice is insufficient to claim its philosophical and indigenous priorities, and its richness, for infant and toddler pedagogy. We invoke a fuller interpretation of *Te Whāriki* to re-assert the status of infants and toddlers as complex, mysterious learners, and to re-vision the specialised role of the infant teacher as inter-subjective partner in an ethical quest for uncertainty and awe. Such a quest takes the teacher deeper into the language of *Te Whāriki* and gives voice to the mysterious infant and toddler in time and space. Through this journey we suggest there will be a coming of age for infants and toddlers in curriculum; a curriculum that lives and breathes a contemporary Aotearoa New Zealand pedagogy.

Note

We acknowledge the need for concise English translations of Māori terms in an academic context and have provided these in brackets after the Māori terms. However, we are also quick to indicate that such economical translations can be colonising in nature (Mika, 2011a) as they do not reflect the nature and breadth of objects that the Māori terms refer to. The reader is asked to keep this problem in mind when noting the English equivalents.

Acknowledgements

The writers wish to acknowledge Helen May, Margaret Carr, and Tilly and Tamati Reedy for their inspiration through the text of *Te Whāriki*; and Jean Rockel, for her constant watch over its implementation in infant and toddler practice and policy over the years since it was written.

References

Akast, D. (2012). "Through the other's look I *live* myself": Power relations and the infant-toddler curriculum. *The First Years Ngā Tau Tuatahi: New Zealand Journal of Infant and Toddler Education, 14*(1), 14–19.

Bakhtin, M.M. (1990). *Art and answerability.* (K. Brostrom, Trans.), Austin: University of Texas.

Beier, J.S. & Spelke, E. (2012). Infants' developing understanding of the social gaze, *Child Development, 83*(2), 486–496.

Biesta, G.J. (2010). Why "what works" won't work: Evidence-based practice and the democratic deficit in educational research. *Educational Theory, 57* (1), 1–57.

Brownlee, P. (2012). Possums or possibilities: Pondering children, culture and cultural imports. *The First Years Ngā Tau Tuatahi: New Zealand Journal of Infant and Toddler Education, 14*(1), 24–27.

Brownless, J. & Berthelson, D. (2007). Personal epistemology and relational pedagogy in early teacher education programs. *Early Years: An International Journal, 26*(1), 17–29.

Browne, M. (2005). *Wairua and the relationship it has with learning te reo Māori within Te Ataarangi.* Unpublished Master of Educational Administration thesis, Massey University, Palmerston North.

Carroll-Lind, J., & Angus, J. (2011*). Through their lens: An inquiry into non-parental education and care of infants and toddlers.* Wellington: Office of the Children's Commissioner.

Christie, T. (2011). *Respect: A practitioner's guide to calm and nurturing infant care and education.* Johnsonville: Childspace Early Learning Institute.

Cullen, J. (2003). The challenge of *Te Whāriki*: Catalyst for change? In J. Nuttall (Ed.), *Weaving Te Whāriki: Aotearoa New Zealand's early childhood curriculum document in theory and practice* (pp. 269–296). Wellington: New Zealand Council for Educational Research.

Dalli, C. (2006). Re-visioning love and care in early childhood: Constructing the future of our profession. *The First Years Ngā Tau Tuatahi: New Zealand Journal of Infant and Toddler Education, 8*(1), 5–11.

Dalli, C., & Doyle, K. (2011). Eyes wide open: How teachers of infants and toddlers recognize learning. *The First Years Ngā Tau Tuatahi: New Zealand Journal of Infant and Toddler Education, 13*(2), 15–18.

Dalli, C., Rockel, J., Duhn, I., Craw, J., with Doyle, K. (2011). *What's special about teaching and learning in the first years?: Summary report.* Wellington: Teaching and Learning Research Initiative.

Dalli, C., White, J., Rockel, J., Duhn, I., with Buchanan, E., Davidson, S., Ganly, S., Kus, l., & Wang, B. (2011). *Quality early childhood education for under-two-year-olds: What should it look like?: A literature review.* Wellington: Ministry of Education. Retrieved from http://www.educationcounts.govt.nz/ publications/ece/quality-early-childhood-education-for-under-two-year-olds-what-should-it-look-like-a-literature-review

Deleuze, G. (1995) *Negotiations.* New York, NY: Columbia University Press.

Duhn, I. (2011). Being a community: A relationship-focused pedagogy for infants and toddlers. *The First Years Ngā Tau Tuatahi: New Zealand Journal of Infant and Toddler Education, 13*(2), 24–28.

Education Review Office. (2009). *Early childhood monographs: The quality of education and care in infant and toddler centres.* Retrieved from http://www.ero.govt.nz/National-Reports/Early-Childhood-Monograph-Series-The-Quality-of-Education-and-Care-in-Infant-and-Toddler-Centres-January-2009/Conclusion

Elfer, P. (2006). Exploring children's expressions of attachment in nursery. *European Early Childhood Education Journal, 14*(2): 81–96.

Farquhar, S. & White, E.J. (in press). *Philosophy and Pedagogy of Early Childhood, Educational Philosophy and Theory.*

Fox, S.E., Leavitt, P., & Nelson, C.A. (2010). How the timing and quality of early experiences influence the development of the architecture of the brain. *Child Development. 81*(1), 28-40.

Gaffan, E., Martins, C., Healy, S. & Murray, L. (2009). Early social experience and individual differences in infants' joint attention, *Social Development, 19*(2), 369-393

Greve, A., & Solheim, M. (2010). Research on children in ECEC under three in Norway: Increased volume, yet invisible. *International Journal of Early Childhood, 42*(2), 155–163.

Hannikainen, M. (2010). 1 to 3-year-old children in day care centres in Finland: An overview of eight doctoral disserations, *International Journal of Early Childhood, 42*, (2), 101–115.

Jenkins, K., Harte, H. M., & Ririki, T. (2011). *Traditional Māori parenting: A historical overview of literature of traditional Māori child-rearing practices in pre-european times.* Auckland: Te Kahui Mana Ririki.

Johansson, E., & White, E. J. (Eds.). (2011). *Educational research with our youngest: Voices of infants and toddlers.* Dordrecht, The Netherlands: Springer.

Johnston, K. V. (2011). *How do educators establish sensitive relationships with infants (six weeks to twelve months of age) in an early childhood context of Aotearoa/New Zealand.* Unpublished Master of Education thesis, AUT University.

Kidwell, M. (2005). Gaze as social control: How very young children differentiate "the look" from a "mere look" by their adult caregivers. *Research on Language and Social Interaction, 38*(4), 417–449.

Lokken, G. (1999). Challenges in toddler peer research. *Nordisk Pedagogik, 19*(30), 145–155.

Manning-Morton, J. (2006). The personal is professional: Professionalism and the birth to threes practitioner. *Contemporary Issues in Early Childhood, 7*(1), 42–52.

Marsden, M. (2003). *The woven universe: Selected writings of Rev. Māori Marsden*. Otaki: Estate of Rev. Māori Marsden.

May, H. (n.d.). *Preliminary thoughts towards developing a curriculum for infants and toddlers in early childhood centres in Aotearoa/New Zealand*. Hamilton: Centre for Early Childhood, School of Education, Waikato University.

Mika, C. (2011a). Overcoming Being in favour of Knowledge: The fixing effect of mātauranga. *Educational Philosophy and Theory*. v-online, doi: 10.1111/j.1469-5812.2011.00771.x, pp.1–13. Wiley-Blackwell, 2011.

Mika, C. (2011b). Unorthodox assistance: Novalis, Māori, scientism, and an uncertain approach to 'whakapapa'. In N. Franke & C. Mika (Eds.), *In die Natur—Naturphilosophie und Naturpoetik in interkultureller Perspektive* (pp. 89–108). Munich, Germany: Goethe Institut.

Ministry of Education. (1996). *Te Whāriki: He whāriki mātauranga mō ngā mokopuna o aotearoa: Early childhood curriculum*. Wellington: Learning Media.

Ministry of Education. (2009). *Te whatu pōkeka: Kaupapa Māori assessment early childhood exemplars*. Wellington: Learning Media.

Ministry of Education. (2010). *ECE changes: Information for parents: Budget fact sheets*. Retrieved from http://www.minedu.govt.nz/theMinistry/Budget/ Budget2010/Factsheets/ ECEInformationForParents.aspx

Morss, J. A. (2003). A rainbow of narratives: Childhood after developmentalism. In B. Van Oers (Ed.), *Narratives of childhood: Theoretical and practical explorations of the innovation of early childhood education*. Amsterdam, The Netherlands: VU University Press.

Musatti, T., & Picchio, M. (2010). Early education in Italy: Research and practice. *International Journal of Early Childhood, 42*(2), 11–153.

Noddings, N. (1998). *Philosophy of education*. Boulder, CO: Westview Press.

Noddings, N. (2011). *Philosophy of education*. (3rd ed.). Boulder, CO: Westview Press.

Nuttall, J. (Ed.). (2003). *Weaving Te Whāriki: Aotearoa New Zealand's early childhood curriculum document in theory and practice*. Wellington: New Zealand Council for Educational Research.

OECD. (2006). *Starting strong II: Early childhood education and care*. Paris, France: OECD.

Ormond, M. (2010). *Transitions: Shifting from what we comfortably know to new possibilities*. Retrieved http://elp.co.nz/EducationalProject

Page, J. (2011). Do mothers want professional carers to love their babies? *Journal of Early Childhood Research, 9*(3), 310–323.

Reedy, T. (2003). Toku rangatiratanga na te mana-matauranga: "Knowledge and power set me free...". In J. Nuttall (Ed.), *Weaving Te Whāriki: Aotearoa New Zealand's early childhood curriculum document in theory and practice* (pp. 51–78). Wellington: New Zealand Council for Educational Research.

Ritchie, J. (2003). Te Whāriki as a potential lever for bicultural development. In, J. Nuttall (Ed.), *Weaving Te Whāriki: Aotearoa New Zealand's early childhood curriculum document in theory and practice* (pp. 79–110). Wellington: New Zealand Council for Educational Research.

Rockel, J. (2003). "Someone is going to take the place of Mum and Dad and under-stand": Teachers' and parents' perceptions of primary care for infants in early childhood centres. *NZ Research in Early Childhood Education, 6*, 113–126.

Rockel, J. (2009). A pedagogy of care: Moving beyond the margins of managing work and minding babies. *Australasian Journal of Early Childhood, 34*(3), 1–8.

Rockel, J. (2010). Infant pedagogy: Learning how to learn. In B. Clark & A. Grey (Eds.), *Perspectives on early childhood education: Ata Kitea Te Pae—Scanning the horizon: Perspectives on early childhood education.* (pp. 97–110). Auckland: Pearson.

Royal, T. (2008). *Te ngākau.* Te Whanganui-a-Tara: Mauriora Ki Te Ao Living Universe.

Royal, T. (2011). *Whenua: How the land was shaped. Te Ara—The encyclopedia of New Zealand.* Retrieved from http://www.TeAra.govt.nz/en/whenua-how-the-land-was-shaped

Schleiermacher, F. (1969). *Über die religion: Reden an die gebildeten unter ihren Verächtern.* Stuttgart, Germany: Reclam.

Semetsky, I. (2012). Living, learning and loving: Constructing a new ethics of integration in education. *Discourse: Studies in the Cultural Politics of Education, 33*(1), 47–59.

Stephenson, A. (2011). Taking a 'generous' approach in research with young children, In E. Johansson & E.J. White. (Eds.). *Educational research with our youngest,* Dordecht, The Netherlands: Springer, 135–160.

Tardos, A. (2012). "Let the infant play by himself as well". *The First Years Ngā Tau Tuatahi: New Zealand Journal of Infant and Toddler Education, 14*(1), 4–9.

Thrupp, M., & Mika, C. (2011). The politics of teacher development for an indigenous people: Colonising assumptions within Māori education in Aotearoa, New Zealand. In C. Day (Ed.), *The Routledge international handbook of teacher and school development.* London, UK: Routledge.

Victorian Curriculum and Assessment Authority. (2008). *Analysis of curriculum/learning frameworks for the early years (birth to age 8).* Author. Retrieved from http://www.deewr.gov.au/Earlychildhood/Policy_Agenda/EarlyChildhoodWorkforce/Documents/AnalysisofCurriculum_LearningFrameworksfortheEarly.pdf

Vygotsky, L. (1976). *Mind in society: The development of higher psychological processes.* Cambridge, MA: Harvard University Press.

Walker, R. (2008). The philosophy of Te Whatu Pōkeka: Kaupapa Māori assessment and learning exemplars. *The First Years Ngā Tau Tuatahi: New Zealand Journal of Infant and Toddler Education, 10*(2): 5–10.

White, E. J., & Nuttall, J. (2007). Expanding intersubjectivity: The potential of Bakhtinian dialogism to inform narrative assessment in early childhood. *The First Years Ngā Tau Tuatahi: New Zealand Journal of Infant and Toddler Education, 9*(1), 21–25.

White, E. J. (2009) *Assessment in New Zealand early childhood education: A Bakhtinian analysis of toddler metaphoricity.* Unpublished doctoral thesis, Monash University, Melbourne, Australia.

White, E. J. (2011). Aesthetics of the beautiful: Ideologic tensions in contemporary assessment. In E. J. White & M. Peters (Eds.), *Bakhtinian pedagogy: Challenges and opportunities across the globe* (pp. 47–69). New York, NY: Blackwell.

White, E. J. (2012, March/April). *At the 'heart' of pedagogy: Aesthetic love.* Paper presented to mini-Bakhtinian conference Promises and Challenges of the Bakhtinian Pedagogy, University of Delaware, Newark, DE.

White, E. J. (in press, a). Chronotope spaces in ECE: A dialogic encounter with people, places and things. In J. Sumsion & L. Harrison (Eds.), *The lived spaces of infant and toddler settings*. Dordrecht: Springer.

White, E. J. (in press, b). Cry, baby, cry: A dialogic response to emotion. *Mind, Culture and Activity* [special edition].

Yates, L. (2009). From curriculum to pedagogy and back again: Knowledge, the person and the changing world. *Pedagogy, culture and society, 17*(1), 17–28.

CHAPTER 6

Progressing *Te Whāriki* from rhetoric to reality for children with disabilities and their families

Bernadette Macartney, Kerry Purdue and Jude MacArthur

ABSTRACT

In this chapter we suggest that inclusion in early childhood settings and communities involves understanding and identifying exclusion; removing barriers to presence, participation and learning; and practising from an open and listening orientation. Within this context, an inclusive pedagogy emerges out of a critical understanding and use of *Te Whāriki*. We discuss frameworks and approaches that can help teachers and others in early childhood communities to notice, recognise and respond to exclusion in productive ways.

Utilising a listening orientation, we begin with the experiences and perspectives of disabled people and their families/whānau in education. We consider how inclusive education can be understood, and the wider cultural and societal possibilities of an inclusive education system for transforming society. Tensions are identified that create spaces for the exclusion of disabled children and their families/whānau in early childhood education. These include tensions that arise when individual developmental ways of understanding human development and differences are introduced into services where socio-cultural, rights-based views of learning, participation and diversity are valued. The chapter concludes by suggesting some tools and approaches for guiding inclusive *Te Whāriki*-based practice and critical reflection.

Introduction

Te Whāriki (Ministry of Education, 1996) is a progressive curriculum based on values that support equity, social justice and the full community participation of all children. These are critical components in the process of working towards inclusion for children with disabilities, but it is teachers who implement the curriculum and translate values into practice in early childhood settings. In our recent discussions with the parent of a young child successfully included in her second-year class at primary school, the parent reflected back on his daughter's time in early childhood education and commented, "She was like an ornament there". This is a statement about exclusion, about a lack of belonging and participation.

The rhetoric of *Te Whāriki* is inclusive, but the reality of achieving a vibrant and inclusive learning context for all children depends on teachers' values, understandings and actions. Equally, it is apparent that structural supports such as inclusive values and policies, and flexible resources that meet the needs of early childhood communities, are a vital part of the mix if *Te Whāriki* is to make a positive difference for children with disabilities and their families.

The implementation of *Te Whāriki* has challenged early childhood teachers to reflect more critically on theories, philosophies, policies and pedagogies that support or hinder children's and families' rights and inclusion. Our own research and that of others shows that some teachers are working to ensure their early childhood settings and communities are fair and equitable places for all, and are challenging the social, cultural and physical barriers that inhibit children's and families' full participation and inclusion (Carrington & MacArthur, 2012; Gordon-Burns, Gunn, Purdue, & Surtees, 2012; Macartney, 2011; Purdue, 2004). Nonetheless, quality inclusive education in early childhood remains elusive for some children with disabilities and their families in Aotearoa New Zealand.

In this chapter we reflect on the attributes, values, knowledge and skills that *all* early childhood teachers in Aotearoa New Zealand need to have in order to implement *Te Whāriki* as an inclusive curriculum and to promote the learning of all children. We also look at ideological contexts and structural factors that can create pressures for exclusion in early childhood education, and the changes required so that teachers can meet the challenge laid down by *Te Whāriki*: that of weaving a mat for *all* to stand on.

Perspectives of disabled people and their families/whānau

We begin by introducing the social model of disability. The social model has been highly influential internationally because it draws attention to the capacity of *society* to create the experience of disability. The social model distinguishes between the physical or bodily experience of 'impairment' and a person's experience of 'disability', which comes from living in a society that is unprepared to change in order to accommodate and respond in positive ways to people who have impairments (Oliver, 1996). Disabled people experience disability when they and their families encounter structures, ideas, attitudes and beliefs that position them as other, and as not belonging in society. These structures and ideas can be conceptualised as barriers to inclusion, and they can be present in any setting. Within the context of early childhood education, the social model raises questions about the factors that contribute to children's disabling experiences, and about the factors that contribute to children's inclusion in, or exclusion from, the learning experiences afforded by the implementation of *Te Whāriki*.

In Aotearoa New Zealand disabled children and their families can encounter disabling barriers in the form of deficit-oriented perspectives that are taken for granted. Rather than seeing children in terms of their capabilities, strengths and interests, a deficit perspective frames disability in terms of deviation from the norm, and focuses on what children are unable to do. Yet qualitative research that prioritises the perspectives of children and families can counter negative discourses that characterise disabled children as a passive, vulnerable, homogeneous and separate group (Connors & Stalker, 2003; Davis & Hogan, 2004; Kelly, 2005; MacArthur, Sharp, Gaffney, & Kelly, 2007). We begin our discussion, therefore, with a child and family emphasis on thinking about the contexts that can support or supplant disabled children's belonging, participation and learning in early childhood services.

Research with families and whānau of disabled children shows that these families have the same aspirations for their children as the families of non-disabled children (Bevan-Brown, 2004; IHC, 2008; Leithfield & Murray, 1995; MacArthur, 2004; MacArthur, Dight, & Purdue, 2000; Macartney, 2008a, 2008b; Purdue, 2004;). Families want their children to be loved, valued and respected, to make friends and be included, and to learn and develop in a safe, stimulating, supportive and responsive environment. Deficit views make it difficult for these aspirations to be achieved; they restrict the opportunities, outcomes and life chances of disabled children, and they need to be interrupted. Research in New Zealand describes attitudes, fears, assumptions and values in early childhood education that are embedded within discourses of difference, that permeate professional practices, relationships and interactions with children with disabilities and their family members (Gordon-Burns, Purdue, Rarere-Briggs, Stark, & Turnock, 2010; MacArthur & Dight, 2000).

Processes of exclusion within early childhood can be subtle and may not be recognised by teachers. When a child is viewed primarily in terms of their 'special needs', for example, this can become an all-defining characteristic of the child, creating a barrier to their inclusion. An over-emphasis on a single aspect of a child marks them out as not like others and can prevent teachers from developing a supportive relationship with the child, with responsibility for teaching allocated to those considered to be experts or specialists, such as education support workers, early intervention teachers and therapists, and/or the child's family.

Fran, a participant in Bernadette's PhD research, describes her experiences with her disabled daughter Clare and illustrates these processes at work (Macartney, 2011). Clare was 3 years old at the time of this interview and had been attending Crossroads Early Childhood Centre (a pseudonym) since she was two. In relation to Clare starting at the centre, Fran said:

> she was like a little flower, I suppose. She sort of opened up a little bit and realised there were other children around her, from there. That was good … but the teachers never actually took Clare off the teacher aide, and in the holidays, when the teacher aide didn't work and I still had to pay my money, I would go, and I would go and spend the morning with Clare, and she would never be taken off me … They wouldn't have her by herself [at the centre]. Because she was completely dependent. So I either didn't go and Clare didn't go—but I still had to pay— … so me being the stingy person that I am, decided, 'Well, I'm gonna go' … And I didn't mind going, but I used to end up sitting, like on a wet day I'd be sitting in the corner with Clare and five other children. And the teachers would go past and say, 'Oh, you're great! You should come every week!' But they never thought to take Clare off me. And I was not only looking after Clare, I was babysitting the other five children as well … they'd speak to Clare on their way past, and stuff like that, but I don't think, they didn't really integrate her.

Confusion about adult roles and interrupted access to learning experiences became a problem for Clare, who ultimately experienced a barrier to the values, principles, relationships and theories about teaching and learning that form the basis of *Te Whāriki*. When disabled children and their families are physically present, but teachers do not ground their pedagogy and relationships in *Te Whāriki*, disabled children are excluded. Just as importantly, opportunities to develop a vibrant and inclusive culture within early childhood services are lost.

Inclusive education as a framework for thinking about curriculum, teaching and learning in early childhood

One of the enduring purposes of education is to prepare children and young people to be active, involved participants in a democracy where education is a public good centred on ideas about equity and social justice (Goodlad, 2005). Life in an early childhood service is part of life in the larger local community, and inclusive education provides a framework for thinking about how early childhood settings might look when they are actively contributing to inclusive communities and societies. Slee (2011) suggests we might consider *inclusion* to be a prerequisite for a democratic education, inviting us to "think about the nature of the world we live in, a world that we prefer and our role in shaping both of those worlds" (p. 14).

The inclusive early childhood setting can be conceptualised as a community in which teachers work together to meet the challenges of supporting a diverse group of children. These challenges mirror those presented by the diversity of social, family and work relationships in broader society (Carrington et al., 2012; Frankel, Gold, & Ajodhia-Andrews, 2010). *Te Whāriki*, used within an inclusive educational approach, facilitates inclusive practice by providing a critical framework within which teachers can examine and challenge assumptions that inform the way they think and work. Reflection becomes a stimulus for change.

Understanding inclusion

Inclusive education is often associated with the education of children and young people with disabilities in regular community-based early childhood services and schools. However, current understanding positions inclusion as a global concern to ensure all children and young people have the right to access and complete a free and compulsory education that is responsive to their needs and relevant to their lives (UNESCO, 2011). It is a human rights and social justice issue, focused on anyone who may be marginalised and excluded within the education system, from early childhood through to tertiary education. Exclusion may arise from a number of factors, including disability, sexuality, poverty, religion, ethnicity or politics (children in war-torn countries, for example). Key questions for those working in early childhood education are 'Who is on the margins in our early childhood centre?' and 'What do we need to do to ensure all children in our centre fully participate and are supported to be the best they can be?'

Inclusion involves change

British researcher Mel Ainscow (2008) portrays inclusion as one of the most significant challenges we face in education because it requires change at all levels in order for every child and young person to experience a relevant education, and to be welcomed and taught in their local early childhood service or school so that no one is marginalised. Overcoming barriers to children's participation and achievement in education provides a compelling incentive to explore the ways in which early childhood services and schools can respond differently to diversity and reaffirm all children's right to be included as valued, active participants.

Transformation is a vital ingredient in the building of inclusive early childhood services and schools. Early childhood settings and schools working towards inclusion are involved in a continuous process of development and change, because they focus on overcoming barriers to children's learning and participation and share a concern to ensure that all children are *valued, present, participating* and *achieving* (Booth & Ainscow, 2011). Inclusion challenges the attachment of hierarchical values to people whereby some are considered more worthy than others, and in this respect Slee (2011) suggests that inclusion is not something that is done to particular groups of children and young people (such as disabled children); it is something we must do *to ourselves*.

Values are a foundation for inclusion

The values of an early childhood service or school form the foundation for inclusive approaches. The Index for Inclusion (Booth & Ainscow, 2011) describes values as fundamental guides that provide a sense of direction and underpin the actions of children and adults towards others. In developing a framework of values, early childhood settings make a statement about how their community will live together and educate each other. Values are brought to life through the service's policies, practices and structures (Booth, 2005), so it is important that values are made explicit, and that the services community understands what they mean.

On the basis of their work with schools in the United Kingdom, Ainscow, Booth and Dyson (2006) describe a set of values that are the basis for action when working towards inclusion. Some have global significance, such as sustainability and the valuing of international communities; others include equity, participation, community, compassion, respect for diversity and entitlement. Booth (2011) has recently added to the Index the values of honesty, rights, joy, non-violence, trust, courage, love, hope or optimism, and beauty, and asks those working in education to consider what early childhood and school communities might look like when, for example, there is joyful engagement in teaching and learning.

Guidance, policy and curriculum support for inclusion

Inclusion is well supported in Aotearoa New Zealand by policies that protect the right of disabled children to an education. Children and adults are accorded the same human rights through local legislation (New Zealand Government, 1989, 1993) and policies (Minister for Disability Issues, 2001; Ministry of Education, 2010), international agreements (United Nations, 1989, 2006), and the New Zealand early childhood and compulsory school curriculum frameworks (Ministry of Education, 1996, 2007, 2008). Collectively, these statements, laws and agreements describe an ethical framework for and a consensus on the rights of every child and family to an inclusive education that is respectful of, and responsive to, the diversity found in our early childhood services and communities.

The New Zealand Disability Strategy (Minister for Disability Issues, 2001) is an important policy document, which aims for an inclusive society and promotes inclusive education across all sectors of the education system. The first and third of the 15 objectives in the *Strategy* provide another useful framework for critiquing disabled children's educational experiences. Objective 1 aims to

Encourage and educate for a non-disabling society: Encourage the emergence of a
non-disabling society that respects and highly values the lives of disabled people
and supports inclusive communities. (p. 11)

Objective 3 aims to

Provide the best education for disabled people: Improve education so that all children,
youth and adult learners will have equal opportunities to learn and develop in their
local, regular educational centres. (p. 11)

Although the *Disability Strategy* focuses on improving the lives of disabled people in
New Zealand, it also encourages us to consider the extent to which our early childhood
services and schools value diversity and commit to a relevant education that enhances
success for all students.

Aotearoa New Zealand also has obligations to international human rights treaties,
being a signatory to the United Nations Convention on the Rights of the Child (UNCRC,
United Nations, 1989) and on the Rights of People with Disabilities (UNCRPD,
United Nations, 2006). UNCRC is written for all children and highlights the rights
of children and young people to non-discrimination, equitable opportunity and full
participation in community settings, including early childhood services and schools.
Article 3 addresses the "best interests of the child" as a primary consideration in all
actions concerning children; educational decisions should therefore be made with
full consideration of children's rights to receive a high-quality education in their local
community. Article 23 relates specifically to disabled children and asserts their rights
to enjoy a full and decent life, to dignity and independence, and to active participation
in the community. This includes their right to access to education, which is more fully
addressed in Articles 28 and 29 (the right to an education, and to an education that
enhances children's development, respectively). Children's rights to be consulted on
matters that affect them, to express their views and to have their views heard and
taken seriously are addressed in Article 12. We might therefore consider whether
disabled children (indeed all children) contribute to processes and discussions that
pertain to their learning and social experiences, and whether their views are listened
to and acted upon (MacArthur et al., 2007).

UNCRPD sets out the rights of disabled people and provides governments with a
code for implementation. It is based on the social model of disability described earlier
in this chapter and therefore acknowledges the existence of disabling barriers in
society, including those found in educational settings. Article 7 declares that children
with disabilities have human rights and freedoms equal to those of any other child.
Inclusive education is specifically referred to in the Convention as an essential part of
the process of developing inclusive communities, with children's rights to an inclusive
education at all levels of the education system established in Article 24.

Whilst there has been a shift away from segregated education, this chapter alerts readers to challenges in some early childhood settings that can result in the exclusion of children with disabilities (see also Purdue, 2006; Rarere-Briggs, Gordon-Burns, Purdue, Stark, & Turnock, 2012). Although guidance and legislation support inclusion in Aotearoa New Zealand, children's experience of being included or excluded is a function of the values of and relationships among the people who share a learning community. Exclusion can and does occur when a values base is not inclusive, or when there is a disjuncture between an education setting's values and the ideas and practices of people in that setting. This idea helps us to understand why the reviewing and sustaining of inclusive values, and of their translation into practice, is so important in inclusive early childhood settings (Frankel et al., 2010).

Inclusion and *Te Whāriki*

Ideas about inclusion sit comfortably with *Te Whāriki* (Ministry of Education, 1996). The principles and strands of the framework support children's rights to be valued and recognised, and to be part of a culture in which diversity is responded to in positive ways. Teachers have responsibilities to nurture and empower all young children as they learn and grow; to *value, expect and respond positively to diversity*; to recognise and value the integral place of the *wider world, community and family* in children's learning and participation; and to approach learning as an intersubjective process through which children (and teachers) "learn through *responsive and reciprocal relationships* with people, places and things" (Ministry of Education, 1996, p. 14, emphasis added). The strands situate learning and teaching within responsive relationships throughout a setting's community, a theme that is consistent with inclusive practice.

Positive and active participation occurs when all children, whānau and teachers experience a sense of belonging, wellbeing, engagement, exploration, communication, self-expression, contribution and responsibility to and for each other within a service's community. A *Te Whāriki*-based curriculum is relevant to every child, but whether or not inclusion is a priority, how it is offered and which children are eligible are all influenced by the values that inform practice (Frankel et al., 2010). How, then, can teachers collaboratively enact *Te Whāriki* in ways that support the presence, participation and achievement of all children in the setting? We return to this question later in the chapter when we consider tools for progressing change.

Barriers to inclusion: Tensions and dilemmas

Te Whāriki has a strong socio-cultural, bicultural, family- and community-centred, and critical and relational foundation and focus. However, teachers play a central role in creating the curriculum, culture and relationships within an early childhood service. Teachers can understand and challenge social inequalities, and recognise and remove barriers to learning and participation (Dahlberg & Moss, 2005; Gordon-Burns, Gunn, et al., 2012; Robinson & Jones Diaz, 1999; Yelland & Kilderry, 2005). Progress towards inclusion is likely to falter when teachers, families and others in a service's community are operating at cross purposes in terms of their socio-cultural and political perspectives, beliefs and priorities (Frankel et al., 2010). In the absence of a united and democratic belief that all children belong and should be taught together, values, language and practices are likely to conflict when varying interpretations and actions are attached to concepts such as 'disability' and 'inclusion'. New Zealand research on the experiences of disabled children and their families has documented tensions between developmental and socio-cultural discourses, and between ideas about sameness and difference and the language of 'special needs' (MacArthur, 2004; Macartney, 2008b; 2011; Purdue, 2006).

Tensions between developmental and socio-cultural discourses

In contrast to critical and socio-cultural pedagogies, an individualised and deficit-focused developmental discourse requires teachers to fit infants, toddlers and young children into a normalising framework of universal ages, stages and ways of being. When it is the main framework in use, developmentalism promotes an inadequate and impoverished view of children, culture and education (Cannella, 1997; Fleer, 2005; Rogoff, 2003). It has been criticised as an operating theory in early childhood because it can force narrow and restrictive identities on children and, in so doing, deny, punish and work to reduce diversity among learners and their families (Fleer, 2005).

Behind normative approaches to children's learning and development can lie an unquestioned assumption that all children will benefit by conforming to the dominant group's ways of thinking and being. The danger here is that non-dominant groups are silenced and marginalised. Comparing and negatively judging children according to their deviations from (so-called) normal development is the key process for assessing and responding to disability and difference within developmental psychology, and its related field of special education, and disabled children are vulnerable to being viewed through the lens of deficit-based developmental knowledge and practices (Ballard, 2004; Rarere-Briggs et al., 2012). Tensions have been noted when specialist itinerant staff introduce a deficit-oriented approach in a centre and remove disabled children for separate one-to-one instruction, while teachers in the centre attempt to keep children together and participating within the socio-cultural spirit of *Te Whāriki* (MacArthur, 2004). Similarly, disabled children can experience exclusion when a "truckload of professionals" operating on the basis of a range of discourses become involved in the transition of disabled children from early childhood to school (MacArthur & Dight, 2000, p. 39).

Dilemmas of sameness and difference

The Western cultural concepts of sameness (normal) and difference (not normal) are central to teachers' understanding and practices of inclusion and/or exclusion. Key questions for teachers include: 'What is regarded as the same?', 'Who is perceived as different and other?' and 'How is difference responded to?'. Sometimes differences remain unrecognised by teachers or are viewed as a barrier to a child and family's participation in an early childhood setting (Purdue, 2004; Rivalland & Nuttall, 2010). The acknowledgement of difference can also be at a tokenistic or superficial level. When this happens, key ideas about diversity and participation by all can have limited or no impact on the curriculum or culture of the setting, and the diversity of children, whānau and teachers goes unrecognised (Gordon-Burns, Purdue, Rarere-Briggs, Stark, & Turnock, 2012).

Disabled and non-disabled children in regular educational settings do not experience an inclusive education by virtue of sharing the same physical location (MacArthur, Kelly, & Higgins, 2005; Macartney, 2011; Purdue, 2004; Rietveld, 2005; Rutherford, 2009). This point is illustrated in Clare's experience at Crossroads Early Childhood Centre, described earlier in this chapter. Individuals and groups of children experience the curriculum differently, yet Rivalland and Nuttall (2010) have observed a 'sameness as fairness' discourse among teachers and managers in a number of Australian early childhood centres in relation to family diversity. When teachers subscribe to this kind of discourse, they believe that treating every child and family the same is fair and equitable. However, treating everybody the same can lead to the denial of diversity, and may require children and families to fit into existing processes and practices that remain unchanged. Teachers may be discouraged from considering the relevance of the centre's culture and curriculum to *each* child and family. *Te Whāriki* encourages teachers to value and reflect the child *and* their family's culture, norms and ways of being, as this is how each child is supported to belong, learn, fully participate and contribute (Ministry of Education, 1996; Macartney & Morton, 2011).

By contrast, an over-emphasis on perceived differences through, for example, the language of 'special needs' and practices of 'special education', is also problematic, because this constructs disabled children as 'special' (negatively different) and 'needy' (passive). Viewing a child primarily in terms of their impairments or the label of their disability creates and maintains space for a separate view and treatment of them as learners (Ballard, 2004; MacArthur, 2004; Macartney, 2008a). We look at this issue more fully in the section below and raise the possibility that *Te Whāriki* has the potential to exclude children because it retains the language (and therefore may be considered to legitimate the practices) of special needs and special education.

A different way of thinking is to view differentness or diversity in children as an ordinary part of human experience (Ballard, 1995), and to see a task of teachers as learning to become comfortable as they build inclusive early childhood communities where diversity is valued. Carrington et al. (2012) argue that the socio-cultural construction and understanding of difference is represented in the personal beliefs, attitudes and values that shape how teachers interact with students, families and broader society. Separating children on the basis of perceived differences, or stereotyping differences, leads to divisions and status systems that undermine the democratic nature of an early childhood community and the dignity of its participants—both children and adults. Communities in inclusive early childhood settings, on the other hand, view difference as ordinary, and co-operate and collaborate for the common good of all.

Te Whāriki and the language of special needs

The term 'special needs' is criticised in this chapter as contributing to deficit-oriented thinking that distinguishes disabled children from their peers. While *Te Whāriki* sits comfortably with our discussions about inclusion, the use of the term 'special needs' within the early childhood curriculum remains an anomaly that may be a barrier to inclusive early childhood education. In returning to the social model of disability introduced at the beginning of this chapter, we can see that labelling children as 'special needs' suggests that the experience of disability is a result of individual impairment and deficiency rather than arising from institutional barriers and from the discriminatory attitudes and actions of others (Macartney, 2008a; Purdue, 2006).

The construction of children with disabilities as 'special needs' is associated with abnormal development, negative perspectives on difference, and exclusion through the practices of special education. Inclusion, on the other hand, anticipates diversity and views difference as ordinary. It values the knowledge of teachers and their capacity to work in collaborative teams to teach all children through the early childhood curriculum. If we are to effectively tackle disability oppression and disabling practices in education and society, we need to question the place of special needs.

Corbett (2001) suggests that "Inclusion means responding to individual needs, with the term 'special' becoming redundant" (p. *xiii*). Booth, Ainscow and Kingston (2006) concur, suggesting that the phrase 'special educational needs' should be replaced with "barriers to play, learning and participation" (p. 5). They explain their stance as follows:

> The idea that the difficulties children experience can be resolved by identifying some of them as 'having special educational needs' has considerable limitations. It confers a label that can lead to lowered expectations. It deflects attention from the difficulties experienced by other children without the label, and from sources of difficulty that may occur in relationships, cultures, the nature of activities and resources, the way practitioners support learning and play, and the policies and organisations of settings. (Booth et al., p. 5)

We view the movement away from the language and thinking of special needs as an important step in conveying to all teachers that *Te Whāriki* was written—and intended —for all children, their families and teachers.

Tools for progressing change: Putting inclusive values and concepts into practice

The negative workings of power on different groups throughout society influence children's learning, participation and inclusion (Bishop & Glynn, 1999; MacNaughton, 2005; Macartney & Morton, 2011). Critical and ethics-based pedagogies can open the way for society to respond in positive ways to the diversity and complexity that exists within education. In this section we explore orientations and tools that teachers can use to help them engage ethically and critically with *Te Whāriki* and other pedagogical frameworks, and to recognise social inequality and diversity as a central focus of their work with children and families (Carr, May, & Podmore, 2000; Ministry of Education, 1996, 2007; Podmore, May, & Mara, 1998; Rinaldi, 2006; Ritchie, 2010).

An ethic of care and a pedagogy of listening

A 'pedagogy of listening' (POL) is a social constructionist, democratic and ethical approach to early childhood education that originated from early childhood services in Reggio Emilia, in Italy (Rinaldi, 2006), and has been taken up by early childhood educationalists from Sweden and the United Kingdom (Dahlberg & Moss, 2005; Dahlberg, Moss, & Pence, 2007; Moss & Petrie, 2002). Teachers base their orientation to children and families on an 'ethic of care' and an obligation to the 'other' (Dahlberg & Moss, 2005; Moss & Petrie, 2002; Rinaldi, 2006; Veck, 2009). A POL involves conscious resistance to traditional views of teaching, such as the application of pre-defined, normalising knowledge and beliefs.

In a POL, teaching becomes an ethical pursuit in which listening is used as a process for understanding, respecting and responding with openness to others. A key aspect of the teacher's role is to identify and remove barriers to learning and participation through 'attentive listening' within relationship-based contexts. Veck (2009) suggests that

> What is attended to in listening is not, then, what we think we know about a speaker, but the possibilities for newness that dwell within their personhood whose mystery precludes full knowing. Attentive listening thus involves an existential leap, a transformation in being that moves the listener beyond the security of the known. It requires listeners to prepare for change and to allow themselves to be changed by the words they hear. (p. 148)

A listening orientation is based on the understanding that—rather than being a pre-defined and individual process—learning, truth, knowledge and participation are co-constructed within relational, material and socio-cultural contexts (Rinaldi, 2006;

Rogoff, 2003). In response to this situated and provisional view of learning, a POL requires teachers to develop an orientive and curious—rather than norms-based and expert—approach to children's participation and learning. Rinaldi (2006) describes a listening orientation as

> welcoming and being open to differences, recognising the value of the other's point of view and interpretation ... Listening that does not produce answers but formulates questions; listening which is not insecurity but, on the contrary, the security that every truth is such only if we are aware of its limits and its possible 'falsification'. (p. 65)

The Learning and Teaching Story framework

We are fortunate that an orientation to and practice of attentive listening as a process for teaching, learning and transformation is reflected in New Zealand's narrative Learning and Teaching Story approaches to assessment, documentation, critical reflection and teaching (Carr, 1998, 2001; Carr, et al., 2000; Carr, Hatherly, Lee, & Ramsay, 2003; Greerton Early Childhood Centre, 2010; Ministry of Education, 2005, 2006; Te One, Barrett, & Podmore, 2010). However, the post-*Te Whāriki* emphasis of teacher development in Aotearoa New Zealand has been more on assessing individual children's learning ('Learning Stories'), with much less attention being directed towards critical reflection on teachers' thinking and practices ('Teaching Stories') (Meade, 2002). We suggest that an (over-) emphasis on the assessment of individual children's learning without teachers critically reflecting on their assumptions, values and influence is problematic. This is especially so in relation to children and families who do not conform to dominant Western cultural views of what is normal, and therefore familiar, comfortable and desirable for many teachers (Macartney, 2007). Keeping in mind the tendency to privilege assessment over critical reflection, we now turn to considering the potential of the Learning and Teaching Story framework for growing more ethical, responsive and democratic environments.

The framework was developed through a series of qualitative research projects that investigated what teaching and learning looked like in terms of the principles and strands of *Te Whāriki* in action in a diverse range of Aotearoa New Zealand early childhood services (Carr, et al., 2000; Podmore et al., 1998; Podmore, May, & Carr, 2001). The Teaching Story aspect of the framework links children's learning and participation to adults' actions, responsibilities and obligations within the early childhood education setting. It begins with questions, posed from the child's perspective or voice, aligned with the principles and strands of *Te Whāriki*.

The shortened version of the child's questions are: Do you know me? Can I trust you? Do you let me fly? Do you hear me? Is this place fair? Is there a place for me here? These questions are intended as points of entry, or provocations, for teaching teams to develop and consider further questions and tools for inquiry in their context, rather than as an exhaustive list to be universally applied (Ministry of Education, 2006; Podmore et al., 2001). The questions can provide a powerful starting place for teachers and other adults to reflect upon and gather data about barriers and supports for the learning and participation of the children, families, whānau and teachers within their early childhood education setting. Used critically, the child's questions can encourage teachers to listen to and learn from others, and to engage with a diverse range of experiences and perspectives. Developing a deeper and more open orientation to others can help teachers recognise and challenge negative assumptions and beliefs about difference, even when these are unconsciously informing practices and environments.

The following example from Bernadette's doctoral thesis (Macartney, 2011), followed by Bernadette's reflection, illustrates how a Learning and Teaching Story framework can be used to identify processes of exclusion, and as a prompt for teachers to critique their practice and reconsider how Clare (and Fran) experience belonging as it is envisaged by *Te Whāriki*.

Do you know me?

The strand of Belonging—"Children and their families experience a sense of belonging" and the critical, reflective question "Do you appreciate and understand my interests and abilities and those of my family?—Do you know me?"—are central to Fran and Clare's experiences at Crossroads. *Te Whāriki* and the Learning and Teaching Story Framework interweave children and families' sense of belonging and wellbeing with each child developing the dispositions to take an interest in the people, places and things in their environment, and to become involved in the relationships, happenings and life of the centre. Fran's description of Clare opening up 'like a little flower' when she 'realised there were other children around her' at the centre, indicates that Clare was disposed to taking an interest in what was happening around her. Although Fran was aware of the significance of Clare's discovery and interest in the people in her new surroundings, the teachers' behaviour didn't indicate their awareness of being obliged to get to know and include Clare. Rather than listening attentively to Clare, viewing her holistically and seeing it as their role to foster her empowerment within the setting, Clare's "otherness" became a disincentive or reason for her not to be fully included in the life and relationships of Crossroads Early Childhood Centre.

Clare's sense of belonging as a fully participating member of the centre was also influenced by her attendance at Crossroads for only half a day each week. Fran based her choice about the number of hours that Clare was enrolled for on the limited funding that had been allocated by the Early Intervention Specialist for an ESW [Education Support Worker] for Clare. This is an example of a common structural barrier that acted against Clare developing relationships in the centre. Had Fran not spent the mornings during school holidays at the centre with Clare, the amount of time she was there would have been even less. Fran's experiences at Crossroads suggested that the teachers saw Clare as being the responsibility of someone else—her

ESW and her parent when the ESW wasn't present. Without the benefits of being heard and developing reciprocal and meaningful relationships, Clare's opportunities to learn, contribute and participate to the best of her ability were impaired by her environment. Clare's identity as being "special"/other became a reason for teachers not to get to know her or to see it as their role to include her in the relationships and life of the centre. This situation occurred and continued even when a stated goal of the teachers was for Clare to become more part of the centre. It appears that Fran and Clare's voices were not fully sought, listened or considered in these planning discussions and reflections.

In addition to asking the question, "Do you know me?", this situation prompts me to ask: "Do you want to know me?", "What do you want to know about me?", "Why do you seem uninterested in important things about me and my family?" and "Why do you say you want to know me and for me to be part of the centre, and then do nothing different to encourage my influence, participation and connections with others?" What the teachers seemed to focus on in terms of "knowing" Clare was her label, "deficits" or impairments, not who she was as a person and a learner within their setting. Without critical attention being paid to responsive and reciprocal relationships between a child and her family, ESW, teachers, and peers, the possibilities for learning and participation within a context are significantly diminished. In the absence of teachers exercising their obligation to develop a respectful and reciprocal relationship with Clare, the answer to the questions—"Can I trust you?", "Do you let me fly?", "Do you hear me?", "Is this place fair?" and "Is there a place for me here?"—must be no (Macartney, 2011, p. 257).

Forming strong, positive relationships with children with disabilities and their families/whānau

It is important for all children attending early childhood settings to have teachers who form close relationships with them and their family, and who respond to their daily needs with care and sensitivity (Ministry of Education, 1996). *Te Whāriki* argues that responsive, reciprocal and caring teacher–child interactions and relationships are necessary to support all young children's learning and development. Establishing effective relationships and partnerships with families is also seen in successful inclusive practice. Parents and whānau hold a wealth of information about their children, which teachers can then use to guide and enhance assessment, curriculum and teaching decisions. Family accounts and perspectives retain and communicate the complexities, richness and diversity of their child's identity and experiences. Families live with, and are usually well aware of, their child's individual attributes, strengths, weaknesses, ways of communicating and expressing their preferences, desires and needs, and families are likely to view their child as much more than their disability or the label of their impairment. Porter and Smith (2011) position families as central in their child's education team and suggest that:

Educators that possess the belief that parents are a valuable and essential resource and partner in the educational process will ensure that parents are invited and included to participate in the teaching and learning process. These educators respect and privilege the active involvement of parents. The authentic inclusion of parents becomes a key component in the pedagogical practices of these educators. Conversely, educators that do not recognize or respect the lived experience and knowledge of parents, as valuable educational resources, may implicitly and explicitly exclude parents. This exclusion often results in limiting the educational experiences and opportunities for learners. (p. 173)

To nurture and promote children's wellbeing and belonging, children with disabilities and their families (like all children and families) need to know that teachers and other staff in early childhood settings care about them, want them there and want to teach them (Gordon-Burns et al., 2010). As members of the same early childhood education community, families also need to know that teachers are prepared to work alongside them to recognise, challenge and overcome the barriers to inclusion that inevitably arise from time to time.

Implementing inclusive pedagogies

Irrespective of the location or size of an early childhood education setting, the children attending it will have a wide range of learning needs. Teachers can learn to notice, recognise and respond effectively to difference in order to support and enhance children's learning and participation alongside their peers. *Te Whāriki* emphasises that the

care and education [of children with disabilities] will be encompassed within the principles, strands, and goals set out for all children in early childhood settings … [and that the] programmes of each centre will incorporate strategies to fully include them. (p. 11)

When responding to children with disabilities, teachers can confidently draw on their generic knowledge of early childhood education and care. They can also adapt strategies or use differentiated teaching approaches; modify the curriculum, programme and environment; and collaborate with other professionals to enhance learning and participation. The overriding concern must be to ensure that approaches to teaching and learning support children's inclusion and do not isolate, stigmatise or exclude them. Teachers play an important role in ensuring that other professionals and visitors (including family members) work and interact with children and staff in ways that are consistent with the service's philosophy, curriculum and practices (Giangreco & Doyle, 2007, MacArthur, Purdue, & Ballard, 2003).

Sapon-Shevin (2011) encourages teachers to seize—not ignore—teachable moments for social justice. Children from a very early age notice the similarities and differences between people. They also learn quickly who and what to accept and include, and who or what to reject and exclude (Glover, 2001; Turnock, Gordon-Burns, Purdue, Rarere-Briggs, & Stark, 2011). If young children are not exposed to positive understandings and experiences in relation to disability, it is likely that they will grow up contributing to the injustices and inequities experienced by disabled people and their families in society (Minister for Disability Issues, 2001). This is why *Te Whāriki,* and commentators and researchers such as Sapon-Shevin (2011) and Slee (2011), encourage us to turn our educational settings into sites of justice, inclusion and caring so that we can fully honour the rights of diverse children and families to equitable participation in communities and societies. If this ideal is to become a reality, the theoretical and philosophical underpinnings of social justice and inclusion within *Te Whāriki* "need to permeate the consciousness and pedagogical practices" of all teachers (Porter & Smith, 2011, p. 32).

Establishing and maintaining authentic collaboration and partnerships with other professionals

To progress inclusion for disabled children, all educators and professionals associated with a setting will benefit from opportunities to develop authentic collaborative partnerships with one another and to establish clear roles and responsibilities. Teachers, administrators, early intervention teachers, education support workers, teacher-aides, physiotherapists, occupational therapists, speech–language therapists, case workers and others all need to be on the same page and, in the words of Frankel et al. (2010), have a "solidarity of philosophy [that] represents unity and the democratic belief that all children belong and should be educated within their communities" (p. 4).

Establishing and maintaining effective relationships and partnerships takes time, commitment, open-mindedness and effective communication skills—as well as plain hard work. Having a shared vision and being prepared to work together towards this outcome are essential. Working within the parameters of *Te Whāriki,* different people will contribute different understandings about what inclusion is and what it looks like in practice. These differences can form part of the ongoing discussion that is necessary in a democratic community working towards the goal of inclusion. As indicated earlier in the chapter, conflicting viewpoints about how best to include and teach children with disabilities can result in team disharmony and jeopardise inclusion efforts (Gordon-Burns, Purdue, et al., 2012; MacArthur, 2004; Porter & Smith, 2011). They are a reminder of the importance of a shared framework based on mutually agreed inclusive values. Equally,

> Mutual respect and effective collaboration can make the difference between success and failure … Open communication and an unwavering commitment to work through challenges is essential. (Porter & Smith, 2011, p. 29).

Teachers as effective leaders for inclusion and social justice

Exclusion and discrimination in early childhood education have been described as growing issues in Aotearoa New Zealand for a range of children and their families (Gordon-Burns, Gunn, et al., 2012). This suggests that teachers need to be prepared to make a difference as leaders for equity and social justice (Slee, 2011). Teachers have the capacity to make their early childhood settings welcoming and inclusive places for all. Sapon-Shevin (2011, p. 167) suggests that an important question for all teachers to ask is, "Will what I am doing here and now move us forward toward creating equity, social justice, and inclusion, or farther away?" Remaining mindful of the principles of *Te Whāriki*, this question can support teachers to maintain an ongoing reflective approach that enhances the development of their service towards inclusion.

The role of teacher education programmes in preparing teachers for inclusion

Although teachers in Aotearoa New Zealand are working to ensure their early childhood settings and communities are fair and equitable places for all who attend and work in them, quality inclusive early childhood education remains elusive for some children with disabilities and their families. In this final section we want to reiterate the critical role that teacher education plays in helping to progress *Te Whāriki* from rhetoric to reality for disabled children and their families.

The New Zealand Teachers Council expects newly graduated early childhood teachers to join the sector with the professional values, knowledge and pedagogies that will enable them to provide high-quality teaching and learning environments for all (New Zealand Teachers Council, 2007). However, New Zealand research suggests that some teachers feel ill-prepared to teach children with disabilities and learning difficulties (Gordon-Burns, Purdue, et al., 2012; Macartney, 2011; Ministry of Education, 2010; Purdue, 2004). In moving *Te Whāriki* from rhetoric to reality for children with disabilities, teacher education appears to be in need of critical review.

Slee (2011) suggests that teacher education programmes offering 'special education' knowledge, discourses and practices to prepare teachers for student diversity and inclusive education are flawed. He singles out programmes that take a "Grey's Anatomy approach" (p. 155) to inclusive education, using this televisual metaphor to describe teacher education programmes where teachers are taught about the range of syndromes, disorders and defects that constitute the population of children with 'special educational needs', leaving them as experts on child defectiveness unable to put inclusive policy into practice (Minister for Disability Issues, 2001). This approach, Slee argues, formalises exclusionary special education discourses as the official knowledge of difference. Slee (2001) concludes that teacher education needs to explore new forms of knowledge about identity and difference and to suggest new questions that invite students to consider the pathologies of schools that enable or disable students. (p. 174)

For 'quality teaching' to mean 'quality teaching for all children', teachers must learn to appreciate the value of their knowledge of child development, curriculum and pedagogy in settings that include a diverse group of children (Gordon-Burns et al., 2010). This viewpoint is endorsed by teachers themselves. Foreman (2011), for example, reiterates that teachers who work in inclusive settings say they do not need special procedures and qualifications to help them understand children with disabilities, nor do they need special techniques in order to teach and include them. Teacher education students can be supported to critically analyse dominant discourses and their implications for policy and practice. Equally, teachers who have the necessary theoretical tools to help them to see injustice and understand the origins of exclusion are, according to various commentators (e.g., Ballard, 2003; Purdue, Gordon-Burns, Gunn, Madden, & Surtees, 2009; Slee, 2011), better prepared to find or create alternatives that ensure all children are included.

Conclusion

In this chapter we have looked at who is included and who is excluded in relation to disability in early childhood education, and why this happens. Now we have to ask ourselves what we are going to do about it. MacNaughton (2005, p. 189) argues that all those who work with young children should possess knowledge and skills "critically informed by the leading edge of social thinking and theory of their time" and that enable them to make a positive difference in children's lives. Teachers need to have

the type of passion for and commitment to their work that enables them to advocate policies based on social justice … and to embed children's rights in all that they do in the name of children.

When fully implemented, New Zealand and international policies and curricula bring the principles of respect, equity and joy into the lives of young children and their families and, in the longer term, help progress social change and extend democracy. Change for inclusion has to be advanced at the political, professional and personal levels if we are to achieve fairness and justice in education for children with disabilities and their families.

Slee (2011) argues that a re-framing of the education system is required because of a widespread belief that blending 'special' education knowledge and practices into 'regular' education will produce an inclusive education system. If real change is to occur, we need to re-vision education by deconstructing and reconstructing early childhood contexts. Re-righting the language of inclusive education is necessary because "Language not only describes the world, it orders and recreates it. Correspondingly, language can frame and mobilize change" (Slee, 2011, p. 156). The challenge for inclusive teachers (and, indeed, researchers) is to ensure that our work does not reinforce the subordination of marginalised people, but rather contributes to their empowerment, reciprocity and gain. Rather than accepting the status quo, we need to critically reflect on what inclusive education is or can be. Inclusive education is about addressing discrimination and the pathologising of difference in society, including educational settings. It is about changing services' cultures, policies, curriculum implementation, pedagogy and organisational practices so that the needs of all children and families are met.

Recent cut-backs in early childhood education have reduced initiatives that contribute strongly to enhancing quality in the sector (Mitchell, 2011). The requirement for children with disabilities to have, as of right, the resources they need to support their learning and development in early childhood settings is a matter of equity and social justice. Teachers and management in early childhood settings need to think about resourcing and funding issues within the context of children's rights and inclusion. Over-emphasising possible staffing, environmental and financial limitations diverts attention from each service's responsibility to transform and change their policies, structures and culture for successful inclusion (Slee, 2011).

We know that government spending on the provision of quality structural conditions for teaching and learning is essential to the learning and wellbeing of young children in early childhood education. Structural factors affecting the capacity of teachers to meet the needs of all learners include levels of qualified staffing, small group sizes, high teacher:child ratios, paid planning and meeting time for teachers, and ongoing professional development (Education Review Office, 2010). A lack of resources can be used as a reason for services to not fully protect the right of every child and family to inclusive education. Services must work to find innovative ways to modify and adapt their setting to make it inclusive, especially in times of limited resourcing. Every early childhood setting needs to address these and other issues through critical dialogue and reflection, an ethic of care, innovation and risk-taking, cooperation and collaborative problem-solving, partnerships, and sharing of responsibilities. Society cannot afford to wait for equitable funding and resources before committing fully to valuing, supporting and celebrating the learning and participation of every child and family.

References

Ainscow, M. (2008). Teaching for diversity: The next big challenge. In F. M. Connelly (Ed.), *The Sage handbook of curriculum and instruction* (pp. 240–259). Los Angeles, CA: Sage.

Ainscow, M., Booth, T., & Dyson, A. (2006). *Improving schools, developing inclusion*. London, UK: Routledge.

Ballard, K. (1995). Inclusion, paradigms, power and participation. In C. Clark, A. Dyson, & A. Millward (Eds.), *Towards inclusive schools* (pp. 1–14). London, UK: David Fulton.

Ballard, K. (2003). The analysis of context: Some thoughts on teacher education, culture, colonisation and inequality. In T. Booth, K. Nes, & M. Stromstad (Eds.), *Developing inclusive teacher education* (pp. 59–77). London, UK: RoutledgeFalmer.

Ballard, K. (2004). Children and disability: Special or included? *Waikato Journal of Education, 10*, 315–326.

Bevan-Brown, J. (2004). *Māori perspectives of autistic spectrum disorder: Report to the Ministry of Education*. Wellington: Ministry of Education.

Bishop, R., & Glynn, T. (1999). *Culture counts: Changing power relations in education*. Palmerston North: Dunmore Press.

Booth, T. (2005). Keeping the future alive: Putting inclusive values into action. *Forum, 47*(2–3), 151–158.

Booth, T. (2011). Curricula for the common school: What shall we tell our children? *Forum, 53*(1), 31–47.

Booth, T., & Ainscow, M. (2011). *Index for inclusion: Developing learning and participation in schools* (3rd ed.). Manchester, UK: Centre for Studies on Inclusive Education.

Booth, T., Ainscow, M., & Kingston, D. (2006). *Index for inclusion: Developing play, learning and participation in early years and childcare*. Manchester, UK: Centre for Studies on Inclusive Education.

Cannella, G. (1997). *Deconstructing early childhood education: Social justice and revolution*. New York, NY: Peter Lang.

Carr, M. (1998). *Assessing children's experiences in early childhood: Final report to the Ministry of Education*. Wellington: Ministry of Education.

Carr, M. (2001). *Assessment in early childhood settings: Learning stories*. London, UK: Paul Chapman Publishing.

Carr, M., Hatherly, A., Lee, W., & Ramsay, K. (2003). *Te Whāriki* and assessment: A case study of teacher change. In J. Nuttall (Ed.), *Weaving Te Whāriki: Aotearoa New Zealand's early childhood curriculum document in theory and practice* (pp. 187–212). Wellington: New Zealand Council for Educational Research.

Carr, M., May, H., Podmore, V., with Cubey, P., Hatherly, A., & Macartney, B. (2000). *Learning and teaching stories: Action research on evaluation in early childhood: Final report to the Ministry of Education*. Wellington: New Zealand Council for Educational Research.

Carrington, S., & MacArthur, J. (Eds.). (2012). *Teaching in inclusive school communities*. Milton, QLD: John Wiley Publishers.

Carrington, S., MacArthur, J., Kearney, A., Kimber, M., Mercer, L., Morton, M., & Rutherford, G. (2012). Towards an inclusive education for all. In S. Carrington & J. MacArthur (Eds.), *Teaching in inclusive school communities* (pp. 3–38). Milton, QLD: John Wiley Publishers.

Connors, C., & Stalker, K. (2003). *The views and experiences of disabled children and their siblings: A positive outlook*. London, UK: Jessica Kingsley.

Corbett, J. (2001). *Supporting inclusive education: A connective pedagogy*. London, UK: RoutledgeFalmer.

Dahlberg, G., & Moss, P. (2005). *Ethics and politics in early childhood education*. London, UK: RoutledgeFalmer.

Dahlberg, G., Moss, P., & Pence, A. (2007). *Beyond quality in early childhood education and care: Languages of evaluation* (2nd ed.). London, UK: Routledge.

Davis, J., & Hogan, J. (2004). Research with children: Ethnography, participation, disability, self empowerment. In C. Barnes & G. Mercer (Eds.), *Implementing the social model of disability: Theory and research* (pp. 172–190). Leeds, UK: The Disability Press.

Education Review Office. (2010). *Quality in early childhood services.* Wellington: Author.

Fleer, M. (2005). Developmental fossils—unearthing the artefacts of early childhood education: The reification of 'child development'. *Australian Journal of Early Childhood, 30*(2), 2-7.

Foreman, P. (Ed.). (2011). *Inclusion in action* (3rd ed.). Melbourne, VIC: Cengage Learning Australia.

Frankel, E., Gold, S., & Ajodhia-Andrews, A. (2010). International preschool inclusion: Bridging the gap between vision and practices. *Young Exceptional Children, 13*(5), 2–16.

Giangreco, M., & Doyle, M. (2007). Teacher assistants in inclusive schools. In L. Florian (Ed.), *The Sage handbook of special education* (pp. 429–439). London, UK: Sage.

Glover, A. (2001). Children and bias. In E. Dau (Ed.), *The anti-bias approach in early childhood* (2nd (2nd ed.), (pp. 1–14). Frenchs Forest, NSW: Longman.

Goodlad, J. (2005). Foreword. In N. Michelli & D. Keiser (Eds.), *Teacher education for democracy and social justice* (pp. xi–xvi). New York, NY: Routledge.

Gordon-Burns, D., Gunn, A. C., Purdue, K., & Surtees, N. (Eds.). (2012). *Te aotūroa tātaki: Inclusive early childhood education: Perspectives on inclusion, social justice and equity from Aotearoa New Zealand.* Wellington: NZCER Press.

Gordon-Burns, D., Purdue, K., Rarere-Briggs, B., Stark, R., & Turnock, K. (2010). Quality inclusive education for children with disabilities and their families: Learning from research. *International Journal of Equity and Innovation in Early Childhood, 8*(1), 53–68.

Gordon-Burns, D., Purdue, K., Rarere-Briggs, B., Stark, R., & Turnock, K. (2012). Key factors in creating inclusive early childhood settings for children with disabilities and their families. In D. Gordon-Burns, A. C. Gunn, K. Purdue, & N. Surtees (Eds.), *Te aotūroa tātaki: Inclusive early childhood education: Perspectives on inclusion, social justice and equity from Aotearoa New Zealand* (pp. 155–174). Wellington: NZCER Press.

Greerton Early Childhood Centre. (2010). A culture of shared leadership. In A. Meade (Ed.), *Dispersing waves: Innovation in early childhood education* (pp. 13-18). Wellington: NZCER Press.

IHC. (2008). *Complaint to Human Rights Commission under Part 1A of the Human Rights Act 1993.* Retrieved 23 April 2010, from http://www.ihc.org.nz/Portals/0/Get%20Information/education-complaint/education-complaint-hrc.pdf

Kelly, B. (2005). "Chocolate … makes you autism": Impairment, disability and childhood identities. *Disability and Society, 20*(3), 261–275.

Leithfield, L., & Murray, T. (1995). Advocating for Aric: Strategies for full inclusion. In B. Swadener & S. Lubeck (Eds.), *Children and families "at promise": Deconstructing the discourse of risk* (pp. 238–261). New York, NY: State University of New York Press.

MacArthur, J. (2004). Tensions and conflicts: Experiences in parent and professional worlds. In L. Ware (Ed.), *Ideology and the politics of (in)exclusion* (pp. 166–182). New York, NY: Peter Lang.

MacArthur, J., & Dight, A. (2000). Transition with a truckload of professionals. *Childrenz Issues, 4*(1), 39–45.

MacArthur, J., Dight, A., & Purdue, K. (2000). 'Not so special': Values and practices in early childhood education for children with disabilities. *Early Education, 24* (Spring/Summer), 17–27.

MacArthur, J., Kelly, B., & Higgins, N. (2005). Supporting the learning and social experiences of students with disabilities: What does the research say? In D. Fraser, R. Moltzen, & K. Ryba (Eds.), *Learners with special needs in Aotearoa New Zealand* (3rd ed.) (pp. 49–73). Palmerston North: Dunmore Press.

MacArthur, J., Purdue, K., & Ballard, K. (2003). Competent and confident children?: *Te Whāriki* and the inclusion of children with disabilities in early childhood education. In J. Nuttall (Ed.), *Weaving Te Whāriki: Aotearoa New Zealand's early childhood curriculum document in theory and practice* (pp. 131–160). Wellington: New Zealand Council for Educational Research.

MacArthur, J., Sharp, S., Gaffney, M., & Kelly, B. (2007). Does it matter that my body is different?: Disabled children, impairment, disability and identity. *Childrenz Issues, 11*(2), 25–30.

Macartney, B. (2007). What is normal and why does it matter?: Disabling discourses in education and society. *Critical Literacy: Theories and Practices, 1*(2), 29–41. Retrieved from www.criticalliteracy.org.uk/journal/table2.html

Macartney, B. (2008a). Disabled by the discourse: Some impacts of normalising mechanisms in education and society on the lives of disabled children and their families. *New Zealand Research in Early Childhood Education Journal, 11,* 33-50.

Macartney, B. (2008b). "If you don't know her, she can't talk": Noticing the tensions between deficit discourses and inclusive early childhood education. *Early Childhood Folio, 12,* 31–35.

Macartney, B. (2011). *Disabled by the discourse: Two families' narratives of inclusion, exclusion and resistance in education.* Unpublished doctoral thesis, University of Canterbury, Christchurch.

Macartney, B., & Morton, M. (2011). Kinds of participation: Teacher and special education perceptions and practices of 'inclusion' in early childhood and primary school settings. *International Journal of Inclusive Education,* 1–17. doi: 10.1080/13603116.2011.602529

MacNaughton, G. (2005). *Doing Foucault in early childhood studies: Applying poststructural ideas.* London, UK: RoutledgeFalmer.

Meade, A. (2002). Remembering: Knowing the moment cannot be repeated. *Childrenz Issues, 6*(2), 12–17.

Minister for Disability Issues. (2001). *The New Zealand disability strategy: Making a world of difference: Whakanui oranga.* Wellington: Ministry of Health.

Ministry of Education. (1996). *Te Whāriki: He whāriki mātauranga mō ngā mokopuna o Aotearoa: Early childhood curriculum.* Wellington: Learning Media.

Ministry of Education. (2005). *Kei tua o te pae: Assessment for learning: Early childhood exemplars.* Wellington: Learning Media.

Ministry of Education. (2006). *Ngā arohaehae whai hua: Self review guidelines for early childhood education.* Wellington: Learning Media.

Ministry of Education. (2007). *The New Zealand curriculum.* Wellington: Learning Media.

Ministry of Education. (2008). *Te marautanga o Aotearoa.* Wellington: Learning Media.

Ministry of Education. (2010). *Success for all: Every school, every child.* Retrieved, from http://minedu.govt.nz/NZEducation/EducationPolicies/ SpecialEducation.aspx

Mitchell, L. (2011). Enquiring teachers and democratic politics: Transformations in New Zealand's early childhood education landscape. *Early Years, 31*(3), 217–228.

Moss, P., & Petrie, P. (2002). *From children's services to children's spaces: Public policy, children and childhood*. New York, NY: RoutledgeFalmer.

New Zealand Government. (1989). *Education Act*. Wellington: Author.

New Zealand Government. (1993). *Human Rights Act*. Wellington: Author.

New Zealand Teachers Council. (2007). *Graduating teacher standards: Aotearoa New Zealand*. Retrieved from http://www.teacherscouncil.govt.nz

Oliver, M. (1996). *Understanding disability: From theory to practice*. Basingstoke, Hampshire, UK: St. Martin's Press.

Podmore, V., May, H., & Carr, M. (2001). *'The child's questions': Programme evaluation with Te Whāriki using 'teaching stories'*. Wellington: Institute for Early Childhood Studies, Victoria University of Wellington.

Podmore, V., May, H., & Mara, D. (1998). *Evaluating early childhood programmes using the strands and goals of Te Whāriki, the national early childhood curriculum: Final report on phases one and two to the Ministry of Education*. Wellington: New Zealand Council for Educational Research.

Porter, G., & Smith, D. (Eds.). (2011). *Exploring inclusive educational practices through professional inquiry*. Rotterdam, The Netherlands: Sense Publishers.

Purdue, K. (2004). *Inclusion and exclusion in early childhood education: Three case studies*. Unpublished doctoral thesis, University of Otago, Dunedin.

Purdue, K. (2006). Children and disability in early childhood education: 'Special' or inclusive education? *Early Childhood Folio, 10*, 12–15.

Purdue, K., Gordon-Burns, D., Gunn, A., Madden, B., & Surtees, N. (2009). Supporting inclusion in early childhood settings: Some possibilities and problems for teacher education. *International Journal of Inclusive Education, 13*(8), 805–815.

Rarere-Briggs, B., Gordon-Burns, D., Purdue, K., Stark, R., & Turnock, K. (2012). "Do I accommodate his developmental age or do I want him to be with his peers?": (In)exclusionary discourses used in early childhood settings and their implications for teacher education. *International Journal of Equity and Innovation in Early Childhood, 10*(1), 37–59.

Rietveld, C. (2005, December). *Teacher responses to children's spontaneous reactions to differences in their classmates with Down Syndrome: Implications for teaching and learning*. Paper presented at the New Zealand Association for Research in Education Annual Conference, Dunedin.

Rinaldi, C. (2006). In dialogue with Reggio Emilia: Listening, researching and learning. In G. Dahlberg & P. Moss (Eds.), *Contesting early childhood series*. London, UK: Routledge.

Ritchie, J. (2010). Being 'sociocultural' in early childhood education practice in Aotearoa. *Early Childhood Folio, 14*(2), 2–7.

Rivalland, C., & Nuttall, J. (2010). Sameness-as-fairness: Early childhood professionals negotiating multiculturalism in childcare. *Early Childhood Folio, 14*(1), 28–32.

Robinson, K., & Jones Diaz, C. (1999). Doing theory with early childhood educators: Understanding difference and diversity in personal and professional contexts. *Australian Journal of Early Childhood, 24*(4), 33–39.

Rogoff, B. (2003). *The cultural nature of human development*. New York, NY: Oxford University Press.

Rutherford, G. (2009). Curriculum matters for all students?: Understanding curriculum from the perspectives of disabled children and teacher aides. *Curriculum Matters, 5*, 90–107.

Sapon-Shevin, M. (2011). Zero indifference and teachable moments: School leadership for diversity, inclusion and justice. In A. Blankstein & P. Houston (Eds.), *Leadership for social justice and democracy in our schools* (pp. 143–168). Thousand Oaks, CA: Corwin.

Slee, R. (2001). Social justice and the changing directions in educational research: The case of inclusive education. *International Journal of Inclusive Education, 5*(2/3), 167–177.

Slee, R. (2011). *The irregular school: Exclusion, schooling and inclusive education*. London, UK: Routledge.

Te One, S., Barrett, S., Podmore, V., with Booth, C., Tawhiti, L., & Broughton, J. (2010). Titiro mai, titiro atu: Looking near, looking far: Curriculum at Otaki Kindergarten. In A. Meade (Ed.), *Dispersing waves: Innovation in early childhood education* (pp. 41–48). Wellington: NZCER Press.

Turnock, K., Gordon-Burns, D., Purdue, K., Rarere-Briggs, B., & Stark, R. (2011). "I'm scared of that baby": How adults and environments contribute to children's positive or negative understandings and experiences of disability in early childhood settings. *New Zealand Research in Early Childhood Education Journal, 14*, 23–37.

UNESCO. (2011). *The hidden crisis: Armed conflict and education*. Paris: Author. Retrieved from http://www.unesco.org/new/en/education/themes/leading-the-international-agenda/efareport/reports/2011-conflict/

United Nations. (1989). *United Nations convention on the rights of the child*. Retrieved from http://www2.ohchr.org/english/law/crc.htm.

United Nations. (2006). *United Nations convention on the rights of persons with disabilities*. Retrieved from http://www.un.org/disabilities/default.asp?id=259.

Veck, W. (2009). Listening to include. *International Journal of Inclusive Education, 13*(2), 141–155.

Yelland, N., & Kilderry, A. (2005). Against the tide: New ways in early childhood education. In N. Yelland (Ed.), *Critical issues in early childhood education* (pp. 1–13). Maidenhead, UK: Open University Press.

7

CHAPTER 7

Te Whāriki and the promise of early childhood care and education grounded in a commitment to Te Tiriti o Waitangi

Jenny Ritchie

ABSTRACT

This chapter draws on over a decade of research that has focused on the implementation of *Te Whāriki: He Whāriki Mātauranga mō ngā Mokopuna o Aotearoa: Early Childhood Curriculum*, with a particular focus on the ways in which educators have been working to uphold the commitment to Te Tiriti o Waitangi (the Treaty of Waitangi)[1] expressed within the curriculum. Through educator enactment of whakawhanaungatanga—building relationships with whānau Māori—and demonstrating the pedagogical integration of other kaupapa Māori values such as manaakitanga and kaitiakitanga, *Te Whāriki* continues to hold promise for social, cultural and ecological sustainability.

---

1 Te Tiriti o Waitangi (the Treaty of Waitangi) was the document signed in 1840 between the British Crown and Māori chiefs, which legitimated British settlement while promising Māori protection of their chieftainship, resources, lands, villages and everything of value to them (such as, for example, their language, values and traditional cultural practices).

Introduction

The ground-breaking recognition by *Te Whāriki* of the status of Māori as tangata whenua (the indigenous people of Aotearoa New Zealand), seen in its introductory proclamation that "all children should be given the opportunity to develop knowledge and an understanding of the cultural heritages of both partners to Te Tiriti o Waitangi" (Ministry of Education, 1996, p. 9), raised huge challenges for the early childhood care and education profession in regard to the extent, integrity and equitability of the provision of kaupapa Māori content by a largely monocultural and monolingual sector. The question for reflection from Goal One of the Belonging strand, "In what ways do the environment and programme reflect the values embodied in Te Tiriti o Waitangi, and what impact does this have on adults and children?" (p. 56), is one that remains an ongoing provocation for the sector.

This chapter draws on a series of studies (Ritchie, 2002; Ritchie, Duhn, Rau, & Craw, 2010; Ritchie & Rau, 2006, 2008) to illustrate some of the ways in which early childhood educators have, in the past 17 years, been moving beyond rhetoric, mechanical checklists and tokenism to find ways to deliver with integrity the intent of *Te Whāriki* in relation to enacting Māori ways of being, knowing and doing (Ministry of Education, 2009). It also explores the ways in which the proactivity of these teachers is contributing to a counter-colonial re-narrativisation (Ritchie & Rau, 2010) that generates space for and validation of te ao Māori epistemologies. This in turn can be seen as contributing to the major shift in discourse demanded by current Māori education policy (Ministry of Education, 2008), which challenges the entire education sector to move away from pervasive, historical, racist deficit modalities to instead view being Māori as a source of potentiality, capability and success. The final section of the chapter will outline the potential of *Te Whāriki* to offer hope for cultural, linguistic, social and ecological sustainability (Ritchie et al., 2010).

Te Whāriki as promise

In this section I argue that the visionary nature of *Te Whāriki*, particularly with regard to the expectations for integrating kaupapa Māori (Māori values and philosophy) and te reo Māori (the Māori language), continues to hold great potential for delivering culturally equitable early childhood care and education programmes. *Te Whāriki* was originally conceptualised by its writers as a curriculum "guideline" (Ministry of Education, 1993). The non-prescriptive nature of the final document (Ministry of Education, 1996) left some teachers initially uncertain as to how to translate its many principles, strands and learning outcomes into practice, and even more confused about how to demonstrate that this was being achieved.

The document was unusual in that it was consciously developed within a Tiriti o Waitangi framework, via a Tiriti o Waitangi partnership of writers (Helen May and Margaret Carr of the University of Waikato, and Tilly and Tamati Reedy, who were delegated by the National Te Kōhanga Reo Trust). This team of writers also consulted widely within their respective networks during the development process to ensure a broad representation of Māori, Pasifika, home-based carers, early childhood educators working with children with diverse needs, and Playcentre parents/whānau (extended family), as well as childcare and kindergarten educators and management (see Chapter One for a detailed description of this process, and Chapter Two for Tilly Reedy's articulation of the Māori underpinnings of *Te Whāriki*).

During the development of *Te Whāriki* the carefully inclusive approach taken by the writers was probably unusual, but very wise, as the input from the various dimensions of this particularly diverse sector not only informed the document, but also created a sense of ownership within the wider early childhood care and education community. In response to a preliminary review by the Ministry of Education (Murrow, 1995), the draft guideline document (Ministry of Education, 1993) was heavily revised in an attempt to make it more "user-friendly" for a sector that, aside from the kindergarten movement, was largely unqualified.

The expectation to uphold and demonstrate commitment to Te Tiriti o Waitangi was not new for many in the early childhood care and education sector, which has always demonstrated a progressive responsiveness to equity issues (May, 1992, 1997). During the early 1990s—the era of the development of *Te Whāriki*—many branches of the early childhood care and education sector were independently confirming their own organisation's recognition of Te Tiriti o Waitangi. The kindergarten, Playcentre and childcare communities all made various statements of their commitment to Te Tiriti o Waitangi, and to the "bicultural development" that would be required in order to demonstrate that commitment (Ritchie, 2002). Both Te Tari Puna Ora o Aotearoa/New Zealand Childcare Association and the New Zealand Playcentre Federation demonstrated their commitment to Te Tiriti o Waitangi by developing partnership models in their decision-making structures and organisational processes (Cubey, 1992).

My doctoral study (Ritchie, 2002), conducted during the period 1996–2002, focused on the work of an early childhood teacher education programme in relation to its stated commitment to honouring Te Tiriti o Waitangi. In my interviews with colleagues lecturing in the early childhood programme, some interesting observations were made about the influence of *Te Whāriki* on their work in early childhood care and education. A Pākehā[2] colleague who had previously had many years of experience in the kindergarten sector was a little indignant when I asked her whether this new curriculum, *Te Whāriki*, was influencing her practice as a teacher educator:

2 The term for a citizen of Aotearoa New Zealand who has European ancestry.

I don't think, oh in here, no, I don't. I think we would have done that anyway. We were already. This, as a team, we were pretty well already committed to that I think. *Te Whāriki* is being woven into that, and *Te Whāriki* is actually being used, but no it was happening before. (Quoted in Ritchie, 2002, p. 204)

Yet a Māori lecturer was very appreciative of the validation provided by *Te Whāriki* for her teaching of Māori content:

The other thing for Pākehā students is *Te Whāriki* makes what you do, or the Māori things you do, "real". Whatever you're doing in class and when you do link it to *Te Whāriki*: "Oh, okay it's real then." (Quoted in Ritchie, 2002, p. 317)

While clearly the kaupapa Māori content that this lecturer was offering to her early childhood education students was 'real', and in fact an integral part of the teacher education programme, her comment is indicative of the struggle faced by Māori lecturers in the face of resistance from some Pākehā students who did not necessarily value, at least at the outset of their studies, the opportunities provided to them to learn about te ao Māori (the Māori world).

During the 1990s a new generation of early childhood care and education teachers emerged that had been schooled in the discourses of *Te Whāriki*. When I interviewed a Pākehā graduate of the early childhood teacher education programme in which I worked, she was teaching in a poorly resourced kindergarten in a working-class suburb with a high percentage of Māori children and families. She identified her key programme planning resources as *Te Whāriki*, which she described as her 'bible', and an English/Māori dictionary. This teacher was aware, however, that in many centres educators were delivering programmes in which the expectations related to te ao Māori contained within *Te Whāriki* were not visible:

You can use *Te Whāriki*, it is so open, yes, it is really difficult. I have seen people use *Te Whāriki* really well, but they are not using the bicultural aspect of it. You know absolutely excellent teachers too. (Quoted in Ritchie, 2002, p. 481)

After the promulgation of *Te Whāriki*, in line with the Ministry of Education's wider Tomorrow's Schools curriculum implementation project (Department of Education, 1988; Openshaw, 2011; Picot, 1988), professional development contracts were funded to provide support for in-service teachers. As part of contract delivery, educators were provided with expertise regarding implementation of the curriculum's expectations for Te Tiriti o Waitangi obligations. Māori facilitators of this professional learning noted children's receptivity to te ao Māori content:

And a really neat thing was the way kids come up and ask for te reo Māori, they'll say 'What's the Māori name for that bird?' Because we were in the bush. And I think that's choice [excellent]. It's non-Māori asking kaiako [teachers] for, 'Can you find out what that word is in Māori?' Powerful depth, it's like saying we want to know, it's valuable. (Quoted in Ritchie, 2002, p. 311)

A Māori colleague described her recent experience on a return visit to an education and care centre as part of supporting the professional learning of teachers, where she had observed children spontaneously dramatising a legend related to the Māori ancestral demi-god Māui. She described this scenario as evidence that these kinds of knowledge, once made accessible to children, were quickly "becoming part of their knowing" (quoted in Ritchie, 2002, p. 311). Participants in the study also reported the receptivity of some non-Māori parents to the Māori knowledge their children were accessing in the early childhood care and education centres committed to this kind of implementation. As a Pākehā teacher reported:

> And the response we get from parents is that, yeah, [their children have begun to] kōrero Māori at home, you know, and that's great too, because the parents will, if they are keen parents, will pick up on that and start working with that as well. (Quoted in Ritchie, 2002, p. 311)

These kinds of responses demonstrate the transformative potential of *Te Whāriki*, by giving access to and generating respect for te ao Māori, to resonate beyond the immediate early childhood care and education setting into homes and the wider community.

Te Whāriki as challenge

In the study *Whakawhanaungatanga: Partnerships in Bicultural Development in Early Childhood Education* (Ritchie & Rau, 2006), my colleague Cheryl Rau and I employed narrative methodologies to give voice to a wide range of early childhood teachers, Playcentre whānau/educators, professional development providers, an iwi education authority, as well as specialist educators and teacher educators. This study was premised on our previous findings that: strengthening the provision of the bicultural aspirations of *Te Whāriki* within mainstream early childhood care and education settings is a central professional responsibility for educators; a key strategy for achieving this objective is for educators to build relationships with the whānau Māori of children in their settings (Ritchie, 2002); and that whanaungatanga is a Māori-preferred pedagogy that empowers Māori through collaborative learning processes (Rau, 2002).

Reflecting on the decade since the promulgation of *Te Whāriki*, Anahera, a Māori early childhood teacher educator (names reported from this study are pseudonyms), expressed her frustration at the lack of progress in implementing kaupapa Māori practices in line with the expectations of the curriculum:

> I mean, we all must be a bit disappointed in the lack of progress in bicultural practices. It hasn't really gone that fast, has it? I could ask this question to you: 'In honesty, did we think that in 10 years' time we'd be up to this stage or a whole lot further along the track?' (Anahera, quoted in Ritchie & Rau, 2006, p. 22)

Katerina, a Māori teacher-educator, revealed the ways in which the hidden power effects of historical Māori–Pākehā relations continue to be experienced by Māori in early childhood care and education settings, placing her in the position of a shy Māori 'mama' who is seeking a sense of whanaungatanga in her first overtures to an early childhood centre:

> Well, if you sit behind the desk, I'm not going to feel comfortable. If you're teaching my babies and you have the privilege of hanging out with my babies, I need you to get away from that desk and come out in front of the desk and sit down with me and just talk as two Mamas, or two women who are having a cup of tea, and like real cups of tea too! Not when you sit there and it's so stiff and formal that nobody wants to talk. It's all very polite and you walk away, and the whānau walk away feeling like they've got nothing out of it, no real connection. I need to connect with you. Because you are in that position of power, they're my babies, but you're the teacher—you need to connect with me because I see you with the power. (Katerina, quoted in Ritchie & Rau, 2006, p. 15)

The explanation in *Te Whāriki* of the principle of whakamana (empowerment) requires that:

> Particular care should be given to bicultural issues in relation to empowerment. Adults working with children should understand and be willing to discuss bicultural issues, actively seek Māori contributions to decision making, and ensure that Māori children develop a strong sense of self-worth. (Ministry of Education, 1996, p. 40)

Effective preparation of pre-service teacher education students to become aware of their positioning in a country with a history of colonisation remains a challenge; this challenge is to offer pedagogical processes that develop in graduates forms of reflexivity that enable critical awareness of historical and contemporary privilege and the effects of power.

Consideration of all the principles of *Te Whāriki*, of *whakamana—empowerment, whānau tangata—families and community* and *ngā hononga—relationships*, as well as the strand of *mana whenua belonging* (the latter, interestingly, being the only strand to include families in its initial statement: "Children and their families feel a sense of belonging"), would suggest that the expectations of the 'mama' voiced by Katerina are entirely in keeping with the principles outlined in the central philosophy of the curriculum document. Yet a very experienced Pākehā kindergarten head teacher, Anne, was critical of the superficial nature of the Māori content she had observed being delivered at many early childhood care and education settings:

> This often amounts to a veneer of biculturalism. It's an outward appearance only. There is often nothing more. I suppose that's called tokenism. (Anne, quoted in Ritchie & Rau, 2006, p. 22)

She went on to evocatively describe her personal/professional journey, tempered by frustration but driven by commitment, towards gaining the knowledge and dispositions that would equip her to move beyond a superficial tokenistic approach:

I have given a lot of thought to my analogy of becoming bicultural as similar to climbing a mountain. It's a mountain where the summit is shrouded in mist so you can't see the top. You climb very slowly, sometimes you can plan the route because you have read and thought about it, sometimes you need somebody who is familiar with it to show you the way. You have to be prepared to be a follower and be led by somebody who knows the route better than you do. You have to respect and trust other people's views and leadership. All the time you need encouragement. You also need your team to come with you. You are roped together so that you can help each other. Sometimes you will need to be the leader.

Sometimes you get knocked back and discouraged. Your travel is very slow because you are carrying so much baggage with you that needs to be discarded on the way and because in order to be safe you can't hurry. When somebody stands on the ledge you are aiming for and stamps on your fingers as you put them over the ledge, or throws a rock at you as you ascend, you could fall and never have the courage to attempt the climb again. You also take the rest of the team down with you. You will need support to keep going and to have another try.

We all make mistakes. Unfortunately these small incidents can have wide repercussions. A little push can mean the whole team landing in a heap at the bottom of the cliff and losing their confidence to attempt the climb again. It also affects their behaviour and attitude towards Māori people. Fortunately also, some people try, and succeed in getting a long way up the mountain.

In a previous "verbal outpouring" I mentioned that we need to be humble and ask for help. The trouble is that some people find it very hard to get rid of the baggage from past hurts that weighs them down and affects their attitude and behaviour. I would love to help to resolve this but don't have the skills. Is it our collective responsibility? (Anne, quoted in Ritchie & Rau, 2006, p. 19)

This demonstrates Anne's reflexivity regarding her long-term professional and personal commitment to a praxis resonant with cultural integrity. In addition, Anne highlights the need for this focus to be a shared, collective and ongoing endeavour within our sector.

Te Whāriki as inspiration

In our subsequent study, *Te Puawaitanga: Partnerships with Tamariki and Whānau in Bicultural Early Childhood Care and Education* (Ritchie & Rau, 2008), we again used narrative methodologies, this time in giving voice to a diverse range of children, families and teachers from 10 early childhood care and education settings from around Aotearoa New Zealand. In these settings the teachers were committed to delivering programmes that gave effect to the expectations of *Te Whāriki* in relation to Te Tiriti o Waitangi. The data showed that when teachers are committed to and skilled at building relationships with Māori families in their centre, as required by the principles of *Te Whāriki*, parents are willing to articulate their expectations for their children. This can be seen in the following data contributed by Māori parents whose children attended a kindergarten. Under the heading, "What I would like in an educational institute for my children", Amiria (one of the mothers in the study; actual names are used here with consent) listed:

- pride in themselves in everything, for example, sex; culture; colour; height; thoughts
- the ability to express themselves and their individuality
- to learn how to socialise and work with others both similar to them or different
- an education, knowledge of their history both nationally and locally
- multicultural experiences with the other children around them
- genuine caring teachers
- the embracing of whānau/families
- a kindergarten that seeks participation and feedback from families and informs them about the goings on in the kindy
- that they love where they attend.

(Quoted in Ritchie & Rau, 2008, pp. 51–52)

Amiria explained what she valued about the kindergarten programme at Belmont–Te Kupenga:

Good use of Māori language through:
- Song: Which is important because it encourages children to memorise Māori words and sentences. Children can then remember something in Māori and sing it at home, maybe even introduce it to the home which is a friendly way of parents becoming familiar to the Māori language. Quite often Māori learnt at this kindergarten will be the most a lot of families will experience, so positive learning through music and song is very important. Also memory of song lasts much longer than speech or writing
- Mihi: Which is important to show children the importance for Māori in showing respect to the mauri (life force) of all things living—Past, Animate, and Inanimate. Also to show our children that the tone of a mihi set the proceeding Pōwhiri/Hui
- Actions and Activities: Rākau and poi, waiata etc help enjoyment and [work] on motor skills and fitness etc which works in well with the mainstream education plan
- Whanaungatanga: Making children and their families feel safe and part of a big family, showing the caring and sharing aspects, both Māori and other cultures.
- Tikanga: To ensure biculturalism, proper Māori ways and rules of engagement should be taught. My belief is if this is taught alongside a mainstream education then when the two major signing cultures of New Zealand's founding document recognise the importance of each other's cultures then we are better equipped to move into appreciating more than two cultures and embracing multiculturalism. (Quoted in Ritchie & Rau, 2008, pp. 52–53)

Lawrence, Amiria's partner, provided the following outline of his dreams/goals for his child in early childhood care and education. He desired an early childhood service that would offer his child:

- confidence/self esteem
- social interaction of bicultural settings
- opportunities to discover his unique significance as tangata whenua
- development of positive routines and relationships with kaiako to foster healthy learning habits
- a place where they feel safe and are encouraged to express themselves
- a stable platform in which they can move on to primary school without having to overcome huge obstacles. (Quoted in Ritchie & Rau, 2008, p. 53)

Lawrence considered that the centre that his children were attending, Belmont Kindergarten—Te Kupenga in Hamilton, "fosters an atmosphere where children are encouraged to reaffirm their identity" through:

- karakia—mo te kai, timatanga, whakamutunga
- waiata which establish links with mana whenua and tangata whenua
- introduction (formally) to new children in class and establishing links with other children already engaged in class (whakawhanaungatanga)
- field trips to make connections with local rohe recognising importance of Te Taiao (e.g.,Te Winika visit and Roger Hamon Bush)
- recognition of the importance of each individual child and of their contribution to the wairua and mauri of the group
- strong use of te reo and mātauranga throughout learning and non-learning situations (e.g., use of posters, pictures, puzzles).

(Quoted in Ritchie & Rau, 2008, p. 53)

Lawrence concluded that:

All of the above mentioned items have (I believe) a profound effect on breaking down perceived barriers which often hinder Māori parents' full involvement in their children's education due to being "whakamā" or shy. These points in fact reinforce kaupapa Māori by observance of tikanga and kawa whilst not impinging on the needs of non-Māori children and families. (Quoted in Ritchie & Rau, 2008, p. 53)

Early childhood educators who create such openings and receptiveness to Māori (and other) parents are realising the potential of *Te Whāriki* as a document capable of transforming the lives of all those involved in the early childhood care and education sector.

In our most recent study, *Titiro Whakamuri, Hoki Whakamua: We Are the Future, the Present and the Past: Caring for Self, Others and the Environment in Early Years' Teaching and Learning* (Ritchie et al., 2010), the focus was maintained on the inclusion of kaupapa Māori philosophies and practices, this time with an emphasis on manaakitanga/caring, as expressed in the project title. *Te Whāriki* served once again as a guiding document for the educators involved in this project. For example, the Belonging strand states that "Liaison with local tangata whenua and a respect for papatuanuku should be promoted" (Ministry of Education, 1996, p. 54), and the Exploration strand affirms that "There should be a recognition of Māori ways of knowing and making sense of the world and of respecting and appreciating the natural environment" (p. 82). The teachers in this study consistently made links to *Te Whāriki*, illustrated in this excerpt from the first set of data contributed by a teacher at Richard Hudson Kindergarten in Dunedin (in this project, once again, actual names were used with permission):

> We consulted with Huata Holmes, our kaumatua, for guidance, expert knowledge and inspiration. The Southern Māori perspective or "flavour" is important. Lee Blackie, our Senior Teacher, accompanied Huata and gave us a practical aspect that could sit side by side with Huata's ideas. In order to add authenticity and depth we arranged for Huata to come and narrate his Southern mythology/stories/pūrākau to the children and whānau (Communication/Mana Reo Goal 3: hear a wide range of stories, *Te Whāriki*, p. 59) as told to him as a child by his grandmothers and great grandmothers (Holistic Development/Kotahitanga: recognition of the significance and contribution of previous generations to the child's concept of self, *Te Whāriki*, p. 41). Huata's kōrero was excellent and by working together we have achieved more of a shared understanding. He told of the great waka of Aoraki coming through the sky down to the South Island. He also used the waiata "Hoea te Waka" to support his kōrero. This has become a real favourite. His kōrero has supported our teaching of the importance of Papatūānuku in our lives. (Teacher, Richard Hudson Kindergarten, quoted in Ritchie et al., 2010, p. 30)

An almost organic connection is evident here, as the teacher skilfully weaves perceptive connections to the specific content of *Te Whāriki* into her narrative.

Kaupapa Māori values of manaakitanga (caring, hospitality) and kaitiakitanga (guardianship) were evident in the everyday discourse of some of the educators as they observed the ways in which children began to take on the role of caring for their immediate and wider environments:

> Kaitiakitanga is looking after places, things and people. We have observed our children gain a sense of pride and respect for our kindergarten environment. We believe that when children have the opportunity to engage and care for the natural environment they will gain the skills, knowledge and desire to care for it in the future. The environment is the third teacher. There is a learning opportunity in every space. We have gardens that are sensory, edible, native and flowering. We have composting and recycling systems, including water conservation and ecosystems. Children are having a shared responsibility to look after our place and this is valued as real work, so everything we do in the kindergarten here is included with the children. (Teachers, Papamoa Kindergarten, quoted in Ritchie et al., 2010, p. 98)

The proactivity of teachers in this study was evident as they modelled the kaupapa of manaakitanga and kaitiakitanga, which was then reciprocated by the children, as seen in this example from Maungatapu Kindergarten:

The care of Papatūānuku became an individual and group responsibility and this shifted the responsibility from the teachers enforcing rules, to empowering children to take ownership for their actions and this changed the motivation for the children. We observed children peer-monitoring each other regularly and role-modelling our agreed options. The children's attitude and willingness shifted from an inward focus to starting to look outwardly—seeing beyond oneself, empowered by the importance of their contribution and responses. By creating a sense of endearment to Papatūānuku the children have an affinity and nurturing attitude, seeing and understanding the value of care and protection to Papatūānuku. The team philosophy valuing relationships has been transferred to the children in our responsibly and interconnectedness to the living and nonliving world. (Teacher, Maungatapu Kindergarten, quoted in Ritchie et al., 2010, p. 44)

Teachers from Papamoa Kindergarten shared their observations about the ways in which kaupapa Māori philosophies and practices were embedded within their praxis, being integral to their ongoing reflexivity as practitioners who pay attention to the transformative possibilities of their work:

The concept of whakawhanaungatanga, a sense of community; through the young child we have the opportunity to influence change in family and community behaviour by involving, connecting and educating them in an environment ... and environmental awareness and sustainable practices; it is so important to create a sense of belonging, a sense of tūrangawaewae, within the kindergarten community, and not working in isolation. The community has a lot to offer that we value being a part of. Whakapapa, Māori genealogy, links us with the whenua, our land, moana, our sea, and cultural concepts working with family and whānau. And our pepeha, the children's genealogy and where that comes from increased our connections, relationships and valuing who people are and where they come from. Children see adults talking and connecting with each other which gives them a sense of mana and pride. (Teachers, Papamoa Kindergarten, quoted in Ritchie et al., 2010, p. 28)

Kaupapa Māori discourses embedded in *Te Whāriki* continued to resonate throughout the data provided by the teachers.

Te Whāriki as transformative

It is not difficult to identify examples of the ongoing legacy of our country's history of colonisation. For Māori, as for other colonised indigenous peoples, there need to be opportunities "to decolonise our minds, to recover ourselves, to claim a space in which to develop a sense of authentic humanity" (Smith, 1999, p. 23). In order to recognise and challenge the subtle power of these pervasive discourses (Lang, 2005), it is equally necessary that those of us who cannot claim Māori ancestry also work to decolonise our thinking and ways of operating, since these may otherwise reflect patterns of 'dysconscious' racism (King, 1994; William-White & White, 2011). This has ongoing implications for teacher education providers in the imperative to foster among future students the awareness of the historicity (Freire, 1972) that underpins a counter-colonial orientation.

Te Whāriki has demonstrated its potential for educators, through deep engagement with the principles of *whakamana—empowerment, whānau tangata—families and community,* and *ngā hononga—relationships* to create counter-colonial spaces and positioning for whānau Māori. This transformative potential of *Te Whāriki* is potentially threatening to the status quo, since it is counter-hegemonic and radically democratic in enabling the voices of those who have previously been relegated through colonisation processes to subjugated positions to reclaim their right to influence the narratives that are reified within our educational settings (Kincheloe, 2003).

We are now nearing the end of the UNESCO Decade for Sustainable Development (UNESCO, 2012), with its inclusive focus on the multiple and overlapping aspects of economic issues (e.g., poverty and sustainable consumption); environmental issues (e.g., biodiversity, climate change, resource depletion and disaster risk reduction); and social and cultural justice issues (e.g., gender equity, and cultural and linguistic sustainability). It is acknowledged, however, that the notion of sustainable 'development' is problematic, oxymoronic even, in the light of the finite resources of our planet (Davidson, 2011). It is clear that dramatic changes are required with regard to the unsustainability of many current ways of living, with over-consumption evident in affluent countries, and the concerning nature of the widening spectrum of disparities, both between nations but also between affluent and struggling populations within developed nations (Wilkinson & Pickett, 2010). As educators we need to give consideration to how we foster in young people the skills to advocate on behalf of their own, their fellow citizens' and their planet's wellbeing (Sustainable Aotearoa New Zealand Inc, 2009). Teacher-educators have the potential to influence both current and future generations of teachers and students in their attitudes towards these issues of sustainability (UNESCO, 2005) and ancient traditional knowledge, such as that of iwi Māori, offers sources of understanding regarding localised sustainability practices (Penetito, 2009; Rose, 2005; Subramanian & Pisupati, 2010).

Likewise, the linguistic and cultural sustainability of te reo me ōna tikanga Māori (Māori language and cultural values and practices), in line with Te Tiriti o Waitangi obligations, locates pedagogical work as a key factor within the domain of the multiple 'sustainabilities' outlined above. Pedagogical responses to these issues require exposing, challenging and destabilising globalised hegemonic discourses and practices, such as those that peddle over-consumption by the rich at the expense of those living in poverty (Jucker, 2004). Collectively generating counter-narratives to dominant discourses that have become entrenched over many generations involves deep personal and social transformation of ways of knowing, being and doing, grounded in an ethic of care and a commitment to social, cultural and eco-justice (Elliot & Davis, 2009; Kahn, 2010; Noddings, 2005; Ritchie, 2011).

As I write this chapter, I am aware that the Ministry of Education has commissioned the Education Review Office to review the implementation of *Te Whāriki*. The Ministry's website states that "When the review is completed, we will make implementation activity more effective, and, if necessary, update the curriculum to reflect best practice" (Ministry of Education, 2012b). Notions of 'best practice' are dangerously problematic in their essentialist, universalising and hegemonic presumptions. It is risky to offer the possibility of reductionist, simplistic recipes for dealing with complex and ever-shifting educational contexts that call for the "wise practice" (Margrain & Macfarlane, 2011, p. 244) and leadership of qualified, experienced practitioners. Recent changes to education policy have reduced the expectations laid out by the (previous) Labour-led government's strategy (Ministry of Education, 2002) for staged movement towards a fully qualified early childhood care and education workforce, originally due to have been achieved in 2012. The back-tracking on this policy to a current ratio of only 50 percent of teachers being required to hold a 3-year-level qualification, along with the ideological shift towards 'teacher accountability' to narrowly defined parameters of 'best practice', as have already been imposed through the introduction of national standards in the primary schools sector, signal that the potential of *Te Whāriki* as a lever for social, cultural and ecological justice is clearly in jeopardy.

Concluding thoughts

This chapter has discussed ways in which *Te Whāriki* continues to offer both challenge and aspiration to the early childhood care and education sector in Aotearoa, with particular regard to the commitment expressed within the curriculum to honouring Te Tiriti o Waitangi responsibilities. In the years since 1996 the importance of the work of early years educators has been given further acknowledgement as neuroscience has confirmed the vital impact of early childhood experiences (Shonkoff, 2010; Shonkoff & Phillips, 2000). Meanwhile, concern continues to be expressed about those children who miss out on attending high-quality (which includes culturally responsive) early childhood care and education settings (Ministry of Education, 2012a), and about the long-term impacts of non-participation and lack of engagement in education on children's achievement (Ministry of Education, 2011).

The glimpses from the research projects outlined above suggest that the Tiriti o Waitangi, relationship-based vision of *Te Whāriki* for respectful, responsive engagement with whānau/families and tamariki/children; for deeply honouring the ways of knowing, being and doing of Māori and of other cultures; for upholding te reo Māori, as well as children's diverse home languages; and for caring for our planet, Papatūānuku, remains a vision that is worthy and capable of sustaining our sector into the future. Over a decade and a half since its promulgation, *Te Whāriki* continues to have relevance and hold promise as a philosophical vision for early childhood care and education pedagogies that reflect and enact a commitment to social, cultural and ecological sustainability and justice.

Acknowledgements

I am deeply grateful for the funding we have received from the New Zealand Teaching and Learning Research Initiative, and also greatly appreciative of the wisdom of my esteemed colleagues, Cheryl Rau (co-director on all three studies), Iris Duhn and Janita Craw (co-directors on the third study). Furthermore, we offer our sincere appreciation to the many teachers, whānau and tamariki who participated in these projects.

References

Cubey, P. (1992). *Responses to the Treaty of Waitangi in early childhood care and education.* Unpublished M.Ed. thesis, Victoria University of Wellington, Wellington.

Davidson, K. M. (2011). Reporting systems for sustainability: What are they measuring? *Social Indicators Research, 100*(2), 351–365.

Department of Education. (1988). *Tomorrow's Schools: The reform of education administration in New Zealand.* Wellington: Department of Education.

Elliot, S., & Davis, J. (2009). Exploring the resistance: An Australian perspective on educating for sustainability in early childhood. *International Journal of Early Childhood, 41*(2), 65–77.

Freire, P. (1972). *Pedagogy of the oppressed.* London, UK: Penguin.

Jucker, R. (2004). Have the cake and eat it: Ecojustice versus development?: Is it possible to reconcile social and economic equity, ecological sustainability, and human development?: Some implications for ecojustice education. *Educational Studies, 36*(1), 10–26.

Kahn, R. (2010). *Critical pedagogy, ecoliteracy, and planetary crisis: The ecopedagogy movement.* New York, NY: Peter Lang.

Kincheloe, J. L. (2003). *Teachers as researchers: Qualitative inquiry as a path to empowerment.* London, UK: RoutledgeFalmer.

King, J. E. (1994). Dysconscious racism: Ideology, identity, and the miseducation of teachers. In L. Stone (Ed.), *The education feminism reader* (pp. 336–348). New York, NY: Routledge.

Lang, S. (2005). 'Decolonialism' and the counselling profession: The Aotearoa/New Zealand experience. *International Journal for the Advancement of Counselling, 27*(4), 557–572.

Margrain, V., & Macfarlane, A. (2011). He tapuwae mō muri: Footsteps to guide the future. In V. Margrain & A. Macfarlane (Eds.), *Responsive pedagogy: Engaging restoratively with challenging behaviour* (pp. 236–254). Wellington: NZCER Press.

May, H. (1992). Learning through play: Women, progressivism and early childhood education 1920s–1950s. In S. Middleton & A. Jones (Eds.), *Women and education in Aotearoa 2* (pp. 83–101). Wellington: Bridget Williams Books.

May, H. (1997). *The discovery of early childhood*. Auckland: Bridget Williams Books/Auckland University Press/ New Zealand Council for Educational Research.

Ministry of Education. (1993). Te whāriki*: Draft guidelines for developmentally appropriate programmes in early childhood*. Wellington: Learning Media.

Ministry of Education. (1996). *Te whāriki: He whāriki mātauranga mō ngā mokopuna o Aotearoa: Early childhood curriculum*. Wellington: Learning Media. Retrieved from http://www.educate.ece. govt.nz/~/media/Educate/Files/Reference%20Downloads/whariki.pdf.

Ministry of Education. (2002). *Pathways to the future: Ngāhuarahi arataki: A 10-year strategic plan for early childhood education*. Wellington: Ministry of Education.

Ministry of Education. (2008). *Ka hikitia: Managing for success: Māori education strategy 2008–2012*. Wellington: Ministry of Education.

Ministry of Education. (2009). *Te whatu pōkeka: Kaupapa Māori assessment for learning: Early childhood exemplars*. Wellington: Learning Media. Retrieved from http://www.educate.ece. govt.nz/~/media/Educate/Files/Reference%20Downloads/TeWhatuPokeka.pdf.

Ministry of Education. (2011). *Briefing to the incoming Minister*. Wellington: Author. Retrieved from http://www.minedu.govt.nz/~/media/MinEdu/Files/ TheMinistry/PolicyAndStrategy/ EducationBIM2011.pdf.

Ministry of Education. (2012a). *Me kōrero: Let's talk: Ka hikitia: Accelerating success: 2013–2017*. Wellington: Author.

Ministry of Education. (2012b). *Statement of Intent, 2012–2017*. Wellington: Author. Retrieved from http://www.minedu.govt.nz/~/media/MinEdu/Files/ TheMinistry/2012SOI/201 2StatementOfIntent.pdf

Murrow, K. (1995). *Early childhood workers' opinions on the draft document* Te whāriki. Wellington: Ministry of Education.

Noddings, N. (2005). Place-based education to preserve the Earth and its people. In N. Noddings (Ed.), *Educating citizens for global awareness* (pp. 57–68). New York, NY: Teachers College Press.

Openshaw, R. (2011). "A long way to go before we win the battle": The propaganda war over the Picot report and Tomorrow's Schools. *History of Education Review, 40*(1), 62–80.

Penetito, W. (2009). Place-based education: Catering for curriculum, culture and community. *New Zealand Annual Review of Education, 18:2008,* 5–29.

Picot, B. (1988). *Administering for excellence: Effective administration in education: Report of the Taskforce to Review Education* [the Picot Report]. Wellington: Department of Education.

Rau, C. (2002). *Te ahutanga atu o toku whanau*. Unpublished master's thesis, University of Waikato, Hamilton.

Ritchie, J. (2002). *"It's becoming part of their knowing": A study of bicultural development in an early childhood teacher education setting in Aotearoa/New Zealand*. Unpublished doctoral thesis, University of Waikato, Hamilton.

Ritchie, J. (2011). Ecological counter-narratives of interdependent wellbeing. *International Journal of Equity and Innovation in Early Childhood, 9*(1), 50–61.

Ritchie, J., Duhn, I., Rau, C., & Craw, J. (2010). *Titiro whakamuri, hoki whakamua: We are the future, the present and the past: Caring for self, others and the environment in early years' teaching and learning: Final report for the Teaching and Learning Research Initiative*. Wellington: Teaching and Learning Research Initiative. Retrieved from http://www.tlri.org.nz/sites/default/files/ projects/9260-finalreport.pdf.

Ritchie, J., & Rau, C. (2006). *Whakawhanaungatanga: Partnerships in bicultural development in early childhood education: Final report to the Teaching and Learning Research Initiative Project.* Wellington: Teaching and Learning Research Initiative. Retrieved from http://www.tlri. org.nz/pdfs/9207_finalreport.pdf.

Ritchie, J., & Rau, C. (2008). *Te Puawaitanga: Partnerships with tamariki and whānau in bicultural early childhood care and education: Final report to the Teaching and Learning Research Initiative.* Wellington: Teaching and Learning Research. Retrieved from http://www.tlri.org.nz/ pdfs/9238_finalreport.pdf.

Ritchie, J., & Rau, C. (2010). Kia mau ki te wairuatanga: Counter-colonial narratives of early childhood education in Aotearoa. In G. S. Cannella & L. D. Soto (Eds.), *Childhoods: A handbook* (pp. 355–373). New York, NY: Peter Lang.

Rose, D. (2005). An indigenous philosophical ecology: Situating the human. *Australian Journal of Anthropology, 16*(3), 294–305.

Shonkoff, J. (2010). Building a new biodevelopmental framework to guide the future of early childhood policy. *Child Development, 81*(1), 357–367.

Shonkoff, J., & Phillips, D. (Eds.). (2000). *From neurons to neighbourhoods: The science of early childhood development.* Washington, DC: National Academy Press.

Smith, L. T. (1999). *Decolonizing methodologies: Research and indigenous peoples.* London, UK, and Dunedin: Zed Books and University of Otago Press.

Subramanian, S. M., & Pisupati, B. (2010). Introduction. In S. M. Subramanian & B. Pisupati (Eds.), *Traditional knowledge in policy and practice: Approaches to development and human well-being* (pp. 1–11). Tokyo, Japan; New York, NY; Paris, France: United Nations University Press.

Sustainable Aotearoa New Zealand Inc. (2009). *Strong sustainability for New Zealand: Principles and scenarios.* Wellington: Nakedize. Retrieved from http://nz.phase2.org/strong-sustainability-for-new-zealand

UNESCO (United Nations Educational, Scientific and Cultural Organisation). (2005). *Guidelines and recommendations for reorienting teacher education to address sustainability: Education for sustainable development in action: Technical paper No 2 —2005.* Paris, France: UNESCO.

UNESCO (United Nations Educational, Scientific and Cultural Organisation). (2012). *Shaping the education of tomorrow: 2012 report on the UN Decade of Education for Sustainable Development: Abridged.* Paris, France: UNESCO. Retrieved from http://unesdoc.unesco.org/ images/0021/002166/216606e.pdf

Wilkinson, R., & Pickett, K. (2010). *The spirit level: Why equality is better for everyone.* London, UK: Penguin.

William-White, L., & White, J. (2011). Color marks the site/sight of social difference: Dysconscious racism in the "Age of Obama". *Qualitative Inquiry, 17*(9), 837–853.

CHAPTER 8

Te Whāriki and assessment:
A case study of teacher change

Karen Ramsey, Wendy Lee and Margaret Carr

ABSTRACT

This chapter describes teacher change in assessment practice following the introduction of *Te Whāriki*. It focuses on one early childhood centre, and much of the story is told through the eyes of one teacher, Karen. It is structured around two opportunities that supported the teachers and built on the 1996 curriculum: a professional development programme and practitioner research projects. The story is analysed in terms of four major features of teacher professional learning and development experiences that have been shown to change teacher practice and improve student outcomes in schools, as identified by Timperley and colleagues in 2007: assessment practice; leadership; existing theories about the learner; and the professional learning community. In this story, consistent with the central metaphor in *Te Whāriki* and in this book, all four features are woven together.

Introduction

In 1993 the draft *Te Whāriki* framework signalled the beginning of a very different approach to early childhood education for Aotearoa New Zealand. Many teachers at that time were using an informal curriculum framework: an implicit or explicit array of PIES (physical, intellectual, emotional and social skills) to keep in mind without too much deliberate or purposeful teaching. The BWECCian approach taken by *Te Whāriki* (belonging, wellbeing, exploration, communication and contribution) was something of a surprise. *Te Whāriki* emphasises a view of learning as being about responsive and reciprocal relationships between people, places and things (Ministry of Education, 1996, p. 43), and a view of outcomes as "learning dispositions" and "working theories" (p. 44). It also set out some ground rules for a bicultural and socio-cultural approach to curriculum, one that emphasises whakamana, kotahitanga, whānau tangata and ngā hononga, and that aims to be empowering, holistic, ecological and interactive, framed around what has been called "individual(s)-acting-with-mediational-means" (Wertsch, 1991, p. 12).

A mandatory national early childhood curriculum, and the increased funding for early childhood that followed, suggested that attention would need to be paid to assessment practices. Together with the metaphor in *Te Whāriki* of curriculum implementation as a local 'weaving', and Bronfenbrenner's ecological framework (also in *Te Whāriki*), this in turn suggested that teacher change would be a feature of early childhood education in the next decade. This chapter tells the story of teacher change in one centre, Roskill South Kindergarten. It is also a story of professional development and practitioner research that, in concert with *Te Whāriki*, supported that change.

Teacher change and professional development

Early stories of teacher change with a focus on assessment that followed the introduction of *Te Whāriki* have already been told. They include Keryn Davis's story of the journeys of a number of teachers in childcare settings as they tried out new ways of doing assessment (Davis, 2002). She identified three central shifts in assessment practice:
- taking up new possibilities for thinking about what to give value to in assessments
- including multiple voices
- developing a new "assessment consciousness" (becoming more aware, for instance, of the power of both documented and undocumented assessments).

In 1998 one of the authors of this chapter (Margaret) and a group of teachers described five case studies of teachers in very different settings exploring assessment with *Te Whāriki* in mind (Carr, 1998b). This research identified some of the possibilities of narrative modes of assessment, and was followed by a set of three videos (now DVDs) and a professional development programme (Carr, 1998a). The story related in this chapter is about a teacher and her colleagues in one kindergarten as they developed assessment practices that took on board the BWECCian array of outcomes and the assessment principles in *Te Whāriki* (Ministry of Education, 1996, p. 30). The chapter is written by the teacher (Karen), the director of the professional development programme that supported the teacher and her colleagues (Wendy), and a researcher (Margaret), who, with Wendy, was from 2003 to 2005 and 2007 to 2008 an associate director of two research projects with Karen and her co-teachers.

Kiri Gould, in a 1997 review of the literature on professional development and teacher change, pointed out that teacher change involves not only change to teaching behaviours and practice, but also to teachers' attitudes and beliefs. She added:

> It is often presumed that getting teachers to change their beliefs will lead to a commitment to change and specific changes in classroom practices. A commitment to change however, is an additional factor. It is sometimes referred to in the literature as 'ownership' of change and has been identified as an important factor in achieving significant change ... For this to happen teachers must feel dissatisfaction with their existing practice, find the innovation plausible and intelligent and be convinced that they are gaining more than they are giving up. (Gould, 1997, p. 3)

Ten years later, Helen Timperley and colleagues prepared a Best Evidence Synthesis of teacher professional learning and development for the New Zealand Ministry of Education (Timperley, Wilson, Barrar, & Fung, 2007). They commented on the evidence relating to a number of issues relevant to teacher change. Four of these are also relevant to the early years (the fifth commented specifically on secondary school contexts):

(i)   the multiple roles of *assessment*

(ii)   the role of the *leadership*

(iii) teachers' existing *theories*

(iv) *professional learning communities*.

They summarised these four features as follows (we have added the italics).

(i) Assessment
"Learning to understand and use assessment information was part of the professional learning experience in about half the core studies associated with substantive impact on student outcomes. Uses of assessment information included *determining the next steps* for teaching and learning, *reviewing the effectiveness of teaching*, and *motivating the teachers to engage in professional learning*. For assessment information to be used in this way, teachers needed to undertand that *assessment was about informing the teaching–learning relationship*, not about labelling students." (Timperley et al., 2007, p. 191)

(ii) Leadership

"We have identified four different roles that leaders may adopt: *developing a vision* of how teaching might impact on student outcomes, *managing* the professional learning environment, *promoting a culture of learning* within the school, and *developing the leadership of others in relation to curriculum or pedagogy*. In no core study did leaders take on all four roles. All, however, were adopted by leaders in various ways that led to positive outcomes for students."(p. 196).

(iii) Teachers' existing theories

"[W]e have noted that the most effective theories [teachers' theories of practice] are integrated around *the notion of responsiveness to students*" (p. 201). [We include responsiveness to families as well.]

(iv) Professional learning communities

"Communities that promoted professional learning in ways that impacted positively on student learning had a set of definable qualities. These included a focus on *opportunities to process new understandings* and their implications for teaching, *the introduction of new perspectives and challenging of problematic beliefs*, and *an unrelenting focus on the impact of teaching* on student learning." (p. 205)

These are the four themes to which we return in this chapter. We begin, however, by describing the context for Karen's story of teacher change, both in terms of the programme in which she participated and the focus on assessment within that programme.

The Education Leadership Project

Roskill South Kindergarten, under Karen's leadership, began their journey with a professional development provider in 2000 when they signed up with the Educational Leadership Project (ELP) directed by Wendy Lee. In Aotearoa New Zealand, professional development funded by the Ministry of Education accompanied the introduction of *Te Whāriki*, and this was followed by evaluations of these initiatives (Foote, Irvine, & Turnbull, 1996; Gaffney & Smith, 1997). ELP was one of the professional development providers that received funding from the Ministry of Education to support the implementation of *Te Whāriki*. Involving centres and teachers in Auckland, Waikato and the Bay of Plenty, the ELP programme had several main features.

For a start, the aim was—and still is—to develop professional and pedagogical leadership within the teachers themselves (Lee, 2008). This means that, in the later phases of the ELP, teachers whose professional development journeys reflect extensive teacher change become part-time facilitators, working with teachers who are just beginning to contemplate changes that might strengthen their practice. Second, teachers informally share ideas and formally present aspects of their practice to each other at cluster meetings. Third, teachers are given opportunities to visit other centres;

and fourth, readings and references to other readings are provided for the teachers, reflecting the expectations of the ELP that teachers should be prepared to make connections between theory and practice, because effective professional development requires more than the acquisition of off-the-shelf solutions.

In recent years ELP programmes have included a research component. Teachers choose a research question they are keen to pursue, and this component, often with the assistance of an outside researcher, adds (in the words of Timperley et al., 2007) a focus on "opportunities to process new understandings" and their implications for teaching, and "the introduction of new perspectives and challenging of problematic beliefs". The ELP experience of professional development in early childhood education recognises that professional development is often a complex, evolving journey. It also supports, and views as powerful, the notion of 'purposeful practice', not only for children but for adults as well:

> Purposeful practice is about striving for what is just out of reach and not quite making it; it is about grappling with tasks beyond current limitations and falling short again and again. Excellence is about stepping outside the comfort zone, training with a spirit of endeavor, and accepting the inevitability of trials and tribulations. Progress is built, in effect, upon the foundations of necessary failure. That is the essential paradox of expert performance. (Syed, 2011, p. 85)

Early childhood professional development programmes have been severely diminished by budget cuts in recent years. Universal access to professional development programmes is no longer a part of New Zealand's early childhood landscape, and new professional development programmes are primarily targeted at centres in low-participating and low-income communities. Some national early childhood professional development remains for a significantly reduced number of participants, focused on pedagogical leadership and working with children under the age of 2 years. There is now a greater urgency for professional learning programmes that build sustainability of reflection, dialogue and experimentation in a range of ways. There are a variety of potential focuses for such professional learning, but, for us, the key one has been the issue of assessment of children's learning in early childhood settings.

The focus on assessment practices within the ELP

In 2000 the ELP began to support and develop the narrative modes of assessment that had been introduced in 1998. Together with teachers like Karen and her team, ELP projects developed a range of formats and highlighted a range of purposes. They also won a contract with the Ministry to implement *Kei Tua o te Pae*, a professional development resource of 20 books that provided exemplars of assessment for learning in early childhood (Carr, Lee, Jones, & Ministry of Education, 2004, 2007, 2009). The

Roskill South teaching team contributed a number of assessments to these books. By 2009 narrative assessments had become a secure part of the early childhood assessment practice repertoire in New Zealand (Gunn & de Vocht van Alphen, 2011; Hatherly & Sands, 2002). Writing about the theoretical positioning and outcomes in three different curriculum documents for the early years—the *Early Years Learning Framework* (EYLF) (Australian Government Department of Education, Employment and Workplace Relations, 2009) from Australia; the *Early Years Foundation Stage* (EYFS) (Department for Children, Schools and Families, 2008) from England and Wales; and *Te Whāriki*—Helen Hedges and Joy Cullen commented:

> In terms of outcomes, the EYFS is the most explicit about knowledge outcomes, including these among others: personal, social and emotional development; communication, language and literacy; problem solving, reasoning and numeracy; knowledge and understanding of the world; physical development; and creative development. In contrast, *Te Whāriki* specifies the concepts of dispositions and working theories as main outcomes. These incorporte knowledge, skill and attitudinal components. In other writing, Carr (2005) identifies the strands of *Te Whāriki* as its outcomes for children; namely, well-being, belonging, contribution, communication and exploration. In similar vein, the EYLF details five learning outcomes related to identity, contribution, well-being, confident learners and effective communicators. These notions challenge traditional conceptions of outcomes as domain-based. Instead, reflective of sociocultural theories, outcomes are more holistic than subject domains and reflect a more synergistic view of learning.
>
> Nevertheless, while the EYFS comes closest to providing specific and measurable cognitive and behavioural outcomes and provides a 13-scale summative profile to be assessed prior to school entry, none of these documents indicate how children might be assessed as achieving the wider participatory goals or aspirations of each curriculum. In keeping with sociocultural approaches, a narrative form of assessment has since evolved in NZ, that of 'learning stories' (Carr, 2001a; MOE, 2004, 2007, 2009). Australian teachers have also found this approach appropriate (e.g. Nyland & Ferris 2009); indeed the approach has found international recognition (e.g. Karlsdóttir & Gararsdóttir, 2010). (Hedges & Cullen, 2012, pp. 928–929)

The value of Learning Stories for the assessment of learning in mathematics has been described from Australian contexts (Perry, Dockett, & Harley, 2007), and in *Learning Stories: Constructing Learner Identities in Early Education* (Carr & Lee, 2012) there are Learning Stories from Australia, England and Germany. Karen and her colleagues from Roskill South also contributed to the examples of children's learning journeys, over time, in the 2012 book. We turn now to Karen's story of coming to this level of engagement with assessment in early childhood education.

Karen's story

Roskill South Kindergarten's community is set in a low-income suburb of Auckland. The families belong to a wide range of cultural communities, and at any one time they represent about 17 different home languages. For many of the families, therefore, English is an additional language. Many of the families have come to New Zealand for the opportunity of a good education for their children but they keep close links with family outside New Zealand, keen to send news of their children's educational experiences back to family at home. Roskill South is a 'sessional' (i.e., half-day) kindergarten, with 45 children in a daily morning programme and 45 children in the 3-day afternoon programme: up to 90 families in all.

Karen's journey of professional development with ELP began more than 12 years ago, and the journey is continuing. When Roskill South Kindergarten was first enrolled in ELP, Karen began to keep a log of their progress towards a manageable and meaningful assessment framework. What follows is an abridged version of the written component of this log, annotated at the side using the four features of teacher change outlined by Timperley and colleagues and listed above. It begins with two entries from 1998 and 1999, written in hindsight.

Early assessment practices	*July 1998.* As a new teaching team, we decided it was time to review the assessment system and develop a system that was workable for us. The assessment system that was developed at the time involved writing incidental observations on what the children were learning through play. These short observations were recorded on post-it notes. Children had their own cardboard folder. Inside the folders were a booklet and any photos taken of the child while at kindergarten. At planning meetings, we would discuss the child/children involved and decide if we would use the individual observations as a basis for our group planning. Each observation was linked to a Te Whāriki strand, the post-it was stuck into the booklet and the strand that we thought the child had achieved was highlighted. Children's folders were kept in the office in a locked filing cabinet. Parents and children had access to them but had to ask a teacher first.
The establishment of a professional learning community	*Term 4 1999.* When we were writing the incidental observations, it was becoming apparent that we wanted to record more detail about the process of the child's learning. We had heard the term 'Learning Stories' when we had gone to various meetings but didn't know anything about it. We thought this might be the answer to our questions. Maryanne from Hillsborough Kindergarten told us that they had been using learning stories and had found it very beneficial. They had been working with Wendy Lee and recommended the courses she offered. We applied to be part of the 'Education Leadership Project 2000'.

Teachers' theories of responsiveness	*Term 1 2000* Successful in gaining a place on the project, a great start to the millenium! We mapped where we were at and where we wanted to go! Then came the development of our project focus. The focus had 2 parts. The first was to consult with parents, families and community to find out what they value for children's learning so we could then use this as a base for assessment. The second part was to investigate current theories of assessment and develop a workable system for our kindergarten.
	Term 2 2000 A change in team dynamics as one of our teachers resigned. We had a relieving teacher. We attend the Learning Stories workshops. A combination of staff illness, a string of relievers and a busy kindergarten saw our project work put on the back burner! However, we informed parents and families about the new system we were trying, we created a display to share this information.
	Term 3 2000 We were back on task and dedicated to trying the learning stories framework in our centre. We decided we would make a concentrated effort to write learning stories and lots of them. We needed practice in this skill and as the weeks went by we could see our styles of writing the children's learning stories change the more experience we gained. We used some photos to record the children's learning process as well.
Assessment that informs the teacher-learner relationship	We were excited about the progress we were making and the positive feedback we were getting from parents when we shared their children's learning stories with them. We were finding learning stories were allowing us to know the child at a much deeper level. We could see that this assessment framework was easy for all our families to understand, especially with the use of photos to illustrate the child's learning process. (Hence the increase in the chemist account.)
	We reviewed the layout of the children's files and redesigned the front introduction pages to include information about the new system (learning stories) we were using (this included forms asking parent's permission to have their child's file accessible in the centre). During a centre visit Ann helped us to formulate a draft version of this which we then asked parents to read and give us their feedback on. We asked the questions: Was it easy to understand? Would they read it? Some parents gave written comments. [*Authors' comment: These are included in the log.*] Parent support was encouraging and we went into Term 4 full steam ahead.
Leadership consolidating curriculum	*Term 4 2000* We had a new reliever join us for the term. During the year there had been many changes and we decided to spend this term consolidating what we had learnt, continue to write stories and just enjoy where we were at in our journey.
A professional learning community processing new understanding	I attended a workshop and gave a presentation on our project work for the year. This was a new challenge for me. As a team we were buzzing from the feedback we got from parents each time we shared their child's learning story with them, we had made great progress on our journey and found it rewarding to share with follow teachers. [*Authors' comment: A copy of this presentation is included in the log*]. The workshop also gave the opportunity to listen to other people's journeys.

Challenging problematic beliefs	A couple of days after the workshop I was watching two children reading their files to each other. They were having to sit in the doorway as the files were stored in a bookcase just inside the door. Did this show the children we value their stories? As a team we thought it didn't and decided to create a learning stories corner! We ended the year with a family night [*Authors' addition: log includes photographs of children sharing their files with their parents*]. What a great way to end the year!

Term 1 2001 We started the year with a permanent teaching team. We spent Term 1 consolidating our developments of last year – we were back into the full swing of recording children's learning. We were successful in gaining a position on Year 2 of the Educationa Leadership Project. We were excited about this opportunity and looked forward to our continuing journey. |
Theories of practice integrated around responsiveness to students (children)	Last year we had made greater use of photographs in documenting children's learning. This meant the children's learning stories had meaning for them and they could re-visit and share their experiences with their friends – very motivating for oral, visual and written literacy. Photographs were also extremely powerful for our families and especially those with English as an additional language. During Term 4, I regularly talked to the committee about our need for a digital camera. They came on board and it was decided that the profit from our annual Monster Garage Sale would be targeted for a camera. The Garage Sale was a huge success. We raised $1500! Our dream was coming true. A digital camera meant learning stories could be written up quicker rather having to wait for a film to be processed.
Assessment informs the teacher–learner relations hip; it is not about labelling the students (children)	*Term 2 2001* We were finding our sessions becoming busier and busier because the children were now directing their learning and we were putting more emphasis on interactions with children as a result of the closer relationships we were developing through Learning Stories. Once we focused on children's strengths and interests we found we recognised the importance of listening to children (genuinely) and having meaningful conversations with them (child's voice). As a team we talked about the need for a more formal parent/whanau help system and so our Parent/ Whānau involvement system was born. We kicked it off at the start of Term 2. A visual display of parents helping around the kindergarten and reasons why we were asking for help was put together. Basically the more support we got from parents and families meant more learning stories for their children! It sounded like bribery but parents valued our assessment system and so were keen to help during session. Two weeks into Term 2 we said goodbye to Michelle, who was leaving on her big overseas adventure! And the hunt was on again for another team member.
Widening the professional learning community	Auckland Kindergarten Association was developing a pilot programme for computers in kindergartens. There were 6 computers for allocation and we were desperate for one! We had raised enough money for a digital camera but had found out they weren't compatible with our PCs at home. Our kindergarten couldn't afford to buy a computer and camera as well, so we applied to be part of the pilot programme and kept our fingers crossed !!!!!! Soon the good news that we had been hoping for came ..... We were successful in being selected for the computer pilot programme. This was a huge boost for our team. We had worked hard developing our assessment

	system during the past year and were passionate about documenting our children's learning. Having a computer and digital camera meant we could take our assessment system to a higher level!
Challenging current practice	Term 2 also saw a change in our planning system. We were interested in the 'Longterm project' approach and had begun to investigate this model. Our first project was from an interest the children had in Aliens—this project ran for 2 terms. Not long into the start of the project we were beginning to notice many of our children for whom English is an additional language were coming on board and contributing to group discussions and becoming involved.
Widening the professional learning community

The wider professional learning community introduces new perspectives | We began inviting parents to contribute to their child's learning in the form of 'Parent Voice'. The response was encouraging and a great way to share information between home and kindergarten. This empowered parents to be involved in their children's learning. During Term 2 we had attended a course about the Quality Journey. We decided to use this document to review our new parent/whanau system. We drew up a survey and asked parents to fill it out at the end of sessions. The feedback was interesting and we were able to make changes to improve the system.

Term 3 2001 A permanent appointment was made and Jane joined our teaching team in the last 2 weeks of Term 3. Finally a full teaching team with no babies or overseas trips in sight! As a development from the feedback we received about parents helping in Term 2 we began to develop a parent help information book. The aim of the book was to give parents practical ideas about how they could help the children at kindergarten. |
| Responding to challenge: a theory of responsiveness

Becoming a hub for a professional learning community | *Term 4 2001* From a parent's concern about their child's transition to school we began a case study and trialled a new procedure. I went on a school visit with George and his mum. This was an invaluable experience; we were able to video George in his classroom, his teacher, things in his classroom, the playground. The next day at kindergarten George was able to re-visit this experience by watching the video; he watched it many times and shared his new school with his friends. A book was then made on George's school visit, which he could take home and re-visit during the Christmas holidays. We also made a copy for the centre so other children could benefit. It is our vision that this process will become part of our centre's Transition to School Policy. How? I'm not quite sure yet! [*Authors' addition: By this stage in their journey, several teachers from other centres and other regions are coming to visit to see the assessment documentation.*]

Well What a Year! |
| An unrelenting focus on the impact of teaching on student learning | Where to for 2002?
• Develop our long-term project documentation further. Involve families and the community in the projects.
• Encourage children to re-visit and self evaluate planning boards.
• Weekly reflection on learning stories board and sharing of children' stories at staff meetings. This will ensure children are 'not missed'. |

	• To be more constant in recording children's learning and writing up children's Learning Stories.
	• Develop children's self-reflection and self-evaluation skills.
	• And who knows what else. . . ?
	Term 1 2002 We begin Term 1 with notification of our ERO visit on Wednesday 20th February. We looked forward to the review and receiving feedback on the assessment and planning systems we had woven into our curriculum. The day of the review came and we were a 'little nervous'. But by end of the visit we wrapped up with a feedback session, their comments were positive and encouraging. The day the draft ERO report arrived arrived I read it out from cover to cover during our lunchtime. Comments like 'Children are highly motivated, self-directed learners' and 'The relationship between teachers and parents is an outstanding feature of the kindergarten' are the essence of our teaching philosophy. ERO had clearly seen this in our daily practice. We were excited. [*Authors' addition: The ERO Report included the following summary of the centre's assessment practice: 'Ongoing individual assessment underpins the curriculum. The assessment process is a result of collaboration between the teachers, the children and parents. On a daily basis teachers record children's experiences in narratives which identify learning dispositions that link to*
Assessment designed to increase children's outcomes	*the strands of Te Whāriki. An analysis in the form of a short term review and identification of "what next", informs future programme decisions. Learning stories are illustrated with photographs and form the basis of the individual assessment files. Children and parents are encouraged to access and contribute to the files with their own stories, comments and reflections. Teachers have a highly effective system to ensure that learning stories for each child are maintained and that individual goals and interests are tracked. These very well developed systems result in high quality, formative assessment material that clearly demonstrates individual progress and the effectiveness of teaching strategies.']*
	Term 3 2002 We had a vision to develop the use of the video camera – children would have written learning stories in their files and for some stories they would also have the footage on their own videotape. In June, I was writing up Ben and Daniel's learning story about a diesel train they had made out of boxes. I watched the video footage to download the photos for the story but couldn't decide what frames to choose as it all seemed so important. It was becoming clear to me that the time had come to
Leadership focused on relationships	begin our video documentation. A very exciting time, especially when we hadn't planned on this development until the following year. A newsletter was written to tell the parents about our exciting new development and to explain that it will be a slow process; children will get their own tape as learning stories evolve.
	The first time we introduced the children to their stories being on tapes, it was an exciting day. Once the video was playing and children saw themselves they automatically went and got their files and began to look through them as they watched the footage. The videos sparked children's conversation as they revisited and talked about the learning experience. I thought this was amazing; children had made very clear links with their files to their videotapes.

Extending the learning community into the home	Parent feedback was encouraging. Ben's mum made a copy of Ben's tape because she was scared he was going to wear it out he watched it so often. Diane, Glen's mum made the comment 'Thanks Karen we had to watch it 10 times last night!' I received some feedback from Fay, Ryan's mum. When I asked what she thought about Ryan's tape she said his grandmother had it. She had had the tape for 3 days....... After watching the tape she now thinks Ryan is clever! Wow, I hadn't realised how powerfully this new innovation was going to impact our families and how they view children. I knew we were on the right track.
Extending the professional learning community to other centres	We edit the video footage in a software programme called iMovie. This enables us to bring in early literacy by adding titles and written commentary to the video footage. When children take home their videotape to share with their families it is extending their learning, involving their family and developing a community of learners. Someone at home will read the words on the footage, extending literacy into the home. As well as children's individual videos, we also began a video library of trips and experiences. Children and families are able to take home and re-visit these experiences, once again extending learning and involving families in their children's interests. [*Authors' addition: By this time Karen is being asked to facilitate a number of workshops for other teachers on her kindergarten's assessment journey.*]

Plans were under way for a Parent/Whanau evening on Learning Stories. We also extended the invitation to local schools. Teachers from four schools attended, we were so pleased with the response. We read some learning stories, making links to Te Whāriki. The evening was a great success; it was wonderful to share our passion for documenting children's learning with families and primary school teachers. |

Karen's log to this point traces the work at Roskill South up until the end of 2002. Since 2002 this work has taken on a new dimension as opportunities for funded teacher research have been taken up by Karen and her teaching team. These opportunities have been a logical extension of the teaching and learning journey experienced by Karen and her colleagues along the four dimensions of shifts in teaching-and-learning practice that were strengthened during the early years of ELP and that are evident in her log book. In the final part of this chapter we describe the move to teacher development through engagement in teacher research by reflecting on our collaboration in two major teacher research projects.

Teacher change and teacher research

Two practitioner research programmes were available in New Zealand after the publication of *Te Whāriki*, both funded by the Ministry of Education: the Centres of Innovation (COI) programme, and the Teaching and Learning Research Initiative (TLRI, administered by the New Zealand Council for Educational Research). These programmes recognise the value of practitioner inquiry or action research projects, a value articulated by Greenwood and Levin (2008):

> Action research aims to solve pertinent problems in a given context through democratic inquiry in which professional researchers collaborate with local stakeholders to seek and enact solutions to problems of major importance to the stake-holders. We refer to this as cogenerative inquiry … The professional researcher often brings knowledge of other relevant cases and of relevant research processes. The insiders have extensive and long-term knowledge of the problems at hand and the contexts in which they occur, as well as knowledge about how and from whom to get information. (p. 72)

Greenwood and Levin's argument supports many of the points made by Timperley and her colleagues in 2007, used in the previous section of this chapter as an analytical framework for Karen's log book entries. The new opportunities offered by the two research programmes also enhanced the teachers' abilities to use assessment information to inform the teaching–learning relationship, enact a culture of responsiveness to learners, develop the leadership of others in relation to curriculum and pedagogy, focus on opportunities to process new understanding and its implications for teaching, introduce new perspectives for discussion, and challenge problematic beliefs. A further value of action research in this context is that it allows for the contribution of the teachers' knowledge of the wider context, the families and the local communities to the research process.

Centre of Innovation, 2003–2006

In 2002 the Roskill South teachers applied for a 3-year Centre of Innovation (COI) project and invited Margaret and Wendy to be their research associates. Their bid was successful for a project entitled Strengthening Learning and Teaching Using ICT (Ramsey, Breen, Sturm, Lee, & Carr, 2005, 2006b). The project was designed to strengthen children's agency and competence with information and communication technologies and to explore the ways in which these technologies could deepen and broaden assessment for learning (Lee, Hatherly, & Ramsey, 2003). One of the requirements of COI projects was that the teachers disseminate their findings, and Roskill South held visitors' days, ran workshops and prepared professional development resources for visitors and the workshops.

During the COI project we began to see the early childhood centre as a network or system in which teaching and learning are distributed across a range of artefacts (including the ICT tools, a curriculum document and assessment formats) and routines, greater sharing of responsibility for teaching and learning with the children and the families (a consequence of their beliefs about the image of a learner and the process of learning), and family participation. We borrowed the unit of analysis from activity theory (i.e., the centre itself as an activity system) to explain how this network of elements, individually and in concert, worked to enhance the agency of the children and the participation of the families (Ramsey, Breen, Sturm, Lee, & Carr, 2007). The executive summary of the final report (Ramsey, Breen, Sturm, Lee, & Carr, 2006a, p. i) noted:

> The integration at Roskill South Kindergarten of ICT and *Te Whāriki* with Learning Stories has been a powerful combination for enhancing learning within all five strands of *Te Whāriki*. The combination developed a culture in which each of the children was recognised as a competent child by the teachers, by the children themselves, and by the families. Children could use the digital camera to prepare their own Learning Stories, and they could explain their learning to others in slide shows and powerpoints. *Te Whāriki's* vision, principles, and strands provided the framework for the aims of the learning and teaching. *Te Whāriki* was foregrounded, with ICT as a mediating tool. At the same time, children families and teachers were developing considerable ICT knowledge and skill, inside meaningful enterprises.

The computer, the camera and the other ICT resources (e.g., photocopier, laminator, printer, fax machine) in the kindergarten made this ICT development possible. Making it *probable* depended entirely on "the pedagogical approach of the adults, and the teaching strategies that are put in place accordingly" (Visser, 2000 p. 11). The teachers were determined that the computer was just another tool for learning, and slotted the digital technology into their view of learning as belonging, wellbeing, exploration, communication and contribution. Central to this integration was their view of assessment as "noticing, recognising and responding", later extended to "noticing, recognising, responding, recording and revisiting" (Carr et al., 2004, Book 1; Carr & Lee, 2012; Cowie, 2000). Assistance with the digital technology was also provided by the ELP facilitators.

In 2009 the Ministry of Education halted funding for the COI programme, despite its being a flagship for practitioner research that had reached out to many early childhood teachers in New Zealand which had been followed with interest internationally. The editor of the five volumes of papers from the 20 COIs, Anne Meade, wrote in the final volume (Meade, 2010 p. 4):

> The collective impact of the COI programme has exceeded all expectations. In a valedictory letter, Peter Moss, professor of Early Childhood Provision at the University of London, commended the 'hard work, vision and commitment' of COI who have contributed 'something very precious in the field [internationally] in the practice of innovation … and played a critical role in enabling services to flourish and grow even better'. … Through their talks and workshops, the teacher-researchers have stimulated—indeed, inspired—hundreds, possible thousands, of teachers to:
> - engage in critical thinking based on research findings that challenged their previously held assumptions about teaching and learning

- improve their planning and assessment for children's learning
- be far more creative in using ICT to communicate how and why early childhood education is beneficial for children's learning and development.

At the end of the 3 years, when asked what being involved in the COI project meant to her, Karen said,

> I remember the day we received the phone call from Anne Meade notifying us that we had been selected as a COI. It was a dream come true. Being selected as a centre of innovation was going to give us support to achieve our vision for integrating ICT into our teaching and learning practice. This was a journey we had already began, but we could see that the COI project was going to have huge benefits for our children, families/whānau, and us the teaching team. [As a consequence of this COI experience], my reflective practice has deepened and I have absolutely loved having time and opportunities to discuss, ponder and wonder about children's thinking and learning, with our teaching team and research associates. I have truly embedded the framework [of] noticing, recognising and responding into my teaching and learning practice and have a greater understanding of how this looks in practice.

Participation in a Teaching and Learning Research Initiative project

In 2007 the Roskill South team took up another opportunity to participate in a practitioner research project, this time with eight other centres. The team was invited to join a TLRI project, led by Margaret and Wendy, exploring the ways in which children could articulate their learning, within the particular context of revisiting documentation. Research at the University of Otago on mothers reminiscing with very young children (Reese & Newcombe, 2007) and research by Katherine Nelson (1996, 1997), and by Robyn Fivush and Catherine Hayden, had emphasised the contribution of revisiting events and event knowledge to social intent and to making meaning of storylines in young people's lives:

> Children have individual episodic memories from infancy, but it is only in the light of social sharing that both the enduring form of narrative organization, and the perceived value to self and others become apparent. (Nelson, 1997, p. 111)

> As narrative skills develop, so do skills for representing events in more elaborate, coherent and evaluative forms. Narrating the past is a critical part of representing the past. It is through narrating the personal past that we come to understand and represent the events of our lives in ever more meaningful ways. (Fivush & Hayden, 1997, p. 195)

This project was also built on five principles for improving formative assessment in schools, which had been outlined by Black and Wiliam (1998), key commentators on assessment for learning, in a research summary for teachers. Two of these principles are: *dialogue* between learners and teachers, in which learners talk about their understanding in their own ways; and *learners understanding the main purposes* of their learning (Black & Wiliam, 1998 pp. 10, 11; see also Black, Harrison, Lee, Marshall, & Wiliam, 2003). We argue that these ideas are just as relevant for young children in early childhood centres.

We described this as the Learning Wisdom project, introduced by Sternberg's comment that:

> When schools teach for wisdom, they teach students that it is important not just what you know, but how you use what you know—whether you use it for good ends or bad. (Sternberg, 2003, p. 7)

The teachers met regularly to share experiences and ideas, and the findings formed a substantial part of a subsequent book (Carr & Lee, 2012). A Learning Story by Karen in Chapter 4 of the book (p. 82) illustrates some of the increased complexity in modes of documentation at the early childhood centre and the opportunities they provided for children to revisit their learning. A *Temple Design Story* from Devya's portfolio

> illustrated his referring to the pictures from a website to inform his block-building. His portfolio also included a DVD of his work, and Learning Stories were prepared as wall displays and PowerPoints for groups of children to revisit and plan together. Included here [in chapter 6] is another Devya story, the Mandir, which describes Devya explaining and sharing ideas with other children as they watch a DVD of a temple in England, and Devya then referencing the images on the screen to make more temple drawings. (Carr & Lee, 2012, p. 114)

Another Learning Story by Karen (Carr & Lee, 2012, pp. 53–54) describes Thenusan taking on the role of an illustrator, author and, finally, publisher of a book. He dictated a story to accompany a series of drawings and Karen wrote it down. He laminated the pages then used the kindergarten's book binder to turn it into a book. Finally, he read the story to the entire kindergarten group at the end of the day.

Both of these practitioner research projects enabled the team at Roskill South to deepen their understanding of ways to implement the empowerment principle in *Te Whāriki*, distributing the leadership across the teachers, the materials, and the learners themselves. Thus, three key aspects of professional development—assessment, leadership, and teachers' theories—were strengthened and re-shaped during these projects, while the fourth aspect, professional learning communities, was broadened to include more specifically a research community at a university.

Conclusion

This chapter has recounted the story of one teacher's journey in formative assessment since the publication of *Te Whāriki*. It is a story of teacher change, as Karen and her teaching team explored the possibilities of the new curriculum. It is also a weaving together of four features of teacher professional learning and development: assessment practices that inform the teaching–learning relationship, supportive leadership, a questioning of existing theories of teaching and learning, and a broadening and strengthening of engagement with professional development communities, both inside the kindergarten (seeking advice from families and engaging in dialogue about learning with the children, for instance) and outside it. The key threads of the weaving were the changes in assessment practices as the teachers, with the children and the families, explored the ways their documentation could highlight valued learning and give them the information they needed to plan and review the next steps for teaching and learning. The Centre of Innovation project and participation in the Education Leadership Project enabled Karen to develop, in particular, the leadership of others in relation to curriculum and pedagogy.

As we look ahead, we can do no better than quote the final paragraph in a section entitled 'Bringing it all together' (Timperley et al., 2007, p. 225) in the Best Evidence Synthesis that provided the structure for this chapter:

> A key finding of this synthesis has been that teachers need to have time and opportunity to engage with ideas and integrate those ideas into a coherent theory of practice. Changing teaching practice in ways that have a significant impact on student outcomes is not easy. Policy and organisational contexts that continually shift priorities to the 'next big thing', with little understanding/evaluation of how current practice is impacting on desired outcomes for students, undermine the sustainability of changes already under way. Innovation needs to be carefully balanced with consolidation if professional learning experiences are to impact positively on student outcomes.

We have found these words to be appropriate for early childhood services as well as for schools. They are especially true 5 years on from when they were written, and should provide a touchstone for the sustainability of teacher change in years to come.

Acknowledgements

We acknowledge, with thanks, the New Zealand Ministry of Education's funding support for the Centres of Innovation programme, the Teaching and Learning Research Initiative (TLRI) and the professional development programmes that have funded the Educational Leadership Project. The TLRI projects are administered by the New Zealand Council for Educational Research, and we have appreciated their support and guidance. Thank you, too, to the teachers and families who have given permission to be quoted and cited in this chapter.

References

Australian Government Department of Education, Employment and Workplace Relations. (2009). *Belonging, being and becoming: The early years learning framework for Australia.* Canberra, ACT: Commonwealth of Australia.

Black, P., Harrison, C., Lee, C., Marshall, B., & Wiliam, D. (2003). *Assessment for learning: Putting it into practice*. Maidenhead, UK: Open University Press.

Black, P., & Wiliam, D. (1998). *Inside the black box: Raising standards through classroom assessment*. London, UK: King's College, University of London.

Carr, M. (1998a). *Assessing children's learning in early childhood settings: A professional development programme for discussion and reflection* [DVD and support booklet]. Wellington: New Zealand Council for Educational Research.

Carr, M. (1998b). *Project for assessing children's experiences in early childhood: Final report to the Ministry: Part 2: Five case studies*. Wellington: Ministry of Education Research Division.

Carr, M. (2001). *Assessment in early childhood settings: Learning stories*. London, UK: Sage.

Carr, M. (2005). The leading edge of learning: Recognising children's self-making narratives. *European Early Childhood Educational Research Journal*, 13(2), 41–50.

Carr, M., & Lee, W. (2012). *Learning stories: Constructing learner identities in early education*. London, UK: Sage Publications.

Carr, M., Lee, W., Jones, C., & Ministry of Education. (2004, 2007, & 2009). *Kei tua o te pae: Assessment for learning: Early childhood exemplars*. Wellington: Learning Media.

Cowie, B. (2000). *Formative assessment in science classrooms*. Unpublished doctoral thesis, University of Waikato, Hamilton.

Davis, K. (2002) "It's evolving over time": Some reflections on shifts in assessment practices through the voices of infant toddler practitioners. *The First Years: Ngā Tau Tuatahi: New Zealand Journal of Infant and Toddler Education*, 4(2), 32–35.

Department for Children, Schools and Families. (2008). *Statutory framework for the early years foundation stage*. London, UK: Author.

Fivush, R., & Hayden, C. A. (1997). Narrating and representing experience: Preschoolers' developing autobiographical accounts. In P. W. Van den Broek, P. J. Bauer, & T. Bourg (Eds.), *Developmental spans in event comprehension and representation: Bridging fictional and actual events*. Mahwah, NJ: Erlbaum.

Foote, L., Irvine, P., & Turnbull, A. (1996, June). *Professional development programmes for curriculum implementation in early childhood*. Paper presented at the New Zealand Council for Educational Research Conference, Wellington.

Gaffney, M., & Smith, A. B. (1997). *An evaluation of pilot early childhood professional development programmes to support curriculum implementation: Report to the Ministry of Education*. Dunedin: Children's Issues Centre.

Gould, K. (1997). *Teacher professional development: A literature review. Position paper 4*. Hamilton: Department of Early Childhood Studies, University of Waikato.

Gunn, A. C., & de Vocht van Alphen, L. (2011). Seeking justice and equity through narrative assessment in early childhood education. *International Journal of Equity and Innovation in Early Childhood*, 9(1), 31–43.

Hatherly, A., & Sands, L. (2002). So what is different about learning stories? *The First Years: Ngā Tau Tuatahi: New Zealand Journal of Infant and Toddler Education*, 4(1), 8–12.

Hedges, H., & Cullen, J. (2012). Participatory learning theories: A framework for early childhood pedagogy. *Early Child Development and Care*, 182(7), 921–940.

Karlsdóttir, K., & Garǎrsdóttir, B. (2010). Exploring children's learning stories as an assessment method for research and practice. *Early Years*, 30, 255–266.

Lee, W. (2008). ELP: Empowering the leadership in professional development communities. *European Early Childhood Education Research Journal, 16*(1), 95–106.

Lee, W., Hatherly, A., & Ramsey, K. (2003). Using ICT to document children's learning. *Early Childhood Folio, 6,* 12–18.

Meade, A. (2010). Introduction. In A. Meade (Ed.), *Dispersing waves: Innovation in early childhood education* (pp. 3–4). Wellington: NZCER Press.

Ministry of Education. (1996). *Te whāriki: He whāriki mātauranga mō ngā mokopuna o Aotearoa: Early childhood curriculum.* Wellington: Learning Media.

Nelson, K. (1996). *Language in cognitive development: The emergence of the mediated mind.* Cambridge, UK: Cambridge University Press.

Nelson, K. (1997). Cognitive change as collaborative construction. In E. Amsel & K. A. Renninger (Eds.), *Change and development: Issues of theory, method and application* (pp. 99–115). Mahwah, NJ: Lawrence Erlbaum.

Nyland, B., & Ferris, J. (2009). Researching children's musical learning experiences within a learning story framework. *New Zealand Research in Early Childhood Education, 12,* 81–94.

Perry, B., Dockett, S., & Harley, E. (2007). Learning stories and powerful mathematical ideas. Early Childhood Research and Practice, 9(2). Retrieved from http://ecrp.uiuc.edu/v9n2/perry.html

Ramsey, K., Breen, J., Sturm, J., Lee, W., & Carr, M. (2005). Roskill South Kindergarten Centre of Innovation. In A. Meade (Ed.), *Catching the waves: Innovation in early childhood education* (pp. 25–30). Wellington: NZCER Press.

Ramsey, K., Breen, J., Sturm, J., Lee, W., & Carr, M. (2006a). Roskill South Kindergarten COI team reflections. In A. Meade (Ed.), *Riding the waves: Innovation in early childhood education* (pp. 38–44). Wellington: NZCER Press.

Ramsey, K., Breen, J., Sturm, J., Lee, W., & Carr, M. (2006b). *Strengthening learning and teaching using ICT: Final report to Ministry of Education.* Wellington: NZCER Press.

Ramsey, K., Breen, J., Sturm, J., Lee, W., & Carr, M. (2007). Weaving ICTs into *Te whāriki* at Roskill South Kindergarten. In A. Meade (Ed.), *Cresting the waves: Innovation in early childhood education* (pp. 29–36). Wellington: NZCER Press.

Reese, E., & Newcombe, R. (2007). Training mothers in elaborative reminiscing enhances children's autobiographical memory and narrative. *Child Development, 78*(4), 1153–1170.

Sternberg, R. (2003). What is an 'expert student'? *Educational Researcher, 32*(8), 5–9.

Syed, M. (2011). *Bounce: Mozart, Federer, Picasso, Beckham, and the science of success.* New York, NY: Harper Perennial.

Timperley, H., Wilson, A., Barrar, H., & Fung, I. (2007). *Teacher professional learning and development: Best evidence synthesis iteration.* Wellington: Ministry of Education.

Visser, J. (2000). Integrating the early childhood curriculum and information communication technology. *Early Education, 22*(Autumn), 11–17.

Wertsch, J. V. (1991). *Voices of the mind: A sociocultural approach to mediated action.* Cambridge, MA: Harvard University Press.

CHAPTER 9

Curriculum concepts as cultural tools: Implementing *Te Whāriki*

Joce Nuttall

ABSTRACT

This chapter discusses some of the influences on early childhood teachers' co-construction of the enacted curriculum—not the curriculum imagined in documents such as *Te Whāriki* (Ministry of Education, 1996), but the curriculum teachers actually provide. These influences include teachers' initial preparation for teaching, their awareness of various curriculum traditions and models in early childhood education, and their ideas about which aspects of children's centre-based experience constitute part of 'the curriculum'. The chapter argues that these influences constitute cultural tools that mediate teachers' cognitive processes and practical actions. Examples are drawn from a study of teachers' co-construction of the enacted curriculum in one New Zealand child-care centre (Nuttall, 2004). The chapter concludes by discussing some of the constraints teachers face when exploring their co-construction of curricula and suggests some strategies for exploring the concepts teachers bring to the task of enacting curriculum in early childhood settings.

Introduction

The development of the early childhood curriculum document *Te Whāriki* (Ministry of Education, 1996) marked an important shift in early childhood education in Aotearoa New Zealand, since the term 'curriculum' was not commonly used in early childhood education prior to the 1990s (May, 2001). A feature of *Te Whāriki* is the way it encapsulated the understanding about curriculum not only of its writers, but also of the wider early childhood community, due to the broadly consultative way in which it was developed (see Chapter 1, this volume). As a consequence, it received widespread support from teachers, even in its draft form (Murrow, 1995).

Curriculum is defined in *Te Whāriki* as

> the sum total of the experiences, activities and events, whether direct or indirect, which occur within an environment designed to foster children's learning and development. (Ministry of Education, 1996, p. 10)

This definition of curriculum as 'everything that happens' is described in the curriculum theory literature as the 'enacted' curriculum, distinguishing it from the 'specified' curriculum (the curriculum described in curriculum documents) and the 'experienced' curriculum (the curriculum learners actually encounter) (McCormick & Murphy, 2008, p. 3). The notion of enacted curriculum resonates with the holistic, child-centred philosophy of early childhood education in New Zealand. It is, however, an image of curriculum that is extremely difficult to operationalise, since it demands simultaneous attention to every aspect of the learning environment.

The central expectation of *Te Whāriki* is that early childhood centres and services will articulate their curriculum in a conscious, culturally situated way. This is reflected in the metaphor of the document's title, a whāriki being a woven mat. This view of curriculum as "distinctive patterns" (Ministry of Education, 1996, p. 11), 'woven' from highly local, particular and socially situated thinking and circumstances, rejects more traditional notions of curriculum as a set of prescribed aims and content (sometimes called a 'syllabus view' of curriculum); instead, teachers, parents and children collaboratively explore their own perspectives on what counts as teaching, learning and knowledge, an approach to curriculum construction that Shaw (2009) calls a "post-syllabus condition". In order to do this, each early childhood centre or service must make explicit the adults' images of children and childhood, their shared beliefs about the purposes of early childhood education, and their understanding of the role of the teacher in children's learning.

Te Whāriki positions children as active participants in their own learning, capable of developing their own "working theories about themselves and about the people, places and things in their lives" (Ministry of Education, 1996, p. 44), and of bringing rich prior experience to the centre setting. The purpose of early childhood education is seen as allowing children to fully express these capabilities

> to grow up as competent and confident learners and communicators, healthy in mind, body, and spirit, secure in their sense of belonging and in the knowledge that they make a valued contribution to society. (Ministry of Education, 1996, p. 9)

The work of the teacher is less clearly defined (Nuttall, 2002). The socio-cultural constructivist bases of *Te Whāriki* mean that teachers' negotiation of their curriculum enactment, including those practices they consider more or less appropriate in implementing a socio-culturally based curriculum, is itself part of the 'weaving' of life in the centre.

My doctoral research (Nuttall, 2004) was concerned with this aspect of centre life. It was an attempt to understand how groups of early childhood teachers *intersubjectively* construct and enact their definitions of 'curriculum'. One aspect of this co-construction is the way in which teachers monitor and proscribe each other's enactment of the curriculum; that is, how they negotiate with each other the beliefs, understanding and practices that constitute 'teaching'. By regularly observing a group of teachers at work in one child-care centre across a period of 5 months, interviewing them, analysing their curriculum documentation and attending their staff meetings and professional development workshops, I was able to discern something of how they attempted to influence each other's ideas about, and practice of, the teacher's role in enacting the curriculum.

This chapter discusses some of the cultural tools that early childhood teachers in Aotearoa New Zealand might bring to the co-construction of the enacted curriculum. Three of the influences that were evident in the centre participating in the study were the teachers' initial preparation for teaching, their awareness of various curriculum traditions, and their ideas about which aspects of what they provide for children count as curriculum. While these factors may seem self-evident to experienced early childhood teachers and teacher educators, particularly those working within a socio-cultural constructivist framework, I believe they are not always addressed—or even acknowledged—when teachers set out to negotiate their practice. I conclude the chapter by briefly describing some of the constraints on this negotiation and suggesting some ways in which these influences might be explored within a socio-cultural framework, including through the use of *Te Whāriki* itself.

Theoretical framing: The role of cultural tools in socio-cultural theory

Within socio-cultural understanding of teaching and learning, originating in the work of L. S. Vygotsky (1978) and his colleagues in Russia in the first half of the 20th century (van der Veer, 2007), cultural tools are understood to have an important and specific function in shaping human action. These tools may be concrete artefacts, such as pencils, computers and furniture, but they can also exist entirely in the mind, in the form of concepts, including knowledge of the way concrete artefacts can be used. Pre-eminent among cultural tools is language.

Socio-culturalists understand cultural tools to exist first in the wider culture, from where they are progressively internalised by members of the culture (Vygotsky, 1978). Newcomers to the culture—either as visitors or because they are very young—become enculturated as they internalise the concepts and master the artefacts valued by the culture. Once internalised, these cultural tools can be adapted by individuals and groups to new and better uses, thereby changing not only the culture *but their own mental structures.* This was—and remains—a revolutionary idea in psychology:

> For him [Vygotsky], the very development of the higher mental functions rests on the mastery of nature through the creation of psychological tools to control our own psychological processes. Because this involves the creation of external technology—in the form of symbolic systems established in the environment—the task of mastering ourselves is one with [the] project of the control of nature outside us. (Bakhurst, 2007, p. 66)

The specific function of cultural tools, however, is to mediate between the actor (e.g., the teacher) and the object of their activity (e.g., teaching a child how to recognise their printed name). In the case of early childhood teachers, the process of teacher education is, in large part, one of exposure to new cultural tools in the hope these will mediate their subsequent work with children. These tools may take the form of distinctive materials (playdough, dressing-up clothes, sand) and the pedagogical purposes to which they may be put, as well as conceptual tools specific to educational theory (e.g., in the case of socio-cultural theory, concepts such as scaffolding, intent participation and intentional teaching). Either way, they provide mental structures through which teachers can make decisions about how they will enact the curriculum and, in turn, how they should adapt their thinking and practice.

These tools appear not only within theories of learning but also as part of complex aggregations known as curriculum models or 'approaches'. Most experienced early childhood educators entering a Montessori-based kindergarten would immediately recognise the nature of the programme without advance warning, simply by noticing the distinctively Montessori combination of artefacts available to the children (e.g., sensory apparatus, child-scale household equipment) and the concepts given priority by the teachers in their language and practice (e.g., order, inner discipline, self-worth). In the case of *Te Whāriki*, the curriculum exists both as a concrete artefact—the published version of the document—and as a set of inter-related concepts represented symbolically within the document in the form of words and diagrams. The core concepts of *Te Whāriki* (i.e., the privileged cultural tools teachers are expected to enact) are somewhat abstract: belonging, wellbeing, empowerment, communication and contribution. At the same time, the pedagogical strategies to be employed by the teachers—observable as the enacted curriculum—are left up to the teachers to determine, rather than being explicitly suggested within the document. My doctoral research was therefore an attempt to understand how teachers in child-care settings enact such abstract concepts, what other concepts they may be drawing upon to assist in this process, and—crucially for early childhood education settings—how they do this *with their colleagues from moment to moment*. Such a research endeavour requires a very particular research methodology.

The research methodology

The research drew on the theoretical and philosophical principles of symbolic interactionism (Blumer, 1969). Symbolic interactionism understands knowledge as being constructed both within the self (through a process known as self-indication) and through interaction with others. 'Generalised' and 'significant' others serve as points of reference for important ideas about the self. Symbolic interactionists believe that we make meaning in our lives by constantly attempting to see our 'selves' as these important others see us. Cognition is therefore both a personal, covert activity and a group activity; social actors (individuals) strive to align the meanings they hold about social objects (such as curriculum) in order to perform socially defined and mediated acts (such as teaching) (Blumer, 1969). Edwards (2007) has pointed out the similarities between the work of Vygotsky and that of George Herbert Mead, the originator of symbolic interactionism: both

> aimed at offering a reflective version of a problem-solving human science with profound implications for understanding dynamic interrelationships between people and their worlds. (p. 78)

One difference, however, is that symbolic interactionists pay closer attention to the psychology of the individual rather than to the wider culture.

Symbolic interactionists ask the kind of broad questions typically explored through ethnographic approaches (What is going on here? How do these people organise themselves?) as well as social-psychological questions that focus on interaction between individuals, such as 'How do these people create a learning environment for each other?' For teachers in early childhood education, the processes of curriculum decision making are complicated by the need for constant negotiation with other teachers. Early childhood teachers, particularly in child care, work together in groups, and decisions about teachers' actions have an immediate impact on the experiences of other teachers as well as on children. As Burton and Halliwell (2001) point out, maintaining coherence and direction in curriculum encountered by children when they work alongside adults with differing work orientations is a major concern for teachers in centre-based child care. (p. 27)

The study was informed by a body of research, emerging in the early 1980s, that investigates teacher thinking about curriculum in early childhood settings (e.g., Ayers, 1989; Burton, 1999; Burton & Halliwell, 2001; Elbaz, 1983; Halliwell, 1992; Hatch & Freeman, 1998; Hedges & Cullen, 2005; Hseih & Spodek, 1995; Wen, Elicker, & McMullen, 2011; Wood, 2004). Much of the current literature on teacher thinking positions teachers within a web of complex inter-related processes of curriculum decision making, rather than as technical experts (see Blank, 2010, for a discussion of this distinction). This perspective sees teachers as active constructors of their own curriculum knowledge and practice (or, indeed, active rejecters of curriculum initiatives; see Burgess, Robertson, & Patterson, 2010). These approaches to understanding teacher decision making about curriculum acknowledge the complex milieu in which teachers operate, reinforcing Grundy's (1998) pedagogical view of curriculum as "a dynamic interaction of a host of factors prevailing at the time" (p. 30).

One characteristic of the literature on teacher cognition is that it refers almost exclusively to teachers who work on their own in individual classrooms. Burton and Halliwell (2001) call this "a blind spot in the teacher research that assumes teachers can act autonomously once classroom doors are shut" (p. 28). For early childhood teachers the process of symbolic exchange with 'significant others' is both a covert mental activity (as it can be for anyone, at any time) and a constant, observable condition of their work. As a consequence, the opportunities to influence each other's understanding about the curriculum are constant and overt, and can have an intensity that is unlikely to be experienced by classroom teachers on a regular basis.

In child care the teacher will work alongside people with a range of qualifications or with no formal training, and may interact with children from groups they are not formally responsible for. Since all contact staff members have some influence over curriculum decisions, this can lead to tension between individual and collective responsibility. These adults bring different understandings to their work and their input … is not an optional extra. (Burton and Halliwell, 2001, p. 29)

Child-care teachers typically have fewer opportunities than other teachers to meet together outside teaching times in order to discuss general pedagogical issues, including understanding of their approach to enacting the curriculum. Instead, these ideas are often accrued individually and on the job, through a constant exchange of speech, gestures and written directives. Clare, one of the teachers participating in the study [all names are pseudonyms], explained this phenomenon:

Just, well, observing what other people do for a start. How they react to different things, being part of the team, going to staff meetings. Yeah, just talking to other staff, asking them if I'm doing something right, just taking it all in really.

In symbolic interactionist terms, I was attempting to understand how the participating teachers aligned the conceptual tools they brought to curriculum enactment through their symbolic exchanges. My theoretical assumptions included the idea that the teachers were constantly attempting to 'see' themselves teaching *as they believed they appeared to the other teachers*. Since it is literally impossible to see oneself through the eyes of another, the teachers were assumed to be engaging in a constant process of mentally interpreting the statements and actions of others (including statements made by the writers of *Te Whāriki*) in order to subtly realign their developing personal constructs of 'teaching'. From where, then, do teachers acquire their cultural tools? And what are these, other than the concepts they encounter within *Te Whāriki*?

The influence of initial teacher education on the co-construction of curriculum

Socio-cultural explanations for the co-construction of knowledge through engagement with culture can also be applied to how teachers develop their ideas about practice in early childhood settings. This co-construction may be explicitly undertaken, such as through centre-based professional development, but my research examined how this process occurs less formally, by assuming that teachers are continuously developing their ideas about teaching through day-to-day interaction with each other. Teacher educators trust that one of the ways in which teachers approach this co-construction is by drawing on what they have learned about teaching during their initial teacher education.

'Long Acres' is the pseudonym for the child-care centre where I conducted my doctoral field work. The centre operated on a full-day licence, and their licence permitted them to accommodate, at any one time, nine children aged from birth until their second birthday, and 24 children from their second birthday until the age of five. Three teachers were assigned to the under-twos part of the centre and three teachers to the over-twos. The centre also had a full-time supervisor, who was frequently involved in teaching duties, and one of the teaching positions was shared between two teachers, meaning that a total of eight teachers participated in the study.

From my first day in the centre I knew about the variety of teacher education backgrounds among the group of teachers who participated in my study because their various diplomas and certificates were prominently displayed in the centre foyer. Two of the teachers were qualified primary school teachers and did not have formal early childhood teaching qualifications. Two others who had also been primary school teachers had re-credentialised as early childhood teachers through in-service programmes. Three of the teachers had originally qualified for early childhood teaching through 3-year Diploma of Teaching programmes. The other teacher had a background in early childhood education through involvement in the Playcentre movement and had later upgraded her initial qualification to diploma-equivalent status.

During individual interviews with the teachers I asked them to describe what they considered to be the *main* role of the teacher in early childhood education, in an attempt to identify the high-status conceptual tools they were bringing to their work. For those teachers who had originally qualified as primary school teachers the dominant concepts were learning and development. Clare, who had not re-credentialised for early childhood teaching, focused on 'education', with an emphasis on social skills:

> Educating the children, probably doing the job that parents would hopefully like to do if they were able to, and [to] extend children's education. Challenge them. It could be just socialising skills, getting them to develop their social skills, cooperative play, sharing, we give them skills for everyday life really.

Sue, the centre supervisor, had re-credentialised as an early childhood teacher after having qualified as a primary school teacher. Sue was concerned with enhancing children's development:

> I would say the most important role is to have a better understanding about the child's development, so that [the teacher] is more able to put into practice [both] the caring and the education side.

Marsha and Leah, by contrast, had both qualified as early childhood teachers upon leaving school and worked in early childhood ever since. Their responses were more focused on the affective aspects of their work. For Leah, the most important feature of enacting the curriculum was to create a 'home away from home':

> To care for the children and make the centre as home-like as possible. To find out from parents what their children like and what they do at home and try and stick to their routines as much as possible. To make the child feel welcome here so that they like coming here.

Marsha characterised the teacher's role as:

> Basically just to be the child's advocate and to love them, give them the love that perhaps they would be getting at home all day.

During the interviews I asked each teacher to identify which other teacher in the centre most closely shared their perspective on teaching in early childhood, to try to identify who acted as their 'significant other' in constructing their image of teaching. I found that the teachers' beliefs about who shared their perspectives were aligned exactly to their qualifications backgrounds. Clare identified Leah as having *least* in common with her perspective, while Leah identified Marsha as being closest to her view. Sue and Marsha did not name individuals but indicated the way a 'generalised other' (the primary-trained teachers) shaped their perspective: Marsha highlighted the way she did not agree with the approach of those teachers on the staff who were primary trained (although she singled out Sue as an exception to this); Sue highlighted the way the primary-trained teachers were making important shifts in their practice. It is possible, of course, that the teachers' perspectives were not the result of their teacher education, but what is important in this context is the way the teachers strongly characterised each other in terms of their qualifications pathways. In other words, specific qualifications acted as cultural 'place-holders' for particular conceptual tools, such as education or love, that were understood to be dominant concepts among the other teachers.

The teachers were aware of how their teacher education backgrounds provided them with different perspectives, and during the research field work it became evident that the diversity of qualifications among the group influenced the negotiations the teachers had about their practice. However, these differences went relatively unexplored by the teachers. For example, during staff meetings the contrast between primary perspectives and early childhood perspectives was often raised, but only in order to provide an example of what an early childhood teacher should *not* do. One area of debate among the teachers, for example, was the extent to which the teacher should pre-determine art activities; detailed preparation was characterised as a 'primary' approach at one staff meeting:

Sue: This is my personal belief about children's work: We should provide the materials and let them go for it. Yesterday I saw children making bees and they were *all the same*.

Ngaire: I think some primary school thinking came in there.

In another staff meeting, the teachers made a similar contrast, again without defining an alternative 'early childhood' approach. The over-twos teachers were attempting to address a question Clare had posed about curriculum, related to the extent to which children's activities should be 'teacher directed'. Sue explained that it [the curriculum] is about which 'areas' are provided in the learning environment whereupon Clare responded, "But it's also about the children's ideas?"

Sue: Yes, but it's quite different from primary or secondary where they have set curriculum.

Clare: So when we make slime it's about us providing it.

Vi: The old way was just to let them play.

Sue: It's also about the children's experience, what they bring.

Clare: It's like there's different levels … But it's also about us setting it up. What would the children do if there was nothing set up? They'd still want the play dough, the … It's so different from primary.

Sue: When I was in primary it was all teacher directed.

In this excerpt we can see a range of cultural tools that are also evident in early childhood teacher education programmes: play, curriculum, environment, 'areas' of play, children's prior experience, and teacher directedness. The ways in which teachers respond to children's interests and guide children's participation in the life of the centre are central to the enactment of a socio-culturally based curriculum. Wood and Attfield (2005, pp. 104–106) characterise these responses as the use of strategies such as "assisted performance" and "sustained shared thinking". The teachers at Long Acres were examining the question of teachers' responses, but their examination was mediated by their images of primary versus early childhood teaching rather than concepts derived from socio-cultural theory.

Not all child-care centres in New Zealand have teachers who initially qualified as primary school teachers, but it is characteristic of child care in New Zealand that teachers rarely share the same teacher preparation background. I do not mean to imply, in selecting the examples described above, that there is a 'correct' approach to curriculum enactment; rather that, since curriculum will inevitably be co-constructed in a child-care setting, it is important to explore the cultural tools that teachers bring from their prior education to that co-construction.

The influence of curriculum knowledge on the co-construction of curriculum

A second factor that needs to be explored is the knowledge teachers hold about specific approaches to curriculum. Early childhood education in New Zealand has embraced a rich mix of curriculum traditions, and this is reflected in the wide range of early childhood services available in New Zealand, each with its own philosophical base. One of the challenges for the writers of *Te Whāriki* was to accommodate the needs and perspectives of these diverse services within a single document (Carr, 1993). These traditions take various forms, including:

- recognisable syntheses of theory, ideology and practice (sometimes called 'programmes' or 'curriculum models' (Montessori-based centre programmes is one example)
- broad theoretical understanding (such as Piagetian ideas about the value of children having free access to a range of challenging materials)
- ideological beliefs about the purpose of early childhood provision (including preparation for formal schooling, support for working women, parent education and empowerment, and compensatory programmes for children from disadvantaged backgrounds).

May (1997, 2000) has traced this rich heritage of multiple ideological, theoretical and pragmatic influences, showing how each successive trend has challenged early childhood teachers to re-examine their practice. When *Te Whāriki* was developed in the early 1990s, it combined these ongoing traditions with the emerging influence of socio-cultural theory. The writers of *Te Whāriki* stated that they drew on the work of theorists such as Vygotsky and Bruner (Carr, 1993) and there has been considerable interest in New Zealand in socio-culturally based programmes such as those of the Reggio Emilia preschools.

The field notes of just one planning meeting at Long Acres revealed the teachers' awareness of the range of influences available to them. Reference to specific curriculum models included: "anti-bias curriculum" (Derman-Sparks, 1989); "that's really Reggio" (the Reggio Emilia Approach [Edwards, Forman, & Gandini, 1993]); examples of the principles, goals and strands of *Te Whāriki* (Ministry of Education, 1996); and "themes" and a "focus" (the Project Approach [Katz & Chard, 2000]). Reference to theories of development included: "So that's co-operative play" (stage theories); a comment about a child's "phobia" (psychodynamic theory); and "I'd like to put [on the planning sheet] ... gender awareness. Non-gender specific roles" (gender theory). Some general principles in early childhood curriculum implementation were also discussed: "Yes, but it's quite different from primary or secondary where they have *set* curriculum" (curriculum theory); "areas" of play (based on Piagetian, free-play approaches); "core curriculum"; and the general issue of striking a balance between "teacher directed" (culturally transmissive) approaches and "ideas emerging from the children" (child-centred approaches). At another meeting the same group touched on theories of applied behaviour analysis, including discussing the kinds of "treats" they might offer as "rewards" to compliant children. Given that the field work for this project was completed prior to 2004, it would be interesting to repeat this exercise to determine whether the teachers' cultural 'tool kit' is now more socio-culturally oriented; I would not be surprised to find, however, that they were still drawing on this rich tool kit of concepts and models.

Any educational ideology, developmental theory or pedagogical approach drawn on by teachers dictates a particular set of pedagogical practices in relation to the child. MacNaughton and Williams (2008) describe some of the distinct approaches to teaching that arise from a range of traditions. The freedom with which the participating teachers referred to available theoretical and curricular models during their staff meetings suggests that the implications of these are only partially understood, since several stand in contradiction to each other. For example, developmental theories based on ideas about 'normal' patterns of maturation imply different actions for teachers to those based in social-constructivist learning theory, a contradiction that Cullen (1996) identified within *Te Whāriki*. Broström (2001) has described the implications of this distinction in the Danish setting (see also Chapter 12, this volume), where curriculum traditions in early childhood are much less diverse. Broström argues that many Danish early childhood teachers have rejected social-constructivist approaches to teaching in favour of developmentally based 'free play' models, based on the implications they see for the role of the teacher. Since they view the active role of the teacher within constructivist pedagogy as too much like the work of teachers in compulsory schooling, they are determined to maintain a firm qualitative distinction between children's experiences before and after school entry. It may be that the traditional reliance on 'free play' as a key cultural tool within early childhood programmes in Aotearoa New Zealand, versus the more hands-on approach of facilitating guided participation, may create similar tensions for teachers here.

Whether an eclectic approach to cultural tools helps or hinders teachers to enact early childhood curriculum in Aotearoa New Zealand remains an open question. It seems important, however, for teachers to explore the implications for practice embedded within the various traditions to which they have been exposed. Without this exploration, alignment around concepts such as curriculum and assessment is likely to be confounded.

Definitions of what counts as curriculum as an influence on curriculum enactment

Throughout the time I was observing at Long Acres I noted a persistent tension the teachers seemed to be experiencing between being an active supporter of children's learning and an enforcer of children's compliance to centre routines. A key centre document exemplified the way in which these were viewed as separate. The teachers had negotiated several lists (effectively a set of duty rosters), which described the relationship between time and tasks for teachers during the centre day. The 'inside-outside' roster (for the teacher who worked with the over-twos children inside the centre in the morning and in the playground in the afternoon) is shown in Figure 1.

There are many possible readings of the rosters. The most obvious one is that they are a logical and pragmatic way for the teachers to communicate their expectations of each other's behaviour at particular times during the day; one teacher told me they were particularly useful for giving direction to relief staff. Adherence to the rosters ensures that everything that needs to be done is done and that children are securely supervised.

A further reading is that the rosters provide powerful definitions of the social act of teaching in the centre, since they were the most obvious evidence of the way the teachers had negotiated the nature of their day-to-day activities. The implication of how tasks had been delineated on the inside-outside roster is that facilitating "children's play and learning" is what teachers do *between* routine events. In negotiating the rosters, the teachers had made explicit the idea that implementing routines is not teaching

---

Figure 1. Inside–outside roster

INSIDE–OUTSIDE

Supervision of children is important at all times.

8.30 Greet children and families. Supervise and facilitate children's play. Write up day's toileting first.

9.10 Help with sharing time.

9.30 Get morning tea ready, staggered or group. Tidy up afterwards and do dishes. Open communication with staff to ensure children's toileting needs are being met.

10.20 Change nappies where needed. Check toileting. Check laundry.

10.30 Reset activity tables. Supervise and facilitate children's play and learning.

11.20 Gather children and encourage them to tidy up inside.

11.30 Mat time. Set up lunches, tablecloths on, lunches out, heated if needed.

11.45 LUNCH. Supervise children in bathroom. (Pick up hot lunches on Friday.) Set up beds. Help with lunch. Stay with sleepers.

12.30 Session ends

OUTSIDE roster now

Remember there MUST be a teacher outside at all times if children are outside, so get another teacher to relieve you if you need to go inside.

When outside, supervise and facilitate children's play and learning.

2.30 Afternoon tea. Staggered groups, inside or outside, weather permitting.

4.00ish Tidy up time, all children to help. Put toys in garage. Empty water trough/messy play. Encourage children to pick up rubbish. Rake and cover sandpit (twice a week). Fridays—wash sandpit toys with hose. Make sure shed is LOCKED.

4.20ish. All children inside to help tidy up.

4.30 – 4.50 Quiet time in the sleeproom. Stories, songs, games and fruit. Farewelling children and families.

5.00 Session ends.

ALL STAFF

Remember to sweep bark and concrete daily.

END OF DAY – Bring chairs and clothes in. Check windows and all doors are closed and locked. Coffee pot is off and everything else. Double check fire exit door.

PLEASE REMEMBER: to use open communication and to be flexible.

(or, paradoxically, that teaching is yet another routine, something to be attended to between other events).

This separation of routines from teaching was a persistent theme in the teachers' negotiations with each other, one that Sue, the centre supervisor, was attempting to overcome. Sue, the newest teacher in the centre apart from one other, was responsible for the insistence on 'flexibility' that appeared on the rosters (in apparent contradiction to their purpose and contents). Sue was concerned at the rigidity of the practices that had developed prior to her appointment and was trying to slowly change the other teachers' thinking. One strategy Sue used was to persistently promote a socio-cultural orientation to thinking about the centre's curriculum (although she did not articulate it to me in those terms). For example, during staff meetings she would make statements such as "Even though this is our focus, there are other ideas emerging from the children. We don't have to just go by this [plan]", and "Greeting parents is more important than routines". She encouraged the other teachers to be 'flexible' in their thinking about what they did during the day, to the extent that, when she made suggestions for practice during staff meetings, the other teachers would sometimes chime "and be flexible!" at the end of her statements. Although teasing, this response suggests that the teachers understood that Sue's suggestions ran counter to the emphasis on structural constraints on teachers' work in the centre, as exemplified by the rosters. Although the teachers were aware of the range of curriculum traditions described earlier, I found that the division they had conceptualised between teaching and caregiving was one that over-rode all their other definitions of curriculum.

The centrality of routine events in early childhood settings is a key emphasis of *Te Whāriki*. Writers such as Rockel (2009) have stressed that caregiving *is* the curriculum in early childhood education, particularly for infants and toddlers. Unless the implementation of routines is understood as central to teachers' work in fostering children's learning, the practical constraints of the child-care day leave little time for other definitions of teaching. Alternatively, a fundamental understanding of the culturally embedded nature of centre practices (however defined) has the potential to relieve child-care teachers of unhelpful distinctions between teaching and routines in their attempts to co-construct the curriculum.

Practical constraints on the co-construction of enacted curriculum

I have written elsewhere (Nuttall, 2003) about some of the characteristics of child-care settings that constrain teachers from exploring *Te Whāriki*. Teachers may simply have insufficient knowledge of the theoretical and ideological bases of the document (Cullen, 1996). Then, even if they do have this knowledge, they may not know how to translate these ideas into day-to-day practice. McNaughton argued in 1998 that *Te Whāriki* lacks sufficient guidance about teaching practices, particularly "specific examples of [co-

constructivist] activities and the educator's role in these" (p. 193). I am not necessarily advocating a more prescriptive version of *Te Whāriki*, but the consequences of having a non-prescriptive curriculum document pose a persistent challenge for teachers, particularly in a sector where preparation for teaching is variable (or non-existent).

A further constraint on teacher enactment of curriculum is the lack of frequent and adequate opportunities to discuss centre curricula, and to study and reflect on *Te Whāriki*. The teachers who participated in this research met just once a month, for 1 hour, for programme planning. In this time they were expected to evaluate the previous month's plans, plan for the next month, discuss the progress of individual children, and discuss any other matters affecting their planning, such as the revision of centre policies.

Finally, the nature of the child-care day itself, and the heavy demands on teachers throughout the day, may be the aspect of teaching in child care that most effectively undermines teachers' attempts to reflect on their curriculum implementation. As the programme plan and rosters at Long Acres suggest, multiple tasks have to be repeated with multiple children throughout the day simply to ensure the children's continued physical wellbeing. These tasks are repetitive, physically demanding and create a pattern of continuous disruption to children's play. At the same time, few child-care centres provide conditions of service that allow teachers lengthy periods of non-contact time for professional learning and reflection. Although many child-care centres in New Zealand steadily improved in aspects of structural quality during the 1990s and 2000s, particularly in terms of ratios and group size (Meade et al., 2012), the ability to simply prioritise tasks from minute to minute remains the cornerstone of teacher thinking and decision making in child care.

Conclusion: Strategies for exploring curriculum co-construction within socio-cultural pedagogy

In this chapter I have identified some of the cultural tools teachers bring to the negotiation of curriculum enactment in early childhood education when curriculum is conceptualised as a process of constant co-construction, framed by social and cultural contexts. Most obviously, teachers can only negotiate their actions within the constraints and possibilities of their existing definitions of curriculum. The theoretical bases, ideological positions, curriculum models and other cultural tools to which the teachers have been exposed during their teacher education and ongoing professional development inevitably mediate these symbolic exchanges. I have also described some of the difficulties that may arise when teachers have to construct and enact their notions of curriculum when working as a group. But these are difficulties that can only be addressed by teachers continuing to work together and exploring their work collaboratively.

As Brown and Jones (2001) point out, teachers have an obligation to continually examine their own practice in order to identify the assumptions they hold and perpetuate. They ask, "How, then, may things be different?" but their suggestions are vague: reconsideration of "attachments to particular beliefs" so that "what might then be avoided is mindless or static adherence to self-normalizing practices" (p. 724). How might such reconsideration occur? How might teachers free themselves from this "static adherence" in order to co-construct practices that realise the socio-cultural underpinnings of *Te Whāriki*?

Some investigation of how teachers can work together to liberate themselves from ineffective ideas about curriculum construction is occurring through strategies that consciously expose the beliefs and assumptions upon which teachers' co-constructions are based. The growing use of teacher research in early childhood settings is one such strategy (e.g., Meade, 2007). Participatory action research (Mills, 2000), in particular, has become influential in the early childhood sector in New Zealand and the method for reviewing practice in centre settings advocated in Ministry-produced resources (Ministry of Education, 1998, 2000) is closely modelled on the action research 'spiral' (Kemmis & McTaggart, 1988; Mills, 2000). Action research demands a close examination of current practice and the systematic exploration of alternative strategies. Action research can also offer empirical rigour to the (sometimes ephemeral) process of reflective practice, identifying the discrepancies that arise between what teachers say they do and what they are seen to do.

A second possibility is to explicitly examine the cultural tools early childhood teachers bring to their exploration of *Te Whāriki*. For example, successful implementation of *Te Whāriki* depends upon teacher exploration of sophisticated, abstract concepts such as empowerment. As Britzman (1998) points out, discourses on empowerment frequently rely on the concept of the 'disempowered subject'. In these discourses, power is viewed as a quantum, something to be amassed for, and distributed to, the less powerful. In early childhood, such discourses position adults as 'knowing' and children as rich receptors for established discourses of power and knowledge. This model of learning is inconsistent with socio-cultural theory, which views learning as an active co-construction between children and adults.

The complex understanding required to confront discourses of empowerment/ disempowerment requires a great deal of teacher dialogue, reflection and investigation. Brown and Jones (2001) draw on the work of Foucault to explore some of "the complexities that are embedded in any discursive power relations" (p. 713) and argue that this "necessitates not only challenging dominant social practices but, additionally, it obliges the practitioner-researcher to confront his/her own complicity in such arrangements" (p. 714). Ryan and Grieshaber (2005) describe how they work with early childhood education students in their practice as teacher educators, using postmodern-inspired strategies such as engaging with visual images and situating knowledge in the historical context of its production to challenge the dominance of child-centred, developmentally appropriate orientations in early childhood teacher education.

Te Whāriki itself contains many useful reflective questions, linked to the strands and goals of the 'woven curriculum' described in the document, which serve as starting points for teacher exploration of their images of themselves and each other. Questions such as "What kinds of role do adults have when children are playing, and how do these roles promote children's learning?" (Ministry of Education, 1996, p. 84) and "What do adults do when children are excluded by others, and what effects do the adults' actions have?" (p. 66) can stimulate vigorous discussion between teachers about how they can best foster children's learning. Indeed, the metaphor of the woven curriculum—the most obvious cultural tool offered by *Te Whāriki*—offers teachers a wonderful tool with which to examine the social act of teaching itself.

References

Ayers, W. (1989). *The good preschool teacher: Six teachers reflect on their lives*. New York, NY: Teachers College Press.

Bakhurst, D. (2007). Vygotsky's demons. In H. Daniels, M. Cole, & J. V. Wertsch (Eds.), *The Cambridge companion to Vygotsky* (pp. 50–76). New York, NY: Cambridge University Press.

Blank, J. (2010). Early childhood teacher education: Historical themes and contemporary issues. *Journal of Early Childhood Teacher Education, 31*(4), 391–405.

Blumer, H. (1969). *Symbolic interactionism: Perspective and method*. Upper Saddle River, NJ: Prentice-Hall.

Britzman, D. (1998). *Lost subjects, contested objects: Towards a psychoanalytic inquiry of learning*. Albany, NY: SUNY Press.

Broström, S. (2001). Constructing the early childhood curriculum: The example of Denmark. In T. David (Ed.), *Promoting evidence-based practice in early childhood education: Research and its implications*. London, UK: JAI.

Brown, L., & Jones, A. (2001). 'Reading' the nursery classroom: A Foucauldian perspective. *International Journal of Qualitative Studies in Education, 14*(6), 713–725.

Burgess, J., Robertson, G., & Patterson, C. (2010). Curriculum implementation: Decisions of early childhood teachers. *Australasian Journal of Early Childhood, 35*(3), 51–59.

Burton, J. (1999). *Teacher dilemmas and workplace relations: Discretionary influence and curriculum deliberation in child care*. Unpublished doctoral thesis, Queensland University of Technology, Australia.

Burton, J., & Halliwell, G. (2001). Negotiating curriculum: Discretion and collaboration in teaching teams. *Curriculum Perspectives, 21*(1), 27–34.

Carr, M. (1993, March). *Choosing a model: Reflecting on the development process of* Te whāriki: *National early childhood curriculum guidelines in New Zealand*. Paper presented to the First Warwick International Early Years Conference, Warwick, UK.

Cullen, J. (1996). The challenge of *Te whāriki* for future developments in early childhood education. *Delta, 48*(1), 113–126.

Derman-Sparks, L. (1989). *Anti-bias curriculum: Tools for empowering young children*. Washington, DC: NAEYC.

Edwards, A. (2007). An interesting resemblance: Vygotsky, Mead and American pragmatism. In H. Daniels, M. Cole, & J. V. Wertsch (Eds.), *The Cambridge companion to Vygotsky* (pp. 77–100). New York, NY: Cambridge University Press.

Edwards, C. P., Gorman, G. E., & Gandini, L. (1993). *The hundred languages of children: The Reggio Emilia approach to early childhood education*. Norwood, NJ: Ablex Publishing.

Elbaz, F. (1983). *Teacher thinking: A study of practical knowledge*. London, UK: Croom Helm.

Grundy, S. (1998). The curriculum and teaching. In E. Hatton (Ed.). *Understanding teaching: Curriculum and the social context of schooling*. Sydney, NSW: Harcourt Brace.

Halliwell, G. (1992). Practical curriculum theory: Describing, improving and informing early childhood practices. In B. Lambert (Ed.), *Changing faces: The early childhood profession in Australia*. Watson, ACT: AECA.

Hatch, A. J., & Freeman, E. (1998). Kindergarten philosophies and practices: Perspectives of teachers, principals and supervisors. *Early Childhood Research Quarterly, 3,* 151–166.

Hedges, H., & Cullen, J. (2005). Subject knowledge in early childhood curriculum and pedagogy: Beliefs and practices. *Contemporary Issues in Early Childhood, 6*(1), 66–79.

Hsieh, Y., & Spodek, B. (1995, April). *Educational principles underlying the classroom decision-making of two kindergarten teachers*. Paper presented to the annual meeting of the American Educational Research Association, San Francisco, CA.

Katz, L., & Chard, S. (2000). *Engaging children's minds: The project approach*. Stamford, CT: Ablex Publishing.

Kemmis, S., & McTaggart, R. (1988). *The action research planner*. Melbourne, VIC: Deakin University Press.

May, H. (1997). *The discovery of early childhood: The development of services for the care and education of very young children, mid eighteenth century Europe to mid twentieth century New Zealand*. Auckland: Auckland University Press/Bridget Williams Books/New Zealand Council for Educational Research.

May, H. (2001). *Politics in the playground: The world of early childhood in postwar New Zealand*. Wellington: Bridget Williams Books/New Zealand Council for Educational Research.

MacNaughton, G., & Williams, G. (2008). *Techniques for teaching young children: Choices in theory and practice* (3rd ed.). Frenchs Forest, NSW: Longman.

McCormick, R., & Murphy, P. (2008). Curriculum: The case for a focus on learning. In P. Murphy & K. Hall (Eds.), *Learning and practice: Agency and identities* (pp. 3–18). London, UK: Sage Publications.

McNaughton, S. (1998). Co-constructing curricula: A comment on two curricula (*Te whāriki* and the English curriculum) and their developmental bases. *New Zealand Journal of Educational Studies, 31*(2), 189–196.

Meade, A. (2007). *Cresting the waves: Innovation in early childhood education*. Wellington: NZCER Press.

Meade, A., Robinson, L., Smorti, S., Williamson, J., Carroll-Lind, J., Meagher-Lundberg, P., et al. (2012). *Early childhood teachers' work in education and care centres: Profiles, patterns and purposes*. Wellington: Te Tari Puna Ora o Aotearoa New Zealand Childcare Association.

Mills, G. E. (2000). *Action research: A guide for the teacher researcher*. Upper Saddle River, NJ: Merrill.

Ministry of Education. (1996). *Te whāriki: He whāriki matauranga mō ngā mokopuna o Aotearoa: Early childhood curriculum.* Wellington: Learning Media.

Ministry of Education. (1998). *Quality in action: Te mahi whai hua: Implementing the revised statement of desirable objectives and practices in New Zealand early childhood services.* Wellington: Learning Media.

Ministry of Education. (2000). *The quality journey: Improving quality in early childhood services: He haerenga whai hua.* Wellington: Learning Media.

Murrow, K. (1995). *Early childhood workers' opinions on the draft document 'Te whaariki'.* Wellington: Ministry of Education.

Nuttall, J. (2002). Negotiating the meaning of curriculum: Can we awaken the 'sleeping beauty'? *Early Education, 28,* 5–9.

Nuttall, J. (2003). Early childhood curriculum in theory, ideology and practice: Using *Te whāriki. Delta, 54*(1/2), 91–104.

Nuttall, J. (2004). *Why don't you ask someone who cares?: Teacher identity, intersubjectivity, and curriculum negotiation in a New Zealand childcare centre.* Unpublished doctoral thesis, Victoria University of Wellington, Wellington.

Rockel, J. (2009). A pedagogy of care: Moving beyond the margins of managing work and minding babies. *Australasian Journal of Early Childhood, 34*(3), 1–8.

Ryan, S., & Grieshaber, S. (2005). Shifting from developmental to postmodern practices in early childhood teacher education. *Journal of Teacher Education, 56*(1), 34–45.

Shaw, P. (2009). The syllabus is dead, long live the syllabus: Thoughts on the state of language curriculum, content, language, tasks, projects, materials, wikis, blogs and the world wide web. *Language and Linguistics Compass, 3*(5), 1266–1283.

van der Veer, R. (2007). Vygotsky in context: 1900–1935. In H. Daniels, M. Cole, & J. V. Wertsch (Eds.), *The Cambridge companion to Vygotsky* (pp. 21–49). New York, NY: Cambridge University Press.

Vygotsky, L. S. (1978). *Mind in society: The development of higher psychological processes.* Cambridge, MA: Harvard University Press.

Wen, X., Elicker, J. G., & McMullen, M. B. (2011). Early childhood teachers' curriculum beliefs: Are they consistent with observed classroom practices? *Early Education and Development, 22*(6), 945–969.

Wood, E. A. (2004). A new paradigm war? The impact of national curriculum policies on early childhood teachers' thinking and classroom practice. *Teaching and Teacher Education, 20,* 361–374.

Wood, E., & Attfield, J. (2005). *Play, learning and the early childhood curriculum* (2nd ed.). London, UK: Sage Publications.

CHAPTER 10

Te Whāriki: Weaving multiple perspectives on transitions

Sally Peters and Vanessa Paki

ABSTRACT

This chapter explores issues related to the transition from early childhood education to school. *Te Whāriki*, the early childhood curriculum (Ministry of Education, 1996) aims to develop capable and competent learners by weaving together the four principles of *whakamana* (empowerment), *kotahitanga* (holistic development), *whānau tangata* (family and community) and *ngā hononga* (relationships). The strands of *Te Whāriki* align closely with valued learning at school through the key competencies, and children's interests and working theory development lead them to develop expertise in the subject areas included in *The New Zealand Curriculum* (Ministry of Education, 2007). Nevertheless, the move to school can be challenging for some children, and the approaches to learning and teaching in early childhood education and school may be very different.

This chapter is based on initial findings from a 3-year Teaching and Learning Research Initiative (TLRI) project, which is exploring children's learning journeys from early childhood education to school. We conceptualise some of the philosophical and theoretical underpinnings in *Te Whāriki* and what this approach might mean for children's transitions. The chapter draws on surveys and interviews with teachers and families to consider different voices in this process, and we examine how these different perspectives complement and challenge one another. The chapter ends by reflecting on the implications of *Te Whāriki* for weaving together effective and inclusive transition practices.

Introduction

Although *Te Whāriki* was designed for prior-to-school settings, this chapter applies a different lens to the document and explores the relevance of *Te Whāriki* for children's learning journeys as they make the move to school. On the surface this transition might appear quite straightforward. The aspirations in *Te Whāriki* are reflected in the vision for young people in *The New Zealand Curriculum* (Ministry of Education, 2007). The strands of *Te Whāriki* also align closely with valued learning at school through the key competencies, and children's interests and working theory development link to the subject areas included in *The New Zealand Curriculum*. Despite curriculum alignment and synergies, the move to school can be challenging for some children, and the approaches to learning and teaching may be very different in prior-to-school and school settings. In addition, although there is considerable research literature related to starting school (see, for example, reviews by Fabian & Dunlop, 2007; Peters, 2010), there is still much to discover about how children's learning can be enhanced during this time of both opportunity and challenge. In this chapter we argue that there is untapped potential within *Te Whāriki* in relation to this topic.

After exploring some of the more overt alignments with the school curriculum, the chapter focuses on the four principles of *Te Whāriki*: *whakamana* (empowerment), *kotahitanga* (holistic development), *whānau tangata* (family and community) and *ngā hononga* (relationships), and the implications of these for weaving effective and inclusive transition practices. In doing so we will draw on initial findings from a 3-year Teaching and Learning Research Initiative (TLRI) project, which is exploring children's learning journeys from early childhood education to school (Peters & Paki, in progress).

Understanding the transition to school

Our consideration of the transition to school is underpinned by similar socio-cultural and ecological understandings to those described in *Te Whāriki*. This approach recognises the complex interplay of personal and environmental features that help to shape transition experiences (Peters, 2010). Bronfenbrenner and Morris (1997) have identified the ways in which particular forms of interaction between a person and the environment, called proximal processes, operate over time. These interactions between person and environment vary

> as a function of the characteristics of the developing *Person*, of the immediate and more remote *environmental Contexts* and the *Time* periods in which the proximal processes take place. (p. 994, emphasis in original)

Person characteristics include dispositions, resources and demand characteristics. These interact with features of the environment that invite, permit or inhibit engagement. Earlier, Sameroff (1975) had a similar view, describing the interaction between individual and environment, whereby characteristics of both change over time. He saw development not as a set of traits but as "the *processes* by which these traits are maintained in the transactions between organism and environment" (p. 281, emphasis in the original). He argued that rather than one factor leading to a given outcome, outcomes are due to the complex interweaving of several factors. Hence, either positive or negative outcomes for a child result not from a single trait or experience, but as a function of a continuous "organism-environment transaction across time" (pp. 281-282).

When applied to the transition to school, the notion of proximal processes highlights the fact that

> the part played in this transition by any characteristic of the child and family will always depend on the nature of the context they enter. Almost any child is at risk of making a poor or less successful transition if their individual characteristics are incompatible with features of the environment they encounter. (Peters, 2010, p. 2)

Curriculum is an important feature of the contextual milieu that helps to shape the different educational settings that children and families encounter, including what is focused on and valued. In the following section we briefly examine aspects of curriculum development in both sectors.

Two decades of curriculum development

Mutch (2001), May (2001) and others have outlined the history of the development of *Te Whāriki.* This history can be considered alongside developments in the school sector. In the 1990s New Zealand was responding to international trends that led to pressure to develop a national curriculum framework for both early childhood and schools (May, 2001). The draft version of *Te Whāriki* was published in 1993 (Ministry of Education, 1993b), the same year as the *New Zealand Curriculum Framework* for schools (Ministry of Education, 1993a). The final version of *Te Whāriki* was published in 1996. English-language and te reo Māori versions of the school curriculum documents for the seven "essential learning areas" were published between 1992 and 2001 and implemented progressively from 1994 (see Ministry of Education, 2002, for details).

Much of the motivation for developing an early childhood curriculum came from a concern that not defining a curriculum would lead to the school curriculum moving downwards (May, 2001). The resulting *Te Whāriki* curriculum, developed in consultation with the early childhood community, went against the economically driven agenda of the time and "produced an alternative voice in education policy and curriculum" (Mutch, 2001, p. 83). The directors of the curriculum project credited the influential support and commitment of Māori working-group members during the development process for some of these differences (Carr & May, 1993). *Te Whāriki* was New Zealand's first bicultural curriculum development, and this is reflected in many aspects of the document, including the four principles discussed in this chapter and the five curriculum strands, each of which has an emphasis on 'mana'.

As with many Māori words, there is no straightforward translation for the concept of mana. However, Williams (1997) provided an understanding of the ideas involved through related meanings such as authority, control, influence, prestige, power, psychic force, binding, having influence, taking effect, and being effectual. Mana is both inherited and acquired throughout life. It draws on bonds with people, spiritual powers and the land (Shirres, 1997). The mana of a child is inter-related with that of the family and wider social group. Importantly, therefore, while the curriculum looks at developing mana, it also carries with it the requirement to respect the child's existing mana, because, according to Royal Tangaere (2001), to "trample on the mana of the child would place insult on the child's whānau, hapū, iwi, and ancestors" (p. 19). (Again there are no direct translations available, but for the purposes of this chapter whānau, hapū and iwi can be thought of as extended family, sub-tribe and tribe, respectively.)

In the previous edition of this book, Reedy (2003) commented that the five realms of mana in *Te Whāriki* ensured

> that the learner is empowered in every possible way … The child is nurtured in the knowledge that they are loved and respected; that their physical, mental, spiritual, and emotional strength will build mana, influence, and control; that having mana is the enabling and empowering tool to controlling their own destiny. (p. 68)

Te Whāriki drew on complex understandings of learning and development that required new ways of thinking about assessment. With the curriculum in place, Carr (2001) led the way in exploring what assessment might look like in early childhood settings. Later, the *Kei Tua o te Pae/Assessment for Learning: Early Childhood Exemplars* resource (a series of 20 booklets) was published (Carr, M., Lee, W. & Jones, C., 2004, 2007 & 2009). *Kei Tua o te Pae* provided the early childhood sector with information to support teaching and assessment that reflected the principles and strands of *Te Whāriki*. And in 2009, *Te Whatu Pōkeka: Kaupapa Māori Assessment for Learning: Early Childhood Exemplars* (Ministry of Education, 2009) was published to establish the importance of how the development and practice of cultural contexts and methods can contribute significantly to empowering Māori children.

While the early childhood sector had a period of stability, during which it was possible to consolidate and develop greater understanding of *Te Whāriki*, in the school sector, after nearly a decade of curriculum development, the Ministry of Education began a major review of the school curriculum in 2000. The findings and recommendations from this review were published in the *Curriculum Stocktake*

Report (Ministry of Education, 2002). As a result of these recommendations, the New Zealand Curriculum/Te Marautanga o Aotearoa project began redeveloping *The New Zealand Curriculum* and *Te Marautanga o Aotearoa*.[1] Just as there had been during the development of *Te Whāriki*, there was extensive consultation and sector involvement in the school curriculum project (see Rutherford, 2005, for details). This led to quite substantial changes and a much slimmer curriculum document (published in 2007 for English medium and 2008 for Māori medium), which includes all eight learning areas (as opposed to having a separate document for each).

Curriculum alignment through the key competencies

Although alignment with the school curriculum had been resisted when *Te Whāriki* was developed in the 1990s (Carr & May, 1993), in the following decade the school curriculum project opened up new possibilities to create a shared understanding of valued learning across the sectors. Early in the consultation phase the Ministry of Education proposed that the new school curriculum should include key competencies (Brewerton, 2004). This reflected the OECD's notion of competencies "that contribute to a successful life and a well-functioning society" (Rychen & Salganik, 2003, p. 54). During the curriculum consultation phase, the OECD key competencies were eventually adapted to five key competencies for the New Zealand context. These align with the five strands of *Te Whāriki*, and a diagram showing the connections from early childhood education through school to tertiary and beyond was included on p. 42 of the school curriculum (Ministry of Education, 2007).

Unlike *Te Whāriki*, the school curriculum was written in English, with the Māori-medium *Te Marautanga o Aotearoa* undergoing separate development. However, as part of the consultation process a group was commissioned by the Ministry of Education to comment on whether the proposed competencies would make sense from within a Māori world view (Macfarlane, Glynn, Grace, Penetito & Bateman, 2008). Five cultural constructs were placed alongside the five proposed key competencies, and their meanings were explored. Macfarlane et al. (2008) commented that:

> while there is evidence of some commonality in meaning between particular key competencies and particular Māori constructs, there is more evidence of where the Māori constructs did not 'match', because they were coming from quite different knowledge and value bases, and their meaning within a Māori worldview was both wider and deeper than the meaning within the majority European cultural worldview. However, these differences in meaning and understanding should not be seen as sites of conflict, but rather as opportunities for improving and enriching the quality of education of all New Zealanders, though [sic] improving the quality of education for Māori New Zealanders. (p.123)

---

1 The curriculum for Māori-medium kura (schools).

A number of teachers in different settings around the country explored what the key competencies meant for their contexts and many of their stories were shared on the Ministry of Education's curriculum websites. In research by Carr et al. (2008, p. 26), teachers from a school where Māori-medium and English-medium classes worked side by side said they felt that the key competency of *belonging* (later named *participating and contributing*) was central to learning:

> I think it is really important that they [students] do realise that they have a place here and I think if you have got the belonging part instilled in them, then the rest of these: managing self, relating to others sort of fall into place. (Frances)

> Probably, the *belonging*. That's the one in our school itself, it's deep, hōhonu [deep]. I believe that if the child knows that they *belong* in some way ... they'll just thrive, you know. Like most of the children in my class, I know their parents. So that sense of *belonging* and they know that if they play up I could just see Mum or Dad. That's that whānau, that sense of *belonging*. (Judy)

> *Belonging* is something that is very important and I feel I *belong* here, even though I am from a different culture. It is the *belonging* thing, to be part of a cultural institution, that is really, really important. (Auntie)

Curriculum alignment through working theories and learning areas

Although the links between the strands of *Te Whāriki* and the key competencies are identified in the school curriculum as the main alignment between early childhood education and school, Davis and Peters' (2011) research into *working theories* highlighted that these could potentially provide another connection (the main outcomes of *Te Whāriki* are learning dispositions and working theories; see Ministry of Education, 1996, p. 44). For example, informal contact with schools in one setting highlighted that children's interests in particular topics were engaging them in learning at school. Teachers at the beginning school level were aware that the children had been interested in these topics in early childhood and were keen to find ways of engaging with these ideas more systematically. Close examination of children's theories revealed that they were frequently more sophisticated than adults expected them to be, suggesting that paying greater attention to working theories would allow for much deeper knowledge or "islands of expertise" to be fostered than is usually anticipated for young learners (Davis & Peters, 2011; Peters & Davis, 2011). The school curriculum indicates the importance of "building on learning experience that a child brings with them" (Ministry of Education, 2007, p. 41), and greater knowledge of children's working theories seems to enhance the possibility for this to be done in a rich and meaningful way.

The principles of *Te Whāriki* and transitions

Having considered some of the potential connections between the curriculum documents (and these remain potential unless teachers and others support them to happen in practice), in the remainder of this chapter we return to *Te Whāriki* to examine how the four principles might inform transition practices. As noted earlier, we draw on data from a TLRI project *Learning Journeys from Early Childhood into School* (Peters & Paki, in progress). The quotations come from initial interviews with teachers from two schools and three early childhood centres, and surveys with their associated families/whānau and communities.

The four principles of *Te Whāriki* are *whānau tangata* (family and community), *ngā hononga* (relationships), *kotahitanga* (holistic development) and *whakamana* (empowerment). Earlier work by one of the authors (Paki, 2004, cited in Ward, 2005, pp. 41–42) explored the relevance of these principles for supporting the transition of children from kōhanga reo settings to mainstream schools. Mortlock, Plowman and Glasgow (2011) have also considered the English wording of the principles in relation to transition. Here we extend Paki's (2004) earlier discussion and embrace a deeper understanding of the principles in order to consider their relevance for the transition of all children. Although explained separately, ultimately these ideas weave together, as do the different participants' voices from our Learning Journeys research project.

Whānau tangata

The concept of whānau (extended family) encompasses the verb to be born, and the nouns 'family' and 'offspring'. 'Tangata' is human or person. Together, this first principle, whānau tangata can be described as a

> process of establishing whānau (family) relationships by means of identifying, through culturally appropriate means, your bodily linkage, your engagement, your connectedness, and therefore (unspoken) commitment to other people. (Bishop, Berryman, & Richardson, 2001, p. 41)

When considered in relation to transitions, *whānau tangata* advocates for a collective process; a place where involvement and partnership between children, parents, whānau and teachers move towards establishing a sense of belonging. *Te Whāriki* states

> children's learning and development are fostered if the well-being of their family and community is supported; if their family, culture, knowledge and community are respected; and if there is a strong connection and consistency among all the aspects of the child's world. (p. 42)

Involving parents/caregivers in their child's transition and ongoing learning, whereby families and staff become "co-educators" (Whalley & Pen Green Centre Team, 2001), activates an important partnership for effective practice. These ideas are reflected in the comments of a school principal and one of the teachers in our study, who both made a clear connection with families and communities:

> Happy children, happy parents, happy teachers, happy school. One of the queries I get asked by parents is 'How do you know my child will learn?' and I say, 'The main thing is they get happy and settled and the learning will flow'. Happiness and wellbeing is really important and that's for families as well. (Primary School Principal)

> That connection that we know who you are, so we can walk alongside you. So we can give you a buddy to come and hold your hand, or to be there if you need someone. To have that genuine caring person at the door to welcome you, to build an environment where they [children] feel comfortable. Where they come down the school corridor and they see their name tag up already, we know that they're coming, we know who they are. Not just for the child too but also for the parents, because often the parents have had not a nice experience at school, so they need to feel welcome at any stage. (Primary school teacher)

The teacher went on to add that this is no different to children with special needs:

> Again, we need to know them before they get here; we need to have met their family. We need to hear what their aspirations are for their child. Each child comes with gifts and talents whether they are labelled special needs or not; they all bring something to the culture of the classroom. So yes back to the connection, back to knowing them and hearing them. (Primary school teacher)

Strategies to try to develop knowledge of the children and their families have included sharing portfolios from early childhood education (ECE) with the school (see Hartley, Rogers, Smith, Peters, & Carr, 2012; Peters, Hartley, Rogers, Smith, & Carr, 2009), and, in the present project, sharing life-size annotated images of the child with the school. The children's friends in ECE draw an outline around the child who is about to transition. A photograph of the child's face is added onto the child's head on the drawing. Other children in the early childhood centre describe the child and his/her interests, which, along with the child's own comments, are written on to the body. ECE teachers and the child's family also add comments. These provide the schoolteachers with valuable (and easily accessible) information to facilitate building the new connections. These life-size images transition with the child to school and they have continued on with students and teachers at the primary school adding to the child's whakapapa [personal history]. An extension to this idea has lead to one of the schools exploring the possibility of having this as a transitional tool from one year to the next.

A further layering of *whānau tangata* should also consider what Darder (1998) called the role of culture, and Bourdieu (1971) refered to as "cultural capital"; these concepts suggest that individuals socialise within their family and wider contexts, where they gain linguistic and socio-cultural competencies. As children transition to school as 'individuals', they represent a set of cultural dispositions belonging to a group. Furthermore, Bronfenbrenner (1976, 1979) has argued that there are complex inter-relationships among children, their families and their communities. His view would suggest that transitions could be enhanced if there were close connections between home and educational institutions.

In the following quotation an early childhood teacher highlights the importance of culture and language and offers an example of how connections with previous cultural knowledge and competencies can be made in practice:

> When I recently went to school … it's very whānau based, and you can hear the karakia in the mornings. One of the things that I had done was while the kids were waiting on the mat was I'd pull in a waiata or two, and sing. And these children knew it and you could see that their mana was increasing. Another thing I'd done was have a karakia before kai, and the [school] teacher wanted to do it but she didn't know it, so she said 'Do you know it?' and I said 'Oh yeah ok' and I said 'Whakapiri o ringa. E te …' and out of 18 kids maybe 12 already knew it, and you could see that they were puffing themselves up. So to me, maybe a successful transition does include te reo Māori, it includes acknowledging where they come from, so we include that into our programme. It's about giving them the tools to say what they need to say. (ECE teacher)

Ngā hononga

There are strong connections between whānau tangata and the next principle ngā hononga. To hono is the process of building or breaking a relationship, rather than the relationship itself. The concept of ngā hononga centres around the process of forming relationships, where the concept of whānau (family) merged with whānaungatanga (relationships) acts as a compass such that everyone participates and contributes to the wellbeing of each other, and in particular the child (Pere, 1984; Reedy, 1995). *Te Whāriki* discusses the concept of ngā hononga and states that "children learn through responsive and reciprocal relationships with people, places and things" (p. 43). Research (Ministry of Education, 2009) also tells us that responsive and reciprocal relationships are linked to successful learning.

Transition to school is a time when new relationships are being built and the nature of these relationships has been cited as being "core to a successful transition" (e.g. Dockett & Perry, 2008, p. 275). In a review of literature on starting school, Peters (2010) highlighted research that indicates the importance of a range of relationships. Within this broad picture, the teacher-student relationship seems to be a particularly important factor in terms of the child's adjustment to school (Harrison, Clarke, & Ungerer, 2003; Murray, Waas, & Murray, 2008). Mashburn and Pianta (2006) cite a range of literature which indicates that the nature of the child's relationship with teachers is not only important at the transition time, but can have a long-lasting effect on the child's success at school. Similarly, looking at influences on achievement in schools, a meta-analysis of studies revealed that "the most critical aspects contributed by the teacher are the quality of teaching, and the nature of the student-teacher relationships" (Hattie, 2009, p. 126).

The building of other relationships is also important. Pianta (2004) proposed that the quality of the parents' relationships with teachers, with school staff and with the child's schooling may be a key indicator of the nature of a child's transition. At the same time, developing and maintaining children's friendships has been identified as a crucial aspect of a successful transition to school (Belcher, 2006; Brooker, 2008; Denham, 2006; Docket & Perry, 2005; Ladd, Herald, & Kochel, 2006; Peters, 2004).

Conversely, much unhappiness can result when there are difficulties establishing positive relationships. Of 69 parents/caregivers surveyed in our current study, the most common answer to what they felt a successful transition looked like was that children were happy at school (22 responses) and children who were eager/enthusiastic to go to school (12 responses). This was also reflected in explanations of parent aspirations, such as:

That she be happy and safe and enjoy learning and being part of the school community.

That he feels welcome and can fit in at school, that he has the skills to communicate well with others, and has a personal sense of social confidence.

To be happy in their new learning environment. To achieve to her potential, socially and academically.

To feel safe, confident and familiar enough he will know where to go for help ... Will know teacher prior to starting. Makes friends. Has the knowledge he needs to start school academically speaking.

Being proactive at establishing the kinds of relationships that support these experiences seems to be a valuable strategy for teachers. This can start early. In previous research (Peters, 2004), it appeared that a valuable contribution for later learning is made when early childhood centres empower children with relationship skills (such as how to join in play and what to do when they don't like another person's behaviour).

Establishing positive relationships between families, children and teachers can be challenging. Feedback from the 69 families regarding the schools they had experienced with all the children in their family (not just the research schools) indicated a range of experiences. For example:

[With] the first child the teacher certainly made us feel welcome but at that time there wasn't particularly a community feel at the school—the second child ... the school does have more of a community feel, the principal is always out chatting to people before and after school but 2nd child's teacher didn't make us feel very good ... It's hard to explain!

We did feel welcomed at the school, not sure about valued—when asking questions some staff almost made you feel that we asked silly questions.

I felt welcomed but not valued. I was never asked about my child— strengths/ weaknesses—I am someone who knows her the best so any information I can give would have been helpful.

I did feel valued. I was kept informed and given advice ... I was often asked how I was feeling and my thoughts regarding [child's] feelings.

I felt welcomed but I am an outgoing person so feel comfortable in most situations.

For teachers, central to the care and education of children is the building of authentic and trusting relationships and creating opportunities for partnership and collaboration. Within our project, teachers from both the early childhood and primary settings have highlighted the importance of relationships and the need to understand multiple perspectives. Building on the work of Mangere Bridge's Centre of Innovation project (see Hartley et al., 2012) they are continuing to explore ways of fostering these.

Kotahitanga

The third principle, Kotahitanga, means to bring together as one, unity. Within the context of education, the principle of *kotahitanga* reflects "the holistic way children learn and grow" (Ministry of Education, 1996, p. 14). Holistic development focuses on the concept of viewing the child as a whole rather than as separate developmental components. If we think of *kotahitanga* as speaking about the concept of wholeness, then we have a responsibility to view the holistic nature of each child as the framework that will guide our decisions. The link between *kotahitanga* and narratives focuses on the concept of understanding others for transformative praxis. In the following quote, an early childhood teacher shares her thoughts about connecting with others through what she sees as a process of narratives:

It's getting back to how we speak about people ... as well, the identity of how we speak of each other and other people and also that gives the tools to speak about yourself, so it's a whole kind of storying of a person in a particular way that leads to the helpful outcomes, isn't it? (ECE teacher)

The question here is what might transition look like from a holistic point of view? Durie's (1994) concept of an integrated "wholeness" comprising four domains, known as the 'whare tapawhā', can offer one perspective. The whare tapawhā model—based on the four walls of a house, with each side complementing each other—is a metaphor for creating balance and harmony, thus achieving complete wholeness of the child. The whare tapawhā model includes four key concepts: taha tinana (physical domain), taha hinengaro (mental domain), taha whānau (family domain) and taha wairua (matters of the spirit), where each aspect reflects the child's need to grow competent and happy in mind, body and soul. This suggests that getting to know all aspects of the child is important for teachers in both sectors, and that development in one domain (e.g., literacy) should not be at the expense of the other aspects.

Kotahitanga also directs us to consider the child's whole experience of school, not just in the classroom. Early research (e.g., Peters, 2004) indicated that challenges could arise during lunchtimes and when using the toilets. The importance of the whole experience is now acknowledged in the school curriculum, which states:

Transition to school is supported when the school:

- Fosters a child's relationship with teachers and other children and affirms their identity;
- Builds on the learning experiences that the child brings with them;
- Considers the child's whole experience of school;
- Is welcoming of family and whānau. (Ministry of Education, 2007, p. 41)

Dockett and Perry (2001) also recognised that it should include the journey to school, and school bus drivers were included in transition planning for new children.

Another view of unity links with the previous two principles because it may require the unity of all of those involved in the transition. One of the early childhood teachers explained:

> A successful transition can be like a wharenui [traditional meeting house]. The foundations that hold the wharenui to me represent the tamariki [children], whānau, teachers, and our community ... if we connect as one, support and manaaki [care for] each other then we grow together as a whānau that makes that strong foundation. When this happens the structure of the wharenui is strong and united and our learning is enriched and meaningful. Ummmmmm you know what it is ... it's about whanaungatanga [collectivism] and kotahitanga ... if we get that right ... ka ora ai te katoa [everyone is well].

Whakamana

The final principle is whakamana. When 'whakamana' is separated into 'whaka' and 'mana', 'whaka' is a prefix meaning to do something and 'mana' is translated as prestige or power (Mead, 2003). Whakamana places emphasis on the importance of empowerment for all people to develop, irrespective of their culture, gender, appearance or disability. In an educational context, the principle of *whakamana* is the acknowledgement that the child has the right to be and feel empowered as a valued and unique individual, and as an integral member of the family and community (Ministry of Education, 1996). *Whakamana* requires an act of obligation between adults to provide opportunities for the child to shape and explore his/her own understanding and to discover unlimited possibilities. The role of the teacher is to enhance the mana of all children through providing a place that respects the child and motivates them to reach their potential. As a result, we might look for learning that is appropriately stimulating and challenging.

Csikszentmihalyi (1990), who explored the concept of 'flow', found that when a person is fully immersed in what he or she is doing, characterised by a feeling of great absorption, engagement, fulfilment and skill, this is likely to create dispositions of deep motivation and intrinsic harmony, of being completely involved in an activity. However, if the skill level of the individual is higher than the activity level, the potential to push one's boundaries for growth is prohibited. The reverse is true if the activity is at a higher level than the skill level: this will cause a disruption to the state of flow, limiting the individual's progress.

Peters' (2010) review of transitions literature suggested that children's engagement in learning can be seen as an important part of a successful transition. When Carr et al. (2009) found evidence of deep engagement in new entrant classes, these episodes were characterised by a balance between ability and challenge, and there was usually plenty of time. In contrast, work that is too easy has been shown to be as problematic as work that is too hard (Belcher, 2006; Peters, 2004), especially for gifted students (Gallagher, 2005, 2006).

Empowerment cannot be based only on external and observable behaviours (Macfarlane et al., 2008). For example, achievement may be seen by many Māori as "encompassing physical, emotional, and spiritual as well as intellectual growth" (Hirsh, 1990, cited in McGee, Ward, Gibbons, & Harlow, 2002, p. 61), which link to the holistic approaches discussed under *kotahitang*a. To achieve this we must consider multiple voices as equal partners. As one teacher noted:

> It's knowing the family and what their expectations [are] as well as the child's expectations. It's about those relationships you build; I feel the relationships are the foundation of teaching.

In this project we are shifting the emphasis away from Māori students being responsible for under-achieving in education to look at how education can be delivered in the context of the vibrant contemporary Māori values and norms. Durie (2003) argued that celebrating success is important but that it is more important that Māori progress normalises success. A principal involved in the research commented:

> We're focusing on our Māori and Pasifika, and our achievement information shows they're slightly below the whole school cohort, so one of the strategies for next year is, 'How do we become more inclusive?' 'How do we help our Māori students?' We've instituted an external whānau group, we've instigated an internal whānau tikanga group and I'm going to lead that, not because of my skills but trying to give it status. (Primary School Principal)

Potentially, *whakamana* provides a tool to address disparities in a number of contexts. Within this the reflective practitioner can ensure that the child has the opportunity to "learn about the forces that shape them, the history of their people, their values and customs, their language" (Kirkness, 1992, p. 34).

Māori voices and understandings

One of the key perspectives in this chapter has been a Māori view of the four principles of *Te Whāriki*. The ideas discussed have value cross-culturally for supporting the transition from early childhood education to school. However, they also provide a specific lens for thinking about Māori children. A draft charter of the rights of the Māori child (Early Childhood Development (ECD), 2002) stated that "the Māori child requires specific and positive focus on their wellbeing as descendants of Iwi Māori" (p. 3), to "grow up in environments of nurture and care for their individual needs, talents, and aspirations; and that they may reach personal potentiality in all areas of life" (p. 4). The draft charter positioned traditional knowledge and the rights of the Māori child within a set of fundamental principles and origins of both philosophical and theoretical relevance.

It extends its interpretation by explaining the rights of the Māori child as an ethos, based on the United Nations Convention on the Rights of the Child, and connecting this to a Māori view of the fundamental principles and strands of *Te Whāriki*. The notion of the tapu and mana of the Māori child addresses the importance that the child comes from the blood descendants of "godly origins, from human origins, from earthly origins, from a unique cultural heritage, traditions, and discourse, and from universal and ancient origins" (ECD, 2002, p. 6). The four principles of *whakamana* (empowerment), *kotahitanga* (holistic development), *whanaungatanga* (family and community), and *ngā hononga* (relationships) therefore form a critical bridge to language and culture, and how the cultural transaction between early childhood and school must be reflected within the structures and practices influenced by the existence of the whole child.

Weaving together multiple perspectives

This chapter has focused on the four principles of *Te Whāriki*. In practice the principles interconnect and overlap (Ministry of Education, 2004), and these connections can be seen throughout our discussion. Within the interconnected weaving of principles the many voices involved in transition are evident. These voices require equal respect and attention or the weaving may be skewed. Interestingly, working together across sectors to develop understanding and awareness of the other partners' perspectives may lead to greater awareness of one's own practice. This is summed up in this final quotation from an early childhood teacher in our Learning Journeys project:

> We realised that aspects of shared understanding, language, meaning, pedagogies and philosophies (for all) are important in supporting a child through transitions. We

had opportunities to explore these throughout the first year of the project—exploring the key competencies, shared visits [including 'A day in the life of a teacher in the other sector' observations and conversations] and dialogue with teachers at [a local] school.

Linking the two curriculums took us on a journey, which surprisingly led us back to looking at *Te Whāriki* with fresh eyes. We realised that supporting successful transitions did not necessarily require us 'moving up' to a new curriculum, but fully embracing our own. There were benefits when using both [documents] as a lens to position the child and filter their learning. However, it is the curriculum in action and in context that ultimately makes meaning. (ECE teacher)

Conclusion

The purpose of our discussion in this chapter has been to highlight not the differences between the sectors and their respective curriculum approaches, but rather the possibilities for continuity. Whilst *Te Whāriki* was designed for prior to school settings, the aspirations for children that underpin the early childhood curriculum are a foundation for lifelong learning and are relevant across the child's life span. These aspirations are reflected in the school curriculum, which also shows alignment between the strands of *Te Whāriki* and the key competencies at school. This explicit alignment is complimented by other implicit connections. Nevertheless the transition to school can be a challenging time for children, families and teachers. The complex interaction of personal and environmental features that shape experiences means that there is a wide range of issues that impact on the nature of their learning journeys as children move to primary and beyond. Through the principles of *whakamana, kotahitanga, whānau tangata*, and *ngā hononga*, *Te Whāriki* offers a wealth of knowledge and meaning that can be used to inform transition practices.

We have deliberately unpacked and explored the Māori ideas that underpin these principles. While these may be particularly important for the success of Māori children, they highlight respect for all involved and are widely applicable. The approach recognises the importance of relationships and the value of everyone involved in transitions moving towards a deeper connection by embracing a Māori saying, that, 'ko au ko koe, ko koe ko au' meaning 'I am you, and you are I'.

Macfarlane et al. (2008) commented that *Te Whāriki* "is a clear example where theorizing in education from an indigenous worldview has had a tangible impact on the educational theory and practice of people from a dominant majority culture" (p. 108). As noted earlier, New Zealand has benefited from a period of curriculum stability in early childhood, which has allowed ongoing engagement with this theorising so that the deeper meanings and implications can emerge. Our discussion is an example of this and each engagement suggests that greater depth is possible.

Acknowledgements

We are very grateful to the Teaching and Learning Research Initiative (TLRI) for the funding to support the *Learning Journeys from Early Childhood Education into School* project mentioned in this chapter.

References

Belcher, V. (2006). *"And my heart is thinking": Perceptions of new entrant children and their parents on transition to primary school numeracy.* Unpublished master's thesis, University of Canterbury, Christchurch. Retrieved from http://hdl.handle.net/10092/1970

Bishop, R., Berryman, M., & Richardson, C. (2001). *Te toi huarewa: Effective teaching and learning strategies, and effective teaching materials for improving the reading and writing in te reo Māori of students aged five to nine in Māori-medium education.* Wellington: Ministry of Education.

Bourdieu, P. (1971). Systems of education and systems of thought. In M. F. D. Young (Ed.), *Knowledge and control* (pp. 189–207). London, UK: Macmillan.

Brewerton, M. (2004). *Reframing the essential skills: Implications of the OECD Defining and Selecting Key Competencies project.* Background paper prepared for the Ministry of Education.

Bronfenbrenner, U. (1976). *Research on the effect of day care and child development.* Washington, DC: National Academy of Science, Advisory Committee on Child Development.

Bronfenbrenner, U. (1979). *The ecology of human development: Experiments by nature and design.* Cambridge, MA: Harvard University Press.

Bronfenbrenner, U., & Morris, P. A. (1997). The ecology of developmental processes. In W. Damon & R. M. Lerner (Eds.), *Handbook of child psychology, Vol. 1* (5th ed., pp. 993–1029). New York, NY: John Wiley.

Brooker, L. (2008). *Supporting transitions in the early years.* Maidenhead, UK: Open University Press/McGraw Hill.

Carr, M. (2001). *Assessment in early childhood settings.* London: Paul Chapman.

Carr, M., Lee, W. & Jones, C. (2004, 2007, 2009). *Kei tua o te pae: Assessment for learning: Early childhood exemplars.* Books 1-20. A resource prepared for the Ministry of Education. Wellington: Learning Media.

Carr, M., & May, H. (1993). Choosing a model: Reflecting on the development process of *Te whāriki: National early childhood curriculum guidelines in New Zealand. Journal of Early Years Education, 1*(3), 7–21.

Carr, M,. Peters, S., Davis, K., Bartlett, C., Bashford, N., Berry, P., et al. (2008). *Key learning competencies across place and time: Kimihia te ara tōtika, hei oranga mō te ao.* Teaching Learning Research Initiative final report. Retrieved from http://www.tlri.org.nz/key-learning-competencies-across-place-and-time

Carr, M., Smith, A. B., Duncan, J., Jones, C., Lee, W., & Marshall, K. (2009) *Learning in the making: Disposition and design in the early years.* Rotterdam, The Netherlands: Sense.

Csikszentmihalyi, M. (1990). *Flow: The psychology of optimal experience.* New York, NY: HarperCollins.

Darder, A. (1998, April). *Teaching as an act of love: In memory of Paulo Freire.* Proceedings from the annual meeting of the American Educational Research Association (pp. 1-11). San Diego, CA.

Davis, K., & Peters, S. (2011). *Moments of wonder, everyday events: Children's working theories in action.* Teaching Learning Research Initiative final report. Retrieved from: http://www.tlri.org.nz/moments-wonder-everyday-events-how-are-young-children-theorising-and-making-sense-their-world

Denham, S. (2006). Social-emotional competence as support for school readiness: What is it and how do we assess it? *Early Education & Development, 17*(1), 57–89.

Dockett, S., & Perry, B. (2001). Starting school: effective transitions. *Early Childhood Research and Practice, 3*, 2. Retrieved from: http://ecrp.uiuc.edu/v3n2/dockett.html

Dockett, S., & Perry, B. (2005). "A buddy doesn't let kids get hurt in the playground": Starting school with buddies. *International Journal of Transitions in Childhood, 1*, 22–34.

Dockett, S., & Perry, B. (2008). Starting school: A community endeavor. *Childhood Education, 84*(5), 274–280.

Durie, M. (1994). *Kaupapa hauora Māori: Policies for Māori health: Proceedings of the Hui Ara Ahu Whakamua.* Wellington: Te Puni Kōkiri.

Durie, M. (2003). *Ngā kāhui pou = Launching Māori futures.* Wellington: Huia Publishers.

Early Childhood Development Unit/Ngā Kaitaunaki Kōhungahunga. (2002). *Te mana o te tamaiti Māori: A draft charter of the right of the Māori child.* Wellington: Author.

Fabian, H., & Dunlop, A. (2007). *Outcomes of good practice in transition processes for children entering primary school.* The Hague, The Netherlands: Bernard van Leer Foundation.

Fletcher, J., Parkhill, F., Fa'afoi, A., Tufulasi Taleni, L., & O'Regan, B. (2009). Pasifika students: Teachers and parents voice their perceptions of what provides supports and barriers to Pasifika students' achievement in literacy and learning. *Teaching and Teacher Education, 25*, 24–33.

Gallagher, G. (2005). *"They didn't stretch my brain": Challenged by chance: Factors influencing transition to school for gifted children.* Unpublished master's thesis, Flinders University, Adelaide.

Gallagher, G. (2006). Contact … or communication breakdown: The impact of parent–teacher relationships in the transition to school for gifted children. *Tall Poppies, 31*(2), 10–15.

Harrison, L., Clarke, L., & Ungerer, J. (2003, November). The role of child–teacher relationships in children's adjustment to the first year of school. *Proceedings of the Continuity and Change: Educational Transitions International Conference*, Sydney, Australia.

Hartley, C., Rogers, P., Smith, J., Peters, S., & Carr, M. (2012). *Across the border: A community negotiates the transition from EC to primary school.* Wellington: NZCER Press.

Hattie, J. A. C. (2009). *Visible learning: A synthesis of over 800 meta-analyses relating to achievement.* London, UK: Routledge.

Kirkness, V. J. (1992). *First nations and schools: Triumphs and struggles.* Toronto, Canada: Canadian Education Association.

Ladd, G., Herald, S., & Kochel, K. (2006). School readiness: Are there social prerequisites? *Early Education & Development, 17*(1), 115–150.

Macfarlane, A. (2007). *Discipline, democracy, and diversity: Working with students with behavioural difficulties.* Wellington: NZCER Press.

Macfarlane, A., Glynn, T., Grace, W., Penetito, W., & Bateman, S. (2008). Indigenous epistemology in a national curriculum framework? *Ethnicities, 8*(1), 102–127.

Mashburn, A., & Pianta, R. (2006). Social relationships and school readiness. *Early Education & Development, 17*(1), 151–176.

May, H. (2001). *Politics in the playground.* Wellington: Bridget Williams with New Zealand Council for Educational Research.

McGee, C., Ward, R., Gibbons, J. & Harlow, A. (2002). *Transition to secondary school: scoping the issues.* Hamilton: University of Waikato.

Mead, M. (2003). *Tikanga Māori: Living by Māori values.* Wellington: Huia Publishers.

Ministry of Education. (1993a). *New Zealand curriculum framework.* Wellington: Learning Media.

Ministry of Education. (1993b). *Te whāriki: Draft guidelines for developmentally appropriate programmes in early childhood services.* Wellington: Learning Media.

Ministry of Education. (1996). *Te whāriki. He whāriki mātauranga mō ngā mokopuna o Aotearoa: Early childhood curriculum.* Wellington: Learning Media.

Ministry of Education. (2002). *Curriculum stocktake report.* Wellington: Author.

Ministry of Education. (2007). *The New Zealand curriculum.* Wellington: Learning Media.

Ministry of Education (2009). *Te whatu pōkeka: Kaupapa Māori assessment for learning: Early childhood exemplars.* Wellington: Learning Media.

Mortlock, A., Plowman, N., & Glasgow, A. (2011). Transition to school: A principles approach. *New Zealand Journal of Teachers' Work, 8*(2), 94–103.

Murray, C., Waas, G., & Murray, K. (2008). Child race and gender as moderators of the association between teacher–child relationships and school adjustment. *Psychology in the Schools, 45*(6), 562–578.

Mutch, C. (2001). Contesting forces: The political and economic context of curriculum development in New Zealand. *Asia Pacific Education Review, 2*(1), 74–84.

Paki, V. (2004). *How might the four fundamental principles of the Te Whāriki curriculum support mainstream schoolteachers in the investigation of considering appropriate transition issues for children progressing from Kohanga Reo to mainstream?* Unpublished paper, University of Waikato. Hamilton.

Pere, R. R. (1984). *Te oranga o te whānau—The health of the family.* Wellington: Department of Health.

Peters, S. (2004). *"Crossing the border": An interpretive study of children making the transition to school.* Unpublished doctoral thesis, University of Waikato, Hamilton.

Peters, S. (2010). Literature review: Transition from early childhood education to school. Wellington: Ministry of Education. Retrieved from: http://www.educationcounts.govt.nz/publications/ece/78823

Peters, S., & Davis, K. (2011). Fostering children's working theories: Pedagogic issues and dilemmas in New Zealand. Early Years: International Journal of Research and Development, 31(1), 5–17.

Peters, S. & Paki, V. (in progress). *Learning journeys from early childhood education into school.* Retrieved from: http://www.tlri.org.nz/tlri-research/research-progress/cross-sector/learning-journeys-early-childhood-school

Peters, S., Hartley, C., Rogers, P., Smith, J., & Carr, M. (2009). Early childhood portfolios as a tool for enhancing learning during the transition to school. *International Journal of Transitions in Childhood, 3*, 4–15.

Pianta, R. (2004). Transitioning to school: Policy, practice, and reality. *The Evaluation Exchange,* X(2), 5–6.

Reedy, T. (1995). Knowledge and power set me free. In *Proceedings of the Sixth Early Childhood Convention, Volume 1,* (pp. 13–32). Auckland: Sixth Early Childhood Convention, Tamaki Mataurau.

Reedy, T. (2003). Tōku rangatiratanga na te mana-mātauranga: "knowledge and power set me free..." In J. Nuttall (Ed.). *Weaving* Te Whāriki. *Aotearoa New Zealand's early childhood curriculum document in theory and practice.* (pp. 51–75). Wellington, New Zealand Council for Educational Research.

Royal Tangaere, A. (1997). *Te puawaitanga o te reo Māori: Ka hua te hā o te potiki i roto i te whānau: Ko tōnei te tāhuhu o te kōhanga reo. Learning Maori together: Kohanga reo and home.* Wellington: New Zealand Council for Educational Research.

Rutherford, J. (2005). Key competencies in the *New Zealand curriculum:* Development through consultation. *Curriculum Matters, 1,* 210–227.

Rychen, D. S., & Salganik, L. H. (Eds.). (2003). *Key competencies for a successful life and a well-functioning society.* Göttingen, Germany: Hogrefe & Huber.

Sameroff, A. J. (1975). Early influences on development: Fact or fancy? *Merrill-Palmer Quarterly, 21,* 267–294.

Shirres, M. (1997). *Te tangata: The human person.* Auckland: Accent Publications.

Ward, R. (2005). *Coping with change: Transition events at school: What matters for students, caregivers and educators.* Hamilton: Wilf Malcolm Institute of Educational Research, University of Waikato.

Whalley, M., & Pen Green Centre Team. (2001). *Involving parents in their children's learning.* London, UK: Paul Chapman.

Williams, H. W. (1997). *A dictionary of the Maori language.* Wellington: Government Printer.

CHAPTER 11

Theoretical plurality in curriculum design: The many voices of *Te Whāriki* and the *Early Years Learning Framework*

Marilyn Fleer

ABSTRACT

Internationally, *Te Whāriki* has had an enormous impact on curriculum development in many countries, including Australia. Yet the original research it drew upon for its development and eventual publication in 1996 is clearly quite old. So is it dated? Is *Te Whāriki* a timeless piece, or has it become a relic of the past, living on in practice in Aotearoa New Zealand? Drawing upon published material about *Te Whāriki*, this chapter undertakes a critical theoretical comparison of the research and concepts that inform both this curriculum and the recently released *Early Years Learning Framework* in Australia. There is diversity of theories in both curricula, and this chapter discusses what this might mean for early childhood education in both countries. As a result, it becomes possible to see how *Te Whāriki* was, and still is, a highly significant document that has transformed the landscape of early childhood education in Aotearoa New Zealand.

Introduction

This chapter presents a critical theoretical comparison of the research and concepts that inform *Te Whāriki* (Ministry of Education, 1996) in Aotearoa New Zealand and the *Early Years Learning Framework* (DEEWR, 2009) in Australia. This involves examining the theories that have informed each curriculum, followed by an analysis of how these theories 'speak' to each other, in order to illuminate the curriculum content, the principles that drive their design and the practices that are privileged in each.

Te Whāriki has gained international prominence as a substantial early childhood curriculum of great importance (Cullen, 2008), and its influence can be seen early on in Australia (see A. Roantree, ACT Department of Education and Community Services, personal communication, 2000; Wilks, Nyland, Chancellor, & Elliot, 2008), Denmark (Olsen, 1996, cited in Carr & May, 2000), Germany (Keesing-Styles, 2002) and Norway (Sobstad, 1997, cited in Carr & May, 2000). Although curriculum writers look for different things when analysing curricula (McLachlan, Fleer, & Edwards, 2010), there has been sufficient sustained interest in *Te Whāriki* for international researchers to ask why this document has been so enduring.

The draft version of *Te Whāriki* only remained in circulation for 3 years, and the substantial reference list never made it through to the final published version (Hedges, 2011), yet the many voices of the early childhood community and the diversity of views of child development and pedagogy reflected in the reference list are still with us, like shadows from the past. *Te Whāriki* grew out of a particular cultural and political context (see Duhn, 2006; McLachlan 2011; Mitchell, 2011; Ritchie, 2011; Te One, this volume) and provided a new theoretical direction for early childhood education for the whole of Aotearoa New Zealand (McLachlan 2011; Rameka, 2011; Ritchie, 2008, 2011; Ritchie & Buzzelli 2012; White, 2011). The community was exposed to a curriculum of some sophistication, incorporating broadly based concepts, which meant that an ongoing dialogue around the particularities had to take place within the field if implementation of its intent was to be successful when it was first developed (see Cullen, 1996; Dalli, 2011), and more recently in relation to the concept of working theories (see Hedges, 2010; 2011; Hedges & Cullen, 2005).

It is through dialogue that the curriculum becomes a living document and reaches out into the professional community, giving new perspectives to practice, such that "individuals and centres develop their own curriculum pattern through a process of talk, reflection, planning, evaluation and assessment" (Carr & May, 2000, p. 59). This dialogue has been actively fostered through many innovations, including research programmes and resources (Meade, 2007), as well as ongoing professional development (McLaughlin, 2011) of Aotearoa New Zealand's teachers. However, as noted by Duhn (2006), "*Te Whaariki's* effectiveness as a progressive curriculum depends on teachers' interpretation of it" (p. 196), and on opportunities for engaging in collaborative research and professional learning (see Hedges, 2011) to afford deeper understanding.

Duhn (2006) has suggested that "As a teaching tool, *Te Whaariki* has been widely accepted without much criticism or even critical engagement" (p. 191). Alvestad, Duncan and Berge (2009) have argued that a reliance on the "Principles and Strands can run the risk of teachers simply repeating and reinforcing their traditional practice" (p. 12). Similarly, Cullen (2008) has stated that

> Because *Te Whāriki* is principled rather than prescriptive it relies heavily on teacher qualities to guide teaching practices. Hence it attracts an ideological commitment from teachers, rather than a primary focus on programmes that are grounded in evidence of children's learning. (p. 10)

These are strong critiques by scholars in Aotearoa New Zealand. However, these researchers all point to the importance of the support that surrounds the implementation of a curriculum generally, but particularly for such a sophisticated curriculum framework as *Te Whāriki* (Alvestad, Duncan, & Berge, 2009; McLaughlin, 2011; Meade, 2007).

This has resonance for curriculum development in Australia, where Sumsion et al. (2009) have argued that the *Early Years Learning Framework* (*EYLF*), with its streamlined form, also requires continued dialogue and ongoing expansion of the central concepts through research and theoretical scholarship. The *EYLF*, as a principled curriculum framework, can learn from the critiques by Aotearoa New Zealand authors. These authors have highlighted not just the importance of teacher knowledge, but also the multi-theoretical foundations used (Hedges, 2011), whereby significant gains in practice have resulted from innovative and world-leading policies for supporting ongoing practice (see Alvestad, Duncan, & Berge, 2009).

An exploration of the foundational theories that underpin both curricula will be undertaken in this chapter, drawing upon concepts from cultural-historical theory[1] in order to ask: What can we still gain from *Te Whāriki*, and how does this matter for curriculum development elsewhere? This chapter does not seek to position one curriculum framework in relation another, but rather to learn from the experiences of Aotearoa New Zealand in relation to the challenges that are yet to face teachers and researchers in Australia. Through highlighting both the successes and the challenges identified by Aotearoa New Zealand authors, both countries benefit from this reflection.

---

1 *Socio-cultural* is the label usually applied when drawing upon North American research and scholarship (e.g., Wertsch), and the term *cultural-historical* is used when drawing upon Russian scholarship and research.

Methodological note

The analysis undertaken and reported in this chapter treats curriculum documents, and the curriculum writers' papers and other authors' work, as data. A search of available writings on *Te Whāriki* was undertaken, and from this pool articles related to both the longstanding and recent thinking of authors from Aotearoa New Zealand were selected. In particular, papers that presented a Māori perspective, those that discussed theoretical underpinnings, and those that detailed the curriculum's developmental processes were examined more closely. Some articles duplicated what had been said elsewhere and were not used. The first and the final curriculum were carefully examined.

I acknowledge that as a researcher from outside Aotearoa New Zealand it will never be possible for me to fully understand the context in which *Te Whāriki* evolved, or indeed to appreciate the importance of one article above another from an insider's perspective. As a result, some articles that are important, or weighted more highly by particular scholars within Aotearoa New Zealand, may not appear to an outsider to hold the same significance. Nevertheless, ethnographic research has demonstrated over the years that an outsider's perspective may offer some new insights compared to those who live in a culture, and who may no longer see aspects of the fabric of their existence or historical background.

Te Whāriki beyond its time: the importance of kaupapa Māori

Duhn (2006) argues that

> *Te Whaariki* marked a milestone for early childhood education in Aotearoa/New Zealand. Not only was it the first national curriculum for the sector, but it was also the first national curriculum to 'represent and reflect Māori politics and pedagogy' (Te One, 2003, p. 24). (p. 195)

The *EYLF* in Australia was also the first national curriculum for early childhood professionals. Prior to this a diversity of curricula were used across most states and territories. *Te Whāriki* was developed much earlier than the *EYLF*, yet in Aotearoa New Zealand the same document is still being used, despite most curricula around the world only having a shelf life of about 5 years before there is a period of renewal (McLachlan, Fleer, & Edwards, 2010). This is evidence that *Te Whāriki* was ahead of its time.

Twenty years down the track there is now a growing sophistication in the field of early childhood education in relation to many of the concepts inherent in the document, concepts that Cullen (1996) warned would be difficult to implement without support. So is *Te Whāriki* still sufficiently contemporary to be useful to practitioners? Are the original concepts still ahead of their time? White et al. (2007) found when undertaking close analysis of the national curriculum document, that

Aotearoa New Zealand's early childhood services are guided by multiple and sometimes conflicting cultural and theoretical frameworks. (p. 94)

Yet it is this diversity that is so highly valued in Aotearoa New Zealand, as Reedy (2000) originally stated:

[We sought] Inspiration beyond these lands because we thought that *Te Whāriki* was an ideal name allowing people to weave whatever learnings they might want to have for the children. *Te Whāriki* allows you to have different patterns and *Te Whāriki* allows you to have different colours. We thought a curriculum should have all these things available to it so that any one and everyone can create their own curriculum. (Video interview with Tilly Reedy, 2000)

The joint contributions of Māori and Pākehā to *Te Whāriki* have ensured that two voices have come together in ways that give equal value to these world views. In bringing together two voices, the tools of two cultures are also brought together. Bakhtin (in Holquist, 1981, cited in Wertsch, 1998) wrote that when we speak we are borrowing, or renting, the words of others:

When borrowing, or 'renting' (Holquist, 1981), the words of others, Bakhtin viewed those words as being only 'half someone else's' (1981, p. 293) and hence half the speaker's. He went on to state that the speaker populates the words of others 'within his own intention, his own accent'. (Wertsch, 1998, p. 56)

The words that were articulated by the groups who were consulted in the development of *Te Whāriki* represented much more than what they said. Most cultural tools are historically situated. Wertsch has argued that for every utterance made, two voices are always present: the voice of the speaker and the voice of the speaker's culture, belief system, and value system: "cultural tools are historically situated, and this history typically leaves its traces on mediational means and hence on mediated action (Wertsch, 1998, p. 63).

Te Whāriki represents the strong voices of both Pākehā and Māori. In foregrounding Māori voices, we find that the traditional perspective of early childhood education—as a dominant Western discourse—has been rightfully counterbalanced by a Māori voice. Not only is this important for sanctioning other world views, but it has had the effect of watering down the impact of what has in some circles been referred to as "the early childhood police" (B. Raban, University of Melbourne, personal communication, 2002), whereby traditional early childhood values, beliefs and history have reproduced themselves throughout history. 'Category maintenance' by the establishment ensures that anyone who dares to step outside of the 'accepted voice' is sharply reprimanded. *Te Whāriki*, through the sanctioning of 'other voices', has allowed for new ways of thinking, acting and being to be recorded. Interestingly, this second category maintenance voice is not always recognised or its role fully understood. Wertsch (1998) suggests that "we are unreflective, if not ignorant, consumers of a cultural tool" (p. 29).

Wertsch (1998) has also spoken of "fossilised forms of behaviour", arguing that they are ever present in all interactions. In bringing together different world views to form *Te Whāriki*, fossilised forms of traditional practice within the broader early childhood community are more likely to be contested:

> By using the cultural tools provided to us by the socio-cultural context in which we function we usually do not operate by choice. Instead, we inherently appropriate the derministic screens, affordances, constraints, and so forth associated with the cultural tools we employ. (Wertsch, 1998, p. 55)

In bringing together two world views in the development of *Te Whāriki*, not only does the curriculum speak beyond the cultural tools of the Western élite, but also moves beyond a monocultural curriculum so prevalent elsewhere in early childhood education, with the latter always privileging one group above another (see Cullen, 2001). As Wertsch states:

> A central issue is whether consumers belong to the powerful and cultural elite, in which case they use cultural tools belonging to their group, or whether they belong to marginal groups or a counterculture, in which case they use cultural tools belonging to others. (Wertsch, 1998, p. 147)

What has made *Te Whāriki* unique has been the foregrounding of two cultural voices in the document. But this has not been without its challenges, as noted by Ritchie (2008): "This, then, is the challenge to early childhood services in this country—to move beyond complacent, tokenistic, colonised and recolonising discourses" (p. 206). Research by Ritchie (2011) suggests that enacting Māori knowledges through practice still represents a major challenge to the field, but that

> Dialogue and reflection are tools to expose the ongoing colonialist baggage that we continue to carry and perpetuate unless we challenge ourselves and each other on an ongoing basis. (p. 100)

The challenges of bicultural voices in Aotearoa New Zealand

The consultative phase in the development of *Te Whāriki* foregrounded the importance of a bicultural approach and a deep respect for te Tiriti o Waitangi (the Treaty of Waitangi), while acknowledging—but not necessarily drawing upon— theories and concepts from Pacific Island peoples. As originally noted by Ritchie (2002):

> Their strategy included wide and in-depth consultation with many participants representing the diversity of the early childhood sector in this country, and in partnership with the National Te Kohanga Reo Trust represented by Tilly and Dr Tamati Reedy. (p. 32)

In this process, important Māori voices were brought to the fore. In particular, it has been noted that the contribution of Tilly and Tamati Reedy was an important part of defining *Te Whāriki* (see also Chapters 1 and 2, this volume):

> The partnership with Māori articulated through the participation of Tilly and Tamati Reedy, and the wider consultation with Māori they facilitated, ensured that a commitment to Te Tiriti o Waitangi was a foundational tenet of the document. (Ritchie, 2002, p. 33)

The final version of the curriculum places up front the importance of te Tiriti o Waitangi, as noted in the introduction to *Te Whāriki*:

> This is a curriculum for early childhood care and education in New Zealand. In early childhood educational settings, all children should be given the opportunity to develop knowledge and an understanding of the cultural heritages of both partners to Te Tiriti o Waitangi. The curriculum reflects this partnership in text and structure. (Ministry of Education, 1996, p. 9)

The bicultural focus of the curriculum design process from its very roots signals to the whole early childhood community—in Aotearoa New Zealand and internationally— that the dominant Western curriculum discourse must not be placed centre stage in the document, but should sit alongside Māori curriculum perspectives. As Duhn (2006) states, "*Te Whaariki* is a bicultural document and the guiding principles are informed by Maori aspirations for children" (p. 200). *Te Whāriki* shows this emphasis clearly by showing the Māori and English concepts alongside each other, such as:

Mana atua   Well-being

Mana whenua   Belonging

Mana tangata   Contribution

Mana reo   Communication

Mana aoturoa   Exploration

(Ministry of Education, 1996)

The authors of *Te Whāriki* clearly state that these concepts are not exact parallels, but that there are similarities between them, and in writing in Māori and in English they have signalled to the early childhood community the importance of language as a conceptual tool for navigating complex, rich and culturally contextualised principles that cannot be easily translated. Reedy (1995, cited in Ritchie, 2002) argues that the bicultural paradigm expressed in *Te Whāriki* foregrounds

> the transmission of many cultural values, my language and tikanga, and your cultural values language and customs. It validates my belief system and your belief system also (Reedy, 1995: 17). (p. 36)

Ritchie, drawing upon post-colonial theory, powerfully states that:

Post-colonial theory, in offering us the challenge of theorising 'a process of disengagement with the whole colonial syndrome' (Hulme, 1995, p. 120, in Loomba, 2005, p. 21), seeks to uncover or discover patterns of knowing, being and doing that refute the will to reinscribe the colonizing mindset. Modernist, secular, positivist assumptions give sway to respectful engagement with opportunities that create the 'meadows of possibilities' (Duhn, 2007), allowing for subjective positionings that are validating Māori identities and knowledges. (Ritchie, 2008, p. 208)

While researchers in Aotearoa New Zealand have celebrated the success of *Te Whāriki*, Cullen (2001) insightfully noted early on the problematic nature of implementation when she said that "It is not easy for teachers to recognise and support diverse cultural beliefs and practices' the problem is how to translate it into everyday practices" (Cullen, 2001, p. 6). Ritchie (2008) has also noted this challenge, stating that in meeting the

requirements of the early childhood curriculum, non-Māori teachers have struggled to offer more than token smatterings of Māori language and other content, some mindful of the potential to offend Māori with inaccurate offerings. (p. 203)

The problem, according to Duhn (2006), appears to be that

teachers understood *Te Whaariki* as a reinforcement of their practice ('It's what we do anyway.'), without critically examining their practice in light of *Te Whaariki*. (p. 197)

Duhn suggests that:

As a curriculum framework, *Te Whaariki* functions as a descriptive rather than a prescriptive model. This means that unless teachers make a conscious decision to interpret the document as a challenge to existing power relations by, for example, empowering parents to advocate for their children (Keesing-Styles, 2002) within their communities and, on the next level, within New Zealand society, *Te Whaariki* supports existing power relations by default … With its highly flexible structure and non-prescriptive approach, *Te Whaariki* does not challenge teachers to develop teaching practices from a critical perspective. Rather than enabling teachers directly to work from, for example, social justice perspectives, *Te Whaariki* appears to assume that all teachers will address issues of diversity through their individual interpretations of the curriculum. (Duhn, 2006, p. 196)

Duhn (2006) further suggests that "The possibility of different, perhaps conflicting, interpretations of *Te Whaariki* highlights that power relations are omnipresent in the document" (p. 200). It is only in recent times that these power relations have become more openly contested (e.g., Ritchie, 2008).

Biculturalism in curriculum is more than words: it also represents teacher action. Early on in the implementation of *Te Whāriki*, Cullen (2001) argued that bicultural curriculum statements should be more than rhetoric and that there was a huge gap between these in Aotearoa New Zealand:

The discourse identified in these responses highlights language that has become part of early childhood education rhetoric in New Zealand since the introduction of the national curriculum. In particular, Te Whaariki is used as a rationale for 'accepting all cultures', 'expressing culture' or 'acknowledging family and values' while in reality these explanations do not always correspond to teaching practices (Cullen & Bevan-Brown, 1999). There can be a gap between curriculum discourse and reality which may not be easy to bridge. (Cullen, 2001, p. 6)

Seven years on Cullen (2008) reflected that with the release of *Te Whāriki* came "an impressive amount of Ministry-funded research and development activity aimed at supporting teachers to work effectively with the new curriculum" (p. 9), and noted that the subsequent activity and resource development saw "positive international attention for its focus on diversity and associated research initiatives to develop a socio-cultural pedagogy" (p. 9).

In contrast, the *EYLF* in Australia acknowledges indigenous knowledge systems and ways of knowing, but does not reflect these through a bicultural document. Rather, it suggests that a range of knowledge systems and ways of belonging, being and becoming should be supported. *Te Whāriki,* as a bicultural document, signals through the way it has been conceptualised and written that the knowledge systems of Māori and Pākehā are to be equally valued. Despite the challenges of enacting a sophisticated bicultural curriculum in practice, biculturalism is an enduring design principle that means *Te Whāriki* still leads the way on the international curriculum stage.

Theoretical plurality embedded in curricula in Aotearoa New Zealand and Australia

White et al. (2007) wrote that "The eclectic theoretical underpinnings of *Te Whaariki* reflect Aotearoa New Zealand's diverse society" (p. 94). Carr and May (2000) acknowledged the theoretical roots of the current curriculum as being informed not only by local and cultural informants, but also by originally including 10 pages of "annotated footnotes and references from the national and international literature" (Carr & May, 2000, pp. 60–61). In closely examining the footnotes and the way in which *Te Whāriki* was originally framed through the use of headings such as those shown below, it is evident that the earlier writings were very much influenced by developmentally appropriate practice (Bredekamp, 1987); indeed a whole section is devoted to this perspective:

The early childhood curriculum –
- Humanly appropriate experiences
- Nationally appropriate experiences
- Culturally appropriate experiences

- Developmentally appropriate experiences
- Individually appropriate experiences
- Educationally appropriate experiences.

(Ministry of Education, 1993, n.p.)

However, the authors also drew upon a broad range of literature, including: Bronfenbrenner, 1979; Claxton, 1990; Donaldson, 1978; Donaldson, Grieve, & Pratt, 1983; Gardner, 1983; Paley, 1990; Penn, 1991; Piaget & Inhelder, 1969; Schweinhart, Barnes, & Weikart, 1993; Tizard, 1986; Vygotsky, 1978; and Wells, 1987. These references support the claim made later by the authors that *Te Whāriki* was genuinely located within the international literature as a voice guiding, framing and legitimising the curriculum (see Carr & May, 1993a, 1993b, 1994, 1996, 1997, 2000).

Yet others have suggested that the primary perspective of *Te Whāriki* is socio-cultural, as observed by Cullen (2001) when she stated that "*Te Whaariki*, the early childhood education curriculum, has come to be viewed as a socio-cultural curriculum" (Cullen, 2001, p. 1); and as noted by Ritchie in 2002:

> The theoretical base to the document can be situated within the wider arena of socio-cultural educational theory, as espoused by Wertsch (1995a), Rogoff (1990, 1995, 1998) and others. (Ritchie, 2002, p. 32)

Similarly, Hedges (2010) states that the "curriculum draws on multiple theoretical perspectives but has been recently interpreted largely from a socio-cultural perspective (see Carr, 2001; Ministry of Education, 2004)" (p. 300). In the original draft, references to the work of Vygotsky can be found in the extended footnote at the back of the document.

However, this diversity of theory also has its problems. In order to deal with this diversity—and therefore the lack of theoretical clarity—in *Te Whāriki*, we see a merging of theories, as Nuttall (2003) signals when she brings together socio-cultural theory (Wertsch, 1995a) with constructivist theory:

> The socio-cultural constructivist bases of Te Whaariki mean that it is up to teachers to negotiate their role, including those practices that they consider more or less appropriate in implementing a socio-culturally based curriculum. (Nuttall, 2003, p. 3)

Ritchie (2002), in drawing upon the uniqueness of the Māori perspective in *Te Whāriki*, also highlighted some of the original tensions when she stated that early childhood teachers would be "working at the level of family/whanau rather than being solely child-focused" (Ritchie, 2002, p. 36), where the latter (child-focused) approach was historically more constructivist-driven. Ritchie acknowledges the importance of the collective rather than concentrating always on the individual. The tension between a developmental perspective and a cultural-historical (Vygotsky, 1998) or socio-cultural (Wertsch, 1995b) view was played out early, as noted by Nuttall

(2003) when she described the range of theories invoked by a group of teachers in her doctoral research:

> References to theories of development included: 'So that's cooperative play' (stage theories); a comment about a child's 'phobia' (psychodynamic theory); and 'I'd like to put [on the planning sheet] … gender awareness. Non-gender specific roles' (gender theory). Some general principles in early childhood curriculum implementation were also discussed; 'Yes, but it's quite different from primary or secondary where they are set curriculum' (curriculum theory); 'areas' of play (based on Piagetian, free-play approaches); 'core curriculum'; and the general issue of striking a balance between 'teacher directed' (behaviourist) approaches, and 'ideas emerging from the children' (constructivist approaches). At another meeting, the same group referred to theories of applied behaviour analysis, including discussing the kinds of 'treats' they might offer as 'rewards' to compliant children. (Nuttall, 2003, p. 9)

These tensions continue but are now better understood, as Ritchie (2008) comments:

> The socioculturally framed early childhood curriculum, Te Whāriki, albeit under-layered by its historical roots in Western early childhood theories including undercurrents of developmentalism (Duhn, 2007), holds potential for generating early childhood practices that reflect ethical possibilities for moving beyond historical imbalances (Gandi, 1998). (Ritchie, 2008, p. 203)

And, as Duhn (2006) has noted:

> *Te Whaariki*'s reputation as a progressive early childhood curriculum rests particularly on its ability to accommodate diverse perspectives. For example, *Te Whaariki* promotes both universal and socioculturally specific approaches to early years education through its commitment to key theorists from developmental psychology as well as from sociocultural perspectives. (Duhn, 2006, p. 196)

Clearly there are many theoretical voices present in *Te Whāriki*. This is both a strength and a weakness. It is a strength in the way it moved the discourse of early childhood education away from a universal perspective of 'developmental' early childhood education (Dahlberg, Moss, & Pence, 1999). It is a weakness because of the potential for confusion or misinterpretation. Are these voices in harmony? Are they discordant? Are some voices louder and therefore more privileged? Are some voices so soft that they are not heard? As Hedges (2010) has noted in her research, teachers can have difficulties in "appropriating a new theoretical discourse (sociocultural theory), when they have been embedded in another (developmental psychology) that mediates understanding of the new theory" (p. 308).

This difficulty is not specific to Aotearoa New Zealand: this challenge has also emerged over the same period in Australia (see Fleer, 2010; Fleer & Richardson, 2004). In Australia, the *EYLF* actively advocates for using a broad range of theories, and according to Giugni (2011) this invites deliberate theoretical musing when drawing upon the *EYLF*:

> I deliberately explored my practice first and then turned to the *EYLF* to begin mapping: firstly mapping my practices against the *EYLF* and secondly mapping the *EYLF* against my practice. This afforded me the opportunity to look for the 'leakages' (Deleuze, 1993) that trickled out between the dominant discourses of early childhood that produce the *EYLF* and those I was enacting in my practice. (Giugni, 2011, p. 13)

Theoretical complexity has been designed into the *EYLF* and, as in Aotearoa New Zealand, this has generated a great deal of resource development and professional learning programmes in order to actively support teachers in coming to understand theoretical diversity.

The complexity of *Te Whāriki* and of the *EYLF* arises because of the range of theoretical perspectives that are presented in one document. Back in 1996, 1999, and again in 2001 and 2008, Cullen argued that many teachers originally did not have the necessary theoretical knowledge to fully appreciate the complexity of *Te Whāriki*, and therefore to make use of the document as intended by its authors. Because *Te Whāriki* was written to take account both of local voices and of the international literature, some discordance can be found, such as when the importance of the individual and the importance of the collective are considered. The disjunction between individual and collective could, however, be viewed as an important professional learning opportunity for examining what Duhn (2006) has called the 'meadows in between'. The *EYLF* also affords this challenge, one that the authors have embraced as important for helping professionalise the field (see Sumsion & Wong, 2011). White (2011) nicely captures the importance of positioning the curriculum as a contested document when she says:

> Taking the view of curriculum as a constant ideological battle between order and certainty versus dissensus and disruption makes it possible to engage with and highlight practices and their underlying orientations that are lodged somewhere within the living curriculum. (p. 2)

The shift in curriculum design in Aotearoa New Zealand has signalled a movement away from focusing only on the child and their interests to considering culture as the focus. For instance, from a cultural-historical perspective (Vygotsky, 1987), curriculum is underpinned by the view that children learn with and use the community's tools for thinking and learning. As such, the community's tools become the focus, not just what is of interest to the child (see also Hedges, 2010). One of the interesting features of *Te Whāriki* is the way in which the authors have tried to capture a more community-oriented view of the child's interest through incorporating wellbeing, belonging, contributing, communication and exploration. In the introduction to Part A of *Te Whāriki*, a cultural-historical reading is given:

The curriculum emphasises the critical role of socially and culturally mediated learning and of reciprocal and responsive relationships for children with people, places, and things. Children learn through guided participation and observation of others, as well as through individual exploration and reflection. (Ministry of Education, 1996, p. 9)

However, the authors write from a more developmental perspective:

It is about the individual child. Its starting point is the learner and the knowledge, skills, and attitudes that the child brings to their experiences. (Ministry of Education, 1996, p. 9)

Both a developmental and a sociocultural (Wertsch, 1995b) or cultural-historical (Vygotsky, 1987) perspective are foregrounded in *Te Whāriki* (see Cullen, 1996; 2001; Hedges, 2010; McNaughton, 1996; Smith, 1992, 1996). Finding this tension within *Te Whāriki* is not surprising. In addition, the strength of consulting with the whole community for the development of *Te Whāriki* is at the same time both an advantage, as described earlier, and a disadvantage, because when the starting point is 'existing practice' it is difficult to move outside the reproduction of existing values and beliefs, as noted by Cullen (1996) and McNaughton (1996). According to Cullen (1996),

the valuable and intensive consultation process which produced the document (*Te Whaariki*, 1993; 1996) meant that an outmoded developmental philosophy informed by current practices had been maintained. (p. 192)

Over 20 years have passed and the field has moved on from these original binaries, so that we now find a much deeper knowledge of sociocultural or cultural-historical theory evident within the profession (see Anning, Cullen, & Fleer, 2009; Fleer, 2010; Hedges, 2010). As has been shown by Hedges (2011) and White (2011), teachers are now in a stronger position to manage the diversity of theories that can inform curriculum and curriculum implementation, and the huge investment in research and professional learning in Aotearoa New Zealand (McLachlan, 2011) has had a significant impact on teacher engagement with new theories and practices (e.g., Meade, 2007). Developmental theories are positioned as representing thinking from the past and are no longer debated. Once again, we see that the original move away from developmental theory in *Te Whāriki* signals how innovative the curriculum was when it was first developed—even though there is a residue of developmentalism within it.

Diversity of theories also underpins the *EYLF* in Australia, with a developmental position acknowledged but not heavily drawn upon. This chapter now turns to an analysis of the Australian curriculum development context in relation to the theoretical plurality that was designed into the document from the onset of its development. This will provide a point of contrast in order to better understand the current curriculum development context in which Aotearoa New Zealand and Australia co-exist.

Theoretical plurality in early childhood curriculum in Australia

The *Early Years Learning Framework* explicitly advocates "Different theories about early childhood [in order to] inform approaches to children's learning and development" (DEEWR, 2009, p. 11). In Australia, educators draw upon a diverse range of theories to inform their work (Sumsion et al., 2009), including critical and poststructural perspectives, as well as developmental, cultural-historical and socio-behavioural theories of children's development (see Salamon, 2011) to open up multiple possibilities (see also Goodfellow, 2009).

The diversity of theories that are acknowledged in the *EYLF* is shown in Table 11.1 (with some text drawn from DEEWR, 2009, p. 11). What is immediately evident from this summary is the broad spectrum of theories now used within the field and in the academy. Blaise (2009) has coined the term 'postdevelopmental', which is useful in an analysis of the *EYLF*. A deliberate aim in the *EYLF is* to foreground both developmental and post-developmental theories. As a result of the writers making explicit these theories in the document, the field has engaged in discussion, professional learning, resource development, reading of publications, and explanations of what these theories might mean for planning children's learning and development. Giugni (2011) suggests that the *EYLF* "call[s] for early childhood educators to engage with theory in their everyday practice" (p. 11) and that it challenges them to explicitly choose theories "as a way to talk about practice in new ways" (p. 13). This is directly in line with Ritchie (2008), who suggests that *Te Whāriki* is a tool to engage teachers in new ways with their practices.

Table 11.1: Diversity of theories informing practice in Australia	
Foundational theory	**For informing practice**
Developmental theories	The focus is on describing and understanding the process of change, usually framed around age or stages of predetermined development. Traditional child development domains are usually foregrounded (e.g., social-emotional, cognitive, language, physical).
	"[in a] developmental discourse of early childhood education, the teacher is positioned as someone who sets up developmentally appropriate experiences and provides children with choices and the opportunity to take some authority over their learning. The teacher is a facilitator of children's learning through play. However, within a feminist post-structuralist disclosure, the early childhood teacher is positioned as an interventionist; a teacher 'who takes a proactive and explicit political stance with children against social inequities' (Ryan & Oshner, 1999, p. 15)." (Ortlipp, Arthur, & Woodrow, 2011, p. 57)

Socio-behaviourist theories	"Focus on the role of experience as shaping behaviour." (DEEWR, 2009, p. 11)
Sociocultural or cultural-historical theories	*Sociocultural* is the label usually applied when drawing upon North American research and scholarship (e.g., Wertsch, 1995b); *cultural-historical* is the term used when drawing upon Russian scholarship and research (e.g., Vygotsky, 1987).
	"Processes of change foreground cultural development through children's social situation of development in families and other community interactions and relationships." (DEEWR, 2009, p. 11)
	Ortlipp, Arthur and Woodrow (2011) state that "Early childhood teachers who see themselves as someone who 'scaffolds' children's learning, someone who works with children within their 'zone of proximal development' and leads children's learning rather than following it can be seen to be taking up socio-cultural discourses of education and the subject positions made available within those discourses." (pp. 57–58)
Critical theories	"Invite teachers to challenge assumptions about curriculum, and consider how their decisions may affect children differently." (DEEWR, 2009, p. 11)
Post-structuralist theories	These theories offer insights into issues of power, equity and social justice in early childhood settings. Millei and Sumsion (2011) give the example that in earlier drafts of the *Early Years Learning Framework* (citing DEEWR, 2008, p. 8) "the document [creates] a 'space for politics and power relations, [problematising through the curriculum] where children are excluded on the basis of gender, age, size, skin colour, proficiency with English, class, ethnicity, sexuality and more' (p. 8). It [the Early Years Learning Framework] prescribes that the role of the educator is to 'work with children to challenge power assumptions and create play experiences that promote equity, fairness and justice" (p. 8). (Millei & Sumsion, 2011, p. 74)

These theories are incorporated within the document to serve as tools to help early childhood educators in their thinking about and planning for child development and learning, and can be loosely divided into developmental and post-developmental theories. Developmental theories include those theories that use age as a central criterion for defining development (e.g., milestones), where the child's development is usually understood as divided into particular domains (social-emotional, language, physical, etc), and where the process of maturation drives a child's development. It is generally acknowledged in Australia that this view of child development is limiting and out of date. Extensive critique and discussion of this theory were undertaken within the field quite some time ago, and these arguments are well known to most.

Post-developmental theories now appear to be of interest to the field (see Fleer, in press), but are probably less well understood. Post-developmental theories include a sociocultural (Wertsch, 1995b) or cultural-historical (Vygotsky, 1998) view of child development (see Peers, 2011), critical theory, and poststructuralist theory. Sociocultural theory is generally well known within the field, but critical theory and poststructuralist theory are only known to some. For instance, in a study by Fleer (in press) of 239 early childhood teachers from the south-western part of Australia, it was found that of those who predominantly followed one theory of child development to support their view of play, 65 percent of these drew upon sociocultural or cultural-historical theory, 12 percent used Piaget's theorising to guide their work, 12 percent used poststructuralist theory, 8 percent drew upon socio-behaviourist theory, and 3 percent used behaviourism. However, it was interesting that, of the total number of respondents, 34 percent drew upon multiple theories as advocated in the EYLF; indeed, among those who strongly advocated for one theory, 10 respondents indicated that they had leanings towards other theories for other aspects of their work.

When these figures are compared with Nuttall's (2003) earlier work in Aotearoa New Zealand, and with the discussions put forward by Duhn (2006) and Ritchie (2008), it can be argued that even though teachers in Australia have not had a national curriculum to guide their practices over the past 20 years, there is a familiarity with contemporary theories of child development, auguring well for the uptake of the EYLF. Furthermore, the EYLF, with its focus on a diversity of child development theories, has acted as a catalyst for teachers to re-engage in discussions about theory. Here we see a parallel in Aotearoa New Zealand, where teachers engage with Māori theories and practices, alongside sociocultural, constructivist and ecological theories.

At national forums during the development of the EYLF, the authors of the Framework publicly stated they did not espouse one particular model of child development to inform curriculum design; rather, a diversity of theories was supported. This is in line with what has emerged from the implementation of *Te Whāriki* over the last 20 years. The EYLF, as a poststructuralist document, does not claim to support one theoretical approach and resists a singular regime of theoretical truth (Sumsion et al., 2009); by default it supports a poststructuralist stance. Earlier versions of the document support this claim (see Millei & Sumsion, 2011; Sumsion & Wong, 2011). For instance, in a thoughtful deconstruction of the EYLF (interrogating the concept of 'belonging'), Sumsion and Wong (2011) state that

> It takes as its starting point the premise that the questions asked of curriculum and the contexts of curricular development and implementation are fundamental to curriculum scholarship—a view held by 'mainstream' (for example, Dillon, 2009) and critical (for example, Popkewitz, 2009; Apple, 2010) curriculum theorists alike. For the former, key questions of curriculum centre on 'who, whom, what, where, when, why, how, what results' (Dillon, 2009, p. 347). For the latter, questions of rationalities, discourses and silences are key. Hence curriculum theorists ask: Which discourses

'count'? What rationalities underpin these discourses? Where/what are the silences? What are their effects and implications? (Sumsion & Wong, 2011, p. 28)

Sumsion and Wong go on to suggest that during the curriculum development phase,

A significant feature of that context was a requirement for the use of unrelentingly positive language in documents such as the EYLF. Such requirements leave little official space for the language of problematisation and critique. (2011, p. 38)

The shaping of *Te Whāriki* had similar beginnings (see Te One, this volume), leaving the job of critique until after the curriculum development phase (e.g., White, 2011). In Australia, we are seeing the beginnings of this self-critique of the *EYLF*, and look forward to greater dialogue within the field as Australia also engages with its first national early childhood curriculum framework.

Conclusion

As we have seen in both Australia and Aotearoa New Zealand, poststructuralist theory, post-colonial theory and critical theory provide important tools for reflecting on practice and on curriculum development. They are useful tools for progressing and questioning knowledge generation within practice and within the academy. But these tools do not in and of themselves provide the field with a theory of child development. They have a different role, as has been concisely argued by Ritchie:

Generating these shared spaces represents a movement beyond colonised binaries of coloniser/colonised subjectivities, yet at the same time operates in a place which remains deeply mindful of the pain and trauma still reflected profoundly in the negative social statistics of Māori (Ministry of Health, 2006) that is the ongoing legacy of colonisation. (Ritchie, 2008, p. 208)

When curriculum is viewed as an instrument of government for producing particular kinds of children (Duhn, 2006), or as a site for the problematisation and contestation of existing discourses and teacher identities (Ortlipp, Arthur, & Woodrow, 2011), post-developmental concepts become powerful tools for disrupting taken-for-granted practices. Here we see the spaces or 'meadows' (Duhn, 2006) of dialogue emerging.

Both *Te Whāriki* and the *EYLF* support a diversity of views surrounding theory(ies) about children's development, and both present developmental theories and sociocultural theories for informing child development. Cultural-historical theory provides a theory of child development within each framework, and this allows teachers to actively replace longstanding developmental theories with a cultural-historical view of children's development. In Aotearoa New Zealand critique has occurred over 20 years, enriching both practice and research. In Australia this is only just beginning, with poststructuralist tools affording the developers of the *EYLF* some important new directions. It is the published papers from the authors of each curriculum that make these 'meadows in between' visible (Duhn, 2006), expanding the dialogue and leaving it to the field to go further than what is presented in each of the published curricula (White, 2011). It is the re-theorisation of the original text by the authors and the academic community in Aotearoa New Zealand that continues to refine, expand and re-theorise what matters.

In Australia, it is the authors and the academy who give additional life to the broadly based document, expanding and re-theorising the *EYLF*. These are represented below in Figure 11.1 as *spheres of control,* where government sanctioning determines the final product (government control) but where the academy continues to engage in dialogue about the intent and directions of the original curriculum (academy control). The external sphere of the academy in partnership with practice is what keeps the document a living curriculum. The central circle depicts a static and unchanging document, while the outer circle shows an expansive zone that continues to change with research, practice and theoretical scholarship. With this reading of curricula across both countries as expansive, living documents it becomes possible to see why *Te Whāriki* has been so enduring.

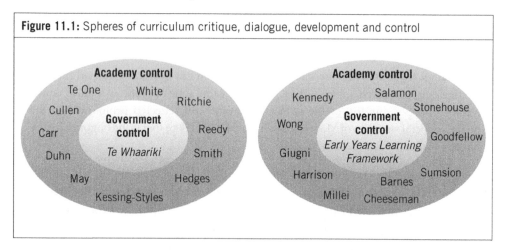

Figure 11.1: Spheres of curriculum critique, dialogue, development and control

References

Alvestad, M., Duncan, J., & Berge, A. (2009). New Zealand early childhood education teachers talk about *Te whāriki. New Zealand Journal of Teachers' Work,* 6(1), 3–19.

Anning, A., Cullen, J., & Fleer, M. (2009). (Eds.). *Early childhood education: Society and culture* (2nd ed.). London, UK: Sage Publications.

Blaise, M. (2009). "What a girl wants, what a girl needs!": Responding to sex, gender and sexuality in the early childhood classroom. *Journal of Research in Childhood Education,* 33(4), 450–461.

Bredekamp, S. (Ed.). (1987). *Developmentally appropriate practice in early childhood programs serving children from birth through age 8*. Washington, DC: National Association for the Education of Young Children.

Bronfenbrenner, U. (1979). *The ecology of human development*. Cambridge, MA: Harvard University Press.

Carr, M. (2001). A sociocultural approach to learning orientation in an early childhood setting. *International Journal of Qualitative Studies in Education, 14*(4), 525–542.

Carr, M., & May, H. (1993a). Choosing a model: Reflecting on the development process of *Te whaariki, National early childhood curriculum guidelines in New Zealand. International Journal of Early Years* Education, *1*(3), 7–22.

Carr, M., & May, H. (1993b). *The role of government in early childhood curriculum in New Zealand*. Paper presented at the New Zealand Council for Educational Research invitational seminar, What is the Government's Role in Early Childhood Education?, Wellington.

Carr, M., & May, H. (1994). Weaving patterns: Developing national early childhood curriculum guidelines in Aotearoa–New Zealand. *Australian Journal of Early Childhood Education, 19*(1), 25–33.

Carr, M., & May, H. (1996). *Te whaariki*, making a difference for the under fives?: The new national early childhood curricula. *Delta: Policy and Practice in Education, 48*(1), 101–112.

Carr, M., & May, H. (1997). Making a difference for the under-fives?: The early implementation of *Te whaariki*, the New Zealand national early childhood curriculum. *International Journal of Early Years Education, 5*(3), 225–236.

Carr, M., & May, H. (2000). *Te whaariki*: Curriculum voices. In H. Penn (Ed.), *Early childhood services: Theory, policy and practice*. Buckingham, UK: Open University Press.

Claxton, G. (1990). *Teaching to learn*. London, UK: Cassell.

Cullen, J. (1996). The challenge of *Te whaariki* for future developments in early childhood education. *Delta: Policy and Practice in Education, 48*(1), 113–125.

Cullen, J. (2001, September). *Assessment dilemmas in a socio-cultural curriculum*. Keynote address to TRCC course on Assessment in Early Childhood, Wellington.

Cullen, J. (2008, December). *Outcomes of early childhood education: Do we know, can we tell, and does it matter?* Jean Herbison Lecture, presented at the New Zealand Association for Research in Education Conference, Palmerston North.

Dahlberg, G., Moss, P., & Pence, A. (1999). *Beyond quality in early childhood education and care: Postmodern perspectives*. London, UK: Falmer Press.

Dalli, C. (2011). A curriculum of open possibilities: A New Zealand kindergarten teacher's view of professional practice. *Early Years: An International Journal of Research and Development, 31*(3), 229–243.

DEEWR (Department of Education, Employment and Workplace Relations). (2008). *Early years learning framework consultation*. Retrieved from http://www.vcaa.viceduau/vcaa/earlyyears/COAG_EYL_Framework20081113.pdf

DEEWR (Department of Education, Employment and Workplace Relations). (2009). *Early years learning framework*. Canberra, ACT: Commonwealth of Australia.

Deleuze, G. (1993). *The fold: Leibniz and the baroque*. Minneapolis, MN: University of Minnesota Press.

Donaldson, M. (1978). *Children's minds*. London, UK: Fontana/Collins.

Donaldson, M., Grieve, R., & Pratt, C. (Eds.). (1983). *Early childhood development and education.* Oxford, UK: Blackwell.

Duhn, I. (2006). The making of global citizens: Traces of cosmopolitanism in the New Zealand early childhood curriculum, *Te whaariki. Contemporary Issues in Early Childhood, 7*(3), 191–202.

Duhn, I. (2007, November). *Honouring the voices of children in early childhood education?: A poststructuralist/socio-cultural perspective.* Paper presented at the Language Education and Diversity Conference, University of Waikato, Hamilton.

Fleer, M. (2010). *Early learning and development: Cultural-historical concepts in play.* Cambridge: Cambridge University Press.

Fleer, M. (in press). Re-theorising play activities: Making room for diverse cultural expressions of play. In O. F. Lillemyr, S. Dockett, & B. Perry (Ed.), *Perspectives on play and learning: Theory and research on early years' education.* Charlotte, NC: Information Age Publishing.

Fleer, M., & Richardson, C. (2004). Moving from a constructivist-developmental framework for planning to a socio-cultural approach: Foregrounding the tension between individual and community. *Journal of Australian Research in Early Childhood Education, 10*(2), 70–87.

Gandi, L. (1998). *Postcolonial theory: A critical introduction.* Sydney, NSW: Allen & Unwin.

Gardner, H. (1983). *Frames of mind.* New York, NY: Basic Books.

Giugni, M. (2011). "Becoming worldly with": An encounter with the *Early years learning framework. Contemporary Issues in Early Childhood, 12*(1), 11–27.

Goodfellow, J. (2009). *The early years learning framework: Getting started.* Research in Practice series. Canberra, ACT: Early Childhood Australia.

Hedges, H. (2010). Blurring the boundaries: Connecting research, practice and professional learning. *Cambridge Journal of Education, 40*(3), 299–314.

Hedges, H. (2011). Connecting 'snippets of knowledge': Teachers' understandings of the concept of working theories. *Early Years, 31*(3), 271–284. doi: 10.1080/09575146.2011.606206

Hedges, H., & Cullen, J. (2005). Subject knowledge in early childhood curriculum and pedagogy. *Contemporary Issues in Early Childhood, 6*(1), 66–79.

Keesing-Styles, L. (2002). A critical pedagogy of early childhood education: The Aotearoa/New Zealand context. *New Zealand Research in Early Childhood Education, 5,* 109–122.

McLachlan, C. (2011). An analysis of New Zealand's changing history, policies and approaches to early childhood education. *Australasian Journal of Early Childhood, 36*(3), 36–44.

McLachlan, C., Fleer, M., & Edwards, S. (2010). *Early childhood curriculum: Planning, assessment and implementation.* New York, NY: Cambridge University Press.

McNaughton, S. (1996). Commentary: Co-constructing curricula: A comment on two curricula (*Te whaariki* and the English curriculum) and their developmental bases. *New Zealand Journal of Educational Studies, 31,* 189–196.

Meade, A. (2007). *Cresting the waves: Innovation in early childhood education.* Wellington: NZCER Press.

Millei, Z., & Sumsion, J. (2011). The 'work' of community in belonging, being and becoming: *The early years learning framework for Australia. Contemporary Issues in Early Childhood, 12*(1), 71–85.

Ministry of Education. (1993). *Te whariki: Draft guidelines for developmentally appropriate programmes in early childhood services: He whariki matauranga mo nga mokopuna o Aotearoa.* Wellington: Learning Media.

Ministry of Education. (1996). *Te whāriki: He whāriki mātauranga mō ngā mokopuna o Aotearoa: Early childhood curriculum.* Wellington: Learning Media.

Mitchell, L. (2011). Enquiring teachers and democratic politics: Transformations in New Zealand's early childhood education landscape. *Early Years: An International Journal of Research and Development, 31*(3), 217-228.

Nuttall, J. (2003). *Influences on the co-construction of teacher role in early childhood curriculum: Some examples from a New Zealand childcare centre.* Unpublished paper.

Ortlipp, M., Arthur, L., & Woodrow, C. (2011). Discourses of the *Early years learning framework*: Constructing the early childhood professional. *Contemporary Issues in Early Childhood, 12*(1), 56–70.

Paley, V. (1990). *The boy who would be a helicopter.* Cambridge, MA: Harvard University Press.

Peers, C. (2011). *Contemporary theories in child development.* Melbourne, VIC: Monash University Professional Learning Program.

Penn, H. (1991). Quality in services: The European approach. In M. Gold, L. Foote, & A. Smith (Eds.), *Proceedings of the fifth early childhood convention.* The Convention: New Zealand Dunedin.

Piaget, J., & Inhelder, B. (1969). *The psychology of the child.* New York, NY: Basic Books.

Rameka, L. K. (2011). Being Māori: culturally relevant assessment in early childhood education. *Early Years, 31*(3), 245–256. doi: 10.1080/09575146.2011.614222

Reedy, T (1995/2003). "Toku Rangatiratanga na te Mana-matauranga: Knowledge and Power Set Me Free …". In J. Nuttall (Ed.), *Weaving Te Whāriki: Aotearoa New Zealand's Early Childhood Curriculum Document in Theory and Practice,* (pp. 55–71). Wellington: New Zealand Council for Educational Research.

Reedy, T. (2000). Interview. In Te whaariki: *Policy to practice—The big picture* [video]. Wellington: Learning Media.

Ritchie, J. (2002). Bicultural development: Innovation in implementation of *Te whaariki. Australian Journal of Early Childhood, 27*(2), 23–41.

Ritchie, J. (2008). Honouring Māori subjectivities within early childhood education in Aotearoa. *Contemporary Issues in Early Childhood, 9*(3), 202–210.

Ritchie, J. (2011). Ma wai he kapu ti?: Being, knowing and doing otherwise in early childhood education in Aotearoa. *International Critical Childhood Policy Studies, 4*(1), 86–106.

Ritchie, J. R., & Buzzelli, C. A. (2012). *Te whariki*: The early childhood curriculum of Aotearoa New Zealand. In N. File, J. J. Mueller, & D. B. Wisneski (Eds.), *Curriculum in early childhood education: Re-examined, rediscovered, renewed* (pp. 146–159). New York, NY: Routledge.

Salamon, A. (2011). How the *Early years learning framework* can help shift pervasive beliefs of the social and emotional capabilities of infants and toddlers. *Contemporary Issues in Early Childhood, 12*(1), 4–10.

Schweinhart, L. J., Barnes, H. V., & Weikart, D. P. (1993). Significant benefits: The High Scope Perry pre-school study through age 27. Ypsilanti, MI: High Scope Press.

Smith, A. B. (1992). Early childhood educare: Seeking a theoretical framework in Vygotsky's work. *International Journal of Early Years Learning, 1*(1), 47–61.

Smith A. B. (1996). The early childhood curriculum from a sociocultural perspective. *Early Child Development and Care, 115,* 51–64.

Sumsion, J., Barnes, S., Cheeseman, S., Harrison, L., Kennedy, A. M., & Stonehouse, A. (2009). Insider perspectives on developing *Belonging, being and becoming: The early years learning framework for Australia. Australasian Journal of Early Childhood, 34*(4), 4–13.

Sumsion, J., & Wong, S. (2011). *Interrogating 'belonging' in Belonging, being and becoming: The early years learning framework for Australia. Contemporary Issues in Early Childhood, 12*(1), 28–45.

Te One, S. (2003). The context for *Te whaariki*: Contemporary issues of influence. In J. Nuttall (Ed.), *Weaving* Te whāriki: *Aotearoa New Zealand's early childhood curriculum document in theory and practice* (pp. 17–49). Wellington: New Zealand Council for Educational Research.

Tizard, B. (1986). *The care of young children: Implications of recent research.* Thomas Coram Research Unit working and occasional paper. London, UK: Thomas Coram Research Unit.

Vygotsky, L. S. (1978). *Mind in society.* Cambridge, MA: Harvard University Press.

Vygotsky, L .S. (1987). Thinking and speech. In R. W. Rieber & A. S. Carton (Eds., trans. N. Minick), *The collected works of L. S. Vygotsky, vol. 1* (pp. 39–285). New York, NY: Plenum Press.

Vygotsky, L. S. (1998). Child psychology. In R. W. Rieber (Ed., English translation, trans. M. J. Hall), *The collected works of L. S. Vygotsky, vol. 5.* New York, NY: Kluwer Academic and Plenum Publishers.

Wells, G. (1987). *The meaning makers: Children learning language and using language to learn.* London, UK: Hodder and Stoughton.

Wertsch, J. V. (1995a). The need for action in sociocultural research. In J. Wertsch, P. Del Rio, & A. Alvarez (Eds.), *Sociocultural studies of the mind.* New York, NY: Cambridge University Press.

Wertsch, J. V. (1995b). *Vygotsky and the social formation of mind.* Cambridge, MA: Harvard University Press.

Wertsch, J. V. (1998). *Mind as action.* New York, NY: Oxford University Press.

White, J. E. (2011). Dust under the whaariki: Embracing the messiness of curriculum. *Early Childhood Folio, 15*(1), 2–6.

White, J., O'Malley, A., Toso, M., Rockel, J., Stover, S., & Ellis, F. (2007). A contemporary glimpse of play and learning in Aotearoa New Zealand. *International Journal of Early Childhood, 39*, 93–105.

Wilks, A., Nyland, B., Chancellor, B., & Elliott, S. (2008). *An analysis of curriculum/learning frameworks for the early years (birth to age 8).* East Melbourne, VIC: State of Victoria Department of Education and Early Childhood Development and Victorian Curriculum and Assessment Authority. Retrieved from http://www.dewr.gov.au/EarlyChildhood/OfficeOfEarlyChildhood/sqs/Docuemnts/AnalysisofCurriclum_LearningFrameworksfortheEarly.pdf

CHAPTER 12

Understanding *Te Whāriki* from a Danish perspective

Stig Broström

ABSTRACT

To help readers understand the context for this chapter I begin with a short outline of the Danish and Nordic early childhood education and care tradition, which emphasises play, care and children's self-activity. This is followed by a description of the present situation, focusing on the implementation of a national early childhood curriculum since 2004. This curriculum attempts to integrate a learning dimension into the prior culture of early childhood education. This has given rise to a struggle to combine play and learning, accompanied by growing political pressure for a more school-oriented preschool, with a tendency to narrow early childhood educational practice to merely an introductory course for school, with a strong emphasis on literacy.

I argue that this situation calls for a reintroduction of critical education, which I examine in part one of the chapter, where I focus on 'critical Didaktik'. I will argue for critical democratic preschool education and care, which understands preschool as a democratic meeting place. I then construct a critical preschool Didaktik with the help of two approaches: a German theory of Bildung, and thus a critical-constructive Didaktik; and a preschool democratic practice based on various versions of child psychology and sociology and postmodern approaches. Based on this theoretical and practice background, in part two I analyse *Te Whāriki* and ask: What kind of curriculum understanding does *Te Whāriki* express? I will address this question in the light of the educational critical democratic approach described in part one of the chapter.

Introduction

In early childhood education and care in Denmark, as in other countries (Cullen, 1996), pedagogues[1] still show a resistance to curriculum theories and curriculum programmes applied to the early years, and they use the concept of curriculum with some reservation (Broström, 2004). In spite of the fact that Denmark now has a national early childhood curriculum (Socialministeriet, 2004), many Danish pedagogues, like other pedagogues around the world, have a strong feeling that early childhood education has to be something quite different from education in school. Danish early childhood education is rooted in a tradition that reaches back to Rousseau, Pestalozzi and Froebel, reformulated by a critical progressive wave early in the 20th century, including the work (among others) of the New Education Fellowship. Together, these approaches provide a background which emphasises concepts such as the importance of play and self-governed activity, self-development, and comprehensive development (Broström, 2003).

These concepts are related to developmental psychology, which in Denmark for almost a century has formed the basis for the development of early childhood education. With reference to humanistic psychology in general, Danish pedagogues embrace the idea that a combination of a rich environment and the child's own activity provides the best opportunities for comprehensive development, defined as an externalisation of the child's self. This realisation of the self comes about through the child's self-governed activity. Consequently, education in Danish preschools is primarily viewed as activity-based.

However, in order to develop, the child also has to interact with adults who are able to understand the child, interpret the child's needs and, in accordance with these, create an environment through which the child can act and develop himself or herself. In other words, the child also needs a recognisable adult with whom they have a secure attachment (Howes & Hamilton, 1992). The pedagogue expresses care, defined through an equal relationship: a subject–subject relationship. Both parties must contribute "[a] connection in which each party feels something towards the other" (Noddings, 1992, p. 15). The pedagogue expresses a caring attitude and the recipient accepts the care. In order to obtain a subject–subject, or I–thou relationship (Buber, 1958), the carer has to express a specific emotional relationship to the recipient (Noddings, 1984).

This tradition, as well as its actual practice, was criticised in Denmark during the 1990s for moving towards an exaggeratedly self-governed approach, where pedagogues only interact in small-scale ways with the children in order to support their learning and development (Vejleskov, 1997). It has been argued that in such a child-oriented

---

1 I use the word 'pedagogue' (Danish: pædagog), which signals a different concept from 'teacher'. However, for the purposes of this chapter it can be translated as 'preschool teacher'.

approach there is a risk of the preschool affording the child so much freedom that learning and development may be compromised in some way. For this reason the Danish approach, and the Nordic model of early childhood education in general, has been discussed and reformed during the last decades of the 20th century in order to ensure equal opportunities and comprehensive development for all children.

Consequently, the Nordic countries, like most European countries, have devised and implemented preschool curricula (Broström & Wagner, 2003), including the Danish curriculum implemented in 2004 (Socialministeriet, 2004). This curriculum requires all preschools to implement six dimensions of aims and content, which are expressed as general themes: personal competencies, social competencies, language, body and movement, nature and natural phenomena, and cultural forms of expression and values. The pedagogues and parents at an individual preschool must discuss and interpret these themes, and once a year they have to create their own curriculum plan, based on their own specific needs and circumstances.

However, because of the introduction of the national curriculum in 2004 and a large number of subsequent resources designed to support its implementation, concepts of learning and curriculum have gained enormous influence. Moreover, during the years following the introduction of the 2004 framework, an increasing number of tools for management have been implemented, including educational standards, language tests and quality reports. Since 2011 local municipalities have had to evaluate the quality of educational activities in their region every second year. Using these quality reports the municipalities construct cross-municipality assessments (Kvalitetsrapporter om dagtilbud nu på nettet [Quality reports on day care now on the net], 2012). In this way, we begin to see a reformulation of early childhood education and care as a form of *efficiency*. Thus the Ministry of Finance and Education (Finansministeriet, 2009) has produced guidance on the skills and knowledge children have to achieve by 3 and 5 years of age. In relation to the six dimensions of aims and content mentioned above, pedagogues also have to test children's learning using about 80 learning indicators.

At the present time in Denmark (and also in most modern neo-liberal countries) we see a tendency to narrow educational practice and reduce preschool to an introductory course for school, with a strong emphasis on literacy and mathematics. In this way, early childhood education and care is under pressure, as expressed through documents such as *The Treaty of Lisbon*.[2] In *Starting Strong 2* (OECD, 2006), which is based on Eurostat, 2000, it is documented that a number of countries

in general introduce structured learning areas to young children from the ages of 4 to 6 years. The preferred domains of knowledge proposed are: nature and the environment; emergent literacy and numeracy; general knowledge; scientific concepts

---

2 See http://europa.eu/legislation_summaries/employment_and_social_policy/community_
employment_policies/c10241_en.htm

and reasoning. The learning areas that receive most focus in official curricula are emergent literacy and numeracy. (p. 135)

This educational change is based on an *economic* interest, as expressed in *The Treaty of Lisbon*, which states that, via efficient education, the European countries (i.e., members of the European Union) will achieve the strongest economy in the world. Such political statements have a strong impact on national initiatives, where we see distinct formulations of goals and objectives closely connected to a number of simplified methods connected with prescribed tests.

Although documents such as *Starting Strong 2* warn against such a narrowing of the notion of early childhood education and care, we see an emerging tendency to focus on readiness for school, learning standards, and the use of narrow goals and objectives, followed by tests. So there is a clear risk of a dominating influence from school, which can lead to the implementation of methods based on evidence, known as the 'what works' approach. This increasing management and political control of the preschool can result in adult-initiated activities focused on preparation for school, with less space for children's self-generated activities such as play and other spontaneous creative activities. A further consequence of this 'efficiency' is a limitation of both children's and preschool teachers' influence, which Biesta (2007) calls a "democratic deficit".

This tendency is in contradiction with the overall aims of the 2004 Act, including, first and foremost, the perspective of democracy and of seeing the child as an active member of society, who participates in a democracy and contributes to the development of culture and society, thereby obtaining knowledge of, and insight into, society (Velfærdsministeriet, 2007). In taking this wording seriously, preschool pedagogues are compelled to interpret these general objectives and implement them in children's everyday life. However, this runs contrary to the actual political pressure for a school-oriented preschool, and there is a tendency to see these overall aims of the Act as a form of rhetoric, bearing no relation to everyday life in preschool. The economic agenda and European competition related to international testing systems appear to be prioritised over democracy in education.

In summary, preschool education in Denmark has changed dramatically during the past decades. We have seen a movement from an outstanding child-oriented approach to a narrow curricular approach. At the present time it seems as if the overall challenge for contemporary Danish early childhood education and care is how to respond to policy that influences curricular and pedagogical practices in narrowing ways. I believe there is a need for a critical early childhood education, which recognises children as active subjects while challenging them to achieve the democratic competence necessary for the future. Such an outline is presented in the next part of this chapter.

A critical preschool Didaktik[3]

A call for critical early childhood education and care that emphasises democracy and children's participation and influence is in agreement with the general aims expressed in important political documents in all Nordic countries, including Denmark:

> [P]reschools must provide children with the possibility to participate in decision making and joint responsibility and understanding for democracy, and to contribute to children's autonomy and abilities to participate in binding social communities. (Velfærdsministeriet, 2007, p. XX, author's translation)

There can be no doubt that these aims emphasise the democratic dimension in education. However, these important words are overshadowed by narrow objectives, tests and quality reports. Democracy and Bildung (a concept I expand upon later in this chapter) are not mentioned at all in the many national and municipal guidelines that have been disseminated over the last 10 years in response to the curriculum. As a result, the effort required to take democracy seriously is crucial. This is the case in the Nordic countries, but my question is: Are such democratic dimensions taken into consideration in preschools in New Zealand, and in *Te Whāriki* (Ministry of Education, 1996)? Before addressing this question, however, it is important to consider the many ways in which it is possible to understand the term 'democracy' and to draw out the consequences for education in the early years. I focus here on two in particular: the need for recognition as a person, and the need for places to meet to forge democratic participation.

Recognition

According to the German philosopher Axel Honneth (1995), human beings have an anthropological and an ontological need for recognition. Without recognition the individual is unable to develop a personal identity. Recognition is a precondition for the individual's self-realisation, for a good life. For this reason, a democratic society has to offer its citizens a fundamental recognition, which is expressed via three *spheres* of recognition—private, legal and community—and three *forms* of recognition—love, rights and solidarity (Honneth, 1995).

In the *private* sphere, symmetrical relations such as *love* and friendship give a basic self-confidence, a kind of emotional recognition. Love is a sphere of recognition, while love between subjects is experienced as a mutual emotional need. In early childhood education and care, attachment theories, for example those of Bowlby (1988) and Stern (1985), have been used to elaborate on this dimension. The Norwegian scholar Berit Bae (2005) has elaborated the concept of recognition and applied it to preschool

---

3 The German term 'Didaktik' (with a capital D, and not didactics) is in accordance with the term 'curriculum', but is much broader as it reflects political Bildung (liberal–political education), with a focus on children's agency and democratic education (see Hopmann & Riquarts, 1995).

practice. Emotional recognition leads to a secure attachment, basic confidence and, as a result, *physical integrity*.

In the sphere of *legal relations*, individuals can invoke their *legal universal rights*; for example, freedom of expression. Engagement as an active member of society—as a recognised, autonomously acting subject—results in *self-respect* and self-esteem. In preschool this is seen when the child uses his or her legal rights to be seen and heard, to participate, and to influence, as promised in the 1989 United Nations Convention on the Rights of the Child.[4] When such rights are realised, the individual gains *social integrity*.

In the sphere of *community of value*, in cultural, political and working communities the individual strives to be an integrated member of a shared solidarity. When the subject is recognised as a special person, *self-esteem* will develop. In preschool such communities are seen in children's play, in their mutual relations, and in their shared exploration of the world. Here children get a form of "honour" dignity (Honneth, 1995, p. 129). However, when a child is expelled from the community, when he or she again and again hears "You are not allowed to take part", they miss out on self-esteem.

Adults and children have a fundamental claim to, and need for, recognition on all three levels: emotional, legal and social. If the individual does not experience recognition, they will not receive emotional attention, cognitive respect and social esteem, with the attendant risk of not developing a positive self-relation. Adults in society, as well as children in preschool, strive for such recognition. But does the modern liberal democratic society offer its citizens recognition on all three levels? One might answer both 'yes' and 'no'. On a formal and rhetorical level, through the supports of family life, the protection of human rights and the social idea of giving people places to meet, society shapes the ground to accomplish all three forms of recognition. However, in all spheres we see a lot of disrespect; in primary relations we see superficial relationships and, in the worst cases, abuse and rape. In legal relations, not only do individuals encounter disrespect in the form of loss of civil rights, but we also see whole groups of people being discriminated against; for example, people with ethnic backgrounds different to those of the majority. Also, in the community, moral injustices occur via daily insults and social disintegration, on a continuum from not being greeted through to being expelled from the community.

When citizens in society—and in preschool—feel no recognition, individuals have to devise alternative ways to get recognition. Some of these forms of recognition-seeking remain private, while others appear as continuous opposition to society, sometimes through violent actions. Thus everyday life in preschool has to address children's need for all three types of recognition, such that the individual child is:
- involved in symmetrical relations with preschool teachers and other children
- able to act as an active subject, getting positive feedback from the other children

---

4 See http://www.CRIN.org.

- an accepted member of the group, in which they play an important role, and are not simply a 'tolerated' member of the children's community.

A fight for democratic meeting places

A possible basis for recognition is a society that is inclusive of all citizens, is open to their participation and gives them a voice. A central part of a critical preschool education is to optimise and democratise children's everyday life: to see preschool as a democratic meeting place. Dahlberg, Moss and Pence (2007) define this as a place where the active citizen can practise democracy by participating in collective actions. This struggle for democracy and its essential practices does not start in adulthood: it must already be expressed in the early years.

Early childhood education must not only be a question of how to learn effectively and how to make an effective transition to school by achieving school readiness; it must also be a tool in the struggle for a radical democracy. Life in preschool is characterised by activities that contain elements of what democracy is all about. For example, when children plan their play they have a dialogue, listen to each other, reach a compromise with each other, and create mutual, goal-directed actions. In some respect their communication is in line with the theory of communicative action developed by the German critical philosopher Jürgen Habermas (1984, 1987). Because the children really want to play, they often make compromises, use non-controlling communication and strive to make the best argument count. These are all practices in a democracy and pave the way for formulating a possible critical preschool education.

Critical preschool education as a future educational approach

There are various ways to transform the broad ideal of democracy into everyday life in preschool. However, a German Bildung-oriented approach (Klafki, 1995, 1998) highlights two dimensions that are necessary in order to fully realise democratic participation. The first dimension is the necessity of reflecting on educational aims in order to formulate a long-term perspective on future people in a future society; in the German educational tradition, this is known as the Bildung ideal (Klafki, 1996). This process of reflection implies an endeavour to bring democracy and participation to the forefront of daily life. According to this first dimension, the aims (or the Bildung ideal), it is not difficult to create a legitimating basis for a critical and emancipatory education. In the *Treaty of Lisbon* and also European Union (2006), eight key competencies for lifelong learning are set out, and social and civic competencies are mentioned in order to "equip individuals to engage in active and democratic participation" (EU, 2006, p. 5). This is in agreement with the thinking in Nordic countries, where democracy is seen as a central value and a set of practices with which children need to be familiar.

These aims emphasise participation, action and democracy, all providing a foundation for legitimate, politically transformative education. Moreover, the aims can be interpreted as viewing children as thoughtful, active participants in a democratic process, not just onlookers. In practice the preschool teacher listens to children, and challenges them to reflect and to express their thoughts and actions and to take initiatives themselves. This is exactly what is mentioned in the Convention on the Rights of the Child. Democracy is characterised, first and foremost, by the constant possibility of people's participation in social action.

However, the Bildung ideal of education for democracy goes beyond the actual situation; it is oriented towards the future and has a global perspective. The democratic person is a political subject, with knowledge and skills, and with a desire to make use of these through transformative practice. This is a person who has the knowledge, skills and will to realise transformation through action, summarised in the concept of "action competence" (Schnack, 2003). In action competence, a critical dimension is evident as the individual uses her or his knowledge to engage in "[p]articipation in decision making and joint responsibility", as it is framed in the Danish Act (Velfærdsministeriet, 2007, chapter 2, § 7). Klafki's (1995, 1996) approach, "critical-constructive Didaktik", defines the critical dimension thus:

> This adjective applies to an interest in knowledge insofar as the concept of Didaktik is oriented to the goal of guiding all children and adolescents to greater capacity for self-determination, co-determination and solidarity. (Klafki, 1995, p. 191)

I have argued so far that the actual democratic society in many respects (in spite of public aims and goals) prevents real democratic education in school and preschool. For example, growing interest in and demands for testing children's knowledge and skills is one obstacle to realising democratic participation. The way in which Klafki uses the term 'constructive' within a critical constructive Didaktik signals that—in spite of hindrances from the environment, and the fact that young children need to appropriate the culture before real critical thinking and acting can be expressed—the teacher has to "suggest models for possible practice, to produce well-founded concepts for reformed or reforming practice, for human, democratic school and instruction" (Klafki, 1995, p. 192). In other words, teachers have a critical role in constructing democratic society and participation in and through preschool education. Elsewhere (Broström, 2006) I have elaborated on the concepts of Bildung and critical-constructive Didaktik as they apply to preschool education. In brief, the term 'Bildung' can be defined through the following three criteria that, at the same time, accord with long-standing traditions of early childhood education and care: an emphasis on children's own activity and dialogue with others; a feeling of mutual obligation and commitment between children and teachers; and participation, action and democratic practices (Broström, 2006).

The educational content in a global world

While the first dimension of the Bildung ideal involves formulating overall aims, the second dimension involves formulating educational content in close connection with the overall aims; in other words, the development of so-called 'critical themes' within children's education. Thus the preschool teacher has to reflect the educational content. As mentioned already, a critical-constructive Didaktik finds it necessary to formulate topics, problems and categories that give children necessary knowledge at the same time as they learn to handle the here and now of everyday life and of society in the long term.

For this purpose Klafki's approach, known as 'category Bildung', can be used as a starting point (Klafki, 1998). In this approach the preschool teacher and the children select knowledge and categories through which the world will be available to the child and, at the same time, the child will be available to the world. For this reason, Klafki (1998) uses the term "double opening" when describing the process of category development (i.e., identification of critical themes in curriculum content). The preschool teacher's selection of such categories is the pivot, and is seen also in Paulo Freire's (1972) concept of "themes of generative character" in emancipatory education. Through this process, the children in the preschool should encounter content that points ahead and helps make the world transparent to them. When the child grows up, they will live in a future world and should be able to solve the problems of *that* world. In order to achieve this, the children have to experience and learn to respond to some fundamental problems of their *present time*. This is the nature of educational 'content' within a category Bildung approach.

This future can be viewed from a dual perspective. On the one hand, it can be described as having the threatening tendencies of a high-risk society (Giddens, 1990); on the other hand, it can be understood in the light of new visionary possibilities in a global world. Anthony Giddens (1990) describes the threatening tendencies as a mutual relationship between growth in the totality of power, conflict over nuclear power, global war, ecological breakdown, and a collapse of the mechanisms of economic development. Correspondingly, Klafki (1994) discusses the relationship between society and decisions about educational content. He outlines a number of core or 'epoch typical' problems, such as questions about war and peace, North–South conflict, problems of nationalism, ecological problems and sustainability, socially produced disparity, and the dangers and possibilities of new communications media. These problems appear to be huge and adult-oriented. Yet every day such core problems are visible in preschools and we can observe how children cope with them in their own ways. For example, children play and ask questions based on watching television news about war in Afghanistan, the Palestinian conflict or a specific terrorism event, all of which influence their thinking and feelings; for that reason they need adults to help them come to terms with these questions.

Preschool teachers have the opportunity to define and select such problems and perspectives as educational content. In one example from a Danish preschool, some children talked about how their friends told them the drinking-water was poisoned and it was dangerous to drink. The truth behind the story was that in the neighbouring municipality there had been problems with the drinking-water, which had led to educational activities focused on pollution. In another preschool two 5-year-old boys had a dialogue during lunch. When Oskar started to eat his bread with sausage, a boy from a different ethnic background burst out, "Ugh this food is unclean, why do you eat such food? My father says this is really unappetising". Oskar replied quickly, "Don't speak about my food" and turned to a boy on his other side, saying, "I like this, and me and my father eat this at home with roasted onion, yum!" In this situation the preschool teacher could *choose* to ask the boys not to speak slightingly about each other's food, and thereby avoid a possible conflict. But she gave the boys the chance to explore each other's culture, norms and values. In this way, the boys are entering into the themes of nationalism, East–West conflict, ethnic difference, etc. They have their own experiences and, during the following days, the preschool teacher can support their appropriation and construction of knowledge and norms.

These examples illustrate the fact that it is not difficult for preschool teachers to identify and mobilise a number of epoch-typical core problems that help children to deal with current *and* future problems through appropriate preschool activity. As Klafki (1994) points out, however, "Such societal risks and possibilities set the education new and big problems and tasks", and here lies an opportunity to challenge the early childhood education and care system. If the preschool teacher continually incorporates such epoch-typical problems, there is the possibility of going beyond the development of a preschool education that simply ends in a smooth transition to school characterised by adjustment to traditional norms. By challenging the tendency to make preschool too school-oriented, I suggest we can move towards a democratisation of children's everyday life and help them to understand the big themes of our time.

Critiques of the Bildung approach

Before turning to how these ideas relate to *Te Whāriki*, it is important to touch on critiques of the Bildung approach. One criticism is that the approach has too much focus on both the Bildung ideal and on content, instead of focusing on process in children's learning. Although Bildung refers to a process whereby the child contributes to their own learning and development, there is still a state of dependence on the educator. This creates a paradox: how can the educator strive to develop a masterful and independent person when there is such an asymmetric relationship between teacher and learner? This paradox is eliminated through two phases. In the first phase the educator opens the door to culture and gives the child new possibilities. In the

Norwegian philosopher Hans Skjervheim's (1992) words, this is expressed through a "natural and actual asymmetric relation". The next phase, the phase of Bildung, is characterised by another type of relationship, whereby the subject strives for liberation from the educator's guidance in order to capture their own independence, thinking and will.

Nevertheless, this critique takes a sceptical view of the focus on the preschool teacher's active role and guidance towards Bildung and liberation. Although the Bildung approach emphasises the idea of children as participants and subjects with their own rights and responsibilities, there is still a need to express a much more radical view, a view that understands the child as a competent person and involves being open to a child's right to take independent decisions. In other words, a view that does not direct children's learning and development toward specific aims, goals and objectives.

Contemporary theories of childhood give voice to these ideas. Elsewhere (Broström, 2006) I have elaborated how numerous sociologists have described changes in various aspects of childhood's structure and content in modern societies (Brannen & O'Brien, 1995; Corsaro, 1997; Honing, 1999; James, Jenks, & Prout, 1998; James & Prout, 1990). These approaches do not view newborn children as either isolated from the surrounding world or as born relatively unskilled; on the contrary, childhood psychology now operates from the perspective that children are born with communicative competencies and interdependent minds (i.e., they are aware that they are dependent on others and that others are dependent on them). Thus, the phrase "the competent child" has gained wide acceptance (e.g., Trevarthen, 1998).

The idea of the child as an active participant is logical within this new understanding of childhood. These sociological as well as psychological perspectives provide an important context for the growing interest in children's perspectives in education and educational research, as well as for increasing general recognition of children's roles and value in modern society. The phrase "children as active participants" emphasises children as subjects, not objects, and as social agents (Jensen & Schnack, 1997). This approach both reflects and contributes to changing perspectives on the nature of childhood and children themselves, especially with regard to children's competence as active participants in their own development and important contributors to society. Moreover, pedagogues are increasingly taking a child's perspective (Qvarsell, 2003; Sommer, Pramling Samuelsson, & Hundeide, 2010), which acknowledges that children *have* a perspective, that it may differ decidedly from adults' perspectives, and that children may have differing perspectives from each other.

Taken together, contemporary perspectives on childhood, coupled with growing faith in children's competence and views of children as 'human beings' rather than 'human becomings' (Qvortrup, Bardy, Srgitta, & Wintersberger, 1994), create potential pathways for children to participate in society with a status that is roughly equivalent to that of adults. From this one general educational principle can be derived: be open to children's actual interest and motivation to have more power, independence and influence on their own life and education. With this in mind, I turn in the final part of this chapter to consider the assumptions about curriculum that underpin *Te Whāriki*.

Te Whāriki considered in the light of a range of Didaktik (curriculum theoretical) models

The development of a curriculum for the early years must be able to take the child's perspective into account while also taking care not to move towards a school-like approach. Although this standpoint might seem somewhat romantic, it is rationally based. To create a curriculum that is neither excessively child-oriented nor excessively school-oriented, academics, politicians and pedagogues must search for new curriculum models. Instead of a child-centred or teacher-directed model, a synthesis could be created between activity- and interaction-based approaches. This could be characterised as a Vygotskian (Vygotsky, 1978) idea of learning, where learning is constructed through the children's activity and social interaction with other (more developed) people. Any theoretical Didaktik/curriculum approach has to overcome both the subject-centred perspective and the child- or learner-centred perspective. In this chapter I have argued that, instead, we should create a society- or problem-centred model (see also Print, 1993; Walker & Soltis, 1997).

The development of *Te Whāriki* can be understood in the light of such a debate. *Te Whāriki* avoids a hierarchical rational/objective model, which is a characteristic of the work of Tyler (1949; see also Print, 1993), for example, which claims a close relationship between goals and means/methods. Such a model gives no room for spontaneity and has a tendency towards narrow goals. So what type of curriculum is *Te Whāriki*? In some respects it adopts a cyclical model (Nicholls & Nicholls, 1978), which begins with a situational analysis in order to formulate goals and objectives and to guide the selection of content. The four principles of *Te Whāriki*—empowerment, holistic development, family and community, and relationships—and the relatively soft presence of educational 'content', suggest such an interpretation. *Te Whāriki* can also be understood in the light of a so-called 'dynamic' model (Print, 1993) or a 'practice-based model' (Skilbeck, 1976), which argue for reflecting the reality of curriculum development within the educational organisation. Stenhouse (1975), for example, creates a process-Didaktik/curriculum, arguing that all factors in the prevailing educational situation have to be taken into consideration. Educational practice is a creative and unpredictable process, characterised by time and place and by children's backgrounds and current situation. It is also subject to the influence of a huge number of experiences outside and inside the educational practices of the institution. Within a process-Didaktik/curriculum, the pedagogue needs to have both a researching and a reflecting attitude towards their own practice, and to take care to avoid the mechanical approach of fixed curricula: their role is to interpret and co-construct the curriculum.

Having examined *Te Whāriki* itself, and through visits to a number of preschools in Auckland and Hamilton back in 2002, I understand the New Zealand approach to early childhood curriculum to have adopted this perspective. Though I am sympathetic toward this adoption, I also detect some problems. First, explicit discussion and formulation of aims, goals and educational content seem to be missing. Any society needs to encourage its inhabitants to involve themselves in democracy in order to change society. Consequently, even in their early years, children have to deal with future-oriented content. Here, I think *Te Whāriki* is too general:

> To grow up as competent and confident learners and communicators, healthy in mind, body and spirit, secure in their sense of belonging and in the knowledge that they make a valued contribution to society. (Ministry of Education, 1996, p. 9)

This formulation is open to very different interpretations. Nor do the principles and the five strands define this perspective sufficiently.

Psychological versus Didaktik approaches

Although practice may have moved on since 2002, in both *Te Whāriki* and in the *Statement of Desirable Objectives and Practices* (Ministry of Education, 1996b) there is a tendency to emphasise an individualistic approach. Although it has been argued (May & Carr, 2000) that the approach of *Te Whāriki* differs from traditional developmental psychology by stressing all dimensions—physical, intellectual, emotional and social—it is easy to see some strong points of resemblance with developmental psychology. This has been mentioned in New Zealand debate about the document (Cullen, 1996). The idea of holistic development, wellbeing, helping children to feel attached and belonging to particular places, being active, contributing to the community, and having opportunities to explore the surrounding world are all elements belonging to the early childhood practice tradition. These dimensions are also expressed in the developmentally appropriate practice approach (Bredekamp, 1987; Bredekamp & Copple, 1997). A curriculum with a developmental orientation describes the development of personal and social competencies, thinking, communication and other psychological characteristics; these are also expressed in *Te Whāriki*.

However, *Te Whāriki* also emphasises responsive and reciprocal relationships, implying a Vygotskian approach that argues for interaction between the child and the pedagogue. This approach understands the individual child as succeeding in handling internalised, as well as externalised, activities in co-operation with adults and other children (Leontjev, 1978). Through such inter-psychological processes, the outside level of action is transformed to intra-psychological processes (e.g., emotional and cognitive structures). Vygotsky (1978, p. 57) states: "First, on the social level, and later, on the individual level; between people (inter-psychological), and then inside the child (intra-psychological)". This approach (social constructionism) argues for the need for interaction in social-cultural settings, where learning and development are seen as co-constructed; in other words, where the learner, together with other people, constructs his/her knowledge. Thus pedagogues play an important role, characterised by Rogoff (1990) as "guided participation" and by Bruner (1985) as "scaffolding", which is also referred to in *Te Whāriki*.

Although *Te Whāriki* takes the ecological perspective of Bronfenbrenner (1989), as well as trying to balance early childhood traditions with a more powerful role for the adults, I understand *Te Whāriki* as a document that helps to support children's general learning and development where the psychological approach is dominant and an educational approach is less stressed. In other words, I believe that it lacks reflection on *what* the children should explore, communicate, think etc.

The issue of educational content

I think clarification of educational content is missing from the document. *Te Whāriki* does not point out particular subjects, giving priority instead to the child's individual interest and activity. Klafki (1958) discusses the 'what' dimension of curriculum—the question of content—identifying one type of content as *material*. Material content means that the curriculum, and therefore the pedagogues, point out a specific subject, problem, or specific forms of knowledge. This understanding of curriculum is typical of schools, where different subjects each have a material role. By contrast, early childhood education traditionally pays attention to the *form* of the curriculum; that is, the learner's activity in itself. This understanding of 'form as content' is defined by Klafki as *formal* education. From my perspective, the text of *Te Whāriki* and the daily educational practice of New Zealand pedagogues tend towards this 'formal' education, which involves believing that any activity the child is motivated for, and involved in, will contribute to the child's development. Here the form or way of acting is more important than the substance. In other words, provided that the four aims and the five strands are taken into consideration, children will learn through whatever activity they have chosen.

To be fair, by closely examining the different goals connected to the five strands, here and there one can find content with a kind of material character. For example "be familiar with the wider world", "caring for the environment", "consciousness of gender and ethnicity", and "knowledge and skills oftechnology and mathematics and symbols" are all goals within *Te Whāriki*. But because they are not formulated as content but as open (diffuse) goals, it is possible to argue that the content neither provides a democratic-critical perspective nor has a binding character. This issue could be resolved if New Zealand adopted interdisciplinary approaches through the use of relevant themes. During visits to a number of New Zealand preschools in 2002 I often observed such a thematic approach. For example, in one preschool a boy started drawing dragons, which the teacher supported with questions and by providing books and other materials. After a while some other children became interested in his project, and this individual interest turned into a collective project. In another preschool a boy's interest in a mountain close to the preschool was transformed into a theme for everybody in the preschool. No doubt many preschools could describe individual themes that have grown into long-lasting shared projects.

To overcome the content problem while maintaining an overall focus on emancipation and democracy, Klafki's approach, known as category Bildung and described earlier, can be used as a starting point (Klafki, 1998). This approach envisions unifying a formal and material education; that is, an integration of the personal subjective experience *and* objective reality. The child acts as a subject in tandem with his or her grasp of objective content. The objective or material aspect is the child's appropriation of concepts and knowledge; the subjective or formal aspect is taken into account if the child is active, engaged and involved in his or her activity. Such discussions of educational content seem not to be reflected in *Te Whāriki*.

I acknowledge that it is easy to criticise a curriculum but not always easy to come to an agreement at a governmental or municipal level. Yet one might argue that a curriculum that does nothing to challenge the culture even of a single preschool has no *raison d'être*. On the other hand, if a curriculum is to be accepted in a society and have a role to play, it needs to avoid being provocative and not promote too much 'border crossing'. If the curriculum is to have a chance to have an impact on practice, it also has to be easy for teachers to read and understand. At the same time, because educational theory and practice are characterised by enormous complexity, it is difficult to reduce curricula to simple terms. I agree with Carr's advice: keep it simple in order to see the big picture, while maintaining a respect for complexity (Carr, 2001).

Conclusion

In this chapter I have criticised the current tendency of narrowing in early childhood education and care in order to a focus on goals and objectives, followed up by tests. In order to go beyond this, I have argued for a critical-democratic preschool education reflecting the big problems of our time, aimed at Bildung and liberation. Such an approach might build on a number of diverse theoretical dimensions, including German-inspired Bildung Didaktik and contemporary theories of childhood. However, above all, the aims and content reflected in a new approach have to be future oriented.

My criticism of *Te Whāriki* is relates to its vague formulation of the critical-democratic dimension. To this one might reply that *Te Whāriki* is not a fixed curriculum; the document expresses an openness, which allows each preschool to draw its own educational conclusions. This is correct. However, seen from a democratic point of view a society has to express its overall values; this is a prerequisite for having a democratic debate. And when a society emphasises the democratic dimension, preschool teachers and parents have to reflect on how to implement democracy in preschool.

I think we need an approach to early childhood education that is able to challenge society, communities, parents, children and pedagogues. This might be a Didaktik with a Bildung perspective, or postmodern preschool approaches with educational and societal content, which deal with epoch-typical problems reaching towards the future. With such an approach we touch on the old—and yet very modern—educational idea of fostering a 'citizen of the world'; in other words, helping children to act in a future society as critical-democratic subjects. We need curricula with such a perspective. This is much more powerful than curricula that only focus on children's comprehensive development —although this is, of course, a necessary component.

Such a democratic dimension is not explicitly expressed in *Te Whāriki*. Because the question of content is rather diffuse in *Te Whāriki*, and because there is no explicit discussion and description of the relationship between aims and content, pedagogues in New Zealand have to make their own content choices. In all probability many pedagogues will carry through sociological and cultural analyses in their search for relevant content, but there is a risk that the old child-centred approach will be maintained, with preschool teachers saying that children have to make their own choices. Although a child's own choice must be a dimension of life in preschool, this is not sufficient. Education has to face the future. This is where *Te Whāriki* most lacks explicit content reflections.

For example, what does it mean to "make a valued contribution to society"? Such a phrase must be discussed, and preschool teachers and society have to discuss and come up with different answers. Where this is missing (in both Denmark and New Zealand) it is very difficult for pedagogues to make choices about content choice related to the overall aims (in Denmark 'responsibility and understanding democracy' and in New Zealand 'make valued contributions to society'). In such a situation, pedagogues in Denmark and preschool teachers in New Zealand might stick closely to the principles and strands without taking steps to go beyond their present situation. From my point of view, on an international level, Didaktik and curriculum researchers in early childhood education and care have to meet this challenge and work to create a critical-democratic preschool Didaktik.

References

Bae, B. (2005). Troubling the identity of a researcher: Methodological and ethical questions in cooperating with teacher-carers in Norway. *Contemporary Issues in Early Childhood, 6*(3), 283–291.

Biesta, G. J. J. (2007). Why "what works" won't work. *Educational Theory, 57*(1), 1–22.

Bowlby, J. (1988). *A secure base: Clinical applications of attachment theory.* London, UK: Routledge.

Brannen, J., & O'Brien, M. (1995). Review easy childhood and sociological gaze: Paradigm and paradoxes. *Sociology, 29*(4), 729–737.

Bredekamp, S. (Ed.). (1987). *Developmentally appropriate practice in early childhood programmes serving children from birth through age 8.* Washington, DC: NAEYC.

Bredekamp, S., & Cople, C. (1997). *Developmentally appropriate practice in early childhood programs.* Washington, DC: NAEYC.

Bronfenbrenner, U. (1989). Ecological systems theory. In R. Vasta (Ed.), *Theories of child development: Revised formulation and current issues.* London, UK: Jessica Kingsley.

Broström, S. (2003). Transition from kindergarten to school in Denmark: Building bridges. In S. Broström & J. T. Wagner (Eds.), *Early childhood education in five Nordic countries: Perspectives on the transition from preschool to school.* Aarhus, Denmark: Systime Academic.

Broström, S. (2004). Modstand mod læring [Resistance against learning]. *Asterisk, 8,* 18–19.

Broström, S. (2006). Children's perspectives on their childhood experiences. In Einarsdóttir, J. & J. T. Wagner (Eds.), *Nordic childhoods and early education: Philosophy, research, policy and practice in Denmark, Finland, Iceland, Norway and Sweden.* Greenwich, CT: Information Age Publishing.

Broström, S., & Wagner, J. T. (Eds.). (2003). *Early childhood education in five Nordic countries: Perspectives on the transition from preschool to school.* Aarhus, Denmark: Systime Academic.

Bruner, J. (1985). Vygotsky: A historical and conceptual perspective. In J. Wertsch (Ed.), *Culture, communication and cognition: Vygotskian perspectives.* London, UK: Cambridge University Press.

Buber, M. (1958). *I and thou.* New York, NY: Scribner's.

Car, M. (2001, July). *Keeping it complex.* Keynote address to Te Tari Puna Ora o Aotearoa/New Zealand Childcare Association Annual Conference, Hamilton.

Corsaro, W. A. (1997). *The sociology of childhood.* Thousand Oaks, CA: Pine Forge Press.

Cullen, J. (1996). The challenge of *Te whāriki*: Future developments in early childhood education. *Delta, 48*(1), 113–126.

Dahlberg, G., Moss, P., & Pence, A. (2007). *Beyond quality in early childhood education and care: Languages of evaluation* (2nd ed.). London, UK: Routledge.

European Union (2006). *Official Journal of European Union. Recommendation of the European Parlement and the Council.* 18 December 2006. On Key Competences for lifelong learning. (2006/962/EC).

Eurostat. (2000). *Key data on education in Europe, 1999–2000.* Brussels: European Commission.

Finansministeriet. (2009). Om project Faglige Kvalitetsoplysninger på dagtilbudsområdet [On project quality information in the day-care sector]. Retrieved from http://www.fm.dk/Arbejdsomraader/Offentlig%20modernisering/Kvalitet%20og%20styring/Faglige%20 kvalitetsoplysninger/~/media/Files/Offentlig%20modernisering/Kvalitetsreformen/Projektbeskrivelse%20paa%20dagtilbudsomraadet.ashx

Freire, P. (1972). *Pedagogy of the oppressed*. Harmondsworth, UK: Penguin Books.

Giddens, A. (1990). *The consequences of modernity*. Cambridge, UK: Polity Press.

Habermas, J. (1984 & 1987). *The theory of communicative action*, Vols. 1 and 2. Boston, MA: Beacon Press.

Honing, M. S. (1999). *Entwurf einer Theorie der Kindheit*. Frankfurt am Main, Germany: Suhrkamp.

Honneth, A. (1995). *The struggle for recognition: The moral grammar of social conflicts*. Cambridge, UK: Polity Press.

Hopmann, S., & Riquarts, K. (Eds.). (1995). *Didaktik and/or curriculum*. Kiel, Germany: Institut für die Pädagogik der Naturwissenschaften an der Universität Kiel.

Howes, C., & Hamilton, C. E. (1992). Children's relationships with caregivers: Mothers and child care teachers. *Child Development*, *63*, 895–866.

James, A., Jenks, C., & Prout, A. (1998). *Theorising childhood*. Cambridge, UK: Polity Press.

James, A., & Prout, A. (Eds.). (1990). *Constructing and reconstructing childhood: Contemporary issues in the sociological study of childhood*. London, UK: Falmer Press.

Jensen, B. B., & Schnack, K. (1997). The action competence approach in environment education. *Environment Education Research*, *3*(2), 163–178.

Klafki, W. (1958, 1974). *Studien zur Bildungstheorie und Didaktik* [Theory on Bildung and Didaktik]. Weinheim und Basel, Germany: Fünfte Studie, Beltz Verlag.

Klafki, W. (1994). Schlüsselprobleme als inhaltlicher Kern Internationaler Erziehung [Key problems as core content in international education]. Aus: N. Seibert & H. J. Serve (Hrsg.), *Bildung und Erziehung: Multidisziplinäre Aspekte*. München, Germany: Prims.

Klafki, W. (1995). On the problem of teaching and learning content from the standpoint of critical-constructive didaktik. In S. Hopmann & K. Riquarts (Eds.), *Didaktik and/or curriculum*. Kiel, Germany: Institut für die Pädagogik der Naturwissenschaften an der Universität Kiel.

Klafki, W. (1996). *Neu Studien zur Bildungstheorie und Didaktik* [New studies on theory of Bildung and didaktik] 5. Auflage. Weinheim und Basel: Belz Verlag.

Klafki, W. (1998). Characteristics of critical-constructive Didaktik. In B. B. Gundem & S. Hopmann (Eds.), *Didaktik and/or curriculum: An international dialogue*. New York: American University Studies, Peter Lang.

Kvalitetsrapporter om dagtilbud nu på nettet [Quality reports on the web]. (2012, 12 January). *Børn & Unge*, *43*(1), 30.

Leontjev, A. N. (1978). *Activity, consciousness, and personality*. Englewood Cliffs, NJ: Prentice Hall.

May, H., & Carr, M. (2000). National curriculum for 'empowering children to learn and grow': *Te whāriki*, the New Zealand early childhood curriculum. In J. Hayden (Ed.), *Early childhood landscapes: Cross national perspectives on empowerment and restraint*. New York: Peter Lang.

Ministry of Education. (1996). *Te whāriki: He whāriki mātauranga mō ngā mokopuna o Aotearoa: Early childhood curriculum*. Wellington: Learning Media.

Ministry of Education (1996b) *Statement of Desirable Objectives and Practices*. Wellington: Author

Nicholls, A., & Nicholls, A. H. (1978). *Developing a curriculum: A practical guide* (2nd ed.). London, UK: George Allen & Unwin.

Noddings, N. (1984). *Caring: A feminine approach to ethics and moral education.* Berkeley, CA: University of California Press.

Noddings, N. (1992). *The challenge to care in school: An alternative approach to education.* New York, NY, and London, UK: Teachers College Press.

OECD. (2006). *Starting strong 2: Early childhood education and care.* Paris: Author.

Print, M. (1993). *Curriculum development and design* (2nd ed.). Sydney, NSW: Allen & Unwin.

Qvarsell, B. (2003). Barns perspektiv och mänskliga rättigheter: Godhetsmaximering eller kunskabsbilding? [Child's perspective and human rights: Goodness or education?]. *Pædagogisk forskning i Sverige: Barns perspektiv och barnperspektiv* [Educational research in Sweden: Child's perspective and child perspective], *8*(1–2), 101–113.

Qvortrup, J., Bardy, M., Srgitta, G., & Wintersberger, H. (Eds.). (1994). *Childhood matters: Social theory, practice and politics.* Aldershot, UK: Avebury.

Rogoff, B. (1990). *Apprenticeship in thinking: Cognitive development in social context.* New York, NY: Oxford University Press.

Schnack, K. (2003). Action competence as an educational ideal. In D. Trueit, W. E. Doll, H. Wang, & W. F. Pinar (Eds.), *The internationalization of curriculum studies.* New York, NY: Peter Lang Publishing.

Skilbeck, M. (1976). *School-based curriculum development and teacher education.* Mimeograph. Paris: OECD publishing.

Skjervheim, H. (1992). Kritik af mistankens hermeneutik. Skjervheim: *Filosofi og dømmekraft.* Oslo, Norway: Universitetsforlaget.

Socialministeriet. (2004). *Lov om ændring af lov om social service: Pædagogiske læreplaner for børn i dagtilbud til børn* [Act on educational curricula]. København, Denmark: Socialministeriet.

Sommer, D., Pramling Samuelsson, P., & Hundeide, D. (Eds.). (2010). *Child perspectives and children's perspectives in theory and practice.* New York, NY: Springer Science+Business Media B.V.

Stenhouse, L. (1975). *An introduction to curriculum research and development.* London, UK: Heinemann Educational Books.

Stern, D. (1985). *The interpersonal world of the infant: A view from psychoanalysis and developmental psychology.* London, UK: Karnac Books.

Trevarthen, C. (1998). The concept and foundation of infant inter-subjectivity. In S. Bråten (Ed.), *Intersubjective communication and emotion in early ontogeny.* Cambridge, UK: Cambridge University Press.

Tyler, R. W. (1949). *Basic principles of curriculum and instruction.* Chicago, IL: University of Chicago Press.

Vejleskov, H. (Ed.). (1997). *Den danske børnehave. Studier om myter, meninger og muligheder.* [The Danish Kindergarten. Studies on myths, meanings and possibilities]. Skrifter fra Center fra Småbørnsforskning Nr. 8. Copenhagen: Danmarks Lærerhøjskole.

Velfærdsministeriet. (2007). Lov om dag-, fritids- og klubtilbud m.v. til børn og unge (Dagtilbudsloven). [Act on day-offer]. Velfærdsministeriet.

Vygotsky, L.S. (1978). *Mind in Society. The Development of higher psychological Processes.* M. Cole et al. (Eds.), Cambridge, Massachusetts: Harward University Press.

Walker, D.F. & Soltis, J.F. (1997). *Curriculum and aims* (3rd ed.). New York and London: Teachers College Press.

CHAPTER 13

Contested concepts in educational play:
A comparative analysis of early childhood
policy frameworks in New Zealand and England

Elizabeth Wood

ABSTRACT

This chapter provides a critical analysis of contemporary versions of play in national curriculum policies for early childhood education and in practice. Focusing on *Te Whāriki* in Aotearoa New Zealand (Ministry of Education, 1996) and the *Early Years Foundation Stage* (EYFS) in England (Department for Education, 2012), the analysis looks at three contested concepts: play as learning, play as curriculum and play as pedagogy. Critical discourse analysis is used to consider these concepts as discursive constructions within the two policy frameworks and to uncover the ways in which discourses operate in the sites of policy and practice. These constructions are juxtaposed with contemporary play scholarship and wider theory. I argue that validations for play as learning, curriculum and pedagogy have been re-formulated in policy texts in ways that align 'educational play' with neo-liberal discourses and, in the EYFS, result in a technicist version of play. Finding a best fit between these positions constitutes a 'problem-space' and a provocation to ask difficult questions about play and its place in early childhood curricula.

Introduction

In early childhood education there is a longstanding international discourse that positions play as education, in as much as play contributes to children's learning, development and progress (Bodrova, 2008; Fleer, 2010; Saracho, 2012; Sutton-Smith, 1997). Within this discourse three concepts have been influential: play-based learning, play-based curriculum and play-based pedagogy, each of which carries assumptions about the ways in which play can be institutionalised within policy frameworks and in practice. (The fourth strand of assessment is the focus of Chapter 10 in this volume).

Play is conceptualised in contrasting ways in the national policy frameworks for England and New Zealand in terms of the theoretical ideas on which they draw regarding children's learning and development, how curricula are constructed, the pedagogical processes that aim to maximise the benefits of play for children, and how practitioners demonstrate those benefits through accountability mechanisms. Although both countries share a similar historical legacy of Western concepts about play and its institutionalisation within early childhood education, this analysis shows differences in their subsequent trajectories; specifically, the extent to which technicist versions of play have been produced within policy discourses. However, as Nuttall states in the Introduction, both countries are facing an intensification of the language of risk, performance, measurement and accountability, and play remains vulnerable to neo-liberal cultures of surveillance and performativity (Broadhead & Burt, 2012; Wood, in press).

The first section of this chapter describes the methods used to uncover the evolution of contrasting policy discourses. This leads on to a comparative analysis of the key concepts relating to play used in the EYFS and *Te Whāriki*, and their theoretical context. The following sections compare and contrast these policy frameworks in relation to the concepts of play as learning, curriculum and pedagogy, drawing on empirical research. The conclusion highlights the tensions and challenges that arise from these positions.

Methods

Critical discourse analysis (CDA) encompasses a range of theories and methods for exploring the language of discourse, particularly the ways in which meanings are produced and conveyed through written and spoken texts, images and graphics (Rogers, 2011). Critical discourse analysis investigates the language of texts and situates their meanings within wider historical, social and political contexts. Intertextuality within CDA refers to the incidence and influence of other texts within a text, such as references to theory, research, reviews or related policy frameworks, as well as systems of beliefs and values (Rogers, 2011). As a theoretical approach to policy analysis, CDA offers the potential for macro- and micro-levels of analysis of specific aspects of social policy and "the underlying issues of power and ideology embedded within the definition of the perceived problem and solution" (Woodside-Iron, 2011, p. 155). Critical deconstruction therefore involves the process of sorting through the possible meanings suggested by policy texts as cultural forms, and as 'expert languages' that connect different forms of language, power and knowledge (Tonkiss, 2004). Deconstruction is not an attempt to destroy the meaning of texts, but is rather a way of looking through, and exposing, their wide-ranging meanings (Henricks, 2011, p. 215) and considering what is involved in the transition from policy texts to policy enactment at different sites.

Critical discourse analysis provides an appropriate framework for a micro-analysis of play in the EYFS and *Te Whāriki* for a number of reasons. For a start, the policy frameworks in both countries have been informed by similar theoretical and ideological concepts (Hedges & Cullen, 2012). Second, the frameworks have evolved over a similar period of time, and have been changed and adapted in response to feedback from stakeholders. Third, this evolution has taken place within the circulation of wider neo-liberal discourses that have influenced international trends in education towards privatisation, marketisation and corporatisation (Ruffolo, 2009), as well as systems of regulation, monitoring and accountability. Fourth, early childhood education and care has evolved in relation to wider social policies such as raising standards and achievement, improving children's life chances, preparing children for school and preventing school failure. These policies reflect neo-liberal concerns with the effectiveness of pre-school provision in relation to quality, costs and long-term outcomes, to the extent that 'effectiveness' has become a dominant authoritative discourse.

Focusing on the two policy frameworks, this textual micro-analysis used electronic search tools to identify statements about play in the online documents for the EYFS and *Te Whāriki*. These were then sorted in relation to aspects of practice such as pedagogy, curriculum, learning, assessment and school readiness in order to examine how these texts are structured to produce particular interpretations of play. Related policy texts that support practice were also examined in order to consider how discourses are constructed and reinforced, and how meanings are controlled by key stakeholders through forms of representation and intertextuality. Notions of educational play were then deconstructed to reveal the influence of neo-liberal discourses and the challenges posed for practitioners in both countries.

Key concepts in educational play: the *Early Years Foundation Stage*

In 2012 a new version of the *Early Years Foundation Stage* was introduced in England, focusing on children from birth to five. This version was the outcome of a 2-year review led by Dame Clare Tickell (Department for Education, 2011), which proposed several changes that reflected a change of government and ideology (from New Labour to the

Conservative–Liberal Democrat coalition in 2010). Developmental theories remain the dominant discourse within the *Statutory Framework for the Early Years Foundation Stage* (Department for Education, 2012) and related policy texts. This discourse promotes a universal view of development, with children following similar pathways in order to achieve the developmental indicators of progress and the learning goals specified in *Development Matters* (Early Education & Department for Education, 2012). The learning goals are "the knowledge, skills and understanding children should have at the end of the academic year in which they turn five" (Department for Education, 2012, p. 2), and these set the educational standards that are expected for this age phase. Summative assessments are based on a developmental check at age two, and on practitioner judgements at age five about whether children are "emerging", "expected" or "exceeding" the learning goals.

Play is positioned as "the route through which the areas of learning should be delivered" (Department for Education, 2011, p. 28) and as one of three characteristics of effective teaching and learning:

- playing and exploring—children investigate and experience things, and 'have a go';
- active learning—children concentrate and keep on trying if they encounter difficulties, and enjoy achievements; and
- creating and thinking critically—children have and develop their own ideas, make links between ideas, and develop strategies for doing things. (Department for Education, 2012, p. 7)

The EYFS has been strongly influenced by the government-funded study on *Effective Provision for Preschool Education* (Sylva, Melhuish, Sammons, Siraj-Blachford, & Taggart, 2010), which recommends that

> effective pedagogy in the early years involves both the kind of interaction traditionally associated with the term "teaching", and also the provision of instructive learning play environments and routines. (Siraj-Blatchford, Sylva, Muttock, Gilden and Bell, 2002, p. 38)

Educational play is privileged within the effectiveness discourse because it is needed to serve age-related developmental purposes:

> Each area of learning and development must be implemented through planned, purposeful play and through a mix of adult-led and child-initiated activity. Play is essential for children's development, building their confidence as they learn to explore, to think about problems, and relate to others. Children learn by leading their own play, and by taking part in play which is guided by adults. There is an ongoing judgement to be made by practitioners about the balance between activities led by children, and activities led or guided by adults. Practitioners must respond to each

child's emerging needs and interests, guiding their development through warm,
positive interaction. (Department for Education, 2012, p. 6)

Although practitioners can exercise judgement about the balance between child-
initiated and adult-led activities, evidence indicates consistently that, in practice, the
balance tips towards the latter. This is because practitioners continue to struggle with
implementing play in ways that lead to defined learning outcomes (Broadhead & Burt,
2012; Roberts-Holmes, 2012). In addition, the emphasis on school readiness means that
play is gradually phased out during the last year (age 4–5 years) of the EYFS:

> As children grow older, and as their development allows, it is expected that the balance
> will gradually shift towards more activities led by adults, to help children prepare for
> more formal learning, ready for Year 1. (Department for Education, 2012, p. 6)

The EYFS codifies a technicist version of play because it is expected to lead to the
achievement of curriculum goals. This is reinforced by the authoritative discourse
within the EYFS review (Department for Education, 2011) about "effective", "good",
"best" and "very best" practices:

> The very best practice in the early years acknowledges the importance of children
> using their curiosity and experiencing the pleasure of learning through play. But
> the best practice also ensures that all children grow up literate and numerate and
> ready for the next stage of their learning. That is why Tickell emphasized that early
> years practitioners should adopt a fluid, flexible approach that includes supporting
> children to be ready for a more formal setting as they get older. Readiness for Year
> 1 and later life depends on an approach to child development which combines play
> and teaching in safe environments in the early years and in which children experience
> warm positive interaction, and can explore and learn, with appropriate support from
> skilled adults. (Department for Education, 2011, p. 14)

Practitioners are therefore caught between two discourses: responding to emerging
needs and interests and preparing children for formal learning. Play has thus been
subordinated to policy agendas that privilege educational effectiveness and school
readiness (Broadhead, Howard, & Wood, 2010; Brooker, 2011), and that assume that
play can be phased out before the transition to compulsory school occurs. Although
there are similar neo-liberal policy discourses operating in both countries, the following
section demonstrates how contrasting responses have been constructed regarding
play within *Te Whāriki*.

Key concepts in educational play: *Te Whāriki*

The development of *Te Whāriki* (Ministry of Education, 1996) occurred through close
collaborations between academics, practitioners, communities and policy makers,
and although it has remained the same, its socio-cultural theoretical framing has

been developed over time, and it now aligns pedagogy and assessment practices with the curriculum strands and goals (Carr et al., 2009). In contrast to the EYFS, there are few explicit statements in *Te Whāriki* regarding the purposes that play must, or should, serve. Play-based learning is socially and contextually situated, and is understood as being mediated by relationships between people, places and things. Play and playfulness are embedded within the strands and goals, notably strand 5 —Exploration—Mana Aotūroa: "Children experience an environment where their play is valued as meaningful learning and the importance of spontaneous play is recognised" (Ministry of Education, 1996, p. 84).

The key to understanding the role of play in *Te Whāriki* lies in the focus on children's learning dispositions and working theories. *Te Whāriki* is informed by 20 years' development of the central concept of learning dispositions, which encompass learning orientation, habits of mind and learning power, all of which are closely tethered to the subject knowledges and domain-specific expertise (Carr et al., 2009, p. 3):

> Dispositions act as an affective and cultural filter for trajectories of learning in the making, and they turn knowledge and skill into action. They can often be traced back through generations of families and students, and are strengthened, adapted, transformed or interrupted through circumstance and experience. They are the source of the recognition (or misrecognition) of learning opportunities and provide strategy and motivation for the inevitable disposition that is learning. (Carr et al., 2009, p. 15)

Learning dispositions are important outcomes in relation to the five strands of the curriculum (Wellbeing, Belonging, Contribution, Communication, and Exploration), and the essential knowledge, skills and attitudes that are the outcomes identified within each area of learning. The outcomes are indicative rather than prescribed: the knowledge, skills and attitudes combine to form children's "working theories" and help the child to develop the dispositions that encourage learning (Ministry of Education, 1996, p. 44; Peters & Davis, 2011). When planning the curriculum, practitioners will have some outcomes in mind, but these are formulated in ways that are responsive to the child or group of children and should reflect dimensions of diversity such as culture, ethnicity, gender, language and special educational needs. Thus the model of assessment is formative, based on pedagogical documentation (Learning Stories, see Carr & Lee, 2012) that involves the perspectives of children, families and practitioners.

In spite of the lack of definitive policy guidance, research shows that play is used as:

- a means of organising activities and promoting learning dispositions (Carr et al., 2009)

- a source for children's interests that drive play or arise from play (Hedges, Cullen, & Jordan, 2011)
- a means whereby children integrate individual goals with group goals (Alcock, 2010)
- contexts for integrating children's knowledge and experiences across home, community and school sites (Hedges & Cullen, 2012).

Although *Te Whāriki* is a bicultural framework, there is flexibility for other ethnic groups who wish to support their cultural heritage within the early childhood curriculum (Ministry of Education, 1996, p. 12). Cultural responsiveness is demonstrated in the exemplars of Learning Stories (Carr, Lee, Jones, & Ministry of Education, 2004, 2007, 2009) that were developed by academics and practitioners, and that include evidence of learning through play and playfulness (Carr & Lee, 2012). In spite of sustained attention to cultural diversities, as Leaupepe (2011) argues, there are a number of critical factors that explain why play remains problematic. Her research at Pasifika centres and with Pasifika student teachers indicates that play may not be valued for a number of reasons, including cultural influences, parental attitudes, teachers' values and beliefs about play, and how student teachers engage with dominant Western ideas about play.

Loveridge, Rosewarne, Shuker, Barker and Nager (2012) conducted a study of two early childhood centres in New Zealand in terms of parents' and practitioners' perspectives of how they respond to diversities. A key finding was the importance of sustained communication for building mutual respect and trust, and creating "a shared space for understanding" (p. 107). This enabled parents to share with practitioners fine-grained details of home and cultural practices in ways that produced culturally sensitive solutions or explanations for children's actions, play, choices and interests. Practitioners were able to communicate the values of their centre settings and to understand what parents and families valued about their practices. However, as Loveridge et al. (2012) argue, deep understanding of diversities requires ethical and socio-political engagement with dominant early childhood discourses, children's biases, the subjectivities of the practitioners, and inequalities in power relationships.

It is difficult to avoid some conceptualisation of child development in early childhood frameworks because of the dominance of developmental theories and their international legacy within the field (Hedges & Cullen, 2012). However, the discourse of development in *Te Whāriki* is less deterministic than in the EYFS. *Te Whāriki* sets out some characteristics of children at different ages (infants, toddlers, young children), which are linked to curriculum requirements, but with the acknowledgement that there are "considerable variations between individual children, as well as different cultural perspectives about appropriate age arrangements" (Ministry of Education, 1996,

p. 20). Formative assessment methods based on pedagogical documentation are a means of reflecting cultural and contextual variations. There is no developmental cut-off at school entry age: during the early school years the principles and strands of the early childhood curriculum continue to apply and can be interwoven with those of the New Zealand curriculum statements for schools (Ministry of Education, 2007).

This analysis has revealed the contexts of influence in which policy discourses about play have been constructed, and the contexts of policy text production in which meanings are controlled by key stakeholders through forms of representation, intertextuality and policy geneaologies. It is argued here that contrasting versions of play as learning, play as curriculum and play as pedagogy are encoded in the EYFS and *Te Whāriki*. Both text and discourse about play within the EYFS are structured to create technicist interpretations, whereas *Te Whāriki* sustains more open-ended approaches. The following sections focus on tensions and challenges in the contexts of practice, and the implications for how early childhood practitioners respond to these policy discourses.

Play as learning

Play has been a rallying position for defending child-centred education against top-down influences that have been exerted through policy intensification (Wood, 2007), in concert with a more assertive focus on the research that links play to learning in the subject disciplines (particularly literacy and numeracy) and domains of development (Saracho, 2012). Much contemporary research draws on socio-cultural theories and demonstrates that play serves educational purposes when it is framed within specific curriculum and pedagogical practices (Fleer, 2010). However, when play is positioned within policy-driven educational discourses, two assumptions are made: first, that the free and spontaneous activities in which children engage are intrinsically valuable for learning and development; and, second, that structured play can be planned, resourced and managed by adults in ways that promote the specific outcomes stated in curriculum frameworks. Both of these assumptions have some credibility in theory but are problematic in practice because they require contrasting pedagogical orientations.

It can be argued that all forms of play in educational settings are structured to varying degrees by macro-level policy influences, and by the micro-level culture, rules, resources, routines and affordances within settings. Contemporary research within a Vygotskian tradition validates the discourse of educational play and indicates that young children benefit from adult scaffolding of pretence and subject knowledge (Bodrova, 2008; Diachenko, 2011; Fleer, 2010). But there are differences between adult-structured play and the structures that children create for themselves in their spontaneous play. Sutton-Smith argues that many theories are used to justify the hegemony of adults over children, which is revealed in the ways in which the theories provide rationalization for the adult control of children's play: to stimulate it, negate it, exclude it, or encourage limited forms of it. (1997, p. 49)

In free play, children's agendas may not be consistent with those of adults because their purposes for playing incorporate issues of identity, status and peer affiliation. Free play activities create opportunities for exercising and affirming group and individual agency because children are acting with imagined power (Wood, 2013). They actively drive their own and each others' development through observation and creative imitation, performing different roles and relating to others in ways that they are not yet fully capable of performing (Holzman, 2009). From a socio-cultural perspective the collaborative nature of play explains some of the ways in which "children are capable of doing so much more in collective activity than in individual activity" (Holzman, 2009, p. 30). Play is thus deeply connected to the different cultural repertoires that children bring from their homes and communities, how these influence their own play cultures, and the different ways in which they represent their knowledge and experiences. Children's motivations to play are focused on becoming a more skilled player, developing play repertoires and engaging in more complex forms of play. Children do things in play that they have not be taught explicitly by adults, and thereby learn what knowledge, skills and dispositions are relevant to managing and sustaining play.

Vygotsky's interpretation of play (1978) drew attention to children's formulation of rules, which become a developmental precursor of children's ability to follow rules in other contexts, in ways that are directed towards the collectivisation of individual action. In contrast, Henricks (2010) argues that the qualities of play are transformative and consummatory. Play activities are transformative because

They represent the efforts of people to assert themselves against the elements of the world, to alter those elements, and in doing so learn about the nature of reality and about their own powers to operate in those settings. From this perspective rules become intrinsic to the purposes and meaning of play as children test themselves against the rules. (2010, p. 192)

Play is consummatory because the players operate inside the boundaries of space and time that mark the play occasion; they are preoccupied with the quality of their experience and the goals that lie within the event; and they are fulfilled or completed within the boundaries of the event (Henricks, 2010, pp. 193–194). Free play has its own purposes and meanings, which may not be accessible to adults, and may be deliberately hidden from adults as children seek to protect some privacy and exercise forms of agency that may not be 'approved', such as inclusion and exclusion (Wood, 2013). Thus from the perspective of pedagogy, the very qualities that make play so attractive for children also create challenges for practitioners when they are expected to align play with curriculum goals. These perspectives go some way towards explaining the challenges that play-based learning continues to pose for practitioners (Aubrey & Durmaz, 2012; Roberts-Holmes, 2012), and raise questions about the concept of play as curriculum.

Play as curriculum

The assertion that the early childhood curriculum should be play-based is deeply embedded in international discourses, and, until recently, there has been a lack of curriculum theorising in the field. Dillon proposes that

> *curriculum is constituted of essential questions to which our practices represent particularized answers.* To know what we are doing, then, is to know the questions that we are answering in action; and to do curriculum rightly, let us say that we may permissibly give certain different yet possibly right answers yet *we must ask the same right questions* to begin with. (Dillon, 2009, p. 357, emphasis in original)

Questions about curriculum in early childhood have centred on dichotomised concepts such as:

- child-initiated versus teacher-directed approaches
- play versus work
- experiences versus subjects
- progressive versus traditional approaches
- informal versus formal learning
- processes versus outcomes.

These debates reflected entrenched beliefs about the universal efficacy of play but did not ask the "right questions" (Dillon, 2009) about established assumptions and ideologies, or how play-based curricula might incorporate social diversity, equity and social justice. To ask critical questions about play risks shaking the very foundations on which early childhood education has been built. At the same time, not asking those critical questions has arguably contributed to the diminished version of play in the EYFS and the 'play as education' discourse that permeates contemporary curriculum frameworks.

Within this discourse there is substantial research evidence that specific environments and activities can be planned to promote learning and development through play. Johnson, Christie and Wardle (2005) take the pragmatic position that play-led curriculum and curriculum-led play create the conditions for flexible approaches that combine freedom and structure. However, both of these concepts can be contested, for a number of reasons. For one thing, it is difficult to prove that play activities, whether free or structured, lead to the specific purposes or goals for which they have been designed. For example, if adults and children play snakes and ladders, the intended outcomes may include curriculum goals relating to counting, socialisation or abiding by rules. Other, and possibly more important, outcomes for the children may include learning what it means to be a player, what is involved in play, how rules operate in play, how to cheat, and how to deal with losing. Therefore children may learn more about play than they do about curriculum goals. Moreover, the curriculum goals may serve future (as yet unspecified) uses, whereas the play goals may be of more immediate use to them in other activities, or in developing their present status within the community.

The concept of play-led curriculum is more complex in the context of freely chosen socio-dramatic play: adults cannot create the goals in advance because they emerge within the dynamic interactions among the players. It is therefore difficult to extrapolate what children are learning that relates directly to the curriculum goals in the EYFS. It may be easier for practitioners to identify the broader working theories, dispositions and competencies in *Te Whāriki* (such as respect for others, self-confidence, resilience, persistence, problem-solving, exploring, thinking, and reasoning). A shared assumption in both frameworks is that in free play children disclose interests and working theories, which form the basis of curriculum planning in ways that support individual development, enabling children to achieve the goals.

However, building a curriculum around children's interests is problematic (Wood, 2007): there is little research that examines the origins of their interests, how they are expressed and developed through self-chosen activities, how they become the basis for learning (Hedges & Cullen, 2012), and what forms of pedagogy support children's working theories (Peters & Davis, 2011). Similar concerns are echoed by Brooker (2010, 2011), who questions whose cultures, interests, goals and activities are privileged in the authoritative developmental discourses of the EYFS. Interests that reflect children's popular cultures, or forms of play such as rough and tumble, may not be approved even though they may be the driving force for free play. Children's interests may also reflect their motivations to create relationships, to develop their unique identities and personalities, and to enact modes of expression that convey imaginative and creative interpretations of everyday events. Central to these processes is human agency—the desire to act in and on the world. Thus freedom to choose is part of a more complex narrative in that children must be able to deal with the effects of their choices, whether these are intentional or unintentional. Children's needs and interests are therefore profoundly social and cultural, and are intrinsically bound up with agency and identity (Hedges, 2010; Wood, in press).

Carr et al. (2009) conceptualise interests, within the dispositional framing of *Te Whāriki*, as the starting points for inter-subjective understanding, dialogue, joint attention, intentionality and knowledge construction. Interests also serve social and cultural purposes because they become the focus for the development of recognition, respect and interdependence. Assessment practices in response to *Te Whāriki* are congruent with these principles and use narrative approaches to document working theories and learning in the context of social relationships. Assessment practices in the EYFS focus on individual progress and attainment, based on the stated developmental indicators and learning goals. However, play provides multi-layered contexts in which children work together on group as well as individual goals, and the fluid, unpredictable nature of free play does not necessarily result directly in the goals or intended learning outcomes that are valued in policy documents. Just as goals and activities are distributed between peers, so too are the shared motivations for play, such as agency, control, and how children exercise power with and over others (Wood, 2013). Therefore, the policy emphasis in the EYFS on planned and purposeful play, and integrated (adult- and child-initiated) activities, is problematic because it is difficult to achieve a best fit between what play means for children and the performativity discourse on what play is expected to deliver. Both the EYFS and *Te Whāriki* pose further challenges to practitioners because of the need for flexible and responsive pedagogical approaches.

Play as pedagogy

Within the play as education discourse, much attention has been given to affirming adults' roles in play (Bodrova, 2008; Broadhead & Burt, 2012), but again there is evidence of inconsistency between policy recommendations and the more nuanced understanding that is evident in research. It is well documented that, although play scholars and early childhood practitioners continue to endorse the many benefits of play, research on practice continues to highlight tensions and dilemmas (Hedges & Cullen, 2012; Roberts-Holmes, 2012). In the context of teaching and learning mathematics in the EYFS, Aubrey and Durmaz (2012) reported a small-scale study of policy and practice in which different pedagogical approaches resulted in wide variations in children's responses and in their mathematical understanding. Aubrey and Durmaz identified multiple and contradictory demands, including the "unchallenged assumptions about connections between play, standards of achievement and learning" (2012, p. 74).

Practitioners struggle to implement good-quality play, both because the concept is itself problematic and also because universal assumptions about what constitutes 'good quality' are derived from the policy-compliant educational effectiveness discourse. Pressures from the standards agenda mean that the role of practitioners is problematic because episodes of child–adult interaction may be influenced by contrasting or even competing intentions, where children intend to pursue their own goals while the adults intend them to achieve curriculum goals. The controlling forms of pedagogy in the EYFS sit uncomfortably with free play, which can seem (un)reasonable, (ir)rational and (un)predictable, depending on the perspective of the child or the adult. Free play poses considerable threats to the virtues of order, stability and regulation that are typical of early childhood settings, because it does not conform to the development of the docile pupil who must learn to act reasonably and responsibly. Nor does play align easily with the assumed logic of a transmission model of pedagogy or with pedagogy as a means of delivering curriculum content. The EYFS positions play as a form of pedagogy, but with caveats about preparing children for more formal learning. Within this discourse, play is understood as the servant to other forms of activity that are not play, and play itself can be phased out as children progress to formal education. In contrast, Bodrova (2008, p. 364) argues that mature or advanced play continues to develop beyond the preschool years, in terms of children's imaginative capabilities, their roles and relationships in play, their ability to create and follow rules, and the quality of roles and scenarios that are created.

In *Te Whāriki* the focus on children's funds of knowledge, dispositions and working theories provides the basis for continuity between early childhood and school settings, with less emphasis on the transition from informal to formal approaches. The expectations are that similar pedagogical approaches will smooth this transition, because New Zealand's curriculum for primary education is aligned with the principles and strands of *Te Whāriki* (Ministry of Education, 2007, p. 42). However, with neo-liberal drivers towards performance, measurement and accountability operating in both countries, transition remains a contentious area; the commitment to play remains tenuous, and the standards agenda exerts considerable leverage. As a result, policy-compliant versions of play are inherently problematic, especially if academic outcomes are privileged as the main content of children's learning. Further attention to children's working theories and funds of knowledge, and how these are used in play, would enable more complex ways of understanding children's goals and trajectories.

Conclusion: Finding a best fit between play in policy and practice

Play has been captured within policy discourses because of the strong advocacy for play-based learning, curriculum and pedagogy within the field. However, policy versions of educational play reflect prevailing neo-liberal ideologies, in which the benefits of play are harnessed as means towards specific ends. The EYFS and *Te Whāriki* construct play in contrasting ways, but with similar assumptions about the value of play to children's learning and development. As a result, play is also subordinated, or at least tamed, within the administrative and regulatory practices these discourses promote. The ways in which play is positioned reflect fundamental tensions between different pedagogical orientations and traditions in early childhood education, ambiguous policy recommendations, and the ways in which policies are implemented in practice (Wood, 2010, p. 10).

Some of the current tensions arise from the ways in which theory has been (mis) interpreted and (mis)used, particularly within educational effectiveness discourses, to convey powerful assumptions about child development, universality, standardisation and objectivity. Therefore it is not surprising that, like Cinderella's glass slipper, finding a best fit for play in policy and practice remains a challenging endeavour. However, there are some interesting sites for progress, as long as the right questions continue to be asked about these discourses and the ways in which they operate in different sites. Based on the foregoing analysis, some of the right questions include a critical focus on play in relation to knowledge, pedagogy, and equity and diversity.

Post-developmental and post-structural theories propose that play is not just a pedagogical site, nor is it the natural and spontaneous activity of childhood that is proposed in much child development theory (Grieshaber & McArdle, 2010; see also Broström, this volume). Play involves complex socio-cultural activity as children engage in cultural interpretations of play in ways that orient them towards active participation. Active participation does not just mean being involved in 'activities': it is through activity that children learn, by organising and reorganising their roles and relationships, using psychological and material tools in creative ways, and inventing new uses, ideas and meanings. Play acts as an integrating mechanism, and different forms of play offer opportunities for children to demonstrate their funds of knowledge, which derive from their school, home and community experiences.

Although play creates many opportunities for children to construct and transfer knowledge, the question remains whether a play-based curriculum can deliver the academic skills that are required for the transition to compulsory school (see also Peters & Paki, this volume). This is not to argue against play, but further research is needed to explore the different purposes that play serves for children and for their learning, particularly the question of whose goals predominate in play activities. This relates to the pressing need for a more complex conceptualisation of progression in play. Children do not progress from play to formal learning (as determined in the EYFS), or from much play to little play: they progress to more complex forms of play and use their play knowledge in increasingly sophisticated ways. Therefore the transition from preschool to compulsory schooling requires more detailed attention to sustaining the qualities that make play so attractive for children, and the knowledge they use and apply in play activities.

From post-structural perspectives, researchers have begun to ask critical questions about play, specifically in relation to assumptions about the universal efficacy of play in relation to multiple dimensions of diversity and the ways in which discourses of effectiveness, quality and child development all contribute to the normalisation and regulation of children and practitioners. Therefore, arguments for play must include greater knowledge about, and responsiveness to, the different values and beliefs found within pluralistic societies. Deeper knowledge of cultural diversity is needed about children, families and communities, and about the beliefs of practitioners at the initial and continuing stages of professional development. This knowledge must come from within those communities as a means of constructing culturally situated understanding of play that can inform equitable practices.

Although policy frameworks within and beyond England and New Zealand are likely to sustain versions of educational play, practitioners need professional knowledge that transcends the limitations of technicist discourses and their different ways in which policy aims to capture play within policy sites. From a CDA perspective, Rogers (2011, p. 7) emphasises the dialectic between individual agency and social structure, including how people use discourses in creative and agentic ways. However, the extent to which such agency can be accomplished within specific sites is likely to vary according to whose ideas and voices are foregrounded, the authoritative impact of policy discourses, and a willingness to engage in critical debates about long-standing assumptions about play. Sutton-Smith (1997, p. 195) emphasises the "incredible structural complexity of the intricate enactment of play" and the wide variations among players, forms of play and play choices. The spaces between structural complexity and intricate enactment remain fruitful areas for enquiry.

References

Alcock, S. (2010). Young children's playfully complex communication: Distributed imagination. *European Early Childhood Education Research Journal, 18*(2), 215–228.

Aubrey, C., & Durmaz, D. (2012). Policy-to-practice contexts for early childhood mathematics in England. *International Journal of Early Years Education, 20*(1), 59–75.

Bodrova, E. (2008). Make-believe play versus academic skills: A Vygotskian approach to today's dilemma of early childhood education. *European Early Childhood Education Research Journal, 16*(3), 357–369.

Broadhead, P., & Burt, A. (2012). *Understanding young children's learning through play: Building playful pedagogies.* Abingdon, UK: Routledge.

Broadhead, P., Howard, J., & Wood, E. (2010). *Play and learning in the early years: From research to practice.* London, UK: Sage.

Brooker, L. (2010). Learning to play, or playing to learn?: Children's participation in the cultures of homes and settings. In L. Brooker & S. Edwards (Eds.), *Engaging play* (pp. 39–53). Maidenhead, UK: Open University Press.

Brooker, L. (2011). Taking children seriously: An alternative agenda for research? *Journal of Early Childhood Research, 9*(2) 137–149.

Carr, M., Smith, A. B., Duncan, J., Jones, C., Lee, W., & Marshall, K. (2009). *Learning in the making: Disposition and design in early education.* Rotterdam, The Netherlands: Sense Publishers.

Carr, M., & Lee, W. (2012). *Learning stories: Constructing learner identities in early education.* London, UK: Sage.

Carr, M., Lee, W., Jones, C., & Ministry of Education. (2004, 2007 & 2009). *Kei tua o te pae: Assessment for learning: Early childhood exemplars.* Books 1–20. Wellington: Learning Media.

Department for Education. (2011). *The early years: Foundations for life, health and learning: An independent report on the early years foundation stage to her Majesty's government.* Retrieved from http://www.dfe.gov.uk.

Department for Education. (2012). *Statutory framework for the early years foundation stage: Setting the standards for learning, development and care for children from birth to five.* Author. Retrieved from http://www.education.gov.uk.

Diachenko, O. (2011). On major developments in preschoolers' imagination. *International Journal of Early Years Education, 19*(1), 19–25.

Dillon, J. T. (2009). The questions of curriculum. *Journal of Curriculum Studies, 41*(3), 343–359.

Early Education & Department for Education. (2012). *Development matters in the early years foundation stage.* Retrieved from http://www.early-education.org.uk

Fleer, M. (2010). *Early learning and development: Cultural-historical concepts in play.* Cambridge, UK: Cambridge University Press.

Grieshaber, S., & McArdle, F. (2010). *The trouble with play.* Maidenhead, UK: Open University Press.

Hedges, H. (2010). Whose goals and interests? In L. Brooker & S. Edwards (Eds.), *Engaging play* (pp. 25–38). Maidenhead, UK: Open University Press.

Hedges, H., & Cullen, J. (2012). Participatory learning theories: A framework for early childhood pedagogy. *Early Child Development and Care, 182*(7), 921-940. doi:10.1080/03004430.2011.597504

Hedges, H., Cullen, J., & Jordan, B. (2011). Early years curriculum: Funds of knowledge as a conceptual framework for children's interests. *Journal of Curriculum Studies, 43*(2), 185–205. doi: 10.1080/00220272.2010.511275

Henricks, T. S. (2010). Play as ascending meaning revisited: Four types of assertive play. In E. E. Nwokah (Ed.), *Play as engagement and communication, play and culture studies, Vol. 10* (pp. 189–216.) Lanham, MD: University Press of America.

Henricks, T. S. (2011). Play as deconstruction. In C. Lobman & B. E. O'Neill (Eds.), *Play and performance, play and culture studies, Vol. 11* (pp. 201–236). Lanham, MD: University Press of America.

Holzman, L. (2009). *Vygotsky at work and play.* Hove, East Sussex, UK: Routledge.

Johnson, J. E., Christie, J. F., & Wardle. F. (2005*). Play, development and early education.* New York, NY: Pearson & Allyn and Bacon.

Leaupepe, M. (2011). Pasifika perspectives of play—challenges and responsibilities. *He Kupu (The Word), 2*(4), 19-33. Retrieved from www.hekupu.ac.nz.

Loveridge, J., Rosewarne, S., Shuker, M. J., Barker, A., & Nager, J. (2012). Responding to diversity: Statements and practices in two early childhood education contexts. *European Early Childhood Education Research Journal, 20*(1), 99–113. doi: 10.1080/1350293X.2011.634998

Ministry of Education. (1996). *Te whāriki: He whāriki mātauranga mō ngā mokopuna o Aotearoa: Early childhood curriculum.* Wellington: Learning Media.

Ministry of Education. (2007). *The New Zealand curriculum for English-medium teaching and learning in Years 1–3.* Wellington: Learning Media.

Peters, S., & Davis, K. (2011). Fostering children's working theories: Pedagogic issues and dilemmas in New Zealand. *Early Years: An International Journal of Research and Development, 31*(1), 5–17. Retrieved from http://dx.doi.org/10.1080/09575146.2010.549107

Roberts-Holmes, G. (2012). "It's the bread and butter of our practice": Experiencing the early years foundation stage. *International Journal of Early Years Education, 20*(1), 31–42.

Rogers, R. (2011). (Ed.). *Critical discourse analysis in education* (2nd ed.). Abingdon, UK: Routledge.

Ruffolo, D. V. (2009). Queering child/hood policies: Canadian examples and perspectives. *Contemporary Issues in Early Childhood, 10*(3), 291–308. Retrieved from http://dx.doi.org/10.2304/ciec.2009.10.3.291

Saracho, O. (2012). *An integrated play-based curriculum for young children.* New York, NY: Routledge.

Siraj-Blatchford, I., Sylva, K., Muttock, S., Gilden, R., & Bell, D. (2002). *Researching effective pedagogy in the early years.* Research report No. 356. London, UK: HMSO.

Sutton-Smith, B. (1997). *The ambiguity of play.* Cambridge, MA: Harvard University Press.

Sylva, K., Melhuish, E., Sammons, P., Siraj-Blatchford, I., & Taggart, B. (2010). (Eds.). *Early childhood matters: Evidence from the effective pre-school and primary education project.* London, UK: Routledge.

Tonkiss. F. (2004). Analysing text and speech: Content and discourse analysis. In C. Seale (Ed.), *Researching society and culture* (2nd ed.). (pp. 367–382). London, UK: Sage.

Vygotsky, L. S. (1978). *Mind in society* (translated and edited by M. Cole, V. John-Steiner, S. Scribner, & E. Souberman). Cambridge, MA: Harvard University Press.

Wood, E. (2007). Play policy and practice: Direction of travel or collision course? *Education 3–13, 35*(4), 309–320.

Wood, E. (2010). Developing integrated approaches to play and learning. In P. Broadhead, J. Howard, & E. Wood (Eds.), *Play and learning in the early years, from research to practice* (pp. 9–26). London, UK: Sage.

Wood, E. (in press). Free choice and free play in early childhood education: Troubling the discourse. *International Journal of Early Years Education.*

Wood, E. (2013). *Play, learning and the early childhood curriculum* (3rd ed.). London, UK: Sage.

Woodside-Iron, H. (2011). Using critical discourse analysis to make sense of public policy. In R. Rogers (Ed.), *Critical discourse analysis in education* (2nd ed., pp. 154–182. Abingdon, UK: Routledge.

CHAPTER 14

The future of *Te Whāriki:*
Political, pedagogical and
professional concerns

Helen Hedges

ABSTRACT

This chapter examines issues that influence the ways in which *Te Whāriki* can continue to act as a catalyst for change in early childhood education (Cullen, 2003). Fluctuating political winds that buffet the sector in New Zealand have, to some degree, constrained the potential of *Te Whāriki* to be realised. Other issues relate to pedagogical concerns about professional knowledge and practice, and associated matters involving professional education and the capability of teacher education and professional learning providers. All three factors affect the potential to build systematically on the positive developments that have occurred in the sector.

The chapter begins by describing the ways in which play-based pedagogy, incorporated in *Te Whāriki*, positions adults in educative roles as important decision makers who need a considerable depth of professional knowledge, exemplified in the notion of children's interests. Next it highlights two elements of professional knowledge—contemporary learning theories and content knowledge—to illustrate the need for ongoing professional learning. I then discuss notions of learning outcomes as they pertain to *Te Whāriki* and challenge the sector to be more responsive to these. Finally, some challenges are raised for teacher education and professional learning providers that result from this examination. The chapter argues that sophisticated professional knowledge is required to interpret *Te Whāriki* in order to provide a catalyst for transformation. Teachers and researchers must remain steadfast about this amidst the vacillations of policy.

Introduction

On the international stage *Te Whāriki* (Ministry of Education, 1996) has been an acclaimed early childhood curriculum (Soler & Miller, 2003). It has been commended for its progressive and non-prescriptive bases, its affirmation of the bicultural nature of New Zealand, its inclusion of attention to infants and toddlers, and its emphasis on learning processes and orientations as outcomes. It was designed so that each early childhood setting could 'weave' its own programme, to reflect the social and cultural context in which the programme is embedded. This inherent flexibility has meant that individual teachers and centres have shouldered the responsibility for interpreting and implementing the curriculum, suggesting there is the potential for this weaving to occur in strong or weak ways. Nearly 20 years after its inception, *Te Whāriki* remains a rich document with much potential yet to be realised. Fluctuating political winds, however, have constrained the sector's ability to deliver on *Te Whāriki*. It has often been a case of two steps forward, one step backwards, as the sector attempts to improve children's experiences.

Six years after the introduction of *Te Whāriki*, an early childhood strategic plan (Ministry of Education, 2002) was released. It focused on improving the quality of services, increasing participation in quality services and promoting collaborative relationships as key goals to develop through to 2012. For the first 5 years steady progress was made towards achieving these goals. Recent policy changes, however, have reversed some of these positive steps. In 2009 the Government announced a reduction of targets for fully qualified teachers from 100 percent to 50 to 80 percent. It also shifted the focus to investing in participation in early childhood education by under-represented groups. This latter policy is designed to boost participation by Māori, Pasifika and other children from lower socioeconomic groups in New Zealand, with the hope that this will somehow address the achievement lag these children often experience later at school. I contend that boosting participation in potentially poor-quality centres with either unqualified or under-qualified staff will not begin to address that gap, nor will it stimulate the relationships necessary with families, communities and schools. Also announced was the removal of funding to assist newly qualified teachers during their 2-year, post-graduation teacher registration period from centres with over 80 percent of staff already qualified. This is a short-sighted move. This 2-year period is vital for embedding and contextualising professional knowledge in a coherent way, and for encouraging ongoing learning and reflection in order to provide the required evidence of quality teaching practices.

An evaluation of the strategic plan (Mitchell, Meagher-Lundberg, Mara, Cubey, & Whitford, 2011) noted that many of the positive shifts in quality that occurred from 2004 to 2009 were for outcomes that had been specific goals of Ministry initiatives. An implied criticism is that the needs of the sector may not be fully addressed by targeted initiatives, and may need to incorporate a comprehensive plan determined by the sector itself. This may also be true of the gradually building research base, which has largely relied on small-scale postgraduate studies and partnerships between researchers and teachers, notably the Centres of Innovation (COI), and Teaching and Learning Research Initiatives (TLRI) initiatives (see Chapter 8, this volume, for discussion of these programmes). There has been evidence that pedagogical shifts occurred in the centres that participated in the COI projects,[1] and dissemination of evidence through conference presentations, the Waves series of publications (e.g., Meade, 2009), and other books (e.g., Hartley, Rogers, Smith, Peters, & Carr, 2012). Yet the COI programme was cancelled by the Government without warning in 2009.

Alongside the successes of this research programme, questions have been raised about the long-term impact of such projects and the potential for greater dissemination. An evaluation of the COI programme (Gibbs & Poskitt, 2009) found that although innovative practices were researched, they were not required to be evaluated; there were, therefore, limitations to judging outcomes for children. Similarly, Nuttall (2012) questioned whether the TLRI projects have made much difference to educational practices beyond the participating centres, whether wide dissemination has occurred, how much these projects have contributed to a cumulative evidence base so far, and whether they have contributed to theory critiquing and building rather than theory confirmation.

In terms of the professional learning that has accompanied the implementation of *Te Whāriki*, the assessment project led by Margaret Carr resulting in the *Kei Tua o te Pai* and *Te Whatu Pōkeka* exemplars (Ministry of Education, 2004, 2007a, 2009a, 2009b), appears to have been the most influential. An evaluation of the impact of the exemplars for those who participated in the associated professional development programme reports that teachers changed their practices to incorporate the use of Learning Stories (Stuart, Aitken, Gould, & Meade, 2008). Nevertheless, there is still further potential in many centres for teachers to move beyond anecdotal recordings and captions on copious photographs to understanding and enact formative assessment, as practices are continually improved.

In 2011 the report of the Early Childhood Education Taskforce suggested that the content of *Te Whāriki* did not need revision due to its forward-looking and innovative origins and intent. The Takforce's report reflected ongoing government interest in the sector being able to demonstrate results, also evident in recent Ministry-commissioned literature reviews on outcomes (Mitchell, Wyllie, & Carr, 2008) and transition to school (Peters, 2010), among others. Although the Taskforce's report generated some questions about how much of *Te Whāriki's* potential might remain to be realised, it was welcomed by the sector because it reiterated the importance of universal early childhood provision

---

1 See http://www.educationcounts.govt.nz/publications/ece/22551

and qualified teachers. At the time of writing it has precipitated two reviews of quality in the sector, as well as a review of funding and a proposal that every child be given a unique identifier so that participation in early childhood services can be tracked, but the findings and implications of these actions have yet to result in further policy decisions. The Taskforce's report recommended an evaluation of teachers' implementation of *Te Whāriki* in order to provide evidence of its effect on teaching practices and outcomes for children. Earlier, Cullen (2008) had also appealed for an appropriate longitudinal study to track the outcomes of *Te Whāriki*. These calls appear pertinent when, as noted above, teachers have considerable autonomy to enact the curriculum.

Notwithstanding the immense value of the research and professional learning programmes to date, there is clearly much work still to do in relation to research and teaching relating to *Te Whāriki*, particularly as the rhetoric of evidence-based practice begins to permeate Ministry of Education discourse. There is a case for teachers to carefully take up the challenge to more explicitly demonstrate the outcomes of this holistic and innovative curriculum. It is not possible in this chapter to address all the social, political and cultural constraints and changes that those in the sector find themselves struggling with in order to respond to such a challenge (for an overview, see Mitchell, 2011). Suffice to say for the focus of this chapter that there is a paucity of research and professional learning funding available to assist professional knowledge building, a situation that must change if New Zealand is to follow international trends of coherent investment in children and their teachers to facilitate positive educational, social and economic outcomes.

A further significant challenge for the future of *Te Whāriki* lies in the diversity of the sector. Parent-led services such as kōhanga reo and Playcentre are an accepted part of service provision. This chapter could be read as focusing on teacher-led centres rather than parent-led centres because of the arguments made about the necessity for depth of professional knowledge, commonly recognised in a qualification that leads to teacher registration. The word 'teacher' is therefore used in this chapter to represent all adults in educative roles. All such adults can contemplate the arguments of this chapter, which considers advances made since Cullen's (2003) chapter in the first edition of this book and raises ongoing concerns about professional knowledge and practice. Also, parent-led services would be part of any evaluation or longitudinal study, thereby making it possible to identify the ways in which various types of, and contexts for, professional knowledge may be a critical variable.

This chapter examines the ways in which *Te Whāriki* could continue to act as a catalyst for change in teacher knowledge and practice in the light of Cullen's (2003) commentary. In particular, I raise issues about the scope and depth of the professional knowledge required to make decisions during play-based pedagogy, exemplified by discussion of the construct of children's interests, learning theories, content knowledge and learning outcomes as they pertain to *Te Whāriki* (see Wood, this volume, for further discussion of issues related to play-based pedagogy). I challenge teacher education and professional learning providers to strengthen their awareness of contemporary theory and research. This awareness is vital for teachers to realise *Te Whāriki's* potential and for them to engage with the complex learning outcomes it describes as they continue to play their part in a variable political climate. I conclude with suggestions about matters overlooked thus far in relation to *Te Whāriki* that I believe warrant further investigation. Taken together, these matters function as constraints on any future evaluation of the implementation of *Te Whāriki* and outcomes for children, because its execution has been constrained by vacillating policy.

These matters are also my chosen foci because I have recently felt a sense of *déjà vu* in relation to *Te Whāriki* and policy. Reflecting on the early implementation of *Te Whāriki*, May and Carr (1997) noted that many constraints affected teachers' ability to deliver the high expectations of the curriculum. These included regulations and funding in relation to teacher qualifications, group sizes, ratios, and the provision of professional education programmes. As May and Carr argued then, policy that champions the effective implementation of *Te Whāriki* is a critical systemic factor in determining whether teachers and researchers can realise its potential and, therefore, provide evidence of the curriculum's effect on teaching practices and outcomes for children. It is timely, therefore, to examine the complexity of professional knowledge required to engage with this innovative and interpretive curriculum.

Play in educational provision

Participation in play has long been accepted as an important way to promote children's learning. Yet the developmental theories that have influenced early childhood pedagogy have often meant that play-based learning has tended to focus on providing children with richly resourced, integrated environments in which they are free to choose their own play experiences from the resources and equipment provided by adults. Learning was viewed within this theorisation as largely an individual activity, little supported by adults in teaching roles. *Te Whāriki* moves beyond the superficial interpretations invited by long-held mantras such as 'learning through play' into more complex, socio-cultural interpretations of play and its place in learning, curriculum and pedagogy. *Te Whāriki* values children as competent learners and highlights play-based learning environments in the principles that guide pedagogy. However, it identifies that every experience children engage in is a potential learning opportunity, whether through play *per se* or, for example, through deliberate planning (such as projects), or through interactions that arise spontaneously, often stimulated by events in families and communities. Socio-cultural theory also emphasises that peers and adults have important roles to play in enhancing teaching and learning.

In 2003 Cullen suggested that *Te Whāriki* may have made little difference to the play-based programmes offered in many centres, where long-held theories, beliefs and practices held sway. In this volume Wood teases out the concepts of play as learning, play as curriculum and play as pedagogy. Wood's nuanced interpretations could help shift teachers' understanding of play-based provision. Teachers can realise learning for children through holistic views of outcomes while maintaining integrated, playful approaches to pedagogy during planned and spontaneous interactions. Teachers can thereby retain both the disposition to be playful and the joy of childhood in pedagogical provision (Broadhead & Burt, 2012).

Complex interpretations of play and its place in learning, curriculum and pedagogy rely on depth of professional knowledge. For example, in interpreting *Te Whāriki*, many settings focus on identifying children's interests as a basis for planning. Interests-based curriculum and pedagogy in early childhood therefore rely on interpretation of what constitutes an 'interest'. Here, the dominance of developmental psychology as a long-standing early foundation for practice has led to a narrow interpretation of play interests. Until recently, international studies all defined children's interests as activities or objects in the play environment, such as playdough, blocks, dolls, trains, trucks (e.g., Cremin & Slatter 2004; Gmitrova, Podhajecká, & Gmitrov, 2009). Similarly, in my study (Hedges, 2010b), when teachers, parents and children were asked about what constituted children's interests, they first referred to activity areas in the learning environment, such as the sandpit, painting or books. The provision of abundant resources and space, organised well to promote integrated learning experiences, continues to be a focus of early childhood pedagogy.

Aligning the notion of children's interests with the disposition to inquire leads to potentially richer socio-cultural interpretations of the concept. Specifically, building on Cullen's (2003) idea of narrow and strong interpretations of children's interests, it may be useful to consider a continuum of children's interests (Hedges, 2010b). This continuum might be a function of their 'funds of knowledge', a credit-based notion of knowledge related to household wellbeing and functioning found in diverse families, which can be used to strengthen centre–family partnerships (González, Moll, & Amanti, 2005). In this continuum, activity-based interests feed back and forward among deeper, ongoing interests and fundamental inquiry questions. Children reveal these interests during their play choices. Providing conceptual frameworks to guide teachers' recognition of and decision making about children's interests encourages deeper interpretations of the concept and helps them to provide contextually appropriate curriculum.

Funds of knowledge is a concept that encourages authentic, sensitive teacher–family partnerships with diverse communities. This may be particularly pertinent given the origins of the research in everyday literacy practices in bilingual communities and the growing number of immigrants to New Zealand who speak more than one language. The funds of knowledge concept is in line with the Taskforce's report, which notes that:

> Early childhood teacher education may need to focus on the family and community aspect more than it currently does. This education should focus on a strengths-based approach, where teachers are able to identify and build on the skills and knowledge every family brings to the setting. However, this wealth is often overlooked, or not recognised, because of negative teacher attitudes toward families. This thinking and practice has to shift, because it is families who have the most influence on a child's life, well-being and growth. (Early Childhood Education Taskforce, 2011, p. 93)

Utilising conceptual frameworks that encourage teachers to empower families as partners in children's learning to guide pedagogical practices suggests that teachers need positive and open attitudes towards families. Positive attitudes can be encouraged by professional learning experiences and a strong, theoretically rich foundation of professional knowledge. Yet, in keeping with many countries internationally, not all early childhood teachers in New Zealand currently hold a teaching qualification, which could be one indicator of a sound grounding in professional knowledge. As Cullen (2003) asked, is such a qualification profile "adequate to deal with the complexities of *Te Whāriki*?" (p. 273).

Professional knowledge

Early childhood teachers are positioned in this chapter as key decision makers who draw on a range of personal and professional knowledge to inform their practice. In studies in the primary and secondary sectors, Shulman (1986, 1987) defined seven multi-faceted categories of teacher knowledge: knowledge of content; pedagogy; curriculum; learners and learning; contexts of schooling; pedagogical content knowledge; and educational philosophies, goals and objectives. These categories are relevant for early childhood teachers if they are contextualised to the teaching of children aged birth to 5 years. In their study, Carr and Kemmis (1986) included informal knowledge, which may include personal and practice-based knowledge, by incorporating the categories they termed teachers' "common-sense knowledge and folk wisdom".

A range of informal personal knowledge, based on life experience, may complement professional knowledge and may be evident in decision making and action. Given that *Te Whāriki* is designed to be applied differently in diverse settings, consideration of the ways in which personal and professional knowledge combine may be particularly pertinent. For example, personal/professional knowledge and competence in te reo and tikanga Māori are likely to be determinants of how well bicultural imperatives are met, alongside how these are valued and enacted in specific contexts of practice (see Ritchie, this volume). Teachers' own interests, life and family experiences may influence the choices they make in co-constructing curriculum and extending children's interests (Hedges, 2012). This may lead much decision making to be tacit rather than explicit, which can limit opportunities to rationalise and justify pedagogical actions that draw on theory and research in matters of implementation (Stephen, 2010).

Te Whāriki has multiple theoretical bases, and early childhood theoretical discourse has evolved in the intervening years since its introduction (see Fleer, this volume). *Te Whāriki* has been increasingly interpreted by academics from socio-cultural, postmodern and post-structural perspectives. But, unless they are recently qualified, teachers may struggle to move from the legacy of developmental psychology to understand and embrace multiple theories and their implications for an active teaching role. In 1996 Cullen argued that a lack of deep understanding of relevant theories and differing orientations to knowledge had accentuated potential theoretical tensions between multiple theories in teaching practices. Cullen placed responsibility for this tension not only on teachers but also on teacher educators, who may be simplifying the theory they present to students. While by 2003 Cullen had become more optimistic about teachers' ability to grapple with multiple theories and adopt more socio-culturally oriented perspectives, she maintained that it remained likely that one of the constraints in the implementation of *Te Whāriki* was the weak theoretical knowledge base and understandings of teachers.

In short, the scope of professional knowledge may be varied and may be drawn on somewhat intuitively. What knowledge, then, would be particularly pertinent to advancing interpretations of *Te Whāriki* in order to catalyse change? The next section addresses two aspects of professional knowledge that have been resistant to change in the sector: theories of learning and content knowledge.

Participatory learning theories

Do teachers have deep understanding both of long-standing learning theories and of more recent post-developmental theories that highlight participation, collaboration and co-construction? Contemporary theories embody a more dynamic orientation to teaching and learning. Consistent with the principles of *Te Whāriki*, it is worth bringing together a range of theories that reflect an emphasis on participation in communities and cultures in order to provide useful guidance for the field. In particular, Rogoff (1998, 2003; Paradise & Rogoff, 2009; Rogoff, Paradis, Arauz, Correa-Chávez, & Angelillo, 2003) has drawn attention to theories that highlight the skills of observation, listening and intent participation, emphasising that children develop through participation in the everyday activities and practices of communities. Consistent with the thrust of *Te Whāriki*, participatory theories highlight the contribution that activities embedded in children's families, communities and cultures make to motivation and learning. It is within the context of this self-motivated participation in authentic activities that meaningful knowledge building can occur.

Children observe and participate, and subsequently re-create and represent their current knowledge in their individual and collaborative play in early childhood settings. In this way they construct identities as competent learners and future citizens. Participatory learning can provide a contemporary framework for understanding young children's learning within a "participation plus" model of pedagogy (see Hedges & Cullen, 2012). In this model, participatory learning can lead to early conceptual and dispositional understanding. It therefore has the potential to drive forward future implementation of *Te Whāriki* through its contemporary focus on learning theories and outcomes, and the ways these might be apparent in children's representations in play of their family and cultural experiences. The issue of how knowledge development is supported is taken up in the next section, followed by considerations of meaning-making through holistic outcomes.

Subject content knowledge

Cullen (2003) suggested that a focus on children's interests and holistic learning had inadvertently de-emphasised "the significance of content and skills in children's learning" (p. 281). *Te Whāriki* is non-prescriptive in relation to curriculum content; instead, hints about content are suggested in some of the goal statements (see also Broström, this volume). Links between children's play-based activities and the role of teachers' subject content knowledge in promoting children's learning have a contentious history in early childhood education. In short, arguments have evolved over the extent to which children are, or might be, supported by teachers during play to construct content knowledge appropriate to their interests and current cognitive capabilities. These tensions also partially lie in the perceived dilemma between the kinds of outcomes promoted by curricula and the pedagogical processes through which these outcomes might be achieved. For many teachers it is simply too difficult to see how play can assist the construction of content learning such as literacy and numeracy within holistic outcomes, when their own experiences of more didactic approaches might be used to achieve this. Teachers may also be seduced by the 'ready for school' discourse that can permeate practice. Activities within this discourse run the risk of promoting a de-contextualised, low-level curriculum content of letters, numbers, colours, shapes and self-care.

Yet skilful engagement in children's play can enhance learning. By engaging naturally with children in matters related to their interests, a range of content knowledge can be drawn on during interactions so that early content learning can be achieved and highlighted. Although it is simply not possible to have the expert subject content knowledge necessary to teach across a range of subject domains, as early childhood (and indeed primary school) teachers might often be expected to do, it is also insufficient to use this as an excuse to know very little. Teachers can reasonably be expected to develop a baseline general knowledge across a range of subject domains or knowledge disciplines, particularly in areas of children's common interests. Research and teaching practices over time, in particular contexts, can determine what these interests might comprise. Developing knowledge and making meaning are essential to achieving the aspirations of *Te Whāriki* to create confident, competent learners and citizens.

When an interaction goes beyond a teacher's current knowledge as children explore and ask questions about something of interest to them, there should not be an immediate and automatic move to locate an answer, especially from potentially unreliable sources on the internet. Such a response ignores the fact that children may already have a range of everyday, intuitive knowledge that could be drawn on to explore the topic, and that the time children and teachers spend puzzling profitably in intellectual inquiry and meaning-making is worthwhile in its own right. In this way, teachers can lead children to more concept-oriented learning during these types of self-motivated interactions.

This chapter now goes on to discuss how meaning-making might also occur through the holistic notions promoted in *Te Whāriki*. It also addresses the ways in which these outcomes might pay greater attention to content learning.

Holistic outcomes

Although this chapter argues that attention be paid to content knowledge, it does not advocate for the educationalisation of play in order to promote academic outcomes. Early childhood education has always been concerned about a potential 'push-down' effect from formal schooling approaches in the compulsory sector. The effect commonly accompanies knowledge and skill-focused 'ready for school' or 'school effectiveness"' discourses (see Mutch and Trim, this volume). In relation to outcomes and content knowledge, in 1996 *Te Whāriki* was very different in structure, style and outcome emphases from its counterpart for the compulsory school sector. Eleven years later a revised *New Zealand Curriculum* (Ministry of Education, 2007b) had much more alignment with *Te Whāriki* in terms of its vision for learners and notions of outcomes. However, its implementation has been hampered by a parallel policy focus on National Standards, with achievement objectives that sit uncomfortably alongside the new curriculum. These standards are used to regularly assess the achievements of primary school-aged children in reading, writing and mathematics, and have raised widespread fears that primary teachers will teach to the standards rather than towards the holistic outcomes of key competencies in the curriculum.

Western, mono-cultural, developmental and subject-based perspectives often dominate such descriptions of outcomes and early standards (e.g., see Bracken & Crawford, 2010). If taught didactically, they may fail to draw on or risk decontextualising children's experiences. This may be of particular concern when teachers take into account the increasingly multi-ethnic population living in New Zealand. At the time of writing there are concerns about the threat of a push-down effect of National Standards to early childhood. If the early childhood sector hopes to resist this pressure, it is no longer justifiable to simply ignore content knowledge. In fact, it is imperative to do the opposite in order to demonstrate the ways in which content can be incorporated within play-based pedagogies. Cullen (2008) has argued that it is time for teachers to take a more systematic approach to teaching skills and content without necessarily adopting formal approaches. She argues that New Zealand has a strong tradition of research and pedagogy related to play-based curriculum alongside a foundation of international guidance.

One of the innovative features of *Te Whāriki* was an alternative conception of learning outcomes. *Te Whāriki's* overall indicative learning outcomes relate to the ways in which knowledge, skills and attitudes combine to develop children's working theories and dispositions that encourage learning. Significant work on the construct of dispositions, links to *Te Whāriki's* strands and ways to assess these have developed from funded research and professional learning projects led by Margaret Carr from 1995 to 2009. Learning Story assessment practices have developed in relation to *Te Whāriki* (Carr, 2001; Carr & Lee, 2012). Using Learning Stories, competent learners are seen to develop positive dispositions for learning in the form of outcomes such as curiosity, concentration, persistence, contribution and communication. Carr et al. (2009) followed children from early childhood centres to their schools and tracked their development of dispositions over that time. The value of dispositions as an outcome was clear in the way children continued to develop and demonstrate reciprocity, resilience, imagination, resourcefulness and agency in the early primary years, capabilities likely to positively influence lifelong learning. Yet the relationship between dispositions and their school achievement outcomes remained unaddressed.

In contrast to the focus on dispositions, the concept of working theories is only beginning to be developed. The major reason for this is likely to be that no programmes of professional development were provided to support teachers to understand the concept, and little research has been carried out on the concept so far. In the draft of *Te Whāriki*, Claxton's (1990) constructivist notion of 'minitheories' was noted as being the theoretical basis for working theories. Nearly 20 years later, working theories might also be considered to be influenced by more complex socio-cultural notions, highlighting the understanding that knowledge construction occurs within a wider framework of social and cultural activities that emphasise active participation and inquiry. From this perspective, working theories represent the tentative, evolving ideas and understanding formulated as children engage with others in their families and communities to think, ponder, wonder and make sense of the world in order to participate more effectively within it (Hedges & Jones, 2012).

There is a strong link between dispositions, working theories and the development of content knowledge. Some knowledge outcomes such as literacy and numeracy are often privileged. There is excellent guidance in the literature about what a disposition to be literate and early literacy content and skills look like, and the ways these can be encouraged in early childhood education (e.g., see McLachlan, Fleer, & Edwards, 2010). I suggest that teachers and researchers could similarly highlight the range of dispositions and working theories involved in 'thinking mathematically' and 'thinking scientifically' in order to demonstrate outcomes more satisfactorily. For example, the disposition to think scientifically can motivate children who are throwing balls or swinging on a swing to construct intuitive theories that will lead to later conceptual knowledge about force, gravity and trajectory. Assessment documentation could address these matters more directly if teachers had the related content knowledge and imperative to recognise and document this learning.

Despite increasing attention to dispositions and working theories, these alternative constructs of outcomes may remain difficult for those inside and outside the sector to understand. There is an emphasis on early literacy and numeracy among the few professional learning contracts still being funded. The issue of whether or not these domains are being incorporated holistically by being developed within the outcomes promoted in *Te Whāriki*, or via more didactic methods as the spectre of National Standards looms, is a major concern for the sector. Effective resistance to any potential downward pressure of achievement-based objectives in literacy and numeracy can only occur when teachers and researchers can provide robust evidence of the value of these alternative process-oriented outcomes. Otherwise, as Cullen (2003) somewhat controversially suggested, policy might go beyond the random possibility of content and skills development through interests-based learning present in *Te Whāriki* to the development of specific content standards, with the associated risk of inappropriate, de-contextualised pedagogy.

While this chapter was being prepared a Ministry of Education-appointed group of academics has been working on a framework of draft learning outcomes based on the strands of *Te Whāriki*. This move inspires confidence that the sector may continue to enjoy appropriate expert input into its own future and develop a layer of outcomes that meet government needs, but which are consistent with the approach and aspirations of *Te Whāriki* and recognise the depth of professional knowledge required to enact them. It is imperative that teachers and researchers address practices that highlight both the parallel and intertwined intent of dispositions and working theories as outcomes, and more explicitly articulate the skills, knowledge and attitudes implicit in dispositions and working theories. This is essential in order to continue to argue for complex outcomes, respond to any new outcomes-based framework and resist the possible downward pressure of standards-based outcomes.

Ultimately, the breadth and depth of professional knowledge and the ability of teachers to realise the potential of *Te Whāriki* and its capacity to catalyse change rely heavily on the quality of the professional education to which teachers have access, and the subsequent constraints of institutional, policy and employment issues that teachers experience. This chapter now picks up Cullen's (2003, 2008) theme that *Te Whāriki* can be viewed as a catalyst for challenging dominant beliefs and practices in early childhood teaching and learning. As Cullen (2008) stated, we need teachers

> who are knowledgeable about learning, who respect young children as learners and above all are themselves excited about learning and who interact with children in ways that will strengthen children's motivation to learn. (pp. 13–14)

This assertion is one reason why this chapter uses the term 'knowledgeable teachers' rather than the policy term 'qualified teachers': the two may not necessarily be the same. As Cherrington (2011) notes, even when teaching teams with several qualified teachers come together to unpack and reflect on video footage of teaching and learning interactions, their ability to draw on any depth of theoretical or research-based knowledge can be questionable. Rather than criticise teachers for this situation, it is simply evidence that policy has not supported systematic professional knowledge development. I turn now to matters related to the responsibilities of those providing professional education.

Challenges for teacher education and professional learning

Te Whāriki was first introduced in draft form in 1993 (Ministry of Education, 1993) and "developed on the assumption that early childhood centres would have funding and the trained staff to operate quality programmes" (May & Carr, 1997, pp. 234–235). The Early Childhood Education Taskforce Report reaffirmed qualified staff, working in partnership with families in well-managed services, as a hallmark of quality. The report also noted that standards of teacher education graduates have been reported to be inconsistent. Earlier, Kane (2008) had reported concerns from teachers and employers about the variable quality of initial teacher education providers and programme graduates. One participant stated that "we need to get a bit more serious about having quality teachers and quality qualifications" (p. 38).

It is not surprising, then, that another recommendation of the Taskforce report is to "review ... the extent to which initial teacher education and later professional development prepare and support teachers to implement *Te Whāriki* effectively"

(p. 106). The Taskforce's vision, which is likely to be shared with the entire early childhood community,

> is for a highly paid, well-qualified and respected early childhood education profession. This begins with two dimensions: (a) teacher education and (b) improving professional development opportunities for all staff. (p. 150)

Cullen's (1996, 2003) question regarding the adequacy of the knowledge base of teacher educators and professional learning facilitators to support teacher knowledge and practice to develop is still relevant. I now examine this concern in the context of the present policy climate.

Teacher education

This chapter criticises a number of aspects of teacher knowledge and practice. This is not a criticism of early childhood teachers, but of the political and policy systems that have constrained teachers' ability to access current research and theory, and have not encouraged professional education to be led by active researchers and educators who will continue to delve into *Te Whāriki* and extend and deepen teachers' understanding. I argue that issues related to professional knowledge and practice mean that any future evaluation of *Te Whāriki* must be cognisant of the policies that have constrained its potential.

There are a large number of early childhood teacher education programmes and providers in New Zealand. It may be questionable how well this serves teachers and children if not all are consistently delivering a thorough grounding in relevant or contemporary professional knowledge, a point Nutbrown (2012) also makes relating to early years professional education in the United Kingdom. It seems obvious that those who educate teachers need to be *au fait* with current research and theory in order for programmes to reflect contemporary understanding and be responsive to a curriculum document. Yet Kane's (2005) review of early childhood teacher education programmes indicated that, 12 years after *Te Whāriki* was mooted, a reliance on developmental theory and play-based philosophies was still prevalent. It may therefore only be very recently that some teacher education providers in New Zealand have altered programmes from being grounded in developmental theories to reflect the socio-cultural leanings of *Te Whāriki*, let alone to address the multiple perspectives and theories indicated earlier.

Many teacher educators were initially part of a teaching practice culture rather than a research culture, and began studying at postgraduate level after joining a teacher education provider. This has meant that, echoing Nutbrown's (2012) concern in the UK, some teacher educators do not hold qualifications significantly beyond the level of the qualification they teach. Coupled with the concern expressed earlier about the potential simplification of theory for students, there may also be a time lag between educators gaining their own qualifications and incorporating new theories and practices. It is vital that teacher educators develop identities as academics with roles to play in advancing and critiquing knowledge through continued active engagement in research alongside the education of future teachers. Furthermore, international moves to recognise teaching as a postgraduate profession may be echoed shortly in New Zealand. How might the early childhood community react and respond to this initiative?

Professional learning

Ongoing knowledge building through professional learning, including support for teacher registration, is essential as educational theory and research progress and as the contexts for, and challenges of, teaching continue to change. It is well known that one-off workshops do little to bring about positive changes to practice. Working with teachers' beliefs, helping teachers to link theory, research, philosophy and practice, and providing opportunities to engage in discussion about new research findings are integral to ongoing efficacy. Government-funded teacher professional development in New Zealand initially focused on the implementation of *Te Whāriki* and associated assessment and evaluation material, transitions for children, the development of management systems and accountabilities, and considerations about quality (Gaffney, 2003). More recently, professional development has focused on the implementation of Learning Stories via the published exemplars and the use of information and communications technologies (Hatherly, Ham, & Evans, 2010). Building professional knowledge through the provision of professional learning programmes to support implementation of *Te Whāriki* was originally widespread but, over time, has become patchy, costly and difficult to access. Mirroring the policy changes in early childhood centres, systemic investment in funding for professional learning has reduced.

Effective professional learning demands that highly qualified and effective facilitation occurs over a sustained period of time and takes into account research-based understanding about effective professional development (Mitchell & Cubey, 2003). Until very recently there appear to have been few well-designed, longer-term programmes of professional learning for early childhood teachers in New Zealand. In addition, as Cullen (2003) pointed out, the degree to which current research and theory are incorporated into professional learning is dependent on the knowledge and skill of the facilitators and the way they view their role. I contend that professional learning facilitators ought to be as highly qualified as university academics in order to effect current, theoretically oriented and evidence-informed change in teacher knowledge and practice. With increasing competition among providers of programmes and the likely tendency for funding bodies to accept low-cost bids, recent contracts for professional learning provision have largely gone to providers other than universities. I question how these programmes, which ought to be designed to support and challenge teacher learning and growth, can consistently access current rich theoretical and research expertise. I also suggest that, within a user-pays model of provision, providers may be unwilling to challenge teachers too deeply. Both factors could constrain the implementation of *Te Whāriki* to catalyse change.

Perhaps different approaches to professional learning might also be considered. These might build on insights from the COIs and from TLRI projects to involve researcher-led collaborative projects and inquiry into practice facilitated by researchers acting as critical friends, with the explicit goals of showcasing, researching and evaluating practice and challenging, deepening and improving practice (Hedges, 2010a; Meade, 2009). Another possibility, related to a current focus in New Zealand policy, would be to provide syntheses of research evidence for consideration by teachers (e.g., Farquhar, 2003). These syntheses, and any subsequent iterations, could usefully be the focus of funded professional learning programmes for teachers if policy makers genuinely want to promote research-informed practice and deep knowledge of the diversity of children, families and communities. Postgraduate study with research-active academics is another important way that, after their initial teacher education qualification, teachers can become part of a research culture and develop new understanding about theory and research.

Research needs to be one of the types of knowledge that teachers use so that local curricular and pedagogical decisions and processes are responsive to contemporary understanding. In the present research funding climate, New Zealand researchers are compelled to prioritise publishing academic, rather than practitioner-oriented, material. Yet unless the academic community takes responsibility for disseminating findings in ways that are accessible to teachers, teachers and professional learning providers may struggle to access fresh ideas to inform their practice. Education researchers wanting to make theory and research germane to practice must write for various audiences and enter into dialogue about new theoretical perspectives in order to make a difference to teachers' practice. In this way, both teacher educators and professional learning providers can access material that can support and challenge teacher learning. Further, academics need to advocate for *Te Whāriki,* including aspects yet to be realised, and continue to critique it in order to challenge unhelpful discourses.

Realising the potential of *Te Whāriki*

Te Whāriki might be described as having been ahead of its time when first introduced. The way it has been able to survive theoretical shifts and to champion alternative conceptions of outcomes is remarkable given that it has gone unrevised even as time has passed and political winds have changed. However, *Te Whāriki* has been largely shielded from critique. New Zealand is a small country and early childhood is a tight-knit sector, likely worried that open critique might result in widespread reform that could well leave the sector worse off. Yet by becoming more critical and research-informed, there must be a willingness among teachers and researchers to critically appraise *Te Whāriki* and its implementation, albeit in ways that do not detract from the positive achievements attained nor threaten hard-won improvements. In this final section some future developments, constraints and trends are briefly proposed.

This chapter has argued that professional knowledge can be enhanced by perspectives in *Te Whāriki* that were forward-looking for their time and that can now be supported further by current research and theoretical developments. In 2003 Cullen identified the way in which postmodern perspectives on early childhood education were beginning to be understood, and this trend has continued. A stronger emphasis on post-structural theories that address issues of culture, power and identity are worth consideration as curriculum frameworks might also highlight the power, privileges and silences that occur within curriculum (Stephenson, 2009; Wood, in press). For example, conceptual frameworks that consider how diverse families might be welcomed and involved, and how family involvement in children's learning and assessment might be enacted authentically, are areas ripe for further progress. In addition, seeking guidance and possible solutions from other sectors is surely also a sign of maturity. In this regard, the work of McNaughton (e.g., 2011) and colleagues to assist children's literacy development, and attempts to cohere schooling practices with social, cultural, political and economic contexts, may hold many useful parallel ideas for action in early childhood.

Early childhood education in New Zealand has a history of being receptive to international trends in education. For example, many centres claim to be adopting, or to be influenced by, the curricular and pedagogical approaches of Reggio Emilia. Similarly, many look to the ideas of Magda Gerber and Emmi Pikler to guide practices with infants and toddlers. Yet it is only recently that an evidence base for these ideas has begun to be developed. It appears that many of these philosophies may be adopted uncritically without reference to *Te Whāriki* or the New Zealand context (e.g., see Cooper, 2012). Looking inside the richness of *Te Whāriki* to lead, or at least complement, these philosophies and practices is a topic for future attention if teachers are to build evidence-informed practices consistent with the *Te Whāriki* framework.

Other somewhat neglected aspects of implementation also remain to be addressed. Pasifika perspectives, in part addressed by the inclusion of Diane Mara's chapter in this volume, have been sadly lacking, despite the increasing proportion of Pasifika children and families living in New Zealand and the current participation goals. Do early childhood teachers yet have the cultural understandings Cullen (2003) noted as necessary to enact appropriate curriculum for Pasifika (and other) children? Ritchie (2008; see also Chapter 7, this volume) has long questioned this in relation to Māori, the group rightly prioritised within policy and practice. Further, while the aspiration statement of *Te Whāriki* clearly highlights being "healthy in spirit" as vital for all children, and Mara (this volume) helps explicate this in relation to Pasifika children, Batchelar (2011) and Bone (with Cullen and Loveridge, 2007) remain lone voices in attempting to tease out an understanding of what this might entail in ways that are not related to religion or ethnicity. In addition, the application of a credit-based curriculum in early childhood education for children with special educational needs remains under-researched.

Conclusion and policy implications

Over time there has been significant government investment in early childhood services, but this has not matched the growth in the number, or indeed quality, of services for children. As in 1997, overall government support "is still inadequate to ensure quality for all children" (May & Carr, 1997, p. 227). The positive steps made in the first 10 years of *Te Whāriki's* implementation have been undermined by recent policy changes, in particular those that have reduced government targets for fully qualified teachers and significantly reduced ongoing professional learning available to early childhood settings. These policy changes have occurred despite the fact that it has long been recognised, as is argued in this chapter, that sophisticated professional knowledge is needed in order to understand and interpret *Te Whāriki* in local settings. Teachers can rightfully have an expectation of contemporary, research-based, professional education programmes and of ongoing professional learning support and dialogue to guide them in this process. In this way they can be responsive to the kinds of research evidence and current theories highlighted in this chapter that are vital to understanding and assessing the outcomes of implementing *Te Whāriki*.

In this chapter I have drawn attention to major issues related to professional knowledge; contemplation of the effects of further policy shifts and changes and their effect on professional education and children's outcomes is a task for the future. Certainly, the commitment of the early childhood sector has always helped to transcend issues and problems related to policy fluctuations. That the government-appointed Taskforce reaffirmed the ground-breaking nature of *Te Whāriki* and the importance of qualified teachers, at the same time that policy changes were brought to bear that undermined the potential for realising *Te Whāriki*, appears somewhat contradictory. An optimist might hope that any evaluation of *Te Whāriki* would recognise the issues raised in this chapter, and that the government of the day would subsequently invest in the appropriate research and professional support required. Certainly, policy winds must change back to systemic support for knowledgeable teachers if the potential of *Te Whāriki* as a catalyst for change is to be realised. Just as May and Carr noted in 1997, "there is still a long journey to turn adult words into realities for children" (pp. 229–230). I close with Cullen's (2003) challenge that still remains for both researchers and teachers: we need to "face up to the question of what *Te Whāriki* means for the lives of children, based on evidence, not simply on belief" (p. 288).

Acknowledgements

Sincere thanks to Joce Nuttall and Joy Cullen for the opportunity to contribute to this volume. Thank you to Sarah Jones for assistance with the preparation of the chapter, and to Joy Cullen, Val Podmore, Sarah Jones and the un-named reviewer for constructive critiques of earlier drafts that have greatly strengthened this final version.

References

Batchelar, S. (2011). *Supporting children's spiritual health in early childhood education.* Unpublished master's thesis, University of Auckland.

Bone, J., Cullen, J., & Loveridge, J. (2007). Everyday spirituality: An aspect of the holistic curriculum in action. *Contemporary Issues in Early Childhood, 8*(4), 344–354. doi: 10.2304/ciec.2007.8.4.344

Bracken, B., & Crawford, E. (2010). Basic concepts in early childhood educational standards: A 50-state review. *Early Childhood Education Journal, 37*(5), 421–430. doi: 10.1007/s10643-009-0363-7

Broadhead, P., & Burt, A. (2012). *Understanding young children's learning through play: Building playful pedagogies.* New York, NY: Routledge.

Carr, M. (2001). *Assessment in early childhood settings: Learning stories.* London, UK: Paul Chapman.

Carr, M., & Lee, W. (2012). *Learning stories: Constructing learner identities in early education.* London, UK: Sage.

Carr, M., Smith, A. B., Duncan, J., Jones, C., Lee, W., & Marshall, K. (2009). *Learning in the making: Disposition and design in early education.* Rotterdam, The Netherlands: Sense Publishers.

Carr, W., & Kemmis, S. (1986). *Becoming critical: Knowing through action research.* London, UK: Falmer Press.

Cherrington, S. (2011). *Early childhood teachers' thinking and reflection within their communities of practice.* Unpublished doctoral thesis, Victoria University of Wellington. Retrieved from http://hdl.handle.net/10063/1893

Claxton, G. (1990). *Teaching to learn: A direction for education.* London, UK: Cassell Educational.

Cooper, M. (2012). *"It's a little tricky": Teachers and families assessing infants' and toddlers' learning dispositions together.* Unpublished master's thesis, University of Auckland.

Cremin, H., & Slatter, B. (2004). Is it possible to access the 'voice' of pre-school children?: Results of a research project in a pre-school setting. *Educational Studies, 30*(4), 457–469.

Cullen, J. (1996). The challenge of *Te whāriki* for future developments in early childhood education. *Delta, 48*(1), 113–125.

Cullen, J. (2003). The challenge of *Te whāriki*: Catalyst for change? In J. Nuttall (Ed.), *Weaving Te whāriki: Aotearoa New Zealand's early childhood curriculum document in theory and practice* (pp. 269–296). Wellington: New Zealand Council for Educational Research.

Cullen, J. (2008, November). *Outcomes of early childhood education: Do we know, can we tell, and does it matter?* Paper presented at the Herbison lecture delivered at New Zealand Association for Research in Education conference, Palmerston North. Retrieved from http://www.nzare. org.nz/awards/herbison/joy_cullen_herbison2008.pdf

Early Childhood Education Taskforce. (2011). *An agenda for amazing children: Final report of the Early Childhood Education Taskforce.* Wellington: Author. Retrieved from http://www. taskforce.ece.govt.nz/reference-downloads/

Farquhar, S. E. (2003). *Quality teaching early foundations: Best evidence synthesis.* Wellington: Ministry of Education. Retrieved from http://www.educationcounts.govt.nz/publications/ series/2515/5963

Gaffney, M. (2003). *An evaluation of Ministry of Education funded early childhood professional development programmes.* Wellington: Ministry of Education.

Gibbs, R., & Poskitt, J. (2009). *Report on the evaluation of the early childhood Centres of Innovation programme.* Auckland: Evaluation Associates Ltd. Retrieved from http://www. educationcounts.govt.nz/publications/ece/22551/report-on-the-evaluation-of-the-early-childhood-centres-of-innovation-programme

Gmitrova, V., Podhajecká, M., & Gmitrov, J. (2009). Children's play preferences: Implications for the preschool education. *Early Child Development and Care, 179*(3), 339–351.

González, N., Moll, L. C., & Amanti, C. (Eds.). (2005). *Funds of knowledge: Theorizing practices in households, communities and classrooms.* Mahwah, NJ: Lawrence Erlbaum.

Hartley, C., Rogers, P., Smith, J., Peters, S., & Carr, M. (2012). *Crossing the border: A community negotiates the transition from early childhood to primary school.* Wellington: NZCER Press.

Hatherly, A., Ham, V., & Evans, L. (2010). *Effective Learning in early childhood education?: The impact of the ECE ICT PL programme: A synthesis repo*rt. Wellington: Ministry of Education. Retrieved from http://www.educationcounts.govt.nz/publications/ece/79138/executive-summary

Hedges, H. (2010a). Blurring the boundaries: Connecting research, practice and professional learning. *Cambridge Journal of Education, 30*(4), 299–314. doi: 10.1080/0305764X.2010.502884

Hedges, H. (2010b). Whose goals and interests?: The interface of children's play and teachers' pedagogical practices. In L. Brooker & S. Edwards (Eds.), *Engaging play* (pp. 25–38). Maidenhead, UK: Open University Press.

Hedges, H. (2012). Teachers' funds of knowledge: A challenge to evidence-based practice. *Teachers and Teaching: Theory and Practice, 18*(1), 7–24. doi: 10.1080/13540602.2011.622548

Hedges, H., & Cullen, J. (2012). Participatory learning theories: A framework for early childhood pedagogy. *Early Child Development and Care, 82*(7), 921–940. doi: 10.1080/03004430.2011.597504

Hedges, H., & Jones, S. (2012). Children's working theories: The neglected sibling of *Te Whāriki*'s learning outcomes. *Early Childhood Folio, 16*(1), 34–39.

Kane, R. (2005). *Initial teacher education: Policy and practice.* Wellington: Ministry of Education. Retrieved from http://www.educationcounts.govt.nz/publications/series/initial_teacher_ education/5159

Kane, R. (2008). *Perceptions of teachers and teaching: A focus on early childhood education.* Wellington: Ministry of Education. Retrieved from http://www.educationcounts.govt.nz/publications/ ece/perceptions-of-teachers-and-teaching-a-focus-on-early-childhood-education/ bibliography

May, H., & Carr, M. (1997). Making a difference for the under fives?: The early implementation of *Te whāriki*, the New Zealand national early childhood curriculum. *International Journal of Early Years Education, 5*(3), 225–236. doi: 10.1080/0966976970050304

McLachlan, C., Fleer, M., & Edwards, S. (2010). *Early childhood curriculum: Planning, assessment and implementation.* Port Melbourne, VIC: Cambridge University Press.

McNaughton, S. (2011). *Designing better schools for culturally and linguistically diverse children: A science of performance model for research.* New York, NY: Routledge.

Meade, A. (Ed.). (2009). *Generating waves: Innovation in early childhood education.* Wellington: NZCER Press.

Ministry of Education. (1993). *Te Whāriki. Draft guidelines for developmentally appropriate programs in early childhood services.* Wellington: Learning Media.

Ministry of Education. (1996). *Te whāriki: He whāriki mātauranga mō ngā mokopuna o Aotearoa: Early childhood curriculum.* Wellington: Learning Media. Retrieved from http://www.educate.ece. govt.nz/learning/curriculumAndLearning/TeWhariki.aspx

Ministry of Education. (2002). *Pathways to the future: Ngā huarahi arataki.* Wellington: Learning Media.

Ministry of Education. (2004, 2007a, 2009a). *Kei tua o te pae: Assessment for learning exemplars.* Wellington: Learning Media. Retrieved from http://www.educate.ece.govt.nz/learning/ curriculumAndLearning/Assessmentforlearning/KeiTuaotePae.aspx

Ministry of Education. (2007b). *The New Zealand curriculum.* Wellington: Learning Media. Retrieved from http://nzcurriculum.tki.org.nz/Curriculum-documents

Ministry of Education. (2009b). *Te whatu pōkeka: Kaupapa Māori assessment for learning exemplars.* Wellington: Learning Media. Retrieved from http://www.educate.ece.govt.nz/~/media/ Educate/Files/Reference%20Downloads/TeWhatuPokeka.pdf

Mitchell, L. (2011). Enquiring teachers and democratic politics: Transformations in New Zealand's early childhood education landscape. *Early Years: An International Journal of Research and Development, 31*(3), 217–228.

Mitchell, L., & Cubey, P. (2003). *Characteristics of professional development linked to enhanced pedagogy and children's learning in early childhood settings: Best evidence synthesis.* Wellington: Ministry of Education. Retrieved from http://www.educationcounts.govt.nz/publications/ series/2515/5955

Mitchell, L., Meagher-Lundberg, P., Mara, D., Cubey, P., & Whitford, M. (2011). *Locality-based evaluation of Pathways to the future: Ngā huarahi arataki.* Wellington: Ministry of Education. Retrieved from http://www.educationcounts.govt.nz/__data/assets/pdf_ file/0017/100916/973_ECE-Strategic-Plan-web.pdf

Mitchell, L., Wylie, C., & Carr, M. (2008). *Outcomes of early childhood education: Literature review.* Wellington: Ministry of Education. Retrieved from http://www.educationcounts.govt.nz/ publications/ece/25158/11

Nutbrown, C. (2012). *Review of early education childcare & qualifications.* Retrieved from https:// www.education.gov.uk/publications/standard/publicationDetail/Page1/NUTBROWN-REVIEW

Nuttall, J. (2012). Challenges, opportunities, and capacity building in early childhood teacher education research in Australia and New Zealand. *New Zealand Journal of Educational Studies, 47*(1), 65–78.

Paradise, R., & Rogoff, B. (2009). Side by side: Learning by observing and pitching in. *Ethos: Journal of the Society for Psychological Anthropology, 37*(1), 102-138.

Peters, S. (2010). *Transition from early childhood education to school: Literature review.* Wellington: Ministry of Education. Retrieved from http://www.educationcounts.govt.nz/publications/ece/78823

Ritchie, J. (2008). Honouring Māori subjectivities within early childhood education in Aotearoa. *Contemporary Issues in Early Childhood, 9*(3), 202–210. doi: 10.2304/ciec.2008.9.3.202

Rogoff, B. (1998). Cognition as a collaborative process. In D. Kuhn & R. Siegler (Eds.), *Handbook of child psychology* (5th ed., Vol. 2, pp. 679–744). New York, NY: John Wiley.

Rogoff, B. (2003). *The cultural nature of human development.* New York, NY: Oxford University Press.

Rogoff, B., Paradise, R., Arauz, R. M., Correa-Chávez, M., & Angelillo, C. (2003). Firsthand learning through intent participation. *Annual Review of Psychology, 54,* 175–203. doi: 10.1146/annurev.psych.54.101601.145118

Shulman, L. S. (1986). Those who understand: Knowledge growth in teaching. *Educational Researcher, 15*(2), 4–14.

Shulman, L. S. (1987). Knowledge and teaching: Foundations of the new reform. *Harvard Educational Review, 57*(1), 1–22.

Soler, J., & Miller, L. (2003). The struggle for early childhood curricula: A comparison of the English foundation stage curriculum, *Te whāriki* and Reggio Emilia. *International Journal of Early Years Education, 11*(1), 57–67.

Stephen, C. (2010). Pedagogy: The silent partner in early years learning. *Early Years: An International Journal of Research and Development, 30*(1), 15–28. doi: 10.1080/09575140903402881

Stephenson, A. M. (2009). *Skirmishes on the border: How children experienced, influenced and enacted the boundaries of curriculum in an early childhood education centre setting.* Unpublished doctoral thesis, Victoria University of Wellington. Retrieved from http://hdl.handle.net/10063/1106

Stuart, D., Aitken, H., Gould, K., & Meade, A. (2008). *Evaluation of the implementation of Kei tua o te pae: Assessment for learning: Early childhood exemplars: Impact evaluation of the Kei tua o te pae 2006 professional development.* Auckland: Cognition Consulting.

Wood, E. (in press). Free choice and free play in early childhood education: Troubling the discourse. *International Journal of Early Years Education.*

Index

Lightning Source UK Ltd.
Milton Keynes UK
UKOW06f0112190913

217478UK00015B/1379/P